TERRENOS

Illustrated History of the Otero Land Grant

Diana Hinojosa DeLugan

Arizonac Publishing Tempe

Arizonac Publishing
P.O. Box 7443
Tempe, AZ 85281

Phone: 602-699-4595
Email: support@arizonacpublishing.com
Web: http://arizonacpublishing.com

Front Cover Image: Lyle Watson
Back Cover Image: Diana DeLugan

ISBN 978-0-9909987-4-7
PRINTED IN THE UNITED STATES OF AMERICA

DEDICATED

To my beloved mother
Celia Sinohui Hinojosa

May 28, 1936 – May 26, 2013

CONTENTS

CONTENTS

LIST OF ILLUSTRATIONS

"Arizona is a young state, even by American standards...Arizona has a remarkable long history: the oldest occupied village in the United States is there, Francisco Vásquez de Coronado first entered what is now the United States there. And the first European words describing its exotic terrain were written over three generations before the Pilgrims landed in Plymouth.

For the National Archives at Riverside, too, the young state provides us with our oldest document. It is a land grant for a rancho granted in the name of the Spanish King to one Torivio de Otero near the Presidio at Tubac, on the Santa Cruz River between Nogales and Tucson.

The Court of Private Land Claims records show that by 1880 Otero's descendants had faced many significant challenges in both working and keeping the land. They survived drought, Indian raids, squatters, and justified their claims to both the Mexican and then the American governments."

~ National Archives and Records Administration Office of Regional Records Services, *The National Archives in the Regions.* September 2011.

This is their story.

THE NATIONAL ARCHIVES IN THE REGIONS...

September 2011

A MONTHLY CALENDAR OF EVENTS OPEN TO THE PUBLIC

La Tierra de los Pioneros (Land of the Pioneers)

Arizona is a young state, even by American standards. Next February, Arizona will be 100 years old. And yet, Arizona has a remarkably long history: the oldest occupied village in the United States is there, Francisco Vásquez de Coronado first entered what is now the United States there. And the first European words describing its exotic terrain were written over three generations before the Pilgrims landed in Plymouth.

For the National Archives at Riverside, too, the young state provides us with our oldest document. It is a land grant for a *rancho* granted in the name of the Spanish King to one Torivio de Otero near the Presidio at Tubac, on the Santa Cruz River between Nogales and Tucson.

In 1789, Torivio de Otero was granted land near the Santa Cruz River by Nicolas de la Erran, commander of the Presidio. The grant is a beautiful document covered in ornate official seals and written in a hand easy to admire. It is, of course, written in the Spanish of the time. We rely on a translation done by the Surveyor General's Office in the 1880s. Erran stated that the land was granted to Otero for the "purpose of pursuing his calling, as an agriculturist." At the end of the grant, Erran records, "I took him by the hand, and gave him possession of said lands; he, according to custom, scattering earth and stones, and pulling up herbage." And the transfer was made from crown to cultivator. The Court of Private Land Claims records show that by 1880 Otero's descendents had faced many significant challenges in both working and keeping the land. They survived drought, Indian raids, squatters, and justified their claims to both the Mexican and then the American governments.

In honor of Hispanic Heritage Month, we salute this story of the Otero family, who farmed the desert for generations before the first Americans journeyed west.

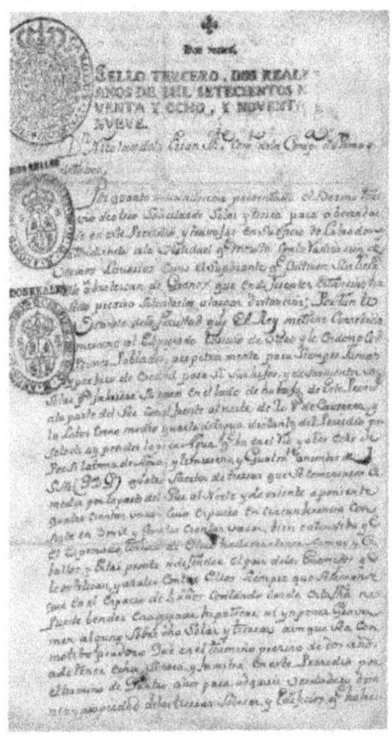

Above: First page of Spanish land grant to Torivio de Otero from the records of the Arizona Court of Private Land Claims, 1798, Record Group 49; National Archives at Riverside.

NATIONAL ARCHIVES AND RECORDS ADMINISTRATION ■ OFFICE OF REGIONAL RECORDS SERVICES

Figure i: NARA. Office of Regional Records Services. *The National Archives in the Region. La Tierra de los Pioneros (Land of the Pioneers)* honoring the Otero family land grant. September 2011.

FOREWARD

Terrenos is a deeply personal exploration of the history of a family —not of the people of their past but of the lands on which they lived. For Diana Hinojosa DeLugan, 8th-generation descendant of the prominent southern Arizona family of the Oteros, it began as a simple quest to answer the question many of her relatives asked her: "What happened to the land?" A question which has been asked by many members of other families who owned and farmed and prospected the land in the Spanish and Mexican eras which in the end ended up in ownership of wealthy immigrants and investors from the eastern United States, and later, in the case of some of the Otero lands, in corporate ownership.

I have been conducting tours of the village of Tubac, the *barrio*, in which the soldiers of the Presidio of Tubac made their homes in the eighteenth and nineteenth centuries for some twenty years. Often these tours begin in Otero Hall, built in the early part of the twentieth century by the Otero Family on the site of the original house. Otero Hall was built as a community center for the inhabitants of Tubac, reflecting the involvement of the Family in the community. In fact, the property on which the Hall was built was part of a Land Grant issued by the King of Spain through the Spanish administrative system to Torivio de Otero in 1789. The other part of the Land Grant was for agricultural lands north of Tubac where the Tubac Golf Resort & Spa now operates. That much was known to people in Tubac, some of whom may not know that the Oteros were also prominent in Tucson: so much so that when the Otero House was destroyed as part of an ill-conceived "urban renewal" project the house porch/front facade was preserved as an exhibit in the Arizona Historical Society Museum in Tucson.

But not much more was known about the Oteros. Some knew that Don Torivio taught, and many who knew that thought he had come to Tubac to establish a school for the children of the soldiers of the Presidio, but this did not affect the notion that the "first school house," (possibly in the state of Arizona) had been built in Tubac in 1885 by a local real estate promoter, T. Lillie Mercer. In fact, there was a general gap in knowledge between the Presidio period of the 1760s and 1770s, dominated by the tenure of Juan Bautista de Anza as commander of the Presidio and the Gadsden Purchase of 1853/54 dominated by Charles Poston and the printing press brought by him from Ohio. After the Civil War the common history of Tubac continues to consist of accounts of immigrants from the East.

Diana DeLugan in *Terrenos* has changed and enlarged that view by showing that the Otero family over generations made the transition through the Presidio/Spanish period, the Gadsden Purchase period and the post-Civil War while farming the same land. Although grounded, literally, in Tubac the family had other lands particularly those acquired by Sabino Otero in the late 1800s. These lands consisted of the whole of the Santa Cruz Valley north from Tubac to the point where the river ceased to provide sufficient water at Reventon. There was land in the Santa Rita Mountains. Sabino also established a cattle raising operation based around strategic supply (water!) points stretching from Florence in the north to Schuk (Santa Rosa) and then south along the Avra/Altar valleys reaching in the south to his operation at "Otero" as it was shown on maps, at the base of Baboquivari. *Terrenos* describes this remarkable operation and thus is a contribution to understanding the cattle business as it operated in Arizona in those days of large-scale, long-distance cattle drives.

Otero is a name most would associate with Tubac, famous for being a military presidio, but remarkably none of the Oteros were from the military. Don Torivio was a brother-in-law of the commander of the post when he came in 1787, but as Diana notes, importantly, he came as a settler— not as a school teacher nor as a soldier. *Terrenos* thus is an account of a history that is neither Mission-based nor military: it is an account of a family of settlers who took up land and farmed it for generations.

Philip Halpenny

Retired Hydrologist/Tubac Historian & Lecturer

INTRODUCTION

I was born and raised in Phoenix, Arizona, a United States citizen of Spanish, Mexican, and German ancestry. When I attended grammar school in Phoenix, Arizona during the 1960's, it never dawned on me that my history curriculum omitted significant mention about Hispanic Arizona. Our history books and classroom lessons focused on English colonists who arrived on the Mayflower, along with rip-roaring stories of cowboys and Indians (as Native Americans were then-called), and the daring Eastern men and women who sacrificed life and limb during the westward gold rush. I imagined my Mayflower ancestors breaking bread with the natives during that memorable Thanksgiving Day in 1621 each time a teacher called the Mayflower colonists our "forefathers." During the past decade, I confirmed my ancestors were European but discovered they had absolutely no connection to the Mayflower. Ah, the deceptions of youth!

My musician father Fidencio Garcia Hinojosa, a native of Veracruz, Mexico, was the first to introduce me to my personal Hispanic history. His dark eyes gleamed beneath his bushy eyebrows each time he recounted his favorite childhood discovery, the moment when he found a silver Spanish Conquistador's helmet as he played in the countryside at Perdenales near Pueblo Viejo (Old Town), Veracruz. He welcomed every opportunity to discuss our Mexican ancestors, their culture, and customs. He spoke of majestic Aztec and Mayan temples at Tenochtitlán and Yucatan, structural icons of Old Mexico located far from the United States, the land that adopted him. Through my father's folk music, I was exposed to Mexican performance arts which instilled in me a strong sense of pride for my cultural heritage.

Unlike my boisterous father, my mother Celia Sinohui Hinojosa was always quiet, reserved about her personal Hispanic history. Occasionally she shared stories about her heritage gleaned from the time when she lived with her grandparents Ricardo and Francisca Otero. I deeply regret that I failed to pay more attention to my mother's ancestry earlier in life because I now know that her family's story is highly important to me, to my own and extended family, and to all of Arizona. I credit my mother for helping me discover the importance of preserving family history. As a great-grandmother entering the golden chapter of my life, I now understand that people, places and names are only remembered when history is documented. Absent documentation, the memory of our ancestors quickly blurs and eventually fades, forever lost to time. This book was written to memorialize the history of a small Spanish land grant in present-day Arizona that belonged to a family whose story is worth telling. It is a true story that starts in Tubac.

Located forty-five miles south of Tucson and twenty-three miles north of Nogales, Arizona, Tubac is a small artisan community. It was once the northernmost settlement of New Spain and the center of commerce. When my mother Celia was a child, her grandfather Ricardo Otero told her stories about how the Otero family of Tubac was once a prosperous stock-raising family during the Spanish and Mexican colonial era and pre-Arizona statehood period. Otero men owned a massive herd of cattle that roamed freely from Sonora to Casa Grande. It was an important family heavily involved in education, business, social, and political matters throughout southern Arizona.

During the spring of 2009, my mother and I strolled together across the white sun-bleached sidewalk at the Tubac Presidio State Park and Museum admiring the colonial artifacts and learning about Arizona pioneer history. We suspected but were unsure of just how deep our connections were to the land at Tubac. Like the centuries old cotton trees that border the Santa Cruz River at the former Rancho de Otero, now known as the Tubac Golf Resort and Spa, the Otero family formally laid its permanent roots at Tubac when Don Torivio de Otero received a Spanish land grant in 1789. Although the land would later become the subject of controversy, the Otero land grant was always the nexus of the Otero family's prosperity and remains a legacy that endures to this day as any visit to the Tubac Golf Resort and Spa at Tubac, AZ would attest.

Figure ii: Tubac Presidio State Historic Park and Museum entrance. Otero Hall is located to the right of the image background. (Photograph by the author).

My mother passed away on May 26, 2013. Before she died, she asked me to research whether her grandfather Ricardo Otero's stories were true. Was she a descendant of the Otero family of Tubac or were her grandfather's stories the skilled inventions of a master storyteller?

To initiate the research, I established *TheOteros.com,* a family history research project founded in 2009. In collaboration with other Otero family descendants, the Project resulted in a three-volume *Otero Family History Collection* that was compiled and donated to the Pimería

Alta Historical Society at Nogales, the Tubac Presidio State Park and Museum at Tubac, and the Arizona Historical Society at Tucson to use for education, research, and other non-commercial purposes. Ultimately, government and vital statistic records report Ricardo Otero was the son of Teofilo Otero, the last Otero family owner of the 1789 Otero Spanish land grant properties.

While conducting Otero family history research I was surprised to be repeatedly asked one question, ***"What happened to the land grant properties?"*** From historical society to state archives, personal interviews to expert lectures, no single source provided the answers needed. This became my mission. This is the central question that this book attempts to answer.

Figure iii: Kiosk behind the Pimería Alta Historical Society at Nogales near the railroad tracks. This is one of several places where abuelo Ricardo Otero share stories about the Otero family of Tubac. (Photograph by the author).

A few modern Arizona history books mention that Don Torivio de Otero received the first land grant in Arizona. This assertion is one this book takes issue with correcting the record to explain how Torivio de Otero was not technically the first land grantee. Modern Arizona history books that give cursory reference to the Otero land grant lack detail about what happened to the land, the family, or what became of the financial prosperity acquired from exploiting the land. The story of the Otero land grant is one shared many other Spanish and Mexican pioneer families. Spanish and Mexican land grant history is a collective experience. It is a culture-rich history of people that flourished or fell once they were subject to United States government rule.

I was hesitant to publish this book because it challenges some long held beliefs about the Otero family and Arizona history. Truth matters. Sometimes documents reveal a family history that is in stark contrast to the way we remember our ancestors, and not all of it is flattering. I grappled incessantly on whether to exclude history that might offend extended family members. Ultimately, I decided to publish the facts as history presents them, naked and unadorned. Like every family that has ever lived, the Otero family was frail due to having existed. Human frailty is part of the human experience. I have faith that my immediate and extended family will understand that our ancestors do not dictate how we live today nor reflect our personal mores and values. My hope is that learning the truth about our mutual family history will bring us closer together. We can accept our ancestors for all their strengths and weaknesses and still celebrate their several personal achievements.

I named this book *Terrenos, An Illustrated History of the Otero Land Grant* because the story of the land is not limited to the boundaries of the original land grant properties. *Terrenos* means "lands" in Spanish. The Rancho de Otero at Tubac was a prosperous ranch. From ranch proceeds, the Otero family acquired numerous other lands throughout southern Arizona. As this book reveals, many Otero properties and structures have been preserved as important Arizona historical sites by public and private entities. Although the land acquired by Don Torivio pursuant to the original Spanish grant of 1789 is no longer owned by the Otero family, the land symbolizes the Otero family's legacy. It is a proud legacy that subsequent land owners have honored well into the twenty-second century.

This book reveals how the Otero family overcame significant challenges to their land grant rights including theft, Apache attacks, and government obstruction. Maps, photos, and images contained in this book bear witness to the family's challenges as it proved and perfected its land grant property rights to the Spanish, Mexican, and United States governments. Operations at the Rancho de Otero at Tubac lasted approximately 148 years, from 1789 to 1936, holding a respected place in Arizona's ranching history.

Terrenos also reveals many firsts: the location of Arizona's first permanent private European residence, names Arizona's first lay teacher, and identifies the first private European land owner to build an irrigation system in Arizona. *Terrenos* connects the history of other families through lands once owned by the Oteros. This Arizona pioneer story begins more than a century before Arizona was admitted into the United States union as its 48th state.

Figure iv: Great Seal of Arizona. (Photograph by the author).

CHAPTER SUMMARIES

Chapter One identifies where Tubac was located during the Spanish Arizona era and how the Otero family received the Spanish land grant. It explains the distinctions of land under Spanish law and introduces Don Torivio de Otero, the land grantee. The chapter also reveals how Don Torivio protected his land against squatters and successfully proved his property title to the Spanish government. Chapter Two focuses on Otero family property at Tubac and Tucson, Arizona as land rapidly transitioned under Spanish, Mexican, and United States territorial government rule. The chapter provides a unique insight into the thriving Tubac community where the Otero family lived and reveals the exact location of where the Otero's *Solar* or house was located. Chapter Three focuses on the Rancho de Otero property, the scope of the Otero cattle empire, and challenges the family faced to preserve the land and the wealth that flowed from the land. Chapter Four identifies other historic *Terrenos* (lands) once owned by the Otero family. These Otero family lands and land transactions throughout southern Arizona reveal the Otero family's pre-statehood financial and social influence.

Finally, Chapter Five introduces some of the subsequent private owners of the Otero Spanish land grant properties who celebrated the Otero legacy beginning the early to mid-twentieth century. Notable owners of the Rancho de Otero include crooner Bing Crosby and acclaimed aviatrix Joanna Fay Shankle Davis. It also references the current owners of the historic land grant property at Tubac. Documents and images included in this book were carefully selected to help illustrate the story of the Otero land grant and affiliated properties.

Several of the documents and images presented here have never been published. Documents include United States Surveyor General's journal entries and field notes that identify the Otero land grant with exacting detail, courtesy of the Arizona State Records and Archives Division. A biofile of memorable Otero family members is provided to give insight into their personal lives and intra-family connections. Finally, I hope the Bibliography will be a starting point for anyone interested in a similar field of research.

ACKNOWLEDGEMENTS

"None of us got to where we are alone. Whether the assistance we received was obvious or subtle, acknowledging someone's help is a big part of understanding the importance of saying thank you."

~ Harvey Mackay

Since research began for this book more than seven years ago, several important individuals who contributed to Otero family history research have passed away. I am heartbroken that they are not with us to see their contributions in print. Thank you to everyone who helped and encouraged me during the research and production of this book. If I have missed anyone, please know it was unintentional and that I remain deeply grateful to you.

A special thank you and deep appreciation goes to Mary Bingham, Tubac Historical Society docent and researcher. Mary is the co-author of "*Tubac: Where Art and*

History Meet" and a celebrated local Tubac area historian. After Mary learned about my Otero land research in 2010, she generously shared her vast knowledge and directed me to multiple resources to further my investigation. Over the years, she personally conducted some Otero research which she provided to me and was the first to suggest that a book be written about the Otero family. As the Tubac Historical Society docent, Mary has remained an invaluable resource over the years and her many contributions are reflected in this book. I have deeply enjoyed our talks and visits together. Mary, you remain my forever friend in history.

During the last few years of my research, Mary Bingham and Shaw Kinsley, former director of the Tubac Presidio State Park and Museum, strongly encouraged me to reach out to Philip Halpenny, retired hydrologist. Philip and I became fast friends and research companions. I cannot overstate how important Philip is to the research and conclusions rendered in this book. His professional background and expertise in land monuments and measurements confirmed important conclusions presented in this book; including the engineering layout of 1882 Tubac, the original location of the Otero family *Solar* or house lot, the origin of the Rojas House at the Tubac Presidio State Park and Museum, and the Sabino Otero land at Baboquivari. Like Mary Bingham, Philip Halpenny is a tireless and passionate historian who shares my interest in Hispanic Arizona history. Words are simply insufficient to thank you for your assistance and the friendship extended me during this important research. Nonetheless, my humble and sincere gracias Phil. I look forward to other research collaborations with you.

My deep gratitude to the late Shaw Kinsley, former director of the Tubac Presidio State Park and Museum, for his unwavering support of all Otero family history research. I deeply appreciate his leadership as we worked together with local historical societies to obtain Governor Doug Ducey's proclamation in honor of Don Torivio de Otero during the 2015 Hispanic Heritage month for Don

Torivio's significant contributions to Arizona history. The gubernatorial proclamation is now permanently housed at Otero Hall within the Tubac Presidio State Park and Museum. Shaw will be remembered as a tireless advocate dedicated to preserving Tubac and Hispanic Arizona history and as a leader in his field. Research for this book reveals that the Otero connection to the Tubac Presidio State Park is far deeper than ever imagined.

The late Teresa Leal, former curator at the Pimería Alta Historical Society (PAHS) and great humanitarian, provided me with copies of important Mexican Heritage Project research related to Manuel and Fernando Otero, son and grandson of Sabino Otero. She also introduced me to an Otero relative, Eduardo Robinson, who gave me my first significant insight into the Otero Arizona-Sonoran connection. In addition to becoming a dear friend, Teresa was also instrumental in gaining PAHS support during the 2015 Otero proclamation project. Teresa, there is a special place in heaven for angels like you. Gracias.

Thank you, Jose Ramon Garcia, author and PAHS Director. You were instrumental in the success of the Don Torivio de Otero proclamation project effort. I appreciate your continued support and interest in Otero family history.

My sincere thanks to the late Don Garate, former chief translator for the National Parks Service at Mission Tumacácori, who gave me a private tour of the mission. We spoke endlessly about the Otero family from the Spanish period to the 1880s, Otero relatives buried at the mission site, and the 1880's preserved graffiti by Fernando Otero, son of Manuel Otero and Maria Clara Martinez de Otero. Don also directed me to the Mission 2000 website and other colonial period research resources that were important during the early stages of my research.

Research of the Sabino Otero lands at Baboquivari was made possible through the help of several individuals. Thank you to David Jesus "Pancho" Valles Ballesteros who shared his personal family story of living at the Sabino

Otero home at Baboquivari, and for his photographs which bring this lost chapter of Baboquivari history to life. I deeply enjoyed our conversations and look forward to our continued friendship. Thank you to Charley and Mary Miller, owners of the Elkhorn Ranch, for sharing your knowledge about the Otero/Elkhorn connection, for your personal tour of the land, and generous hospitality. My husband Jim, Philip Halpenny, and I will always treasure the time spent with both of you along with John and Pat King, of the Anvil Ranch at Altar Valley. Our families will always share a mutual connection because of the land at Baboquivari. Also, on behalf of all Arizonans, thank you for your tireless preservation efforts through the Altar Valley Conservation Alliance.

Research was conducted at multiple institutions including the Arizona Historical Society at Tucson, the Tubac Historical Society, the Tubac Presidio State Park and Museum, and the Pimería Alta Historical Society at Nogales. Anyone in search of Arizona genealogy or land research should visit these repositories. They preserve our important documents and artifacts for the public to enjoy. Thank you to the staff at each of these institutions. Without their assistance and support, this book would not be possible.

Special mention and sincere thank you is extended to the many government entities who aided in this book's research. After I exhausted my research at the various southern Arizona historical societies, the most productive repository by far was at the Arizona State History and Archives Division in Phoenix. Thank you to recently retired Director Dr. Melanie Sturgeon for access to your staff and your encouragement to complete this Otero research. Your knowledgeable staff always went the extra mile to help me. Special thanks go to Wendi Goen for your on-point research guidance. You were central to helping me locate Otero land and court documents.

Thanks to the staff at the Phoenix branch of the United States Bureau of Land Management (BLM) who patiently worked with me in person and explained Otero plats and related land surveys. They guided me on how to use the BLM website and explained how to identify and plot land survey measurements. At Nogales, the staff at the Santa Cruz County Recorder's office helped me search for important plats and deeds used in this book. Thank you Nicolas Fernandez, America Ramirez, and Maria F. Sihas for working with me. Special thanks to Patty Garcia who gave me access to her staff and who went the extra mile to locate and provide me with important difficult-to-locate Tubac historic plats. Thank you Charles R. Eatherly, Arizona State Parks historian, for sharing your quality time with me, gifting me the book you authored on the history of the State Parks, *Arizona State Parks "The Beginning,"* and for directing me to resources that helped identify the location of the original Otero *Solar*.

Also paramount to the history of the *Solar* was research and documents provided by the staff at the Santa Cruz Valley Unified School District No. 35. Thank you to Dr. David Verdugo for giving me access to your staff, Dr. Carol Cullen for your detailed communications, and to especially to Josie Gallo who conducted the actual research of the school district records.

I am deeply thankful for all the unique Hacienda de Otero and Rancho de Otero images provided courtesy of Georgia Bowman Allen and John Shankle. Mrs. Allen shared personal family's photos during the 1940s, while Mr. Shankle shared personal family photos taken during the 1950s. These images greatly complement the Rancho de Otero chapter.

Thanks to the several illustrators whose artistry enhance the pages of this book, especially Najla Kay for the hand drawn map of 18th Century Tubac based on the Joseph Urrutia Spanish map of 1765, Shazeb Turk for the graphic illustrations of the Tubac Presidio and Otero Family Crest of Spain, and Dorotea Cvijanovic for the numerous portrait illustrations. Your talents enriched this book.

Beta readers Martha DeSoto Green, Shirley Pinkerton, James DeLugan and Yvonne Clay provided an invaluable service. Their specific feedback enhanced the final proof copy of this book. Yvonne was particularly instrumental in coordinating help. My sincere *gracias* to each of you.

To my cousins, your contributions elevated this book. I am beholden to Dr. Lydia Otero for your encouragement and interest in this research. The documents you gave me inspired me to contact the Spanish government national archives. Thank you Martha DeSoto Green and Teresa Anita Coenen Seaman for sharing your personal Otero family photographs. Having an image to connect with a name brings the Otero family story to life. I also sincerely appreciate the encouragement and support you have shown me over these grueling years of research. To Lyle Watson, my deepest thanks for allowing me to use your graphic illustration of the Otero land grant for the cover of this book and for your tireless research efforts as we compiled the *Otero Family History Collection*. All of your contributions are significant and help preserve our mutual Otero family history.

More than a decade has passed while relentlessly researching Otero family history. I would not have had the stamina or focus without the support of my loved ones. Thank you, Wendy Jacob, for your unwavering support. You are more than a friend to me. You are my soul sister. To my extended *familia*, you remained in my constant thoughts as I conducted this research in the hope it would help answer many of your questions. We share a proud legacy. It is a legacy that belongs to all Otero descendants. To my children Alma Diana, Christopher, and Reynaldo, I love you to the moon. Thank you for believing in me and for your patience. To my grandchildren Jesse, Cesar, Jorge, Juan, Rosie, Vanessa, Diana, and Christopher Jr.; and my great-grandchildren Cesar, Clara Marie, and Emma Layla, and all future Otero descendants, be proud of your roots! You have a family history worth knowing. I extend my most profound and undying gratitude to my husband Jim. Your sacrifice was the greatest. You never gave up on me or questioned the value of my work. I am a better person because of you. Above all, thank you to my mother Celia Sinohui Hinojosa who is in heaven watching over my every day. My devotion to you has no boundaries. It was your question, your desire to learn about your family history that placed me firmly on this path as a researcher and writer. You remain my greatest inspiration.

Finally, to you the reader. Every time you learn about the past, you become the conduits of knowledge. You elevate our communal consciousness. You matter. You are a living vessel of history.

Figure v: Otero Family Crest of Spain graphic illustration by Shazeb Turk commissioned for *Terrenos* © 2018 Diana DeLugan. All rights reserved.

TERRENOS

Illustrated History of the Otero Land Grant

Diana Hinojosa DeLugan

CHAPTER ONE
THE OTERO LAND GRANT

Adjacent the north-flowing Santa Cruz River, *terrenos* (lands) sustained the first European families of Arizona at a settlement named Tubac. Before Spanish troops and their families lived at Tucson, before Arizona was purchased from Mexico and Mexico gained its independence from Spain, Spanish families traversed the blazing desert with a dream shared by new settlers of all emergent nations. It was a dream to establish a permanent home. It was a dream to see children grow and live as abundant as the alfalfa and *maíz* (corn) fields near the Santa Cruz River. Among those early settlers was the Otero family.

Like most early Spanish settlers, the Oteros may have been all but forgotten had it not been for the *terrenos* granted to them through a land grant under the authority of the King of Spain. The Otero story is a true Arizona pioneer story that reveals many Arizona firsts. It is a story that requires an understanding of the early settlement at Tubac when Arizona belonged to Spain.

The Spanish conquest of Mexico began in 1519 when Hernan Cortés landed at Veracruz and advanced inward towards central Mexico to conquer the Aztec capital of Tenochtitlán. By the end of the 17th century, Spanish trails cut across the sun-drenched Sonoran Desert at northern *Nuevo Mexico* (New Mexico), as missionary Father Eusebio Francisco Kino[1] established missions throughout *Pimería*

Alta, land of the Upper Piman Indians. National Historic Landmark Mission San Xavier del Bac at Tucson, known as the White Dove of the Desert, was established by Kino in 1692 and completed in 1797.[2] San Xavier del Bac was one in a string of missions that included those at Altar, Arivaca, Sópori, Tumacácori and Guevavi.[3] Tubac, Arizona was initially established during the early 18th century as a *visita*, a small community and mission farm served by priests from nearby missions.[4] Located three miles north of Tumacácori, Tubac was a small but highly important community of *Pimería Alta* (land of the Upper Piman Indians). Among the earliest recorded religious ceremonies at Tubac was a baptismal entry for Miguel Ignacio in 1741.[5] Father Augustine Campos, a follower of Kino, visited Tubac from 1726 to 1751[6] and gave Tubac its name.[7] Tubac is a generic name used during the Spanish colonial era.[8] "Bac" like that used in San Xavier del Bac and Tu-bac signifies a spring of water.[9] The Barrio de Tubac Archaeological Preserve brochure explains:

> *The first reference to Tubac is found in Jesuit missionary documents from 1726. Tubac is described as a small O'odham settlement. In 1732, Tubac became a visita of Guevavi where the priest regularly conducted religious services. Soon afterwards, Hispanic settlers began to build the permanent community that may have been located in what is now the Barrio de Tubac Archaeological Preserve.*[10]

This rural *visita* known as Tubac was a prime location for settlement because the topography offered protection for its settlers and the abundant vital resource of water due to the nearby Santa Cruz River. Daily life at Tubac was challenging and often harsh during the 18th century. Due to its distance from nearby missions, the Tubac *visita* was exposed and vulnerable to frequent hostile attack by Native American tribes. Tubac citizens' worst fears were realized in November 1751 when Piman Chief Luis

Oacpicagigua led a revolt against Spanish oppressors. The uprising decimated Tubac, pummeled Mission San Xavier del Bac, and created havoc among the surrounding communities. While Benjamin Franklin invented a lightning conductor and American colonies remained subjects of the English crown, a meeting was held on April 10, 1752 by Spanish frontiersmen to determine the best location to place a *presidio* or military fort to protect the Tubac settlers. These leaders recognized the benefit of Tubac's "permanent water, cultivable lands and other prerequisites for the successful frontier fort."[11] Some of these same factors still attract modern visitors to Tubac.

Figure 1.1. Father Eusebio Francisco Kino illustrated by Dorotea Cvijanovic commissioned exclusively for *Terrenos* © 2018 Diana DeLugan. All rights reserved.

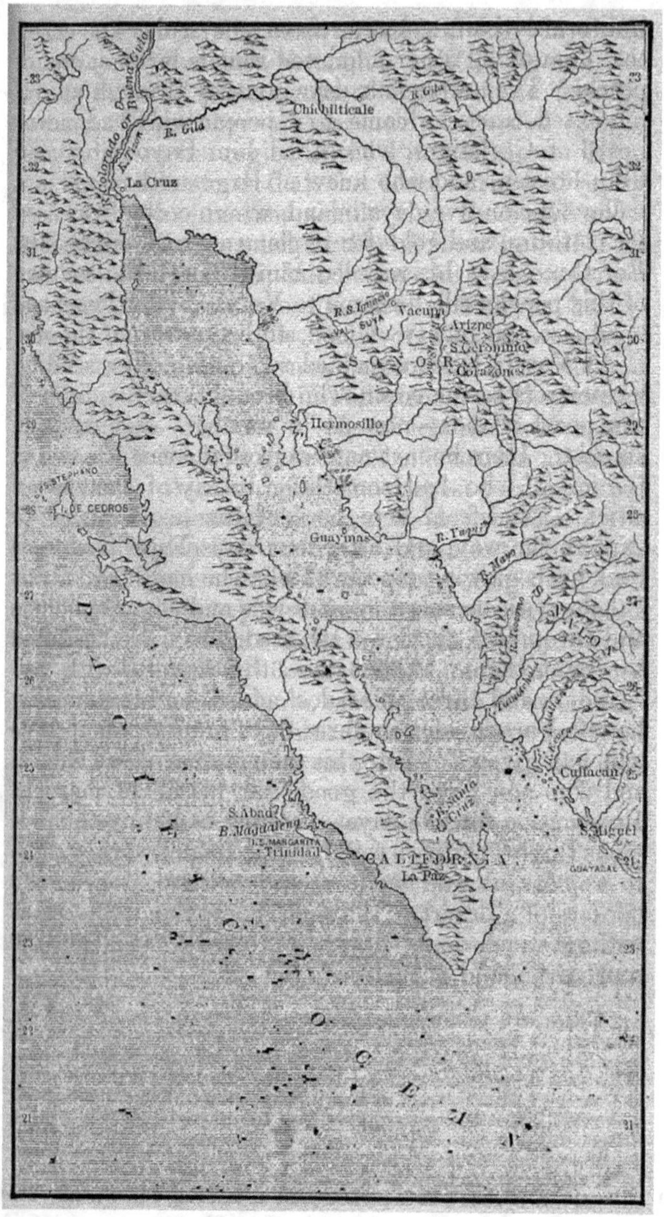

Figure 1.2. 1539 Map of the Spanish Northwest locations. Spanish missionaries explored present-day Arizona. (Public domain).[12]

After Piman Chief Luis accepted terms offered by Spanish Captain Joseph Díaz de Carpio to quell the uprising, the *Presidio San Ignacio de Tubac* was established at Tubac in 1752 to protect Spanish interests.[13]

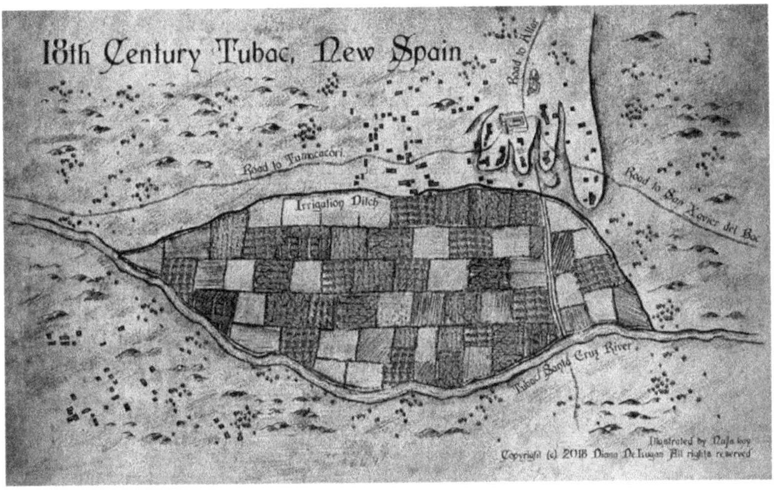

Figure 1.3. Image based on the Joseph Urrutia map of 1765. Illustration of 18th Century Tubac by Najla Kay. Commissioned exclusively for *Terrenos* © Diana DeLugan. All rights reserved.

As mission rule ended at Tubac and throughout *Pimería Alta*, the nature of Spanish land use changed benefitting the Otero family and other early pioneers. Initially when Tubac was a *visita*, settlers resided on *valdios* (vacant) land exclusively owned by the Spanish monarchy.[14] These *valdios* lands were reserved for common use by early settlers to sustain their daily living needs. Natural resources like water, pasturage for grazing cattle, and wood for building or heat benefitted the whole community. A distinct second land right was exercised by the Spanish monarchy after military rule began. *Realengo* land was royal land reserved by the monarchy under right of conquest. After the 1751 Piman uprising at Tubac, the Spanish monarchy issued a royal ordinance on October 15, 1754 that required any petitions for *realengo* land to be made before the local sub-delegates of the province and then approved by the *real audencia*, a judicial tribunal, at Guadalajara, *Nueva España.*[15] This procedure proved burdensome for petitioners as travel was expensive and often precarious. Tubac's government rule at *Pimería Alta* fell under the jurisdiction of the Sonora/Sinaloa province in the Viceroyalty of *Nueva España.*[16]

ARIZONA'S FIRST LAND TRANSACTION

In 1776, the *presidio* of Tubac moved north to Tucson under the name San Agustín de Tucson pursuant to the Royal Ordinance of 1772 to realign the *presidios* on the Spanish frontier as a defense against foreign invaders.[17] Tucson began as a small community with an adjacent village of natives called San Agustín del Pueblito de Tucson. When the *presidio* was established, Tucson became a *rancheria de visita* of the mission San Xavier del Bac.[18] The new Tucson *presidio* supported a population of almost 1,000 - 2,000 persons at its height.[19] Royal Spanish Army Colonel Hugo O'conor was selected to command the military post at Tucson as Inspector Comandante of the Interior Provinces of *Nueva España* under direct orders from the Viceroy. O'conor was a controversial figure, "an object of fear to the savages, who kn[e]w him by the name of el Capitán Colorado or the Red Captain."[20] He established the location for the Tucson *presidio* in 1775.[21] By 1779, a new *presidio* commander Capitán Allande y Saavedra and an estimated twenty-five troops defended against regular Apache attack.

The presidio community was badly outnumbered.[22] Three years after the *presidio* moved from Tubac to Tucson, Arizona's first European land transaction between the Tucson *presidio* military authority and citizen Francisco Nuñez transpired. Despite daily adversity, early Tucson pioneers sought opportunities to enhance the quality of life for themselves and their families. As the American Revolutionary War entered its fifth year, citizen Francisco Nuñez petitioned Tucson presidio commander Don Pedro

Allande y Saavedra for a small parcel of land to use for agricultural purposes. To establish himself at the *presidio,* Nuñez reported he was an experienced farmer. Allande y Saavedra granted Nuñez permission to rent the land for a term of ten years on May 22, 1779 and plant to the south of the *presidio* as was local custom. Later in 1795, Don Torivio de Otero, the central figure of Arizona's land grant history, witnessed a subsequent contract transaction between Francisco Nuñez and Francisco Rivera in front of Tubac *presidio* Commander Nicolás de la Errán. Rivera sought to lease Francisco Nuñez's interest in the Tucson agricultural land for a term of two months.[23]

Figure 1.4. Tucson Presidio first Commander Hugo O'conor illustrated by Dorotea Cvijanovic commissioned exclusively for *Terrenos* © 2018 Diana DeLugan. All rights reserved.

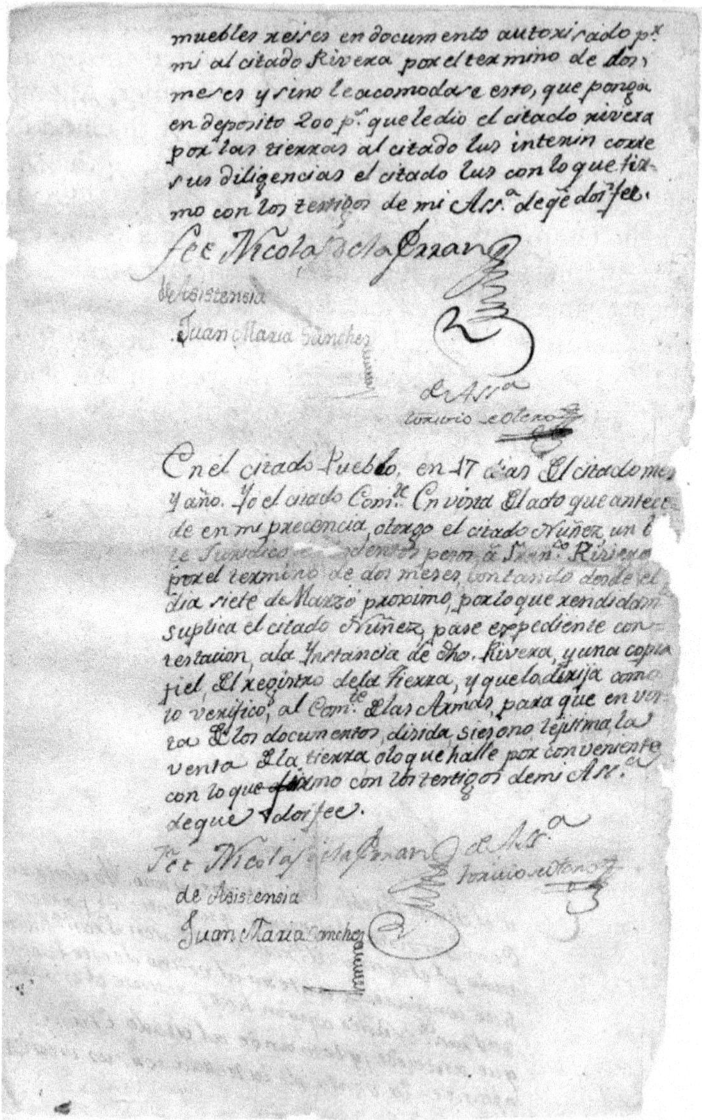
muebles reises en documento autorizado p.r
mi al citado Rivera por el termino de dos
meses y sino le acomodare esto, que ponga
en deposito 200 p.s que le dio el citado rivera
por las tierras al citado Luis interin corre
sus diligencias el citado Luis con lo que firmo con los testigos de mi Asist.a de que doy fee.

Nicolas de la Erran

de Asistencia
Juan Maria Sanchez

de Asist.a
Torivio de Otero

En el citado Pueblo, en 17 dias del citado mes
y año. Yo el citado Com.te En vista del acto que antecede en mi precencia, otorgo el citado Nuñez, un [illegible]
[illegible] Rivera
por el termino de dos meses contando desde el
dia siete de Marzo proximo, por lo que rendidam.te
suplica el citado Nuñez, pase expediente con-
testacion, ala Ynstancia de dho. Rivera, y una copia
fiel del registro dela tierra, y que la dirija como
lo verifico, al Com.te de las Armas, para que en vista de los documentos, decida si es ono legitima la
venta de la tierra o lo que halle por conveniente
con lo que firmo con los testigos de mi Asist.a
de que doy fee.

Nicolas de la Erran
de Asist.a
Torivio de Otero
de Asistencia
Juan Maria Sanchez

Figure 1.5. Page 4 of the Francisco Nuñez Spanish Land Grant. Page reflects the 1795 transaction of land at the Tubac Presidio authorized by Nicolas de la Errán, presidio commander who issued Don Torivio de Otero the first private title to land in 1789, and a witness signature at the lower right of the document by Torivio de Otero. See Appendix D. (Courtesy U.S. National Archives and Records Administration).[24]

Arizona's first European land transaction from the United States National Archives records offers us a glimpse into Spanish procedural requirements necessary to obtain land in colonial Arizona. The Nuñez land grant reveals that land had to be petitioned for at a local level, the transaction had to be witnessed, and land use had to be beneficial to the local community. Issued land was located in close proximity to the *presidio* as similarly reflected in the subsequent Otero land transaction at Tubac. The Francisco Nuñez land grant rightfully deserves recognition as Arizona's first European land transaction.

ARIZONA'S FIRST PRIVATE TITLE TO LAND

After Tubac's *presidio* was moved to Tucson pursuant to the 1772 military order of the *Nuevo Reglamento de Presidios*, Tubac's status under Spanish colonial policy reverted from that of a military fort to "the classification of a *pueblo*, the smallest civilian settlement except a ranch."[25] Suffering constant Apache attack and strained relations with individuals from Tubac who moved to Tucson, Tubac citizens petitioned to join the Tucson *presidio* or have the Tubac *presidio* restored.[26] Other Tubac residents requested permission to leave the country but the Spanish government declined their request and threatened severe penalties for anyone who disobeyed.[27] Tubac's population became severely depleted after some of its residents joined a Colorado River colonization effort and others moved to Tucson.[28] To help Tubac's repopulation efforts and encourage new settlement across Spain's northern frontier, which included present-day Arizona, a royal ordinance was issued on September 10, 1772 that granted *presidio* commanders authority to grant lands to new settlers. Title 11 of the Ordinance "*Gobierno politico*" or political government stated:

> 1. With the fair aim of encouraging the population and commerce in the countries of the Frontera, and also increasing their

strength with the greatest number of inhabitants, I command the commander, captains, officers, and others not to prevent or retreat with any pretext so that people of good living and customs can come and reside within its enclosure, and when [the presidio] cannot contain the additional families, it should be expanded by some on its side, taking this action on behalf of the common good and extend the benefit to all. And I also command the captains to identify and distribute lands and house lots, with the obligation that petitioners cultivate them, they should maintain horses, arms and ammunition to go out against the enemies when dictated by necessity and I order that soldiers who have served ten years of their commitment, whoever is retired due to age or illness, and families of those who have died be given preference to the distribution of lands, giving to some or others according to their situation and 100 pesos from the fund so they can pay for their labor.

2. I expressly prohibit that merchants of goods, food and other effects (which are not prohibited), or artists who wish to go to work at the military forts not be disturbed, nor impede their establishment, sale or temporary work; of which the captain will be responsible as chief and governor of this population.[29]

Figure 1.6. Tubac Presidio Ruins circa 1890. The presidio tower was erected in 1787 when Lt. Commander Pedro Villaescusa arrived with the Pima Company of *San Ignacio de Tubac* to protect Tubac's citizens against Apache hostilities. Public domain. (Courtesy Shaw Kinsley. Director Tubac Presidio State Historic Park and Museum).

Many brave settlers responded to the Spanish government's call to repopulate the dwindling settlement at Tubac.[30] Among them was Don Torivio de Otero. In his heart he carried a dream for land, a home for his family. During this early Spanish settlement period, travel across the Sonoran Desert was difficult but not impossible for Arizona's early colonial pioneers. As Tubac struggled to maintain its existence, Torivio de Otero married Maria Ygnacia Salazar at Santa Ana, Sonora on February 16, 1779.[31] Like other Hispanic pioneer families, the Otero[32] family lived in closely knit communities connected by custom and tradition. Torivio's parents, Joséf Otero and Francisca Granillo de Otero, lived at Cucurpe, Sonora[33] located one hundred and seven miles from Tubac. Torivio's sister Maria Dolores Otero de Salazar and her husband Juan Francisco Salazar lived in Santa Ana,[34] ninety-two miles from Tubac. Juan Francisco's parents also lived in Santa Ana.[35] Juan Francisco and Maria Dolores baptized three of their children at Santa Maria church in Magdalena, Sonora just eighty-one miles south east of Tubac: Joseph "José" Francisco Salazar Otero on July 21, 1774,[36] Maria Guadalupe Salazar Otero in May of 1777,[37] and Jose Ygnacio Loreto Salazar Otero on September 18, 1787.[38]

Don Torivio moved his family to Tubac sometime prior to March 5th of 1782 to make Tubac their permanent home.[39][40] His other brother-in-law, Lieutenant Pedro Sebastián Villaescusa,[41] was busy combating Apache and Seri forces while in charge of The Pima Company of San Rafael de Buena Vista. In 1787, Villaescusa and his company received new orders to protect the embattled *pueblo* of Tubac. With its move, the company assumed a new name: The Pima Company of *San Ignacio de Tubac.* The Piman Company consisted of eighty Pimas and two Spanish officers, Lt. Commander Pedro Villaescusa and Ensign Nicolás de la Errán.[42] Tubac citizens regained a sense of protection, at least for a while. When Villaescusa and his wife Maria Ignacia Otero arrived at Tubac, Don Torivio de Otero was there to meet them.[43]

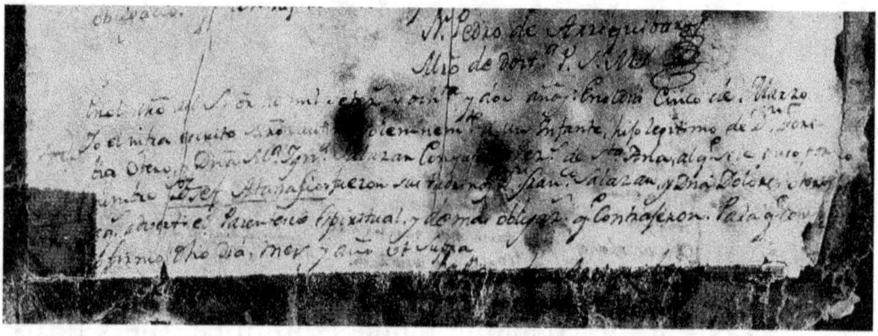

Figure 1.7. Mexican Baptismal Registry of Josef Atanacio Otero, son of Don Torivio de Otero and Maria Ygnacia Salazar. 3/5/1782. Ancient document. (Public domain).

Lt. Commander Villaescusa and his wife left Tubac on March 29, 1788 so Villaescusa could assume command of the Company of San Carlos at the Royal Fort at Buenavista. Through Torivio's family military connections or through his work as a teacher at the Tubac *presidio*, he soon discovered that he could petition the local *presidio* commander to obtain *realengo* (royal) land for private ownership. Nicolás de la Errán assumed command at the Tubac *presidio*.[44]

Saturday, January 10, 1789. Iridescent yellow sun rays would have crowned the crest of the majestic Santa Rita Mountains. Nearby saguaros stood sentry while four men walked together until they reached the spot where land would transfer from crown to cultivator south of the Tubac *presidio*. The group consisted of Don Torivio de Otero, the Tubac *presidio* Lieutenant Commander Nicolás de la Errán, and two witnesses Ramon Erieros and Ignacio Vasquez. The terms of the land grant were read to all present then acknowledged by Don Torivio. Next, a small ceremony was held to finalize the grant. Comandante de la Errán stretched out his arm and intently took Torivio's hand placing within it a handful of loose earth and stone which Torivio ceremoniously scattered. Torivio then reached down and pulled up herbage in a symbolic act to accept the land and acknowledge his new ownership right.[45]

With these small gestures, the first European title to private ownership of land in colonial Arizona was official. Spanish land grant procedures required that the land grant be formally documented. Witnesses affixed their signatures to the grant because no notary was present. The land grant document was stamped with the royal rubric and signed by legal witnesses Ignacio Vasquez and Ramón García Erieros.

Figure 1.8. Illustration of the 1787 Tubac Spanish Presidio by Shazeb Turk commissioned exclusively for *Terrenos* © 2018 Diana DeLugan. All rights reserved.

Records omit whether Don Torivio was granted land because the *presidio* exceeded capacity, or if he fell into one of the specified categories of preferred land grant recipients as stated in the regulations of 1772. Most likely, Don Torivio was an eligible candidate because he was from a military family. Unlike the 1779 Francisco Nuñez land rental document from Tucson, Don Torivio de Otero's land grant at Tubac contained certain mandatory conditions under the Spanish Royal Ordinance of 1772 that had to be satisfied before Don Torivio could receive clear title to the land. After Tubac fell under United States government rule pursuant to the Gadsden Purchase finalized in 1854, the Otero land grant was reviewed for authenticity by U.S. government officials. The following English translation of the Otero Spanish land grant of 1789 was obtained from the United States Surveyor General of Arizona files at the United States National Archives and Records repository.[46] It is important to note that Don Torivio's land transaction was a gift from the Spanish crown, likely granted as an incentive to encourage initial private settlement at Tubac.

No monetary consideration was required unlike later Spanish or Mexican grants.

In the first section of the grant, we discover that the grant of land benefitted the Tubac community once grain could be harvested:

> ***Translation:*** *Whereas; the resident Toribio de Otero*[47] *having presented himself before me, petitioning for a house lot (Solar) on which to establish himself, in this Presidio, for the purpose of pursuing his calling, as an agriculturalist; and in consideration of the utility resulting from the establishment of industrious settlers, such as the petitioner, who will cultivate the soil, thereby furnishing a supply of grain, which, in some seasons, has to be brought from a long distance*

In the next section, the *presidio* commander identifies Torivio de Otero as the first settler at Tubac and identifies the boundaries of the Otero *Solar*, house lot. Of significance, the land was granted in perpetuity for Torivio and all his descendants, meaning the property was private property that no public or government entity or private person could ever take from the Otero family:

> ***Translation:*** *I Therefore, in the exercise of the faculties conferred on me by the King, grant to the said Torribio [sic] de Otero, and donate to him, as a first settler, perpetually forever, and with right of inheritance, to him and his children and descendants, a lot on which to build his house, on the lower side of this Presidio, in the direction of the South, with a front to the north, of twenty varas;*

Next, the land grant specified the location of the ranch land and its boundaries. The ranch was intentionally placed in proximity of water to ensure that Don Torivio's land would be irrigated. The passage reveals that Don Torivio had already built an irrigation system to support his ranch operations resulting in the first documented reference of a European-built irrigation system in Arizona:

> ***Translation:*** *and a tract of land, for cultivation, distant from the Presidio, about one eighth of a league, since only at that point, is found the little water, that runs in the river; and he having made there his irrigating ditch; I grant him also in the name of the King (wherein God preserve) four "suertes" (farming lots) of land; the measurement of the same to be made, from South to North, and East to West, four hundred varas; which tract is embraced in a circumference of 3.400 varas.*

As the permanent first settler and private land owner, Don Torivio was exempt from any future royal order to move with *presidio* troops and families. However, the land grant required he aid the military and defend against any hostile attack. Protection against hostilities may have been why Don Torivio and his family were required to live at the presidio for four (4) years while he built a house and cultivated the land. In addition, the transfer of land to another was restricted during the initial four years of land possession:[48]

> ***Translation:*** *It being well understood, that the said Toribio [sic] de Otero, is required to keep arms and horses, and to be ever ready to defend the country against the enemies thereof, when he is called upon, so to do—It being also understood, that until the term of four years, shall have passed, counting from the present date; the grantee cannot sell; alienate, or mortgage the said land; nor can he impose any encumbrance on the said house lot, or tract of land, although it should be for pious purposes - That within the precise term of two years, he shall have built his house; and that he shall have resided*

> *with his family in this Presidio, for the term of four years, before he can acquire the full dominion of property in the land and Solar (house lot), and the improvements he may have made thereon.*

Explicit in the terms were a few additional requirements not specified in the Royal Order of 1772. Don Torivio was prohibited from alienating his land by sale or devise to any religious organization, beneficial use of the land was required (an issue of later controversy during 1804/1807), and trees had to be planted. The Tubac community was certain to benefit from fruit-bearing trees or the wood for fuel, building and tools:

> ***Translation:*** *And that, when this time shall have passed, he shall have the power, to sell or alienate said land and house lot, and to make such use thereof, as he may see fit, as of a thing belonging to himself; under the condition, that he shall never be permitted to sell the same to the Church or to any monastery, ecclesiastical person or community, nor convey them in mortmain, under the penalty above mentioned; the grantee being also required, to plant upon said land, fruit trees, or other kinds, that may be of some utility; and the said Toribio [sic] de Otero being informed of the foregoing, I took him by the hand, and gave him possession of said lands; he, according to custom, scattering earth and stones, and pulling up herbage—In testimony of which, I give him the present document, which remains copied in the protocol of the archives of this Presidio; signing the same with the assisting witnesses, in the 10th day of the month of January 1789.*
> *Nicolás de la Errán (rubric)*

Ignacio Vasquez (rubric)
Ramón García Erieros (rubric)(8)
(Sealed with the two-real arbitrator's stamp of Charles IV for the years 1788 and 1789)
(Sealed with the two-real arbitrator's stamp of Charles IV for the years 1802 and 1803)
(Sealed with the two-real arbitrator's stamp of Charles IV for the years 1806 and 1807) [49][50]

Don Torivio's historic land grant allowed him to create a home and industry for his family. The *terrenos* were later used by his descendants to expand their land holdings and financially provide for the family for nearly two centuries. The 1789 transaction was the first of two land grants owned by the Oteros.

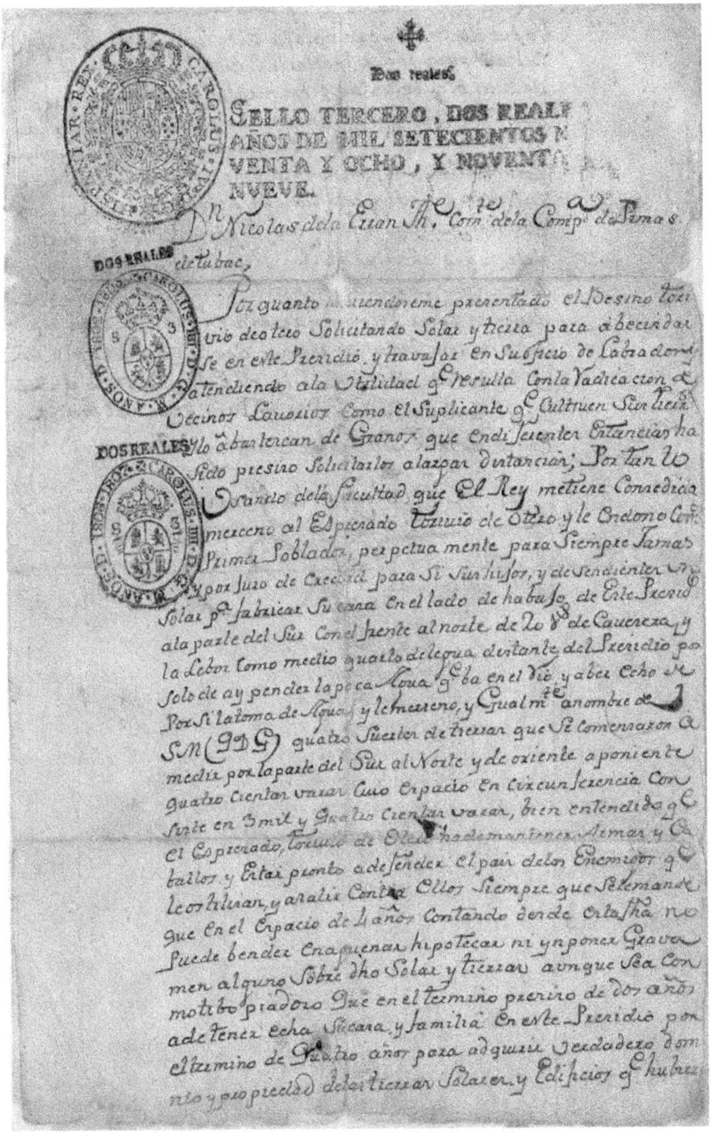

Figure 1.9. Page 1 of the Torivio de Otero Spanish Land Grant of 1/10/1789 issued to Otero by Lt. Comandante Nicolas de la Errán. This document represents the first private ownership of land in Arizona. (Courtesy U.S. National Archives and Records Administration).[51]

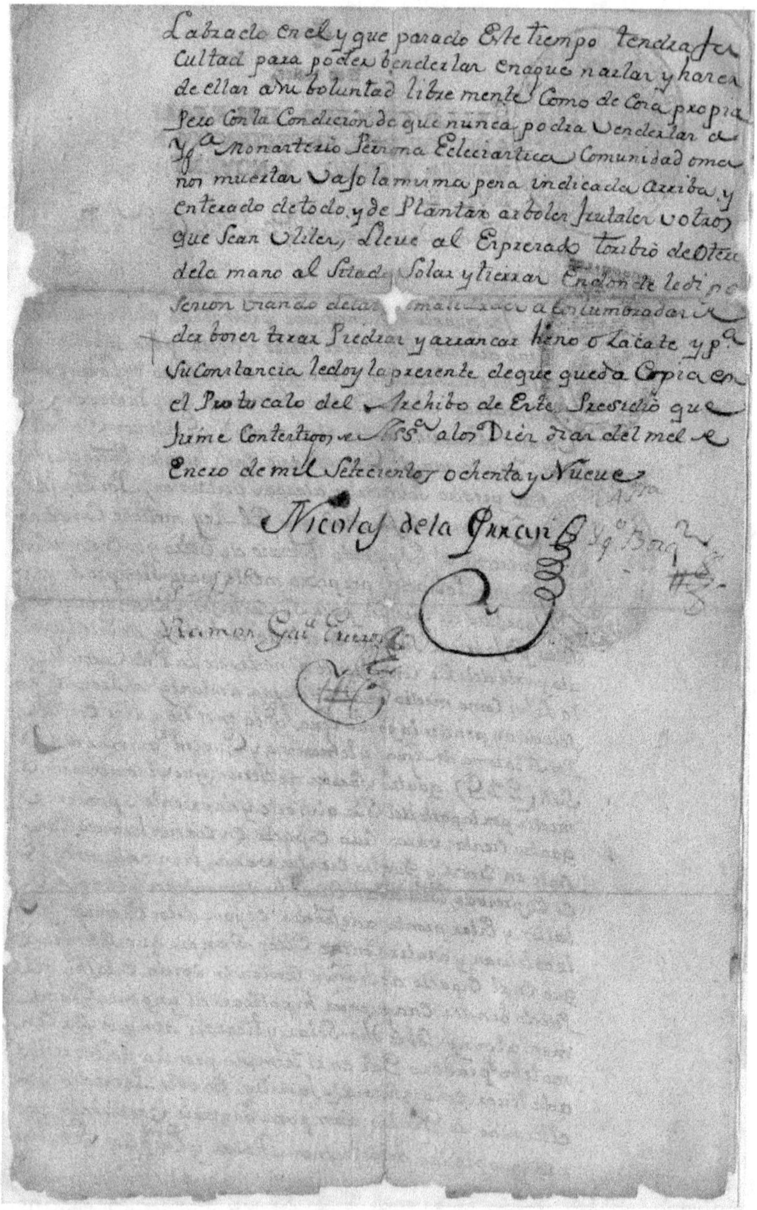

Labrado en el y que pasado este tiempo tendra facultad para poder benderlas en a que nas las y hacer
de ellas a su boluntad libremente como de cosa propia
pero con la condicion de que nunca podra venderlas a
Yg.a Monasterio Persona Eclesiastica Comunidad o ma-
nos muertas vajo la misma pena indicada arriba y
enterado de todo y de plantar arboles frutales u otros
que sean utiles, lleve al expresado Toribio de Otero
de la mano al citado solar y tierras en donde le di po-
session usando de las formalidades acostumbradas
da boses tirar piedras y arrancar heno o zacate y p.a
su constancia le doy la presente de que queda copia en
el Protocolo del Archibo de este Presidio que
firme con testigos en S.n a los Diez dias del mes de
Enero de mil setecientos ochenta y Nueve

Nicolas de la Erran

Ramon Gar.a

Figure 1.10. Page 2 of the Torivio de Otero Spanish Land Grant of 1/10/1789 issued to Otero by Lt. Comandante Nicolas de la Errán. (Courtesy U.S. National Archives and Records Administration).

Figure 1.11. Page 3 of the Torivio de Otero Spanish Land Grant of 1/10/1789 issued to Otero by Lt. Comandante. Nicolas de la Errán. (Courtesy U.S. National Archives and Records Administration).

SQUATTER CONTEST OF 1807

During the same year when Meriwether Lewis and William Clark embarked on their expedition up the Missouri River at the behest of President Thomas Jefferson,[52] a portion of the Otero land grant farm property at Tubac was temporarily abandoned after water became scarce making irrigation impossible. Due to the drought, Don Torivio de Otero moved his farming operations downstream adjacent the Santa Cruz River. After water levels returned to an abundant flow to irrigate his previously cultivated land, Don Torivio returned to his land upstream and discovered to his dismay that three squatters occupied and possessed his land.

Don Torivio promptly appealed to the Commander of the Tubac *presidio* Lieutenant Manuel de León for legal relief requesting that the squatters be immediately removed, and the land returned to him as rightful owner. The commander informed Don Torivio that he, De León, gave the squatters permission to use the land based on the concept of beneficial use,[53] a requirement specified in the original 1789 Otero land grant. Any agricultural land that could produce harvest would benefit the *presidio* and surrounding Tubac community. The commander further explained he knew Don Torivio had previously allowed another individual to cultivate a portion of his farming land that he was not using.

De León advised Don Torivio that he was unable to resolve the squatter land dispute. A dispute of such magnitude had to be resolved by García Conde, the military political Governor and Treasurer of the Province at Arizpe, Sonora.[54]

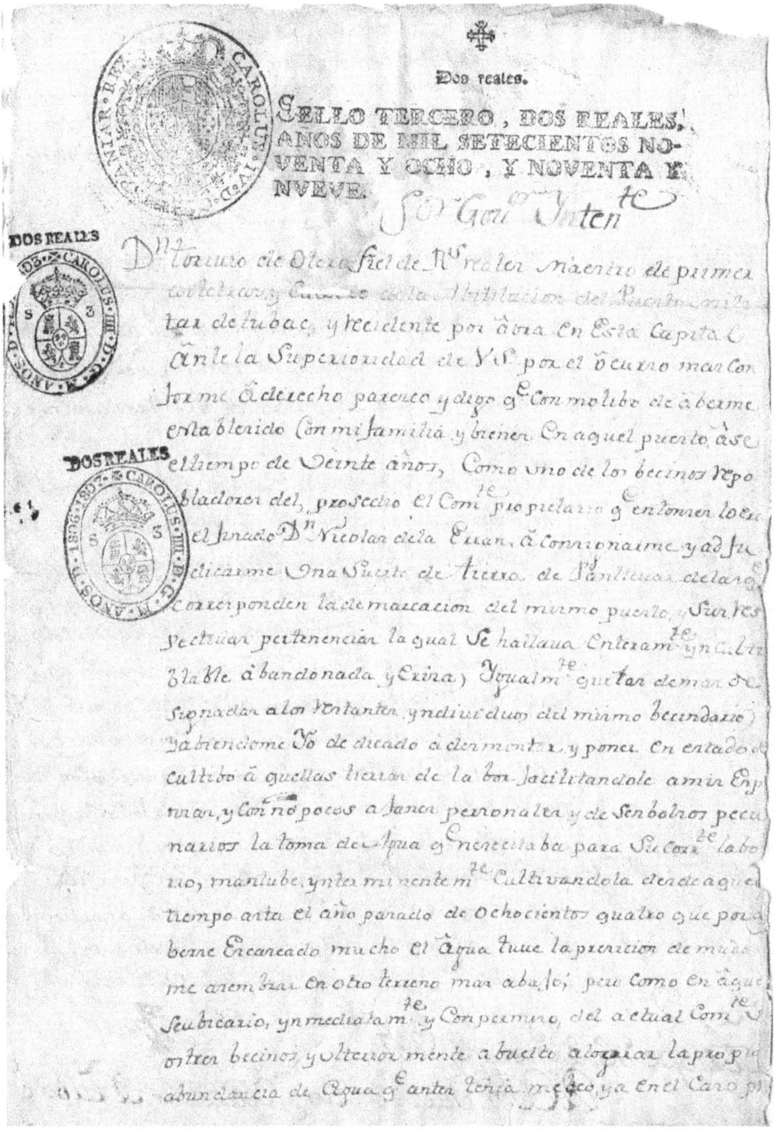
Dos reales.

SELLO TERCERO, DOS REALES, AÑOS DE MIL SETECIENTOS NOVENTA Y OCHO, Y NOVENTA Y NUEVE.

Figure 1.12. Page 1 of the Torivio de Otero Spanish Land Grant Squatter Challenge Petition dated 1807. In the first page of Otero's petition to regain exclusive ownership of his land, he disclosed he went to Tubac for resettlement and worked as a teacher at the Tubac presidio for 20 year. (Arizona Historical Society. MS683).

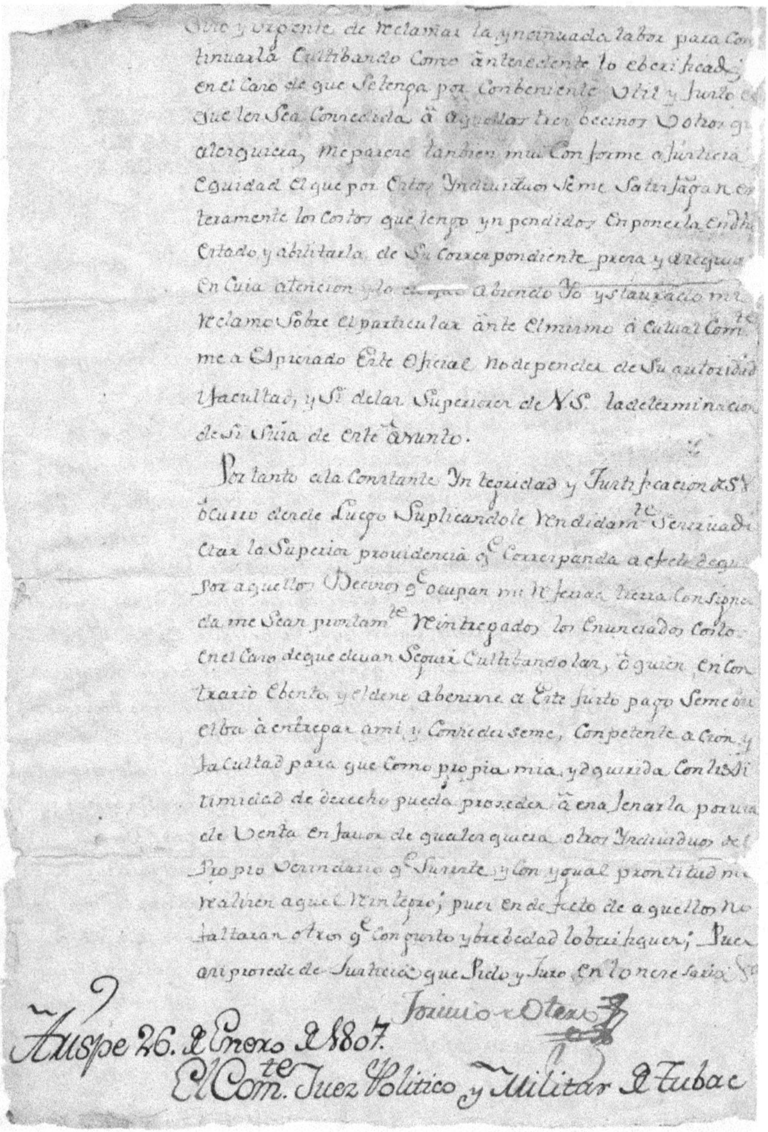

Otro y urgente de reclamar la ynsinuada labor para Con-
tinuarla Cultibando Como antecedente lo eberificado;
en el Caso de que Se tenga por Conbeniente Util y Justo e[l]
que les Sea Concedida a aquellos tres becinos U otros q[ue]
alegueren, me parece tambien mui Conforme a Justicia
equidad el que por Estos Yndividuos Se me Satisfagan en-
teramente los Costos que tengo ympendidos En ponerla En dh[a]
Estado y abilitarla de Su Correspondiente presa y acequia
En Cuia atencion y lo aviendo Yo ynstaurado mi
reclamo Sobre el particular ante el mismo a Cuial Com.te
me a Espresado Este Oficial no depender de Su autoridad
y facultad, y Si de las Superiores de V.S. la determinacion
de Si Suia de este asunto.

Por tanto a la Constante Yntegridad y Justificacion de V.S.
ocurro desde Luego Suplicandole rendidam.te Se sirva di-
ctar la Superior providencia q.e Corresponda a efecto de que
por aquellos Becinos q.e ocupan mi referida tierra Consigna-
da me Sean prontam.te reintegrados los Enunciados Costos
en el Caso de que deuan Seguir Cultibandolas, o quien en Con-
trario Evento y el dene aberirse a Este Justo pago Se me bu-
elba a entregar a mi y Concedaseme, Competente accion y
facultad para que Como propia mia y adquirida Con legi-
timidad de derecho pueda proceder a enajenarla por via
de Venta en favor de qualesquiera otros Yndividuos del
Propio Vecindario q.e Suviente y Con ygual prontitud me
realizen aquel reintegro; pues en defecto de aquellos no
faltaran otros q.e Con gusto y brebedad lo berifiquen; Pues
asi procede de Justicia que Pido y Juro en lo necesario &a

Torivio de Otero

Arispe 26. de Enero de 1807.
El Com.te Juez Politico y Militar de Tubac

Figure 1.13. Page 2 of the Torivio de Otero Spanish Land Grant Squatter Challenge Petition dated 1807. (Arizona Historical Society. MS683).

Don Torivio travelled to Arizpe and submitted a written petition to Governor García Conde. The petition dated 1804 advised the governor that Don Torivio was personally in Arizpe to appear before his Lordship as duly required by law. As evidence of his superior right to the contested land, Don Torivio argued in his petition:

- he arrived at Tubac with his family as a *repoblador*, a person with the intent to help repopulate the dwindling *pueblo* community
- he established ties with the *presidio* community during the previous twenty years
- he was employed as a writing teacher (*primeras letras)* at the Tubac *presidio*
- he was legally granted title to the contested land by former Tubac *presidio* commander Nicolás de la Errán
- the land granted to him by de la Errán was entirely uncultivated, abandoned and fallow
- he cleared and cultivated the contested land with his own labor and at his own financial expense
- he paid for and built an irrigation system to take the necessary water for his fields, and
- he continuously cultivated the land from the time he received the land until 1804, the year prior to submitting his petition to Conde.

Don Torivio also asked to be reimbursed for the use of the land he cultivated in the event the squatters remained on his farm land. Alternatively, he argued that the land should be returned to his sole possession with full right of ownership to dispose of the land as he pleased if he was not reimbursed by the squatters.[55] Any hope for a swift decision was shattered. The next major action in the case occurred on January 26, 1807, nearly two years after Don Torivio filed his petition for justice. Military political Governor Conde ordered military commander and judge at Tubac Manuel de León to provide a truthful and complete report regarding his personal knowledge of Don Torivio's case. De León duly replied:

- he admitted he had personal knowledge that Don Torivio possessed a true copy of his title to land signed by the late Nicolás de la Errán
- he acknowledged Don Torivio as the "first settler" at the Tubac *presidio*
- Conde granted permission for the squatters to farm Don Torivio's land with the understanding that Don Torivio was the legitimate owner of the land, and
- Conde verified that it was self-evident that Don Torivio incurred significant expense to provide water to the contested land evidenced by the existing ditch on the land.[56]

Manuel de León deferred to Governor Conde to render the final decision on whether the squatters or Don Torivio held superior land rights suggesting that, at minimum, Don Torivio should be reimbursed for some of the costs he incurred. Governor Conde issued his long-awaited final order on February 12, 1807. Conde held that Don Torivio's allegations were true and that military commander and judge de León should promptly ensure that Don Torivio be reimbursed by the squatters for costs and expenses.

In the event squatters proved insolvent and unable to pay Don Torivio, Governor Conde decreed that Don Torivio be placed back in possession of his lands expeditiously so that he could cultivate it or lease it as he deemed fit.[57] Available records regarding the land squatter challenge from the Arizona Historical Society Library at Tucson omit whether Don Torivio received payment for the lease of his land, or if the squatters simply abandoned Otero's land. Don Torivio's family retained possession of the Spanish land until after Arizona gained its statehood. Continuous possession of the land reflects that Don Torivio de Otero successfully defended his superior land ownership rights against squatters to the Spanish government.

Communications exchanged between Don Torivio, Governor Conde and Manuel de León, military commander and judge at Tubac reveal several important Arizona historical facts: (1) education was important in colonial Spanish Arizona, (2) Don Torivio, a Spaniard, created a new private irrigation system in Arizona, and (3) the term "first settler" was clarified. Most modern Arizona history generally begins with the Gadsden Purchase. Commonly-held Tubac history focuses on 1752 and the establishment of the Tubac Presidio, then fast-forwards to the 1880s and the establishment of the 1885 Tubac Schoolhouse. The Otero land grant squatter challenge documents fills in details of Tubac life after the reestablishment of the Tubac presidio in 1787.

Spanish government transactions and commerce highly depended on presidial communications. Since the center of Sonoran government was a substantial distance from military outposts, it was imperative that all orders, progress, and transactions be memorialized to ensure that actions taken satisfied directives of the Spanish government. As the *maestro de letras*, or teacher of writing, Don Torivio de Otero was an essential citizen, the very nexus of Tubac's prosperity.

Pre-European Arizona history rightfully recognizes Native Americans for building the first irrigation systems in Arizona. While scholars also acknowledge that Spanish settlers subsequently expanded existing indigenous irrigation systems, few reports reflect that Spaniards built new water distribution systems in Arizona. Spanish Tubac of 1765 had an acequia system of irrigation and water management that reflected a community-centric responsibility for water use. Spanish water rights laws protected both individual and community beneficial use of water. The Otero 1789 and 1804/7 Spanish documents confirm Don Torivio was the first recorded Spaniard to build a new private irrigation system in Arizona[58], as opposed to merely expanding upon systems previously built by indigenous people.

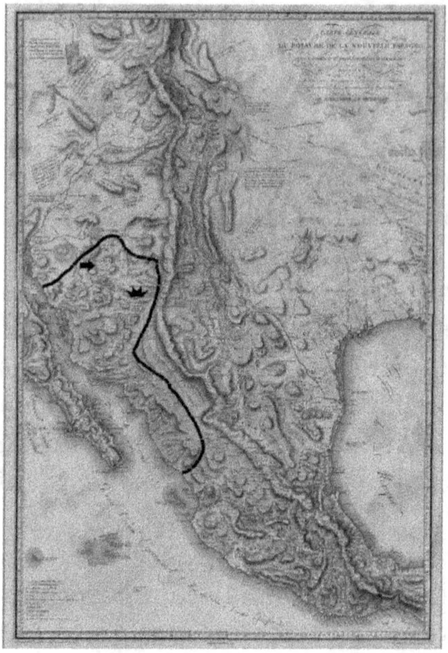

Figure 1.14. 1804 Map of New Spain, Nuevo Mexico. Travel between Tubac Presidio (at arrow) and Arizpe (crown), capital of Sonoran seat of Spanish government would have been precarious. Map shows the distance that Torivio de Otero personally traveled to petition for his land to be returned from squatters.[59] (Public domain. Edited by author).

Figure 1.15. The term for Spanish hacienda owner is *Hacendado.* Don Torivio de Otero was the first *Hacendado* in Arizona. [60] (Public domain).

Further, the use of the term "first settler" in both the 1789 Otero land grant and 1804/1807 land squatter challenge reveals that the Spanish government drew a clear distinction between individuals who lived at Spanish government-own settlements and private individuals who intended permanent settlement. Settlers lived in Arizona, then known as *Pimería Alta, Nueva España*, prior to Otero's arrival at Tubac in 1787. Certainly, Otero was not the first Spaniard to build a home at Tubac. Tubac was first an indigenous settlement then subsequently populated by Spanish families evidenced by the south barrio archaeological site south of present-day Tubac. Since the start of the Spanish conquest of Mexico until prior to the issuance of the Otero land grant of 1789, the land occupied by settlers of Spanish Arizona was *valdios* land, vacant land owned by the King of Spain held in trust for the common use of the people. When the King of Spain granted Don Torivio royal (*realengo*) land with full dominion in perpetuity over the granted land, Torivio's settlement became permanent.

As Tubac's first permanent citizen, Don Torivio de Otero was Tubac's first settler. He had no intent to leave. He was free to build a home and a ranch, to cultivate his land, and raise his family. Don Torivio's dream was to see subsequent generations live in prosperity working the land he fought hard to retain. As we discover later in this book, his dream was heartily challenged after Tubac became part of the United States pursuant to the Gadsden Purchase.

1838 MARTINEZ LAND GRANT ADDITION

Don Torivio and his family maintained continuous possession of the family land at Tubac through the end of the Spanish Arizona era as they witnessed Mexico's independence from Spain in 1821. During this time, local resident Jose Maria Martinez obtained a land grant from the Mexican authorities on November 7, 1838. The Martinez property was located adjacent to the southernmost portion of the 1789 land grant ranch property. This adjacent tract of farming and grazing land was acquired by Manuel Otero, Don Torivio de Otero's grandson, on March 2, 1859. The land conveyance was memorialized in writing. Although the Martinez land grant was issued under the authority of the Mexican government in 1838, its terms were nearly identical to that of Don Torivio's Spanish land grant in 1789, forty-nine years prior. Arms and horses had to be maintained in the event of hostile attack. Martinez had to live at the Tubac *presidio* for four (4) years while he cultivated the land. Like Otero, Martinez was prohibited from alienating his land by sale or devise to any religious organization ever or to any third party during the initial four-year term. Trees for fruit or timber and fuel were also required to be planted on the land boundaries:

> The Alcalde (mayor) of the Presidio of Tubac, Trinidad Yrigoyen, in accordance with Article 33 of the Special Regulations of Presidios. The tract was located west of the river on the road to Tucson. The tract commenced "at the enclosure of Atanacio Otero" and ran thence south twenty-eight *cordeles* of twenty-five *varas* each to the foot of the *mesita* in front of a black mesquite. The tract was seven *cordeles* wide and was extended from the House of Correction on the west to the river bank on the east. Martinez was placed in possession of the tract on November 7, 1838, subject to the same conditions as Otero.[61]

After Tubac became a United States possession pursuant to the Gadsden Purchase ratified in 1854, the Martinez/Otero land grant had to be perfected under U.S. law to prevent the family from losing its lands to government or outside interests. On June 29, 1880, Dario Martinez, sole heir-at-law to the Jose Maria Martinez land grant, sold the land to Manuel Otero's eldest son Sabino for the sum of five (5) dollars recorded in Pima County Book of Deeds.

The Martinez/Otero deed of 1880 reflects the same boundary measurements and monuments as contained in the original 1838 Jose Maria Martinez land grant. According to U.S. Bureau of Land Management Records, the Martinez land grant property consisted of 73.22 acres and thus expanded the initial Otero farm tract from 111.09 acres to 184.31 acres.[62] Given the patriarchal custom both in Spanish and Mexican societies, Sabino Otero likely claimed the land for the benefit of his family with his family's consent as perfunctory head of household after his father Manuel's death. Dario Martinez issued the Deed to prevent the land from being usurped by others. Had Sabino claimed the Martinez land grant property for his sole personal and exclusive use, his mother Maria Clara Martinez Otero, widow of Manuel Otero, and all of Sabino's siblings could have easily exercised their rights under law against Sabino Otero to claim their legal share of the Martinez land grant.[63] History reflects that all Otero family members benefitted from Sabino's claim of the Martinez land.

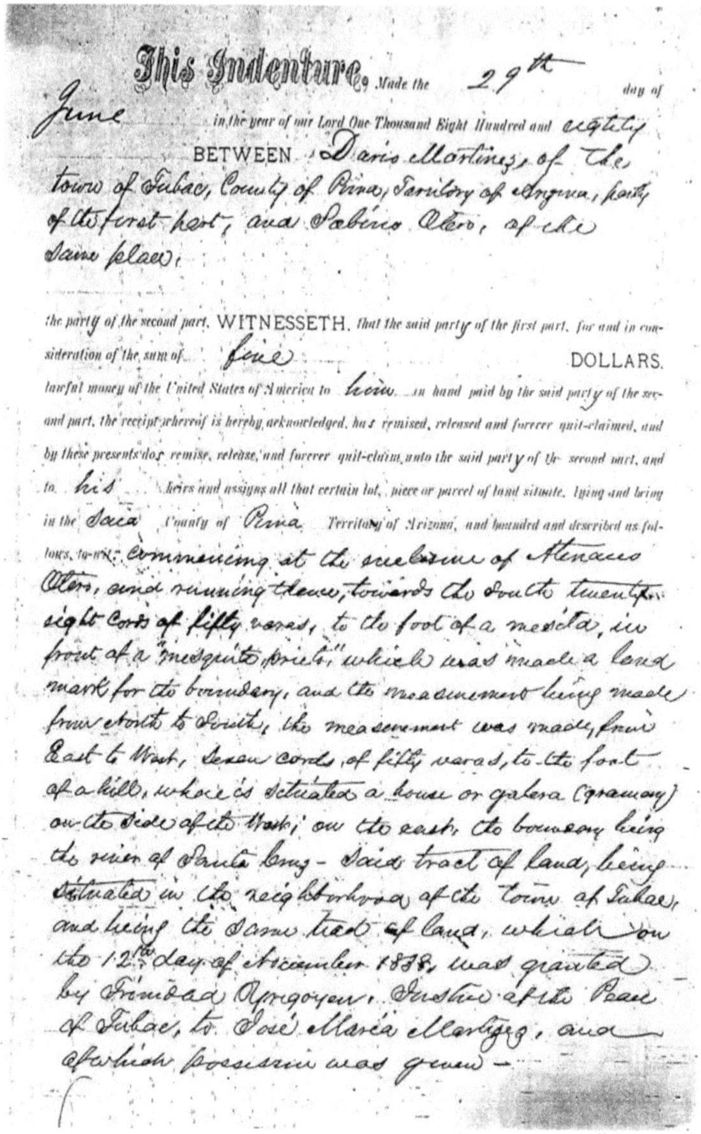

This Indenture, Made the 29th day of June in the year of our Lord One Thousand Eight Hundred and eighty BETWEEN Dario Martinez, of the town of Tubac, County of Pima, Territory of Arizona, party of the first part, and Sabino Otero, of the same place,

the party of the second part, WITNESSETH, that the said party of the first part, for and in consideration of the sum of five DOLLARS, lawful money of the United States of America to him in hand paid by the said party of the second part, the receipt whereof is hereby acknowledged, has remised, released and forever quit-claimed, and by these presents does remise, release, and forever quit-claim, unto the said party of the second part, and to his heirs and assigns all that certain lot, piece or parcel of land situate, lying and being in the same County of Pima Territory of Arizona, and bounded and described as follows, to-wit: commencing at the enclosure of Atenacio Otero, and running thence, towards the South twenty-eight cords of fifty varas, to the foot of a mesita, in front of a "mesquite prieto," which was made a land mark for the boundary, and the measurement being made from North to South, the measurement was made, from East to West, seven cords of fifty varas, to the foot of a hill, where is situated a house or galera (granary) on the side of the West; on the east, the boundary being the river of Santa Cruz - Said tract of land, being situated in the neighborhood of the town of Tubac, and being the same tract of land, which on the 12th day of December 1838, was granted by Trinidad Irigoyen, Justice of the Peace of Tubac, to José María Martinez, and of which possession was given -

Figure 1.16. Page 1 of the Dario Martinez Deed to Sabino Otero on 6/29/1880. From the Book of Deeds U.S. Surveyor General Journal Volume 3, pages 48-50. (Arizona State Library, Archives & Public Records. U.S. Bureau of Land Management Filmfile # 10.1.22. Assorted grants & miscellaneous papers).

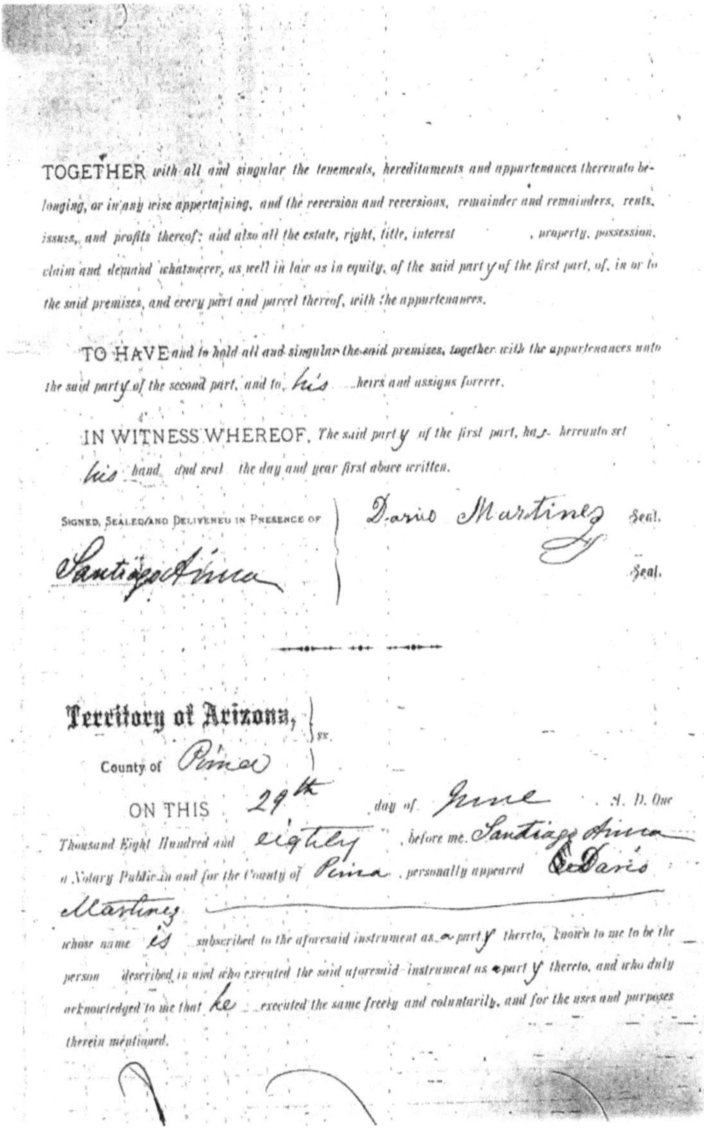

TOGETHER with all and singular the tenements, hereditaments and appurtenances thereunto belonging, or in any wise appertaining, and the reversion and reversions, remainder and remainders, rents, issues, and profits thereof; and also all the estate, right, title, interest , property, possession, claim and demand whatsoever, as well in law as in equity, of the said party of the first part, of, in or to the said premises, and every part and parcel thereof, with the appurtenances.

TO HAVE and to hold all and singular the said premises, together with the appurtenances unto the said party of the second part, and to his heirs and assigns forever.

IN WITNESS WHEREOF, The said party of the first part, has hereunto set his hand and seal the day and year first above written.

Signed, Sealed and Delivered in Presence of

Santiago Ainsa

Dario Martinez Seal.

Seal.

Territory of Arizona, } ss.

County of Pima

ON THIS 29th day of June A. D. One Thousand Eight Hundred and eighty, before me, Santiago Ainsa a Notary Public in and for the County of Pima, personally appeared Dario Martinez whose name is subscribed to the aforesaid instrument as a party thereto, known to me to be the person described in and who executed the said aforesaid instrument as a party thereto, and who duly acknowledged to me that he executed the same freely and voluntarily, and for the uses and purposes therein mentioned.

Figure 1.17. Page 2 of the Dario Martinez Deed to Sabino Otero on 6/29/1880. From the Book of Deeds U.S. Surveyor General Journal Volume 3, pages 48-50. (Arizona State Library, Archives & Public Records. U.S. Bureau of Land Management Filmfile # 10.1.22. Assorted grants & miscellaneous papers).

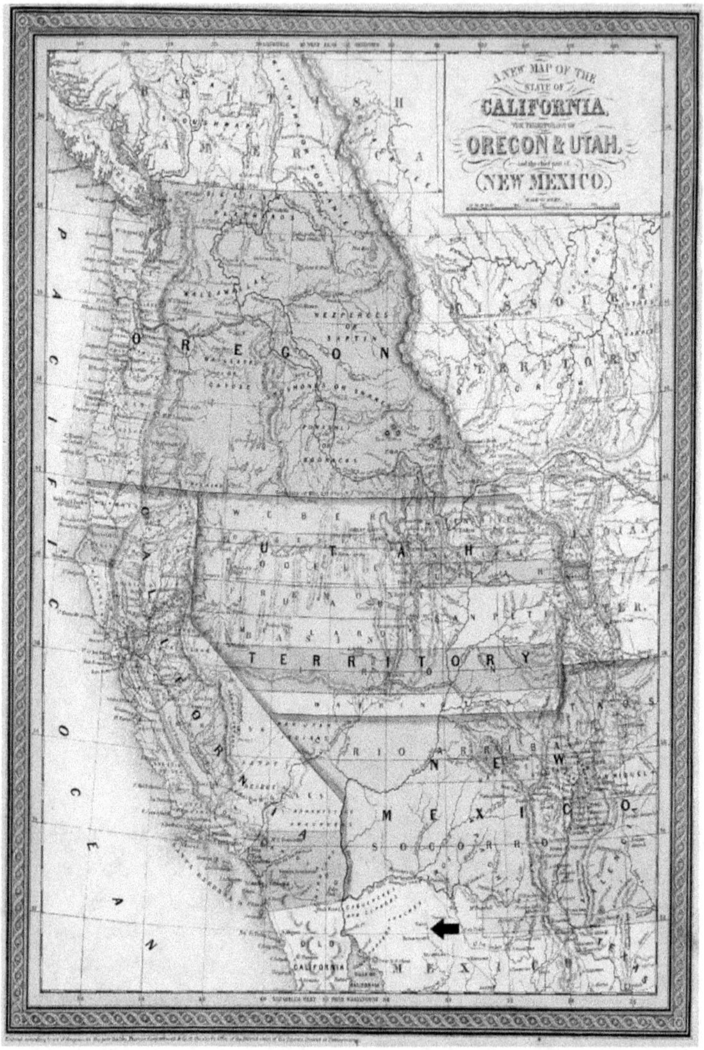

Figure 1.18. A New Map of the State of California: the Territories of Oregon & Utah, and the Chief Part of Mexico. Thomas Cowperthwait & Co. Pennsylvania: 1853. (Public domain image. Edited by the author). Arrow on map depicts location of Tubac in Mexico in the same year Mexico and the United States signed the Gadsden Treaty ceding 29,670 square miles including Tubac to the United States.

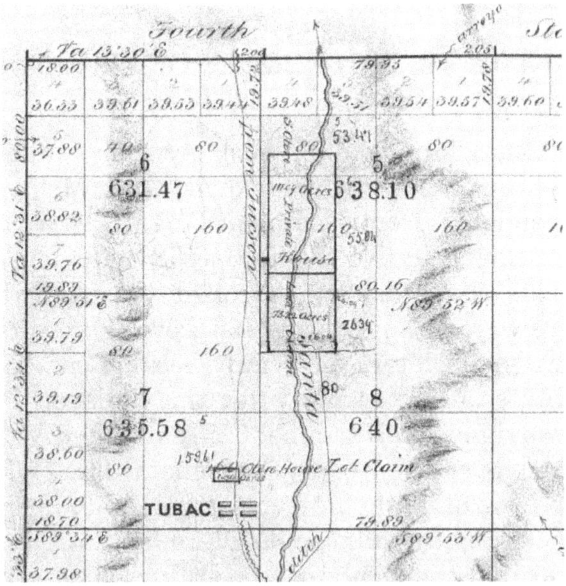

Figure 1.19. Excerpt of Map of Tubac, Township 21 South of Range No. 13 East of the Gila and Salt River Meridian, Arizona filed at the Surveyor General's Office at Tucson, AZ on 2/19/1877 by U.S. Surveyor General John Wasson. (U.S. Bureau of Land Management). The map specifically identifies the location of the Otero lands including the southern expansion of the ranch after the Martinez land grant purchase by Manuel Otero.

Figure 1.20. A modern view of the Martinez Spanish Land Grant facing north towards the Tubac Golf Resort & Spa, Tubac, AZ. (Photograph by the author).

LAND OFFICE AND COURT OF PRIVATE LAND CLAIMS PETITIONS

The Otero family of Spanish Arizona automatically became Mexican citizens by residency after Mexico gained its independence from Spain on August 24, 1821. The family continued to live at the Otero Solar (house lot) at Tubac near the Mexican-controlled presidio while the family grew crops and grazed its growing herd of cattle. Thirty-two years later, the family became citizens of the United States by residency after the Gadsden Purchase Treaty was signed on December 30, 1853. After Arizona fell under U.S. government rule, the General Land Office was tasked to determine the fate of Spanish and Mexican land grants including the Rancho de Otero land at Tubac. "The ownership of the soil in severalty is essential to civilization," reported the Commissioner of General Land Office to the Secretary of the Interior in 1870.[64] The U.S. federal government claimed itself as trustee of all unoccupied western lands: "We find the United States government standing to the immense bodies of our unoccupied western domain in the relation of the trustee of society, holding not only the right of eminent domain but also of individual ownership."[65]

The General Land Office was established in 1812[66] "to handle the business associated with the sale of public lands for private ownership, transforming wilderness to agricultural use, and generating income for the Federal government."[67] It was this division of the federal government that established the procedure to survey lands, subdivide townships, and determine the validity of foreign government land grants.[68] The General Land Office's policy was to ensure that parties who claimed foreign titles to land could secure those lands, "even to premises to which no written title is recorded, where claimants had actual settlements before change of sovereignty."[69]

Figure 1.21. Fernando Otero one of the petitioners to the Tucson General Land Office to claim U.S. recognition of ancestral lands at Tubac under the Torivio de Otero land grant of 1789. Illustrated by Dorotea Cvijanovic commissioned exclusively for *Terrenos* © 2018 Diana DeLugan. All rights reserved.

Otero land records reveal that the land policy of the federal government failed the Otero family of Tubac,[70] much as it failed countless families who owned land grants from Spanish and Mexican governments. Arizona property claimants who wanted their foreign land grant ownership confirmed had to submit a claim according to an Act of Congress of July 15, 1870. The Commissioner of the General Land Office (GLO) explained, "no limit [wa]s placed by law upon the time within which claimants under foreign grants in New Mexico and Arizona must present their claims."[71] To conform with the Act, a claim to perfect the 1789 Otero land grant under U.S. law was filed with U.S. Surveyor General John Wasson at the Tucson General Land Office on December 1, 1879. The petition filed by attorneys "Lindley & Corella" was titled "In the matter of the petition of Sabino Otero and others for confirmation of a pueblo land grant in the town of Tubac." Petitioners for the claim were siblings Sabino Otero, Fernando Otero, Teofilo Otero, Gabriela Otero and Elena Otero Castro.[72] Their sister Manuela Otero was married to Louis Quesse and abstained from the claim.[73]

As lineal descendants of Spanish land grantee Don Torivio Otero through Atanacio Otero and Manuel Otero, son of Atanacio, petitioners asked for confirmation of the marked and enclosed land known as "Otero's Ranch" with land on both sides of the Santa Cruz River. In an apparent exercise of her right of apportionment granted under the Howell Code and Acts and Amendments Chapter 26, Section 1.1 "Of Title to Real Property by Descent," Ana Maria (Comadurán) Coenen claimed her portion of the land as the only surviving child of Francisca Otero Comadurán, deceased.[74] Francisca was the eldest child of Manuel and Maria Clara Otero.

The petitioned for land contained approximately 400 acres situated about one mile north of the center of Tubac.[75] Although the petition failed to explicitly request confirmation of the *Solar* or house lot mentioned in the land grant, the *Solar* was reviewed for confirmation of title throughout subsequent proceedings. U.S. Surveyor General John Wasson was responsible for making a recommendation to Congress on whether foreign title claims in Arizona were valid. Wasson took depositions to adjudicate the merits of the Oteros' claim: Jose Maria Sosa, Nasario Ortiz, Santos Aguirre, Juan Elias and Sabino Otero testified on March 23 and 29, 1880. Wasson also instructed U.S. Surveyor General George J. Roskruge to execute an exact survey of the claimed lands in accordance with GLO guidelines. The contract for the survey was received on February 28, 1881 and fully executed on April 12, 1881.[76] On March 1, 1881, Surveyor General Wasson submitted his Opinion and Recommendation on this case to Congress with a recommendation that the Rancho de Otero and House Lot claim be confirmed.[77] Wasson's full opinion and recommendation on the case was published in the March 6, 1881 edition of Tucson's *Arizona Weekly Citizen*.[78]

In his Opinion, Wasson deemed the Otero title papers genuine and explained that no *expedients* or formal records were available because the archives of the Tubac *presidio* had been destroyed by Apaches. He also held that the Otero claim should be regarded as absolute title to land due to the long and undisputed occupancy and possession of land.[79] U.S. Surveyor General John Wasson was so convinced of the Otero family's vested and absolute title to land that he relied on it in his Opinion and Recommendation of the Rancho de Martinez at San Xavier del Bac petition filed by Jose Maria Martinez. The Martinez claim was ultimately approved by Congress:

> This [Martinez] case presents substantially the same features as that of the "Rancho de Otero and House lot" which this office reported for confirmation on March 1, 1881, except that in this [Martinez case] there is no formal grant of a house lot, nor indeed any reference to the grant of one in the title papers. ¶Even without any title papers, their long, useful and undisturbed occupation, would entitle them to confirmation. Congress has already recognized the right of mere occupants of land in the Santa Cruz Valley...."[80]

Wasson's Recommendation of the Sabino Otero *et al*[81] petition was referred to the Senate Committee on Private Land Claims as "Rancho de Otero and House Lot" claim No. 13.[82] Unlike the Martinez claim that failed to mention a house lot in the title papers, the Otero grant affirmatively specified a house lot. Curiously and despite less persuasive facts than the Otero land grant claim, Congress granted the Martinez grant in its entirety even though no *expedients* or formal records were produced. Both Otero and Martinez held long, useful, undisturbed occupation of their land. Despite U.S. Surveyor General Wasson's belief in "the bona fides of the [Otero] claim,"[83] the Otero land grant claim languished unresolved before Congress for fourteen years.

During this time frame, westward settlers anxiously awaited a prompt resolution of the Otero and other Spanish and Mexican land grants to settle on approximately 6,000,000 acres of contested land.[84] Commercial interests likely hoped the Otero family's claim would fail so that the fertile ranch land located on both sides of the valuable Santa Cruz River could be made available to investors or anxious setters.

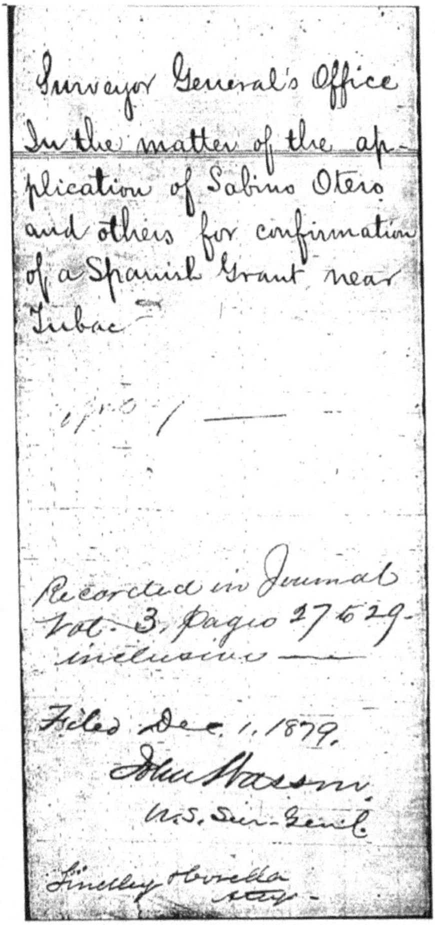
Surveyor General's Office
In the matter of the ap-
plication of Sabino Otero
and others for confirmation
of a Spanish Grant near
Tubac —

No 1 —

Recorded in Journal
Vol. 3, Pages 27 to 29 -
inclusive —

Filed Dec. 1, 1879.
John Wasson
U.S. Sur-Genl.

Figure 1.22. First page of U.S. Surveyor General John Wasson's Journal entry containing the Sabino Otero *et al* petition for confirmation of ancestral lands at Tubac filed 12/1/1879. (Arizona State Library, Archives & Public Records. U.S. Bureau of Land Management Filmfile # 10.1.22. Assorted grants & miscellaneous papers).

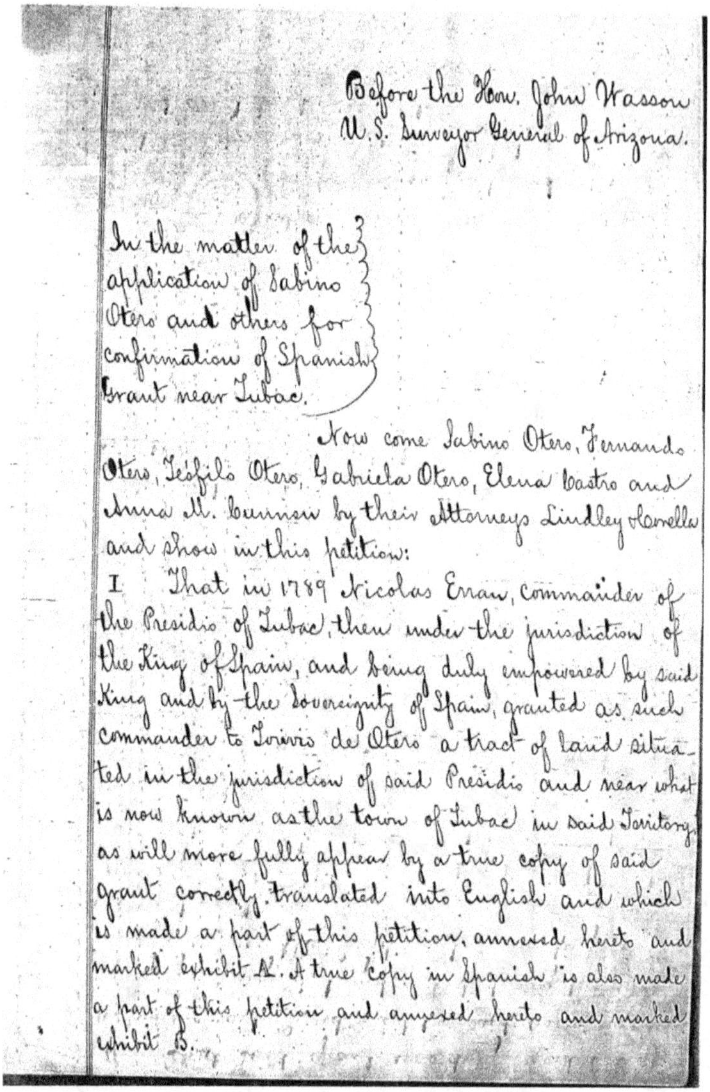

Before the Hon. John Wasson
U.S. Surveyor General of Arizona.

In the matter of the application of Sabino Otero and others for confirmation of Spanish Grant near Tubac.

Now come Sabino Otero, Fernando Otero, Teófilo Otero, Gabriela Otero, Elena Castro and Anna M. Cunnion by their Attorneys Lindley & Lovell and show in this petition:

I That in 1789 Nicolas Erran, commander of the Presidio of Tubac, then under the jurisdiction of the King of Spain, and being duly empowered by said King and by the sovereignty of Spain, granted as such commander to Torivio de Otero a tract of land situated in the jurisdiction of said Presidio and near what is now known as the town of Tubac in said Territory as will more fully appear by a true copy of said grant correctly translated into English and which is made a part of this petition, annexed hereto and marked exhibit A. A true copy in Spanish is also made a part of this petition and annexed hereto and marked exhibit B.

Figure 1.23. First page of the Sabino Otero *et al* petition filed on 12/1/1879 before U.S. Surveyor General John Wasson. (Arizona State Library, Archives & Public Records. U.S. Bureau of Land Management Filmfile # 10.1.22. Assorted grants & miscellaneous papers).

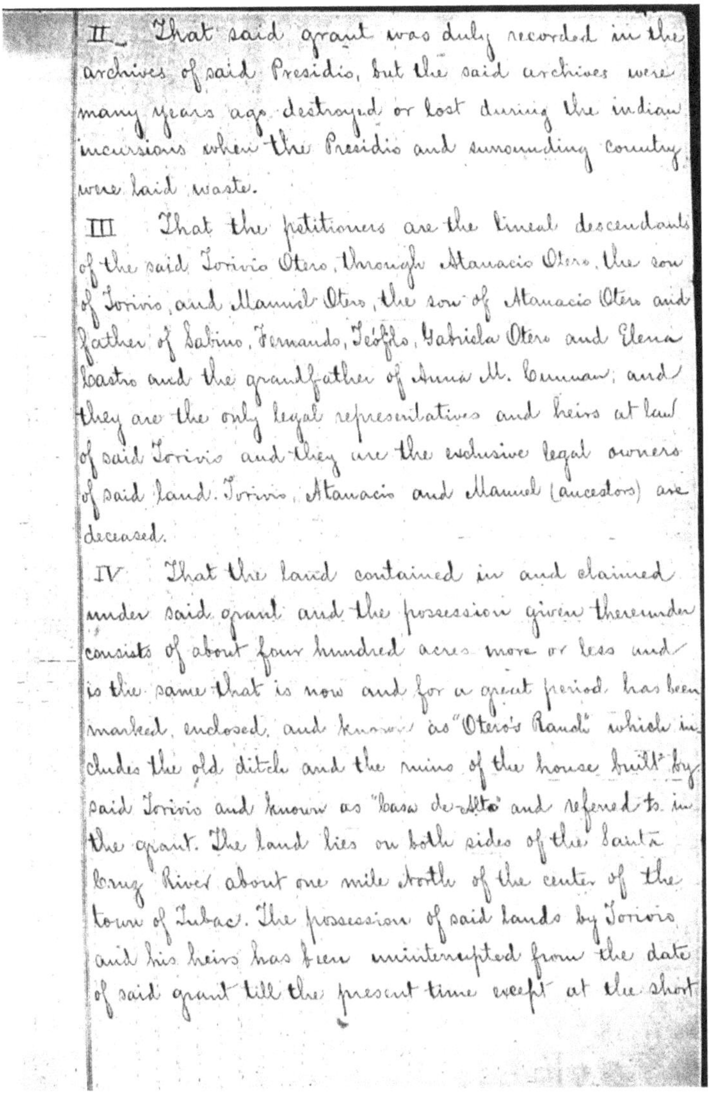

II_ That said grant was duly recorded in the archives of said Presidio, but the said archives were many years ago destroyed or lost during the indian incursions when the Presidio and surrounding country were laid waste.

III That the petitioners are the lineal descendants of the said Torivio Otero, through Atanacio Otero, the son of Torivio, and Manuel Otero, the son of Atanacio Otero and father of Sabino, Fernando, Teófilo, Gabriela Otero and Elena Castro and the grandfather of Anna M. Cumman; and they are the only legal representatives and heirs at law of said Torivio and they are the exclusive legal owners of said land. Torivio, Atanacio and Manuel (ancestors) are deceased.

IV That the land contained in and claimed under said grant and the possession given thereunder consists of about four hundred acres more or less and is the same that is now and for a great period has been marked, enclosed, and known as "Otero's Ranch" which includes the old ditch and the ruins of the house built by said Torivio and known as "Casa de Alto" and refered to in the grant. The land lies on both sides of the Santa Cruz River about one mile North of the center of the town of Tubac. The possession of said lands by Torivio and his heirs has been uninterrupted from the date of said grant till the present time except at the short

Figure 1.24. Second page of the Sabino Otero *et al* petition filed on 12/1/1879 before U.S. Surveyor General John Wasson. (Arizona State Library, Archives & Public Records. U.S. Bureau of Land Management Filmfile # 10.1.22. Assorted grants & miscellaneous papers).

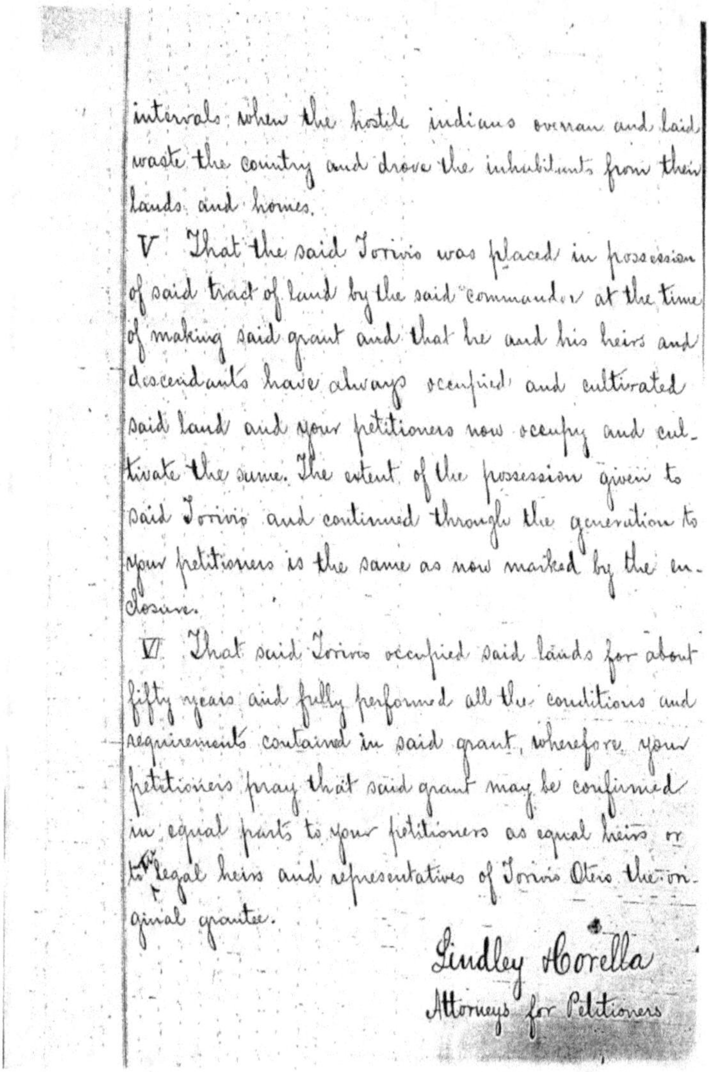

intervals when the hostile indians overran and laid waste the country and drove the inhabitants from their lands and homes.

V That the said Torivio was placed in possession of said tract of land by the said commander at the time of making said grant and that he and his heirs and descendants have always occupied and cultivated said land and your petitioners now occupy and cultivate the same. The extent of the possession given to said Torivio and continued through the generation to your petitioners is the same as now marked by the enclosure.

VI That said Torivio occupied said lands for about fifty years and fully performed all the conditions and requirements contained in said grant, wherefore your petitioners pray that said grant may be confirmed in equal parts to your petitioners as equal heirs or the legal heirs and representatives of Torivio Otero the original grantee.

Lindley & Orella
Attorneys for Petitioners

Figure 1.25. Third page of the Sabino Otero *et al* petition filed on 12/1/1879 before U.S. Surveyor General John Wasson. (Arizona State Library, Archives & Public Records. U.S. Bureau of Land Management Filmfile # 10.1.22. Assorted grants & miscellaneous papers).

If Congress had approved U.S. Surveyor General Wasson's Opinion and Recommendation on the Rancho de Otero and House Lot claim No. 13, the Otero family would have saved time and money prosecuting its claim. Land speculators would also have known the Otero land on the Santa Cruz River was unavailable. In response to the egregious delay in processing foreign land claims, a new United States Court for Private Land Claims was created in 1891 and charged with adjudicating concessions of land from Spain and Mexico which had not yet been confirmed by an Act of Congress.[85] It was intended to be a five-year term court. By 1884, there were eleven known grants in Pima County (these include grants in present day Santa Cruz County): Babocomari, San Rafael de la Zanja, San Ignacio de la Canoa, Tumacácori and Calabasas, Nogales, Sopori, Tumacácori, Tenaca, Torreon and Otero.[86] Unconfirmed land grants "prevent[ed] surveys and settlements of tracts which are really public lands of the United States,"[87] some argued.

Chief Justice the Hon. Joseph R. Reed; Associate Justices Hon. Wilbur F. Stone, Hon. Wm. W. Murrey, Hon. Thos. C. Fuller, Hon. Henry C. Sluss, associate justices; with United States Attorneys Matt. G. Reynolds and Will M. Tipton presided over the Otero case for 185.70 acres.[88] When the federal Court of Private Land Claims initiated its session on February 21, 1893, the Otero land grant acreage was significantly reduced by the U.S. Deputy Surveyor General George J. Roskruge land survey and after the Dario Martinez's deed conveyance of the Martinez land grant to Sabino Otero in 1880.

Figure 1.26. Justices for the Court of Private Land Claims. Court was in existence from 1891-1904. (Public domain).

Due to the prohibitive cost of continuing their land petition and since the 1789 land grant was not located in any Mexican archive, which similarly precluded the Carmen de O'Campos and Heirs of Ignacio Cruz land grants at Tubac,[89] the Otero petitioners withdrew their claim from the court on March 3, 1893 in pursuit of a separate remedy.[90] This proved to be a smart strategy.

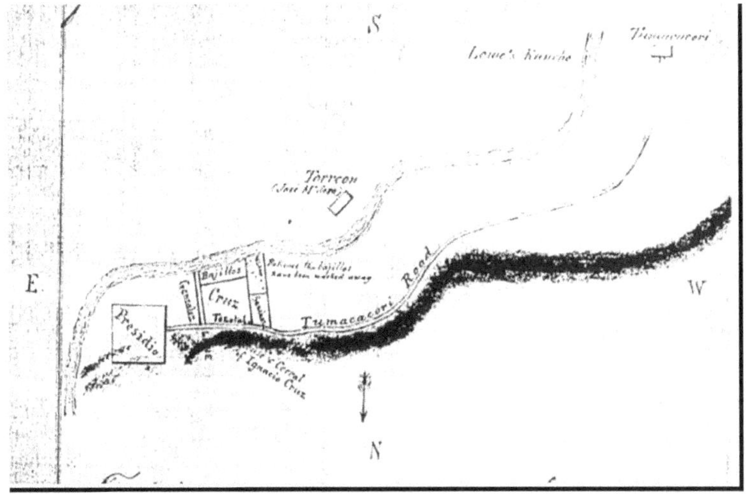

Figure 1.27. Map excerpt from the Ignacio Cruz land grant filed through the General Land Office. Like the Otero grant, the Cruz and O'Campos land grants were withdrawn from the Court of Private Land Claims because original copies of the land grants could not be located in foreign archives. Government records reflect this requirement was arbitrarily applied by Congress. (Arizona State Library, Archives & Public Records. U.S. Bureau of Land Management Filmfile # 10.1.22. Assorted grants & miscellaneous papers).

While other foreign land grant petitioners patiently awaited resolution from the Court of Private Land Claims and most lost their claimed lands, the Otero family launched a new strategy. The family remained on the contested property to maintain their uninterrupted continuous possession, except during short periods of Apache hostilities. It then placed the land into the public domain to assert their right for legally recognized ownership under the 1820 Cash Act. The Act allowed individuals to purchase land from the U.S. government at $1.25 per acre.[91] At such small cost, the savings in legal fees alone made the Otero family's plan a wise and fiscally sound strategy.

On September 3, 1893, Sabino Otero filed homestead application number 011924 on behalf of the *Heirs of Clara Martinez Otero*. The application claimed 126.68 acres for the East ½ SouthEast ¼ of Section 6, SouthEast ¼ NorthEast ¼ of Section 6, and Lot/Tract 11 of Section 5 of Township Twenty-One South of Range Thirteen East of the Gila and Salt River Meridian, Arizona.[92] From the plain language of the September 3rd homestead application, it appears that the Otero land grant was much smaller than stated in the 1789 land grant.

Through a series of land partitions, the original land grant was homesteaded in sections. The Otero Spanish land grant property now claimed by the Otero heirs as a homestead was adjacent to the Martinez/Otero land and two other parcels of land secured through federal land patents that listed Sabino Otero as assignee, effectively expanding the Rancho de Otero to nearly 400 acres. Land Patent Number 251724 of Theophilus A. Bagwell was signed by President William Taft on March 4, 1912[93] and the Robert F. Donaldson Land Patent number 434913 was signed by President Woodrow Wilson on October 10, 1914.[94] The combined acreage of the claims by Otero heirs, Bagwell and Donaldson was consistent with the acreage specified under the terms of the original Otero Spanish land grant of 1789.

On September 19, 1912, the same year Arizona was admitted into the United States of America as its 48th state, President William Taft signed Land Patent Number 292795 in favor of the Heirs of Clara Martinez Otero.[95] President Taft ended the Otero family's fifty-eight-year quest for U.S. recognition of their ancestral lands.

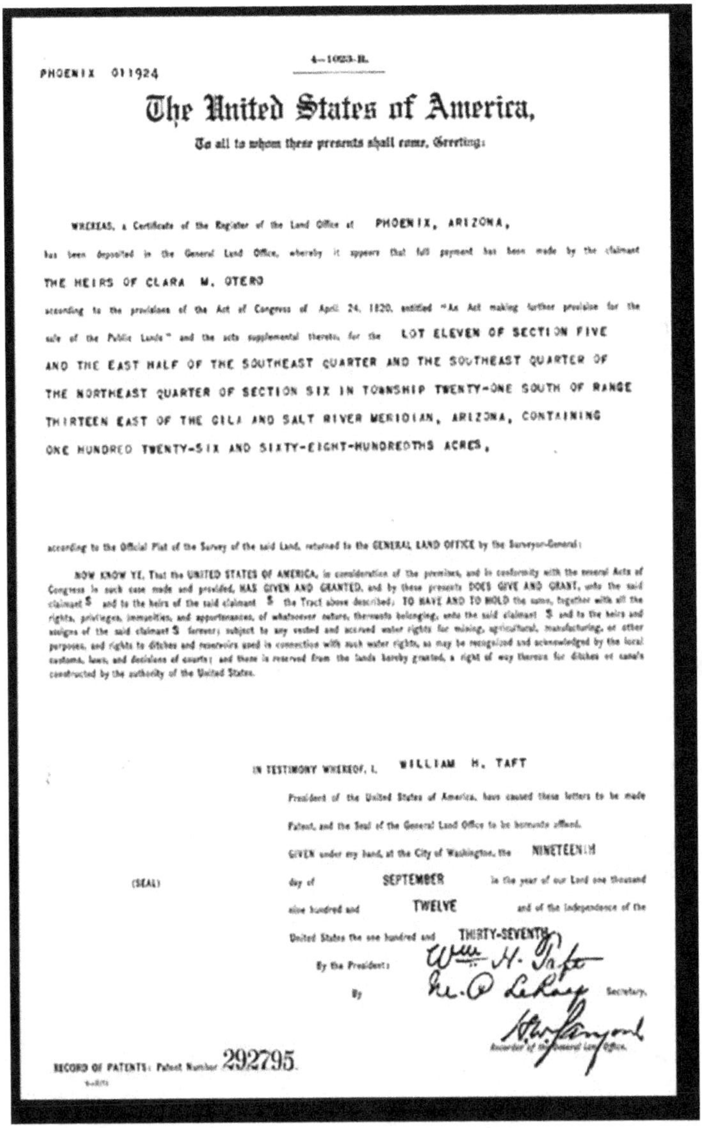

PHOENIX 011924

4—1023-R.

The United States of America,

To all to whom these presents shall come, Greeting:

WHEREAS, a Certificate of the Register of the Land Office at PHOENIX, ARIZONA, has been deposited in the General Land Office, whereby it appears that full payment has been made by the claimant THE HEIRS OF CLARA M. OTERO according to the provisions of the Act of Congress of April 24, 1820, entitled "An Act making further provision for the sale of the Public Lands" and the acts supplemental thereto, for the LOT ELEVEN OF SECTION FIVE AND THE EAST HALF OF THE SOUTHEAST QUARTER AND THE SOUTHEAST QUARTER OF THE NORTHEAST QUARTER OF SECTION SIX IN TOWNSHIP TWENTY-ONE SOUTH OF RANGE THIRTEEN EAST OF THE GILA AND SALT RIVER MERIDIAN, ARIZONA, CONTAINING ONE HUNDRED TWENTY-SIX AND SIXTY-EIGHT-HUNDREDTHS ACRES,

according to the Official Plat of the Survey of the said Land, returned to the GENERAL LAND OFFICE by the Surveyor-General:

NOW KNOW YE, That the UNITED STATES OF AMERICA, in consideration of the premises, and in conformity with the several Acts of Congress in such case made and provided, HAS GIVEN AND GRANTED, and by these presents DOES GIVE AND GRANT, unto the said claimant S and to the heirs of the said claimant S the Tract above described; TO HAVE AND TO HOLD the same, together with all the rights, privileges, immunities, and appurtenances, of whatsoever nature, thereunto belonging, unto the said claimant S and to the heirs and assigns of the said claimant S forever; subject to any vested and accrued water rights for mining, agricultural, manufacturing, or other purposes, and rights to ditches and reservoirs used in connection with such water rights, as may be recognized and acknowledged by the local customs, laws, and decisions of courts; and there is reserved from the lands hereby granted, a right of way thereon for ditches or canals constructed by the authority of the United States.

IN TESTIMONY WHEREOF, I, WILLIAM H. TAFT President of the United States of America, have caused these letters to be made Patent, and the Seal of the General Land Office to be hereunto affixed.

GIVEN under my hand, at the City of Washington, the NINETEENTH day of SEPTEMBER in the year of our Lord one thousand nine hundred and TWELVE and of the Independence of the United States the one hundred and THIRTY-SEVENTH.

(SEAL)

By the President: Wm. H. Taft

By M. P. LeRoy Secretary.

H. W. Sanford Recorder of the General Land Office.

RECORD OF PATENTS: Patent Number 292795.

Figure 1.28. Serial Patent Number 292795 for the Heirs of Clara Otero representing the Hacienda de Otero and surrounding ancestral lands claimed under the Torivio de Otero Spanish land grant of 1789. Patent claimed under the 1820 Cash Act. (U.S. Bureau of Land Management).

CHAPTER TWO
TUBAC AND THE SOLAR DE OTERO

Two parcels of land were provided for in the Otero Spanish land grant of 1789. One parcel was designated for farming lands. During the Spanish Arizona era, it also became a cattle ranch known as the Hacienda de Otero located one mile north of the center of Tubac. The second parcel of land was designated as a *Solar* or house lot. It was on this second parcel of land that Don Torivio de Otero established Arizona's first European privately-owned home. At the *Solar*, Don Torivio and his descendants lived, children were born, some died, as governments changed from Spanish to Mexican rule, then to United States government rule. As government borders shifted, the Otero home remained stationary as an important building at the center of colonial Tubac. When Apache hostilities caused Tubac to be occasionally deserted, the Otero family stayed close protecting their and Arizona's first permanent European home.

The Oteros were not alone. Before the arrival of Charles Debrille Poston, the self-proclaimed Father of Arizona, Hispanic families like the Oteros remained on ancestral lands that successive governments claimed as their own. After the hasty departure of Poston from Tubac, the community remained vibrant, alive with education, commerce, and song. The following brief sketch of Tubac acquaints us with the Tubac inhabited by the Otero family and their contemporaries from its early Spanish days to a mere six years after the ratification of the Gadsden Purchase.

More than thirty years before the First Continental Congress met in 1774 at Philadelphia, Tubac was the most populated settlement in northern *Nuevo México,*[1] present-day Arizona. Military records memorialized the names of the soldiers who traveled there to establish the *Presidio of San Ignacio de Tubac* in 1752.[2] During the 18th century, the *presidio* at Tubac joined a strategic line of Spanish *presidio's* that stretched from the Pacific Coast to the Gulf of Mexico. In an effort to protect early mission and pueblo settlements and to guard against the aggressive incursions of the neighboring savage tribes,[3] Tubac was established in accordance to Book IV, Title 5, Law of Indies. The statute mandated that each settlement provide a "healthy spot" with "pleasant climate, good water, abounding in wood and pasturage."[4] Modern visitors can agree that these features still exist at Tubac.

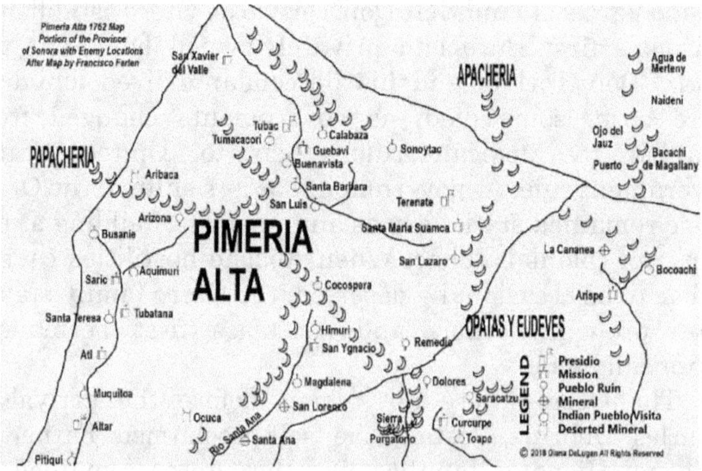

Figure 2.1. Illustration of a portion of the Francisco Ferten Map of 1762. 18th century Tubac was the northernmost military post of New Spain in Arizona. Notice that the Mission of San Xavier del Bac is known as San Xavier del Valle. An old pueblo ruin known as *Arizona* is also depicted. Original map located at the National Library of Spain. (Graphic by the author). © 2018 Diana DeLugan. All rights reserved.

The infrastructure of colonial Tubac also appears to comply with Spanish surveys required by the Law of Indies for the establishment of pueblos. Each pueblo required a minimum of thirty inhabitants and was four square leagues in oblong form with streets "laid out by the authorized engineer in such a manner as to facilitate traffic and the intercommunication of the inhabitants."[5] The Spanish Royal Highway that cuts through Tubac complies with the Law of Indies' basic dictates. It stretches north from Tumacácori mission to mission San Xavier del Bac. At the heart of colonial Tubac, the road intersects at the *presidio* with the coastal road to Altar. Juan Bautista de Anza and his followers used the same Royal Highway in their epic journey as they departed from Tubac to establish the city of San Francisco in 1774-76.[6]

Figure 2.2. Designated the Anza Trail by the U.S. Department of the Interior National Parks Service, this is a portion of the Spanish highway that Juan Bautista de Anza and Spanish colonists traveled from Horcasitas to Tubac on their epic journey to establish San Francisco. The trail is located just south of the Tubac Presidio State Park and Museum and can be viewed during the guided tour of the Barrio de Tubac Archaeological site hosted by the Tubac Presidio State Historic Park. Call the Park for details. (Photograph by the author).

Presidios were government establishments under local *presidio* commanders who acted as subordinates to the governor of the province. Senate records for the Tumacácori and Calabasas land grant petition explain why *presidios* had limited dimensions:

> It was considered that for such a settlement a territory embracing four square leagues was sufficient, to be measured from the center of the presidial plaza, one league to each of the cardinal points; and the captains of presidios were permitted to make grants within these four leagues, but in no case to grant beyond these limits. [7]

Such an engineering layout gave presidial establishments the character of an incipient pueblo, making it a nucleus around which, in time, a pueblo might grow up. [8]

By the end of the 18th century, Tubac's *presidio* and emergent pueblo prospered. Between 1754 and 1757, Tubac's population reached 411.[9] An estimated sixty-four sowing plots or *milpas* had been cultivated near the Santa Cruz River bank with forty-nine dwellings established south of the *presidio* buildings in the area known today as the south barrio at Tubac.[10] These sun baked adobe homes lay scattered in the direction of Tumacácori mission on both sides of the Spanish Highway.[11] Unfortunately, history has forgotten most of the names of the early Spanish settlers who accompanied the military to Tubac and lived in those rustic homes. Although their faces and names have been lost to time, these lay men, women, and children undoubtedly contributed to their community and daily living at Tubac. Many may have sacrificed their lives to protect the fort and its inhabitants.

Spanish colonial settlements usually built their communities around a moral center. With no real church to officiate religious ceremonies at Tubac, a small wood, grass and earth church named Santa Gertrudis was erected in 1767,[12] northwest of the *presidio* to serve the Apachean, Piman, and Spanish settlers.

CHANGE OF GOVERNMENT AND EARLY CORPORATE INTERESTS

Mexican independence from Spain in 1821 did little to interrupt progress at Tubac. Like its Spanish counterpart, the Mexican government retained a small garrison at Tubac sufficient to protect the town's inhabitants as citizens cultivated adjacent fields and worked local mines.[13] Approximately 38 million acres was claimed through Spanish and Mexican land grants in the Territory of New Mexico when the Treaty of Guadalupe-Hidalgo ceded the Southwest in 1848 and after the 1854 Gadsden Purchase. In Arizona, land grants comprised around 12 million acres mostly located in the Santa Cruz Valley, Doña Ana County, New Mexico Territory, USA.[14] Mining, canal, railroad, and ever-increasing speculation in land drew pioneers like a magnet thrust forward by a fundamental belief in Manifest Destiny.

After Tubac was "abandoned by its Mexican garrison after the transfer of the territory...[and] on account of the Apaches,"[15] it became headquarters to Arizona's foremost mining speculator: the Sonora Exploring and Mining Company. Shortly after the Gadsden Purchase, Colonel Charles Debrille Poston of Kentucky and Samuel Peter Heintzelman of Pennsylvania established the headquarters of the Sonora Exploring & Mining Company at Tubac on December 31, 1856.[16] The Sonora Mining and Exploration Company was incorporated on August 13, 1857 under the laws of Ohio for "the purpose of mining and smelting silver and other ores, and manufacturing bars and ingots of the same, and for such other lawful purposes as may be necessary for carrying out the above described objects."[17] Officers of the company were Major S. P. Heintzelman, President; W. Wrightson, Secretary; Edgar Conkling, General Agent; Col. Charles D. Poston, Commandant and Managing Agent at Tubac; Herman Ehrenburg, Topographical Engineer and Surveyor at

Tubac; Frederick Brunckow, Geologist, Mineralogist and Mining Engineer, in charge of Cerro Colorado District; and Charles Schuchard, Geologist, Mineralogist and Mining Engineer in Charge of La Aribac and Smelting Haciendas.[18]

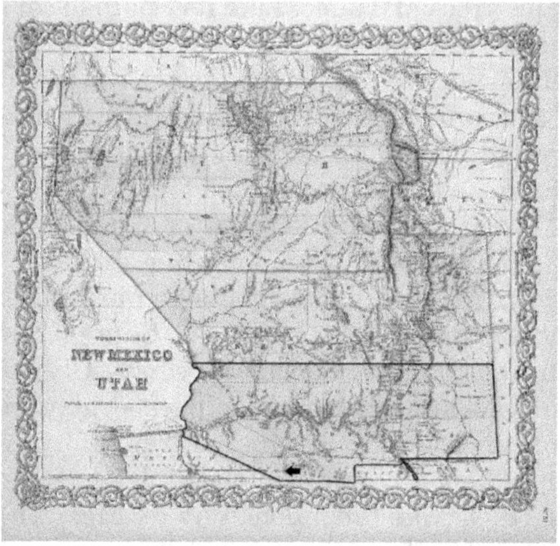

Figure 2.3. After the Gadsden Purchase, Tubac was located southwest section of the Territory of New Mexico within Doña Ana County, identified by the arrow. 1855 Map of the Territories of New Mexico and Utah. J.H. Colton & Co., New York. (Public domain. Edited by the author).

With unlimited terrains to select from, Tubac was chosen as the Sonora Exploring and Mining Company's business location for many of the same reasons that the Spanish had selected Tubac for its first northern *presidio*:

> At Tubac there is pure, mountain water, wood, grass and plenty of game. The barracks occupied by the Mexican government are in a good state of preservation, sufficiently capacious and every way suited to the necessities of our company, so that I immediately determined

> upon taking possession of them and making *'Tubac'* our permanent head-quarters.[19]

Among the mining company's most prized possessions was the Arivaca Ranch located fifteen miles southwest of Tubac. Its natural resources were plentiful to support local mining operations with over seventeen thousand acres of wood, grass, water and agricultural land: [20]

> It [Arivaca Ranch] contains twenty-five Silver Mines, which were worked by the Mexicans previous to the Apache War, and which were famous for their yielding rich ores of silver, lead, and copper, and containing small quantities of gold. The most famous of these mines were Mina San José, Mina Santa Margarita, Mina Basura, Mina Blanca, Mina Arenias, Mina de Los Tajitos, La Mina de Amado, and La Purissima.[21]

The Arivaca Ranch was owned by Tomas and Ignacio Ortiz in 1857. Their father Agustín Ortiz laid cornerstones at Arivaca in 1812 after taking possession of his Spanish land grant.[22] In 1833, Don Torivio de Otero's son Atanacio, [23] first heir-at-law of the Otero Spanish land grant, was the constitutional *alcalde* or mayor of Tubac for the Mexican government. Atanacio received testimony from applicants Tomas and Ignacio Ortiz of Tubac in support of their claim to the 17,000 acres at Arivaca. The Ortiz petition was granted to the Ortiz brothers by the Sonoran governor based in large part on the testimony taken by Tubac mayor Atanacio Otero.[24]

Seizing opportunity, Colonel Poston and Samuel Heintzelman moved quickly. They selected Tubac as the headquarters of the Sonora Exploring and Mining Company then Poston settled in as the territorial *alcalde* (mayor) of Tubac. In 1894, Poston reminisced about his experience as *alcalde* of Tubac in an article for The Overland Monthly Publication, "As Alcalde of Tubac under the government of New Mexico, I was legally authorized to celebrate the rites of matrimony, baptize children, grant divorces, execute criminals, declare war, and perform all the functions of the ancient El Cadi."[25] Corporate prosperity was short lived. Poston and the Sonora Exploring and Mining Company left Tubac abruptly before the start of the 1861 Apache Wars and before the Confederate States of America claimed Arizona as confederate territory in 1862.

Figure 2.4. 1857 Illustration of *Aribaca* [Arivaca] by C. Schuchard des. (Public domain).[26]

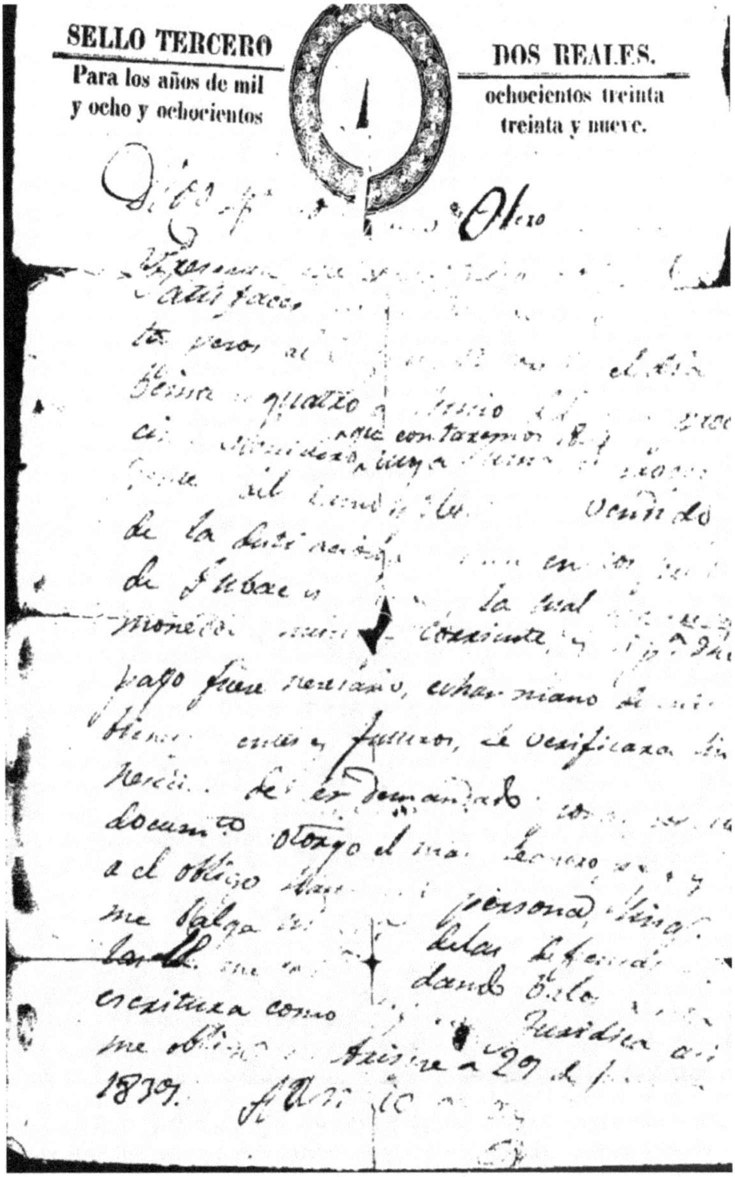
SELLO TERCERO
Para los años de mil
y ocho y ochocientos

DOS REALES.
ochocientos treinta
treinta y nueve.

Figure 2.5. Photocopied image of a promissory note by Atanacio Otero dated 6/29/1839. Besides being a farmer and alcalde of Tubac, Atanacio also profited by distilling mescal brandy. (Arizona State Library, Archives & Public Records. U.S. Bureau of Land Management Filmfile # 10.1.22. Assorted grants & miscellaneous papers).[27]

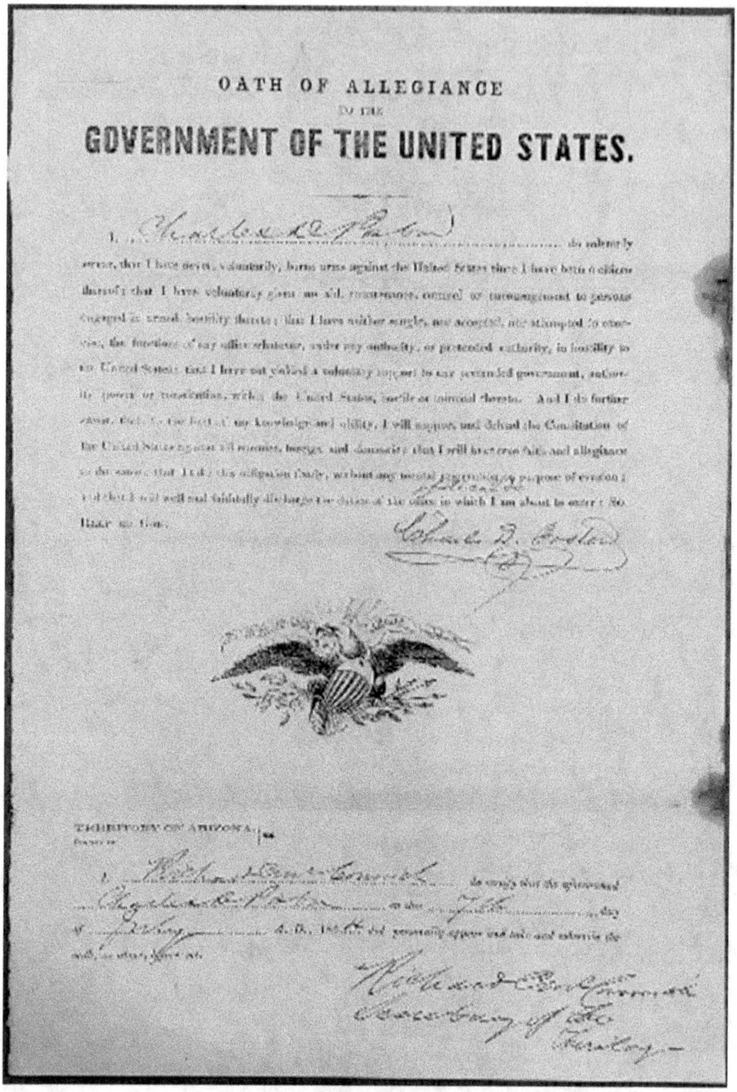

OATH OF ALLEGIANCE

TO THE

GOVERNMENT OF THE UNITED STATES.

TERRITORY OF ARIZONA,

Figure 2.6. On 7/7/1864, Charles Debrille Poston accepted a Territory of Arizona post as Alcalde, location not stated. Appointment was signed by Richard McCormick, Secretary of the Territory of Arizona. One month later, Don Manuel Otero was appointed Alcalde of Tubac by Governor Goodwin. *See* **Figure 2.8.** (Arizona State Library, Archives & Public Records).

Figure 2.7. Arizona Governor for the Territory of Arizona John Noble Goodwin illustrated by Dorotea Cvijanovic commissioned exclusively for *Terrenos*

In 1863, President Abraham Lincoln appointed John Noble Goodwin as the Governor for the Territory of Arizona after the first gubernatorial appointee John A. Gurley died before taking office. Governor Goodwin served from December 29, 1863 to April 10, 1866. In August of 1864, Governor Goodwin made several political appointments including that of Manuel Otero as *alcalde* (mayor) of Tubac. As the grandson of Don Torivio de Otero and son of former Tubac *alcalde* Atanacio Otero, Manuel Otero was the second heir-at-law to the Otero Spanish land of 1789. Manuel and his family lived at Tubac through the 1860s. Manuel and Maria Clara Martinez Otero's children were later tasked to fight for U.S. recognition of Otero ancestral lands.

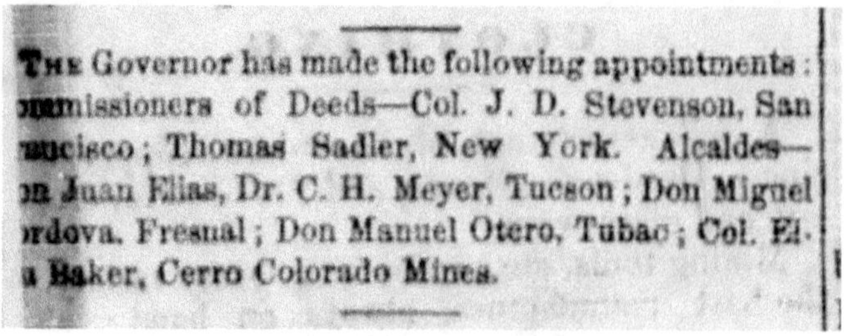

THE Governor has made the following appointments: ommissioners of Deeds—Col. J. D. Stevenson, San ancisco; Thomas Sadler, New York. Alcaldes—on Juan Elias, Dr. C. H. Meyer, Tucson; Don Miguel ordova, Fresnal; Don Manuel Otero, Tubac; Col. El- a Baker, Cerro Colorado Mines.

Figure 2.8. Newspaper clipping announcing Don Manuel Otero as Alcalde (Mayor) of Tubac. (*Arizona Miner*. Fort Whipple, AZ. 8/10/1864).[28] Manuel's father Atanacio Otero was also an Alcalde of Tubac.

TUBAC DURING THE 1860'S

Tubac of 1860 was a community whose colonial past intersected with hopeful prospects under United States government rule. Newly located within the Territory of New Mexico, it was a town in transition. The 1860 United States Federal Census reveals what life was like for the Otero family and other pioneer Tubac citizens just seven years after the United States acquired the town pursuant to the Gadsden Purchase. Sixty-seven occupied dwellings were inhabited by eighty-four families. Several households like that of the Oteros were multigenerational and some were sufficiently affluent to employ servants. Of the twelve servants listed on the census, only one was an Indian, the rest were men and women from Mexico. Irishman P. H. McGovern owned a hotel where cultures and customs were certain to blend. In addition to Mexican nationals and men who had become U.S. citizens due to residency after the Gadsden Purchase, visitors at McGovern's hotel included Abe Lyon of South Carolina, Jno H. Cresser of Heese Kassel, Germany, Louis Seller of France, Jos Moran of Missouri, Carlos Noriel of Italy and Jacob Weddington of Kansas. Other local residents included men from Tennessee, Prussia, Hanover, Mecklenberg, and Ohio. Many prosperous men lived at Tubac: S.H. Lathrop, a 35-year-old merchant from New Hampshire had a combined estate value of $70,000 ($1,944,289.59 value in 2017), followed by the $25,000 estate of Civil Engineer Herman Ehrenberg of Prussia ($694,389.14 value in 2017) and Civil Engineer George D. Mercer of District of Columbia with an estate of $20,000 ($555,511.31 value in 2017).

Although Tubac was sparsely populated, its proud 352 citizens maintained an interesting work-life balance. Six merchants, N. B. Appel, C. A. Hoppin, S. H. Latrop, Theodore Mohran, Fred Hulseman, and Luis Hulseman, offered a variety of goods to the community, in addition to five traders from Mexico: Joaquin Molina, Antonio Gándarra, Francisco Gándarra, Rimigio Rivera, and Francisco Hernandez. Most meals were certain to have been homemade. However, the town was sufficiently progressive to attract culinary professionals: butcher Abe Lyon, baker Louis Seller and cook Jno H. Cresser worked at McGovern's hotel in addition to cooks Jesus Paz and Margarita Granjela both females from Mexico who worked at local homes. Carpentry work was necessary for furniture and buildings. Tubac had three carpenters: Ignacio Vallez, Juan Vasquez and Jesus Mason. Delores Velasquez laid brick while Francisco Salazar made blankets to keep the town's residents warm. Feet were tended to by Tubac's six shoe makers: Rafael Burrel, Eugenio Valenzuela, Cruz Moreno, Eusebio Maduana, Manuel Ibarra, and Manuel Moreno, all from Mexico. Although many of Tubac's residents in 1860 were noted as being from Mexico, we cannot know for certain how the census-taker interpreted country of origin. Like Manuel and Maria Clara Otero who were from Tubac, Mexico, they became United States citizens by residency after the December 30, 1853 signing of the Gadsden Purchase. It is highly likely that the majority of Tubac's citizens who were reported as Mexican were also new U.S. citizens.

In addition to mining and engineering professions, Tubac had nine farmers, Pedro de Herrera, Juan Sombrano, Antonio Carizoza, Ramon Torres, Antonio Bustamante, Henry Alpeng, Eligio Bedoya, Jose M.

Carizoza, and Manuel Otero. Manuel owned the most prosperous farm at Tubac with a combined estate value of $3,000 ($83,326.70 value in 2017). As of 1860, Manuel's farm located just north of Tubac had been in the Otero family for 71 years having been acquired through the January 10, 1789 Spanish land grant. To support the ranches, Tubac's citizens included stock herders, teamsters, an ox driver, a gardener, and scores of farm laborers.

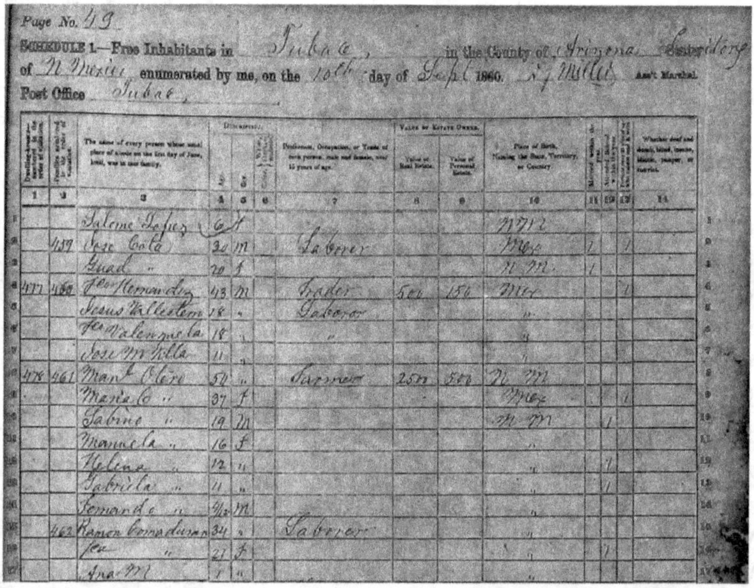

Page No. 49

SCHEDULE 1.—Free Inhabitants in Tubac, in the County of Arizona Territory of N. Mexico enumerated by me, on the 10th day of Sept 1860. Ass't Marshal.

Post Office Tubac,

1	2	3	4	5	6	7	8	9	10	11	12	13	14
		Salome Lopez	6	F					N M				
	459	Jose Cota	30	M		Laborer			Mex	1		1	
		Guad "	20	F					N M	1			
477	460	Jos Hernandez	43	M		Trader	500	150	Mex			1	
		Jesus Villestem	18	"		Laborer			"				
		Jos Valenzuela	18	"		"			"				
		Jose M Villa	11	"					"				
478	461	Man^l Otero	50	"		Farmer	2500	500	N M				
		Maria C "	37	F					Mex			1	
		Sabino "	19	M					N M		1		
		Manuela "	16	F					"				
		Helena "	12	"					"		1		
		Gabriela "	11	"					"		1		
		Fernando "	4/12	M					"				
	462	Ramon Comaduran	34	"		Laborer			"				
		Jos "	21	F					"		1		
		Ana M	1	"					"				

Figure 2.9. The 1860 U.S. New Mexico Territorial Census record of Tubac lists Manuel Otero and Ramon Comadurán families in the same dwelling but separate residences. At the time, Manuel Otero is Tubac's most prosperous farmer. (Public domain).

Women were also instrumental in sustaining Tubac's community. There were eight washerwomen, eleven seamstresses, and the eldest female at Tubac was an industrious 80-year-old Indian midwife known as Guadalupe Maria. 1860s Tubac prepared for its future. Thirty-three youth attended school run by School Masters Fulgencio Hernandez and Antonio Ureangarfin of Mexico. A sizeable Indian Village of forty-one residents was also located at Tubac led by Juan Lena, Governor of the Village. Stories of colonial Tubac were likely told by Tubac's elder male citizen, ninety-five-year-old Estagnio Ramirez, a former Spanish soldier. As the citizens of Tubac, worked, fell in love, had children, and some died, Fandango musicians Ramon Leyba, Jose Ramirez and Jesus de la Huerta strummed their instruments as the sound of music likely danced around the walls of the then vacant Tubac *presidio* and across the former Spanish Royal Highway. This eclectic community was the Tubac where Arizona's first European privately-owned home, the Otero *Solar*, was located.

In 1860, the third generation of Oteros lived at the *Solar*. Manuel and his children Francisca (21yrs), Sabino (19yrs), Maria Manuela (15), Maria Elena de Jesus (12), Gabriela (10),[29] and Fernando (1)[30] were all born at Tubac. Manuel, his wife Maria Clara Martinez Otero, and their first five children gained U.S. citizenship by residence after the Gadsden Purchase as did other Tubac Mexican nationals. Fernando was the first Otero descendant to be born on U.S. soil. Eldest daughter Francisca had married Ramon Comadurán on August 29, 1857[31] and was living with her spouse and daughter Ana Maria as a separate family but in the same dwelling as her parents.

From 1858-61, "Tubac was the most important settlement in Arizona, for good houses had been built, farming had been started and the place was a center of industry and trade."[32] But troubled times were around the bend.

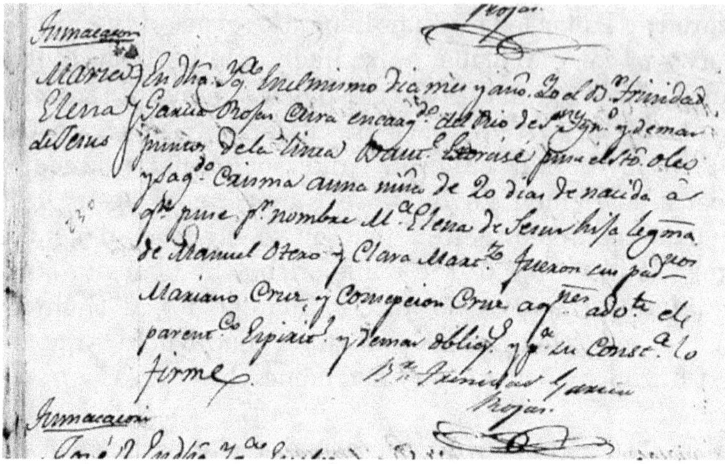

Figure 2.10. 1847 Baptismal record of Maria Elena de Jesus Otero at Tumacácori Mission. Her godparents were Mariano and Concepcion Cruz. (Public domain).

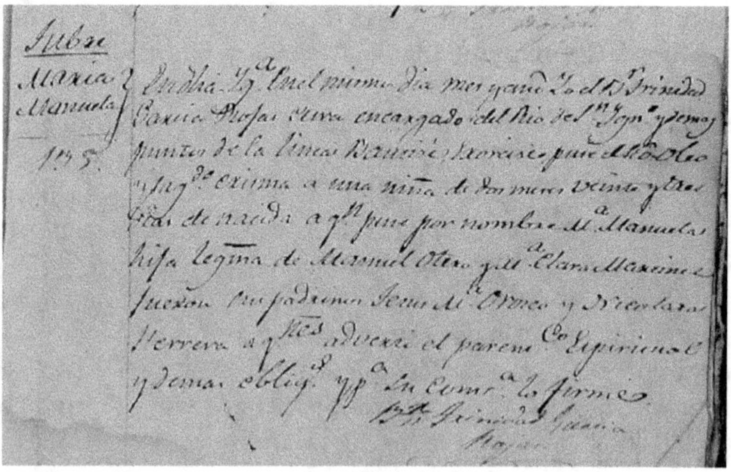

Figure 2.11. 1843 Baptismal record of Maria Manuela Otero at Tubac. Her godparents were Jesus Maria Orozco and Nicolas Herrera. (Public domain).

The American Civil War began. Tensions that often ripped families apart were palpable across the country. Like most of Southern Arizona, Tubac citizens displayed Southern sympathies as employers sought their runaway peons.[33] Southern Arizona was claimed by Confederate

Colonel John R. Baylor, commander of the second regiment of the Texas Mounted Rifles C.S.A. acting as governor, at Mesilla, New Mexico Territory in 1861. A convention was held in 1861 at Tucson to declare the territory of Arizona as part of the Confederacy. The convention was followed by a flag raising by Captain Hunter at Tucson on February 28, 1862 to celebrate Confederate President Jefferson Davis's February 14, 1862 proclamation at Richmond that formalized Arizona as a Confederate territory.[34] During this period, the territory was temporarily open to slavery. At the same time, southern Arizona citizens cried out for protection against ever-increasing Apache hostilities. Out of concern that certain harm was imminent against person and property, many Tubac citizens including the Otero family temporarily moved to other locations. Manuel Otero built a town home at Tucson by 1861. By 1863, Manuel Otero and his family resided intermittently at the Tucson town house. It was a formal residence and the site where Maria Clara gave birth to the couple's last child Joseph Theophilus "Teofilo" Emmanuel Otero on October 22, 1863.[35] After the Union's one thousand eight hundred strong California Column led by Lieutenant Colonel West arrived in the Territory of Arizona towards the close of the Civil War,[36] Tubac's population dwindled to about twenty-five persons.[37]

Cognizant of Arizona residents' mounting concerns for independent governance and a deafening protest for protection against further Apache attack, Congress passed a bill to create the Territory of Arizona on February 12, 1863. President Abraham Lincoln signed the Arizona Organic Act into law on February 24, 1863 that established the Territory of Arizona and abolished all forms of slavery and forced servitude. As the new Territorial Governor John N. Goodwin and his escort troops crossed into the new Territory of Arizona, a decision was made where to establish Arizona's capital:

> Tucson, the logical site for the capital, was considered a hot bed of secession and,

> therefore, entitled to little consideration. The enabling act [to establish the capital for the new Territory of Arizona] did not designate any location for the capital...General J.H. Carlton, in command of the military department, suggested that they strike out into the wilderness to the westward and there, protected by a military post he was establishing, erect a new capital city that be wholly American, without Mexicans or secession influence, within a land where rich mineral discoveries had been made and which, favored by abundant water and timber and by a delightful climate, would seem destined to fill soon with a high class of American resident.[38]

Despite the anti-Mexican sentiment by Arizona's new territorial government, Tubac's primarily Mexican population recovered. Census records report that the Otero family returned to Tubac by late 1864 after Manuel was appointed *alcalde* by Territorial Governor Goodwin. The Otero family maintained its primary residence at Tubac according to the 1866 and 1867 Territory of Arizona Censuses.

Concepcion Ochoa arrived at Tubac according to the 1866 census. That year she likely met 25-year-old Sabino Otero. Concepcion gave birth to their only son Manuel Ochoa Otero who was born out of wedlock on July 14, 1867.[39] At 28-years-old, Sabino Otero assumed the role of functional head-of-household for the Otero family[40] after his father Manuel Otero died of pneumonia in 1870. In the Sabino Otero household, Sabino's eldest sister Francisca[41], resided with her daughter Ana Maria while Sabino's widowed mother Maria Clara Martinez Otero physically cared for her children Gabriela, Fernando, Teofilo, and one grandchild, Maria Elena de Jesus's daughter Brijida Castro.

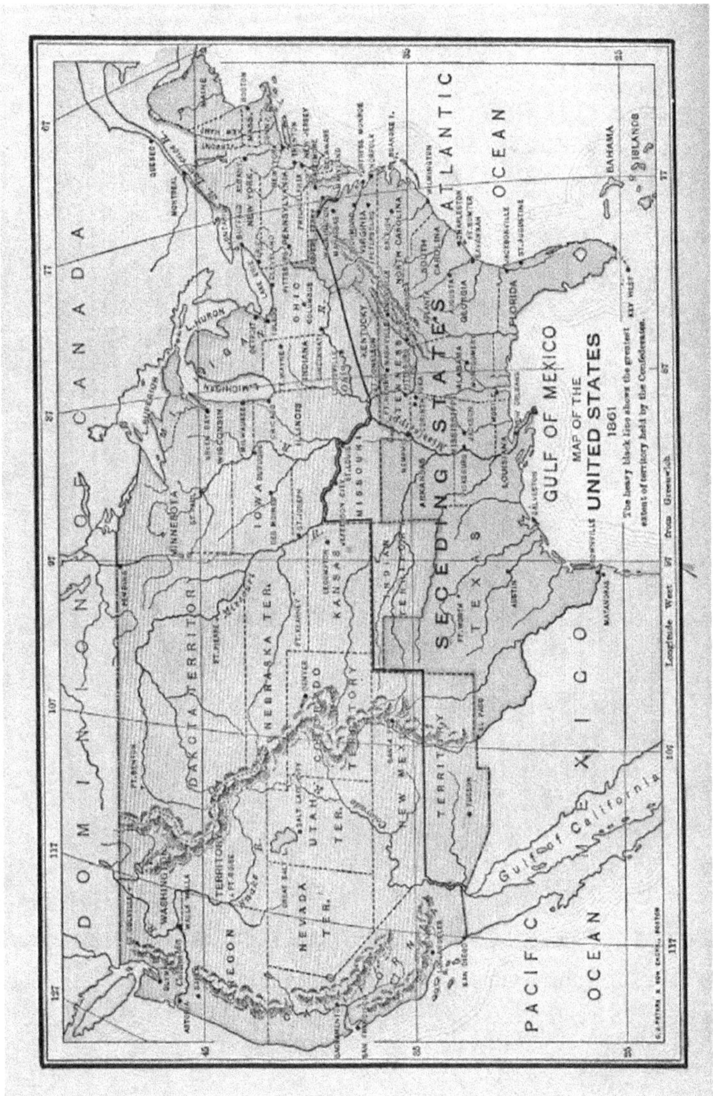

Figure 2.12. Map of the United States 1861. C.J. Peters & Son Engravers. During the U.S. Civil War, Tubac was open to slavery and claimed by Confederate Col. John R. Baylor as Confederate Territory. Map states "The heavy black line shows the greatest extent of territory held by the Confederates." (Public domain).

Figure 2.13. Sabino Otero. Eldest son of Manuel Otero and Maria Clara Martinez de Otero. Twenty-eight-year-old Sabino assumed the role as head of household when his father Manuel died in 1870. (Courtesy Tubac Historical Society).

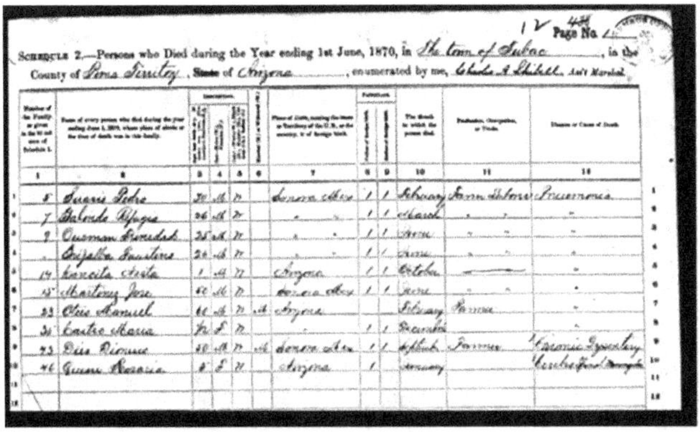
Schedule 2.—Persons who Died during the Year ending 1st June, 1870, in The town of Tubac, in the County of Pima County, State of Arizona, enumerated by me, Charles A Shibell, Ass't Marshal.

Figure 2.14. The 1870 Territory of Arizona Census for Pima County reports Arizona native and farmer Manuel Otero died of pneumonia in February of 1870. He was 60 years old. His granddaughter Rosaria Quesse, daughter of Blacksmith Louis Quesse and Maria Manuela Otero de Quesse, died the same year. She was five years old. (Public domain).

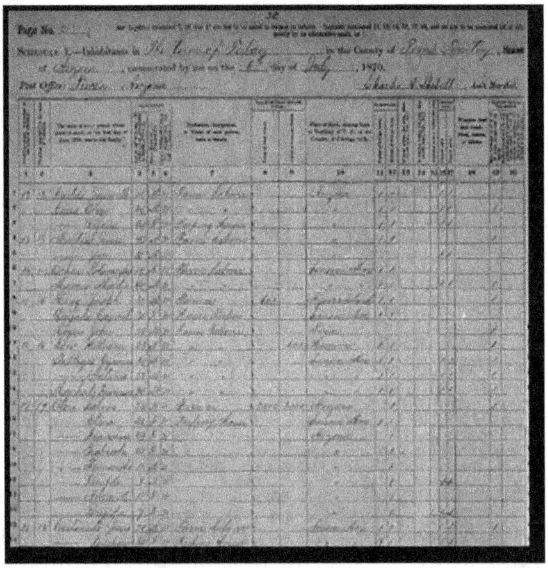

Figure 2.15. The 1870 Territory of Arizona Census for Pima County erroneously lists Sabino Otero as 26-years-old at the time of his father Manuel's death. Ten years prior on the 1860 Census, Sabino was listed as 19-years-old. His Arizona Death Certificate State Index No. 250 lists Sabino's birth year as 1842 placing him at 28-years-old at the time of his father's death. Sabino would have turned 29 in December of 1870. (Public domain).

Figure 2.16. Brijida Castro Coenen and spouse Anthony Coenen. In the 1870 Otero family Census, Brijida was 7-years-old. After her mother Maria Elena de Jesus Otero de Castro passed away, her grandmother Maria Clara Martinez Otero and her children helped raise Brijida. (Courtesy Martha Desoto Green).

THE INITIAL SEARCH FOR THE OTERO SOLAR

The search to locate the original site of the Otero *Solar* (house lot) at Tubac began with an exhaustive review of U.S. Bureau of Land Management (BLM) historical plats both online and at local land offices, particularly the land office at Phoenix, Arizona. To perfect a claim for the ownership of Spanish or Mexican land grants under U.S. law, a petition had to be filed with the U.S. Surveyor-General at the General Land Office or later at the United States Court of Private Claims. Claims were filed at both locations by the Otero land grant heirs-at-law to justify their claims to the United States government. Before confirmation of land could be reviewed, lands had to be surveyed and plats drawn to verify the boundaries of the claimed land. BLM plats provide us with our first major clue to discover the location of the Otero *Solar*.

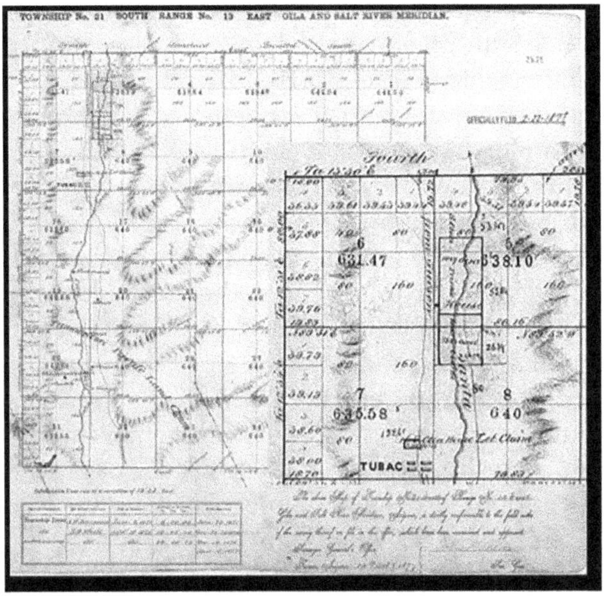

Figure 2.17. U.S. Bureau of Land Management Plat of Tubac by John Wasson filed at Tucson, AZ on 2/19/1877 with superimposed close up of the Otero Solar located north of Tubac. (Graphic enhancement by the author. Original U.S. Bureau of Land Management).

Upon close inspection, the 1877 BLM plat created by the U.S. surveyor depicts the "Otero House Lot Claim" (*Solar*) as located north of the Tubac *presidio*, not south as mandated under the terms of the 1789 Spanish land grant (see Figure 2.16). The 1877 BLM township plat of Tubac reports the plat was filed on February 4, 1877 at the Tucson General Land Office by U.S. Surveyor General John Wasson.[42] Township lines were initially surveyed by S.W. Foreman on January 2, 1871, resurveyed from December 22-28, 1876 by F.F. White, then officially filed on February 22, 1877. Retired hydrologist Philip Halpenny of

Tucson[43] was consulted to clarify why the *Solar* is located north of the Tubac *presidio* site. Halpenny re-measured known Tubac plats and confirmed that the 1877 plat depicts the Otero *Solar* as located north of the *presidio*, but explained that the *Solar* actually measures south of the *presidio*'s Captain's house:

> I used the two attached surveys – orig[inal] and resurvey, and started plotting on a 15-minute map – and it looked like the house was plotting north [of the *presidio*] or at the church. The 1910 plat shows the House Lot at just the north edge of the quarter/quarter line: the same line that separates Lots 3 and 4. The red map shows it in the same location with referred to Lots 3 and 4. I then plotted it on a 71/2 quad and it comes out exactly where it should be: just south of the Presidio buildings. So it plots where it should be....For now, and what I didn't pay any attention to despite using this map on my tours, is that "Tubac" on the 1877 survey is shown as quite a bit south of the House Lot ...The reason Tubac Town is shown as so far south of the House Lot on the 1877 plat is that the Surveyor was using the Tubac Townsite plat of 1872 to indicate Tubac, and the center of this was south of what was Tubac in 1766 and what is Tubac now...So this explains why the House Lot is shown as "north" of Tubac in the Township plat..."[44]

Since the Otero House Lot Claim or *Solar* is located in the southeast quarter of Section 7 in the first original and redrawn Tubac map of 1877 (see Figure 2.16), the township of Tubac was in a different place, not the *Solar*. The township of Tubac in 1877 includes land later claimed by the Baca Float #3[45] which contains what is known today as the south barrio of Tubac. Tubac of 1877 was located south of Tubac's *presidio* ruins precisely as mandated in the 1789

Otero Spanish land grant. On the redrawn 1877 Tubac map, a "Note" informs that the Otero House Lot Claim was also labeled incorrectly. Despite the initial challenge locating the *Solar* using the 1877 Tubac townsite plat, it reveals two important facts. The original *Solar* measured approximately 1.30 acres and the property was rectangular in shape. After the general location of the Otero *Solar* was verified, some important new information surfaced.

Florence Land Office records reflect that the Otero family nearly lost the *Solar* one year after the initial government survey. By 1878, the Otero family had owned and lived in the *Solar* for eighty-nine years. In February of the same year as the Silver Dollar became U.S. legal tender; I. P. Ortiz, Antonio C. Herreras, and Charles D. Poston filed a petition claiming ownership of the township of Tubac. Poston had been the Superintendent of Indian Affairs in 1863 and delegate to the House of Representatives for the Territory of Arizona in 1864. These men petitioned Probate Judge John Woods for 640 acres of Township 21 South, Range 13 East, Pima County[46] for the townsite of Tubac as "Citizens of the United States and claimants occupants and owners" of Tubac. An application was filed with Clerk B.H. Hereford on February 27, 1878 at Florence which asserted that the town was to be held "<u>in trust</u> for the several use and benefit of the claimants occupants and owners thereof" for the following land:

- East ½ of the NorthEast quarter of Section 7
- East ½ of the SouthEast quarter of Section 7
- West ½ of the NorthWest quarter of Section 8
- West ½ of the SouthWest quarter of Section 8
- West ½ of the NorthWest quarter of Section 17
- West ½ of the SouthWest quarter of Section 17
- East ½ of the SouthEast quarter of Section 18, and the
- East ½ of the NorthEast quarter of Section 18.[47]

The lands at Tubac claimed by Poston, Ortiz and Herreras included the East ½ of the SouthEast quarter of Section 7 where the Otero *Solar* was located. If claimants purposefully intended to dispossess the Otero family and other Tubac residents of their property, their attempt was unsuccessful.

Perhaps Poston was simply too fond of Sabino and dropped the claim because he valued Sabino's friendship. Apparently quite fond of Sabino, Poston affectionately referred to Sabino in his poem, "The Battle of Santa Rita" published on August 26, 1885 saying, "Down in there in the valley lives my pretty little page, who came to me when ten years of age."[48] Another theory why Poston and the other claimants reconsidered their application to incorporate Tubac may be they realized that the Tubac town site as claimed would have resulted in legal challenges from the Otero family and other long-standing residents of Tubac. Curiously, Poston apparently had negative views on Spanish or Mexican land grant ownership. He wrote a letter to Territorial John N. Goodwin on July 24, 1864, "By a fiction of law which has no foundation in either justice or reason, we ignore the Indian title to land in the Territories acquired from Mexico, because the Spanish conquerors established that principle of injustice."[49] Although we may never know for certain what motivated Poston, Ortiz and Herreras to renounce their claim to the township of Tubac, history welcomes the creation of the first significant map of Tubac under United States government rule which mapped the location of the Otero *Solar*.

Figure 2.18. Charles Debrille Poston illustrated by Dorotea Cvijanovic commissioned exclusively for *Terrenos* © 2018 Diana DeLugan. All rights reserved.

IDENTIFYING THE OTERO SOLAR AT TUBAC

Given that the general location of the Otero *Solar* was positively identified within Section 7 of the original Tubac town site (present-day south barrio) using U.S. Bureau of

Land Management plats, it was time to dig deeper to locate the modern site of the *Solar*. Four major resources emerged. First was Doris Winifred Bents' University of Arizona thesis in partial fulfillment for a Master of Arts degree completed on May 17, 1949 called *The History of Tubac 1752-1948*. In a footnote, Bents cited the *Reminiscences of Sarah M. Black*, resident of Tubac. Black said Sabino Otero likely purchased the "Goldberg store [at Tubac] and that Mercer kept it."[50] Isaac Goldberg owned a store at Tubac. On October 24, 1876, he filed an intent at the Pima County Recorder's Office to claim 320 acres for the Townsite of Tubac along with Albert Steinfeld, Edward N. Fish, S. Silverberg, and Charles Poppe. Like the subsequent Charles Poston Townsite of Tubac application filed on February 27, 1878, nothing became of Isaac Goldberg claim.[51] Bent's research was the first to suggest that Sabino Otero and family owned two buildings at Tubac, not one. If one building was the *Solar* provided for via the 1789 Spanish land grant, the second building might be the building formerly known as the Goldberg store.

Sarah Black first came to Tubac and took a job as a teacher around 1884[52] making her a contemporary of Sabino Otero. With first-hand general knowledge of Tubac, she appears a credible source. Black said it was "likely" that Sabino purchased Goldberg's store but stopped short of confirming the purchase as a fact. Perhaps her memory dulled by the time Mrs. George F. Kitt interviewed her in 1926. When Mrs. Kitt probed Sarah about forty-two-year-old events, Black was ninety-two years old.[53] Although Sarah Black's statement reveals a new fact that a second Otero building was located at the township of Tubac, the fact was unverified because the purchase and sale of Sabino's store remains speculation absent documentation. Elizabeth R. Brownell's book was the second source used to probe deeper.

Figure 2.19. Conceptual illustration of Sarah Black by Dorotea Cvijanovic commissioned exclusively for *Terrenos* © 2018 Diana DeLugan. All rights reserved.

Elizabeth Brownell (known affectionately by Tubac locals as "Brownie") had a notable career in education before she moved to Tubac in 1865. As the President of the Tubac Historical Society, she had occasion to research volumes of government documents, newspaper and family history files. She even conducted first-person interviews related to the history of Tubac.[54] Published in 1986, she wrote *They Lived in Tubac* which in significant part details the third major attempt to establish the Tubac townsite in 1882. Brownell wrote that Sabino Otero joined forces with T. Lillie Mercer, Dr. H. C. Jessup, Frank Tompkins, Jose A and Jesus Burrel, Pasqual Megory, Abram Salcido, Bernardino Valenzuela, Nicolas Herreras, and Guillermo Reney to petition for the official Tubac townsite.[55] "[O]ld ruins at the north end of the [1882 Tubac Townsite] plat were on the Otero grant still claimed by Sabino Otero and were not allotted to anyone,"[56] continued Brownell.

Contrary to Brownell's assertion that Sabino Otero possessed sole ownership of the Otero lands in 1882, the Otero land grant properties were jointly owned by Sabino, his siblings and niece, Ana Maria Comadurán, all legal heirs-at-law of the Otero 1789 land grant. Their U.S. government petition to confirm the *Solar* and *Rancho de Otero* was pending at the time Sabino applied for the Tubac townsite.[57] Nonetheless, Brownell's statement about the "old ruins" enlightens because it informs that the Otero family owned a third structure at Tubac in 1882, two properties in town and one in ruins north of town. Further research was necessary to discover if the ruins north of town was an early first reference to the original Hacienda de Otero ranch house built by Don Torivio de Otero, land grantee. Before any investigation could begin on the Otero building in ruins north of town, a third source was needed to determine which of the two buildings in Tubac was the Otero *Solar*.

Sarah Black's hypothesis that Sabino Otero had sold his store to T. Lillie Mercer was explored. Research began in earnest for pre-statehood deeds at both the Pima County and Santa Cruz county Recorder's Offices to identify the "Sabino store" and determine if it was the Otero *Solar* mentioned in the 1789 Otero land grant. Given that Tubac belonged to both counties at different intervals in time, the deed from Sabino to Mercer could likely be found at either location. Unfortunately, no deed for any land transaction between Sabino and Mercer has been located to date. This frustrating dead-end prompted a look into a third valuable resource, Wallace Vegors' undated paper "*The Otero Solar at Tubac: 'Home' for 150 Years.*[58]

Vegors was the president of the Tubac Historical Society, director of the Tubac Presidio State Museum in 1967, and spent years as the Assistant Director of Arizona's State Parks system. He was also a tireless advocate for the preservation of Tubac's historic buildings.[59] Vegors arrived at two important hypothesis. First, he suggests that a comparison of the known location of the *Solar* in proximity to then-existing *presidio* ruins suggest the *Solar* was located at the same site as the U-shaped building that appears in the ancient 1766/67 Tubac map by Spanish cartographer Joseph de Urrutia.[60] A review of the Urrutia map of 1766/67 displays a U-shaped building that aligns with the southeast wing of the Tubac *presidio* (see Figure 2.19). Vegors' theory suggests that the Otero *Solar* may have been built over a then-existing structure. Vegors stated:

> There is tantalizing evidence to suggest that the Otero lot on the 1882 map is the original solar granted to Toribio [sic] Otero by Lieutenant Errán in 1789.[61] ¶[I]t appears that the "presidio ruins" of today has been correctly identified. If so, then Otero's solar would lie immediately to the south in a position very like that of the lot shown on the 1882 Tubac Townsite map.[62] ¶The lot was supposed to be 21.30 chains from the quarter section corner of the houselot on a course of North 19° 15'. The direction was found to be exactly correct. However, the distance was insufficient by three chains or 198 feet. The proper distance would be 24.30 chains rather than 21.30 chains, a conceivable misreading of field notes.[63]

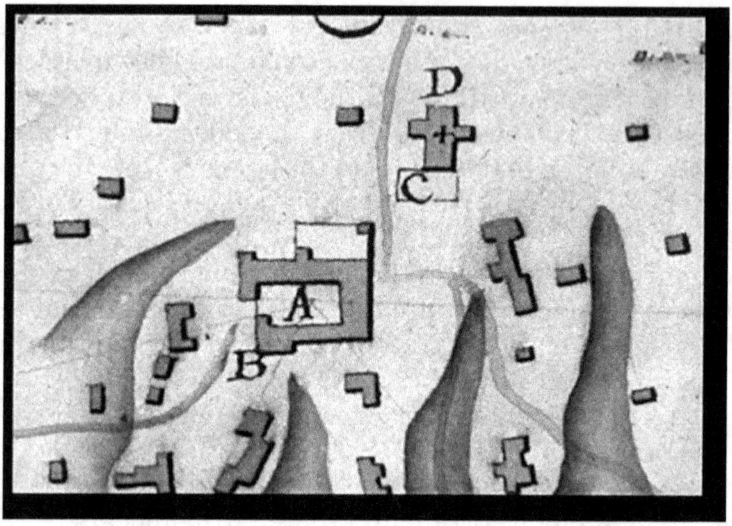

Figure 2.20. Except from Joseph de Urrutia's Map of 1766/77. Close up image shows the location of a rectangular structure located immediately to the south [left on above image] of the U-shaped structure known today as the Tubac Spanish Presidio. Given the Otero *Solar* was required to be built immediately south of the Presidio according to the 1789 Otero land grant, Urrutia's map suggests the Otero *Solar* was likely built upon an existing structure. (Public domain. Edited by the author).

Vegors' argument was compelling. Once the *presidio* ruins were identified, the Otero *Solar* should be located immediately southeast of the *presidio* ruins. Vegors also hypothesized that the *Solar* was likely located at the modern-day site of Otero Hall based on modern map coordinates. To test Vegors' theory, the 1882 Tubac town site plat also known as the Mercer map was obtained from the Arizona State Archives at Phoenix, Arizona. Once the map plat color was inverted from black to white and the business section magnified, exacting detail was revealed.

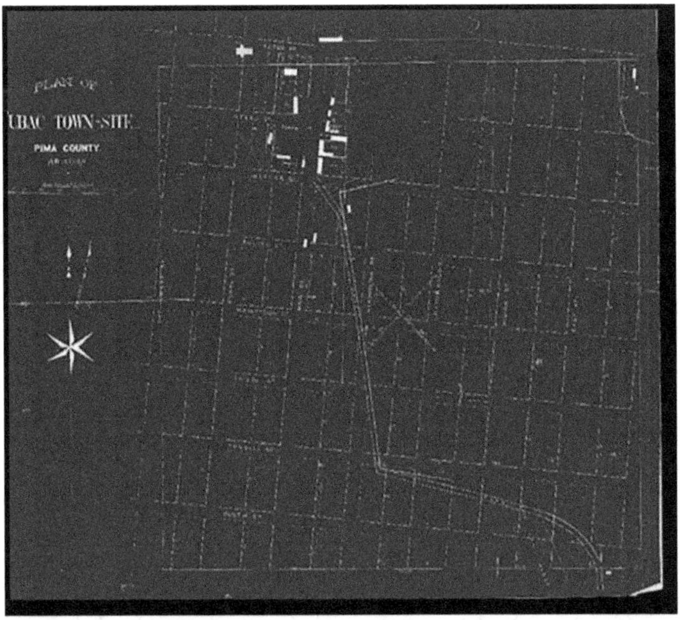

Figure 2.21. Tubac townsite map of 1882 was discovered at the Arizona State Archives. Map negative rendered the image difficult to read. (Arizona State Library, Archives & Public Records).

The 1882 townsite had a "delineated grid pattern of 58 blocks, each roughly 300 by 300 feet. Roadways and streets were laid out in 60 and 80 foot widths."[64] The business section of 1882 Tubac was located at the intersection of Otero Street and the Royal Spanish Highway renamed Main Street, just southeast of the Tubac *presidio* ruins. It included nine lots. Two building structures were labeled as owned by Otero, five by T. Lillie Mercer, one by Glassman and one by E. N. Fish. Lots and roads were designated in anticipation of the town's expansion.[65] Some suggest that Mercer, who directed the townsite effort, Henry Glassman and Sabino Otero fit the grid to their building locations and disregarded the other buildings in the townsite of lesser importance to their own objectives.[66] Residential areas were platted in a southern direction similar to the location of the Tubac's colonial south barrio.[67] Fortunately, the *presidio* ruins were clearly identified on the map located immediately north of a large rectangular building marked "Otero." After the color on the Mercer 1882 map was inverted using Photoshop for readability then laid over the 1913/15 GLORE map, it confirmed Vegors' assertion that "block three, lot 5 closely corresponds rather closely to the location of the Sabino Otero lot on the Mercer map of 1882 both in location and dimensions, measuring 128 feet square in 1913 and about 120 by 100 feet in 1882." Vegors continued:

> The earlier Main Street, a.k.a. the Colonial Highway, was called Broadway Avenue. A roadway called Salero Avenue extended east-west about 300 feet south of the plaza area. River Street formed the other east-west street aligning with existing buildings that faced the north side of the presidio ruins. Six of the large blocks [including the Otero block] were subdivided with lots. Those blocks were located with boundaries adjoining Broadway and Solero [sic] Avenues and River Street. The shape of many of the lots suggest strongly that buildings existing in those parcels and the plat survey were made to accommodate the structures and ownership patter. Most likely the townsite contained between 20 and 25 structures in 1913.[68]

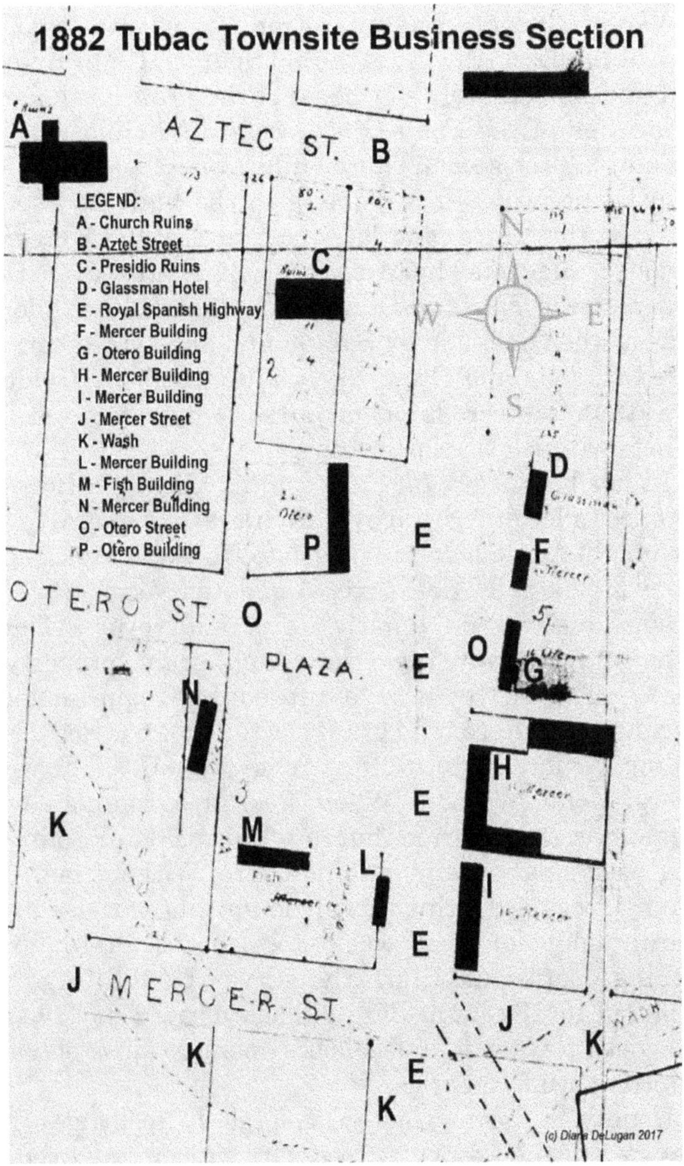

Figure 2.22. Once the 1882 Map of the Tubac Townsite was inverted from black to white, it revealed the names of the building owners. Letters "G" and "P" are two buildings owned by Otero. (Graphic illustration and map excerpt by the author).

Wallace Vegors analysis strongly suggests that the Otero building northwest of the old Spanish Highway/Anza Trail and immediately southeast of the *presidio* should be the location of the *Solar*. By process of elimination, it is possible that the second Otero building northeast of the old Spanish Highway[69] may have been the building used by Sabino as the "store" and later sold to T. Lillie Mercer, as previously suggested by Mrs. Sarah Black. However, Doris Bents believed Tubac was simply too small to have had two stores at the time, one by Sabino and one by Mercer. She argued that Sabino Otero likely purchased the Goldberg Store that Mercer later acquired.[70] Further research conflicts with Black's latter theory.

In her book *They Lived in Tubac*, Elizabeth Brownell references a letter written by U.S. Surveyor General for the Territory of Arizona John Wasson to United States Deputy Surveyor George F. Roskruge, Esq. dated March 25, 1881. Wasson instructed Deputy U.S. Surveyor General Roskruge to survey the Otero land grant property at Tubac.[71] The survey was a procedural requirement to determine the Otero land grant's actual boundaries for the pending General Land Office review by U.S. Surveyor-General John Wasson. When Roskruge completed the *Solar* survey, he reported that the "House Lot" or *Solar* was being used as a store by Sabino Otero. Without more, we can only speculate if this was an actual store for use by the general public or if it was "storage" for Otero family ranching operations. Since the survey by Roskruge was completed in 1881 and Sarah Black arrived at Tubac in 1884, both Roskruge and Black's memory give plausible but incompatible theories.

Deputy Surveyor General George J. Roskruge's field notes was the fourth necessary resource used to affirmatively clarify the location of the *Solar*. Roskruge's survey of the Otero *Solar* was completed on April 12, 1881. The field notes reported that Roskruge commenced measurements of the Otero *Solar* at the "SE corner of Sabino Otero's Store…[and proceeded] along front of Store to the N.E. Cor[ner]."[72] Roskruge's field notes confirm that the Otero *Solar*, original home of the Otero family of Tubac located immediately to the southeast of the Tubac *presidio* ruins and now the modern site of Otero Hall at the Tubac Presidio State Park and Museum, was used as a store in 1881.

Figure 2.23. Illustration of Deputy Surveyor General George J. Roskruge by Dorotea Cvijanovic commissioned exclusively for *Terrenos* © 2018 Diana DeLugan. All rights reserved. *See* Appendix E for full copy of Deputy Surveyor Roskruge's Otero Land Grant Field Notes.

OTERO HALL CHAIN OF TITLE

Wallace Vegors' believed that Otero Hall located immediately southeast of the *presidio* at the current Tubac Presidio State Park is the location of the original Otero *Solar* mentioned in the 1789 Otero land grant. Land deeds and patents were traced to determine if Vegors' suspicions were true. When T. Lillie Mercer, Sabino Otero, and others sought to establish the Tubac townsite, all the town land was deeded to Probate Judge John Wood to hold the land in trust for the petitioners. Judge Wood had the land resurveyed by S. M. Allis,[73] then he petitioned for 160 acres of land under the authority of the 1820 Cash Act. United States Bureau of Land Management land patent details report that BLM serial patent number AZAZAA 010528 was issued to Wood on December 30, 1884. The Wood patent included Block 7 in the Township of Tubac,[74] suspected location of the Otero *Solar*.

After Sabino Otero's death in 1914, Sabino's youngest brother Teofilo Otero built Otero Hall on Lots 19, 25, and 26 in Block 7 of the Tubac Townsite in response to Tubac community's needs for a gathering place. Otero Hall is located immediately south of the *presidio*'s east wing. Weekly Saturday evening dances and other social events were a regular occurrence at Otero Hall.[75] Then four years later on December 23, 1918, W.A. O'Conner (Judge of the Superior Court of Arizona and ex-officio Trustee of the Townsite of Tubac land patent) conveyed a deed to Teofilo for Lots 19, 25, 26 in Block 7 and all of lot 32 in Block 7, lying north of the north boundary line of Baca Float No. 3 as delineated on Glore map of 7/6/1916. [76] Teofilo soon allowed Otero Hall to be used as overflow teaching space for the Tubac State School.

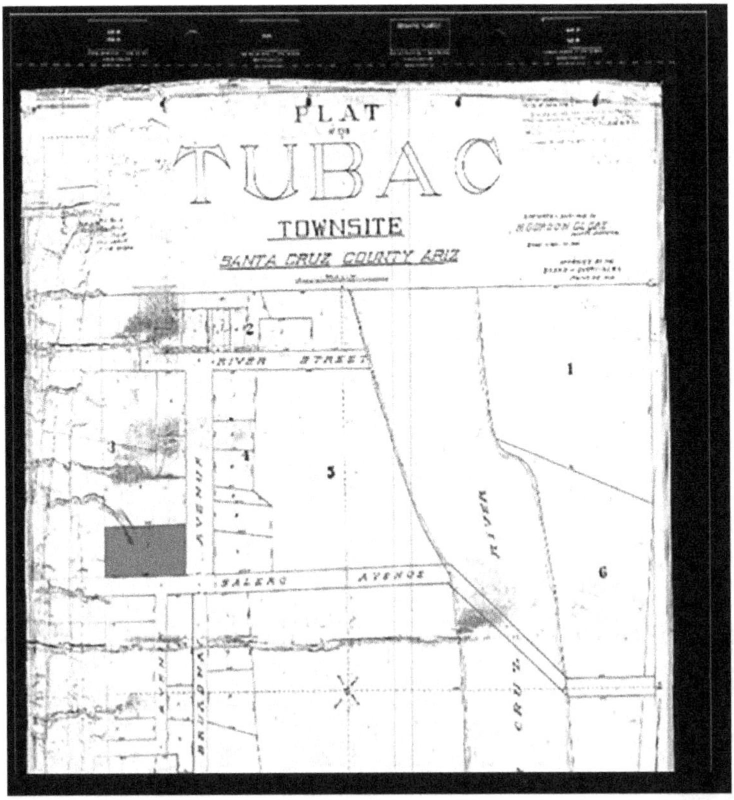

Figure 2.24. H. Gordon Glore Tubac Townsite Plate of 3/3/1914. Shaded lots owned by Teofilo Otero. (Courtesy Santa Cruz County Recorder's Office). 77

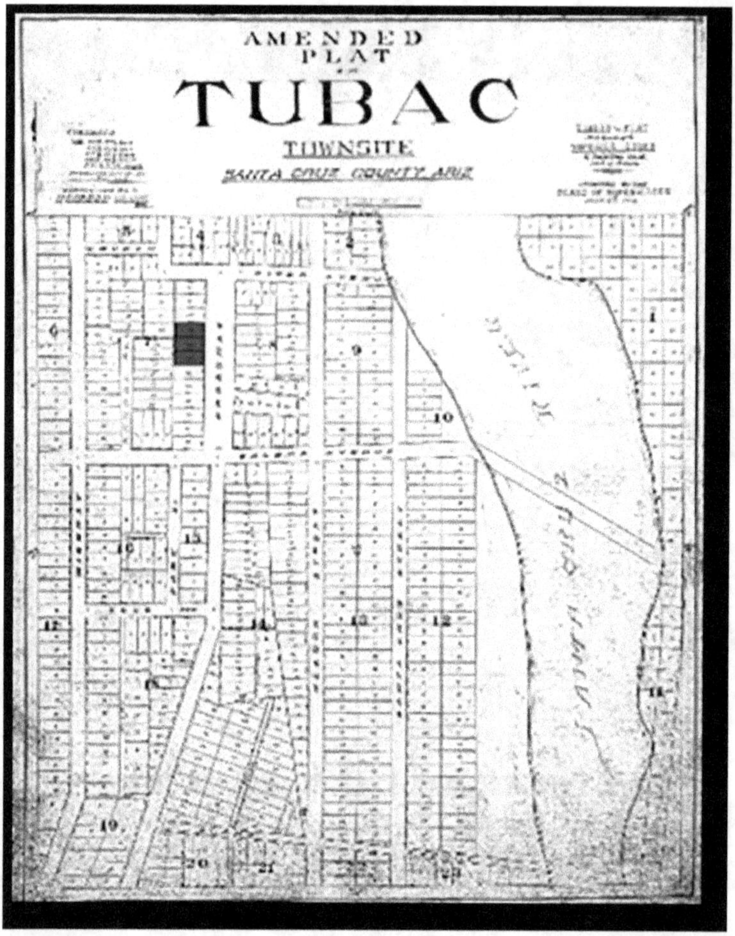

Figure 2.25. In 1916, the Townsite of Tubac was redrawn by H. Gordon Glore for a more uniform appearance and town expansion. Shaded lots owned by Teofilo Otero. (Courtesy Santa Cruz County Recorder's Office).

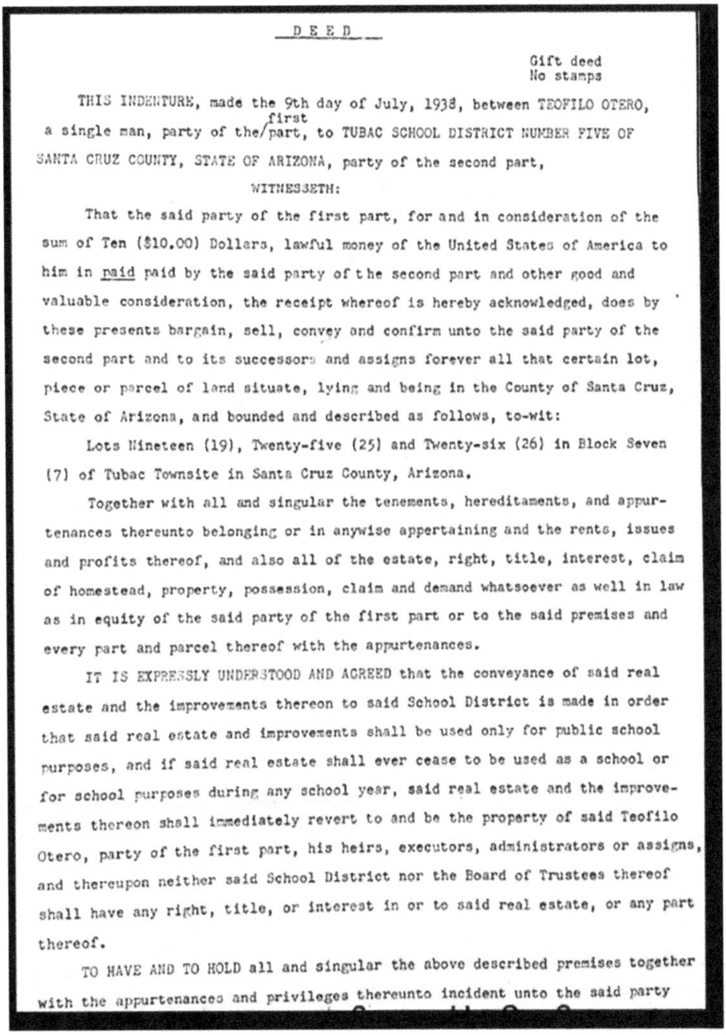

D E E D

Gift deed
No stamps

THIS INDENTURE, made the 9th day of July, 1938, between TEOFILO OTERO, a single man, party of the first part, to TUBAC SCHOOL DISTRICT NUMBER FIVE OF SANTA CRUZ COUNTY, STATE OF ARIZONA, party of the second part,

WITNESSETH:

That the said party of the first part, for and in consideration of the sum of Ten ($10.00) Dollars, lawful money of the United States of America to him in paid paid by the said party of the second part and other good and valuable consideration, the receipt whereof is hereby acknowledged, does by these presents bargain, sell, convey and confirm unto the said party of the second part and to its successors and assigns forever all that certain lot, piece or parcel of land situate, lying and being in the County of Santa Cruz, State of Arizona, and bounded and described as follows, to-wit:

Lots Nineteen (19), Twenty-five (25) and Twenty-six (26) in Block Seven (7) of Tubac Townsite in Santa Cruz County, Arizona.

Together with all and singular the tenements, hereditaments, and appurtenances thereunto belonging or in anywise appertaining and the rents, issues and profits thereof, and also all of the estate, right, title, interest, claim of homestead, property, possession, claim and demand whatsoever as well in law as in equity of the said party of the first part or to the said premises and every part and parcel thereof with the appurtenances.

IT IS EXPRESSLY UNDERSTOOD AND AGREED that the conveyance of said real estate and the improvements thereon to said School District is made in order that said real estate and improvements shall be used only for public school purposes, and if said real estate shall ever cease to be used as a school or for school purposes during any school year, said real estate and the improvements thereon shall immediately revert to and be the property of said Teofilo Otero, party of the first part, his heirs, executors, administrators or assigns, and thereupon neither said School District nor the Board of Trustees thereof shall have any right, title, or interest in or to said real estate, or any part thereof.

TO HAVE AND TO HOLD all and singular the above described premises together with the appurtenances and privileges thereunto incident unto the said party

Figure 2.26. Page 1 of the Teofilo Otero Deed of Otero Hall to the Tubac School District Number 5. (Courtesy Santa Cruz Valley Unified School District No. 35).

IN WITNESS WHEREOF the said party of the first part has hereunto set his hand the day and year first above written.

TEOFILO OTERO

STATE OF ARIZONA)
) ss.
County of Pima:)

This instrument was acknowledged before me on this 9th day of July, 1938, by TEOFILO OTERO who stated to me that he executed the same for the purposes and consideration therein expressed.

My commission expires: April 21, 1939.

LUCILLE VEASE
Notary Public

(SEAL)

#1019 - Filed and recorded at the request of James V. Robins, July 11th, A.D. 1938, at 1:25 P.M.

Lucy T. Mitchell
LUCY T. MITCHELL
County Recorder.

STATE OF ARIZONA,)
County of Santa Cruz, } ss.

I, County Recorder, in and for the County of Santa Cruz, State of Arizona, do hereby certify that the attached and foregoing is a full, true and correct copy of......
GIFT DEED - Teofilo Otero to Tubac School District #5, Santa Cruz County, recorded in Book 23 of Deeds, Page 303
as the same appears of record .... in this office.

IN WITNESS WHEREOF, I have hereunto set my hand and affixed my Official seal at Nogales, Arizona, this ......20th.... day of .....November....... 19...47.

Mary Bettwy
Mary Bettwy County Recorder

Deputy.

Figure 2.27. Page 2 of the Teofilo Otero Deed of Otero Hall to the Tubac School District Number 5. (Courtesy Santa Cruz Valley Unified School District No. 35).

The Tubac State Graded School was originally established in 1885. School had been taught at Tubac subsequent to the Gadsden Purchase of 1854 and likely taught continuously since Don Torivio de Otero first taught at the 1787 Spanish presidio, as education was necessary for government and commerce. However, 1885 ushered in the first designation of a formal school site under the Territory of Arizona. By 1935, school enrollment substantially increased to one hundred and thirty-seven students rendering the old schoolhouse inadequate. To house the new student body and newly hired fourth grade teacher, the school rented Otero Hall from Teofilo Otero to act as a fourth classroom for primary grade students.[78] On July 9, 1938, Teofilo Otero executed a Deed to the Tubac School District Number Five of Santa Cruz County, State of Arizona for land that included Otero Hall. The property was situated on "Lots Nineteen (19), Twenty-five (25) and Twenty-six (26) in Block Seven (7) of Tubac Townsite in Santa Cruz County, Arizona."[79] The deed contained a reverter clause which allowed the property to be returned to Teofilo's heirs if the property ever ceased to be used for a school:

> IT IS EXPRESSLY UNDERSTOOD AND AGREED that the conveyance of said real estate and the improvements thereon to said School District is made in order that said real estate and improvements shall be used only for public school purposes, and if said real estate shall ever cease to be used as a school or for school purposes during any school year, said real estate and the improvements thereon shall immediately revert to and be the property of said Teofilo, party of the first part, his heirs, executors, administrators or assigns, an thereupon said School District nor the Board of Trustees thereof shall have any right, title, or interest in or to said real estate, or any part thereof.[80]

Twenty-five years later, the Tubac School District Number 5 merged with the Amado School District No. 13 in 1963. The Santa Cruz Valley Unified School District was created in June of 1973 after the Calabasas School District No. 3 merged with Tubac School District No. 5 in the same month and year.[81] Before Otero Hall could be condemned and title vested in the State of Arizona, Otero family descendants were contacted by State Parks officials to determine who might have ownership under the deed's reverter clause. They argued among themselves to determine who had superior title to Otero Hall and the contiguous lots. These were uncertain times. Suspense loomed and no one was certain of what might become of the land. There was even talk of building a new home on one of Teofilo's lots.[82] Teofilo's heirs eventually agreed to cede the land to the state and Otero Hall land was condemned on August 27, 1973. Once title vested in the State of Arizona, Otero Hall became a permanent addition of Tubac Presidio State Park and Museum's building inventory.[83]

The location of the Otero *Solar*, Arizona's first European privately owned home, was properly identified thanks to Wallace Vegors' paper *The Otero Solar at Tubac: 'Home' for 150 Years.* Vegors' findings were independently confirmed by this author with the assistance of retired hydrologist Philip Halpenny by tracing land titles and analyzing Tubac Townsite plats. The *Solar* is an important Arizona historic site. It was once a store, community center, and school that served Tubac's residents. Otero Hall is preserved as part of the Tubac Townsite Historic District at the Tubac Presidio State Park and is listed on the National Register of Historic Places. It continues to be used for private and public events.

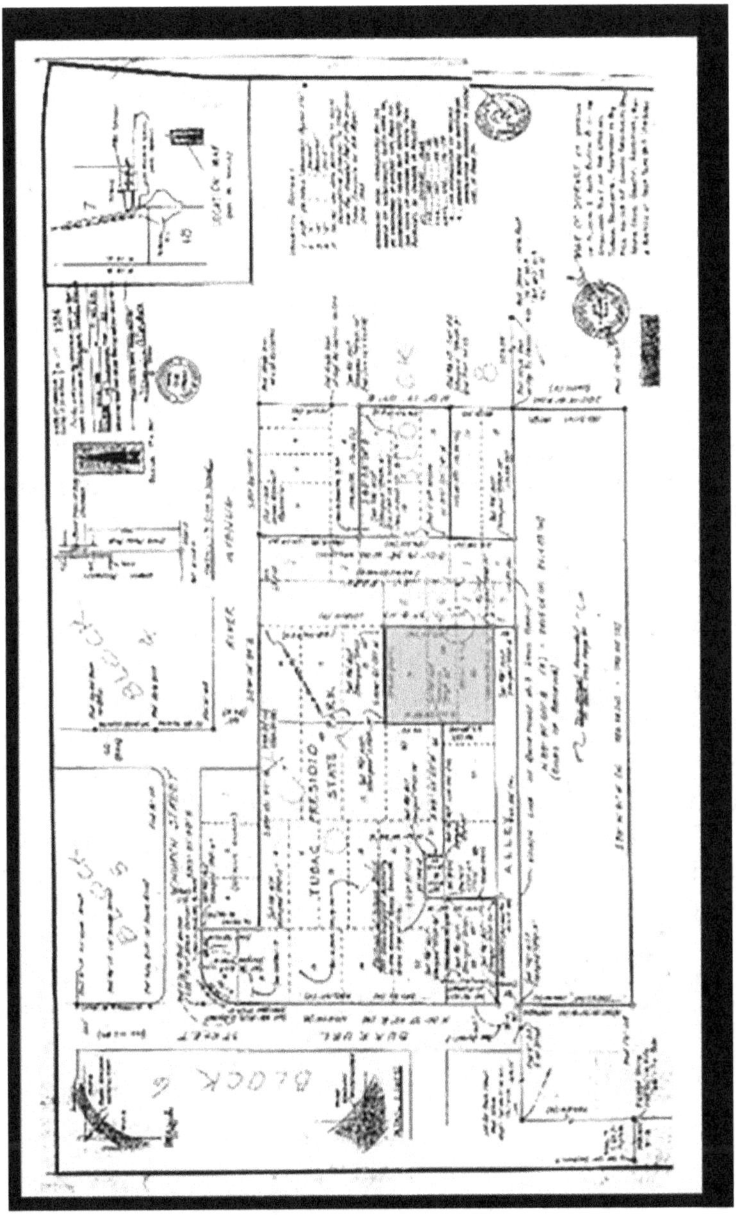

Figure 2.28. Tubac Presidio State Park map filed by the Arizona State Parks Department after the 1973 Otero Hall land condemnation order. Shaded lots deeded to the Tubac School District, subsequently ceded to the State of Arizona. (Courtesy Santa Cruz County Recorder's Office).

The existing Otero Hall structure appears to have been built over the Otero *Solar*, which itself was likely built over an ancient structure located immediately south of the east wing of the Tubac Presidio identified in the Joseph de Urrutia 1766/67 Map of Tubac. (*See* Figure 2.20). Because the exact location of the *Solar* has been revealed, a significant discovery emerged.

When the Sonoran Mining & Exploration Company moved into Tubac, it commissioned an engraving to capture 1857 Tubac and its existing buildings as a visual aid for the corporation's stockholders. The engraving titled *Tubac & The Santa Rita Mtns From the S.E. Side* by C. Schuchard reveals a depiction of the Otero *Solar* in 1857.[84] The image reflects a southeast view of Tubac. Located just right of center next to a large tree, south of the east *presidio* wing, stands the original adobe Otero *Solar*, Arizona's first privately-owned European home. (*See* Figure 2.29). An adobe building identified as owned by Sabino Otero in 1882 is visible immediately to the east of the Otero Solar. It is location of the modern historic building known as the Rojas House. The Schuchard engraving of 1857 is the earliest known image of the Otero *Solar* and the second adobe building in Tubac once owned by Sabino Otero.

Visitors to modern Tubac can experience Spanish and Mexican colonial influence mixed with that of pioneer Arizona in the architecture of its buildings, the food, and history.

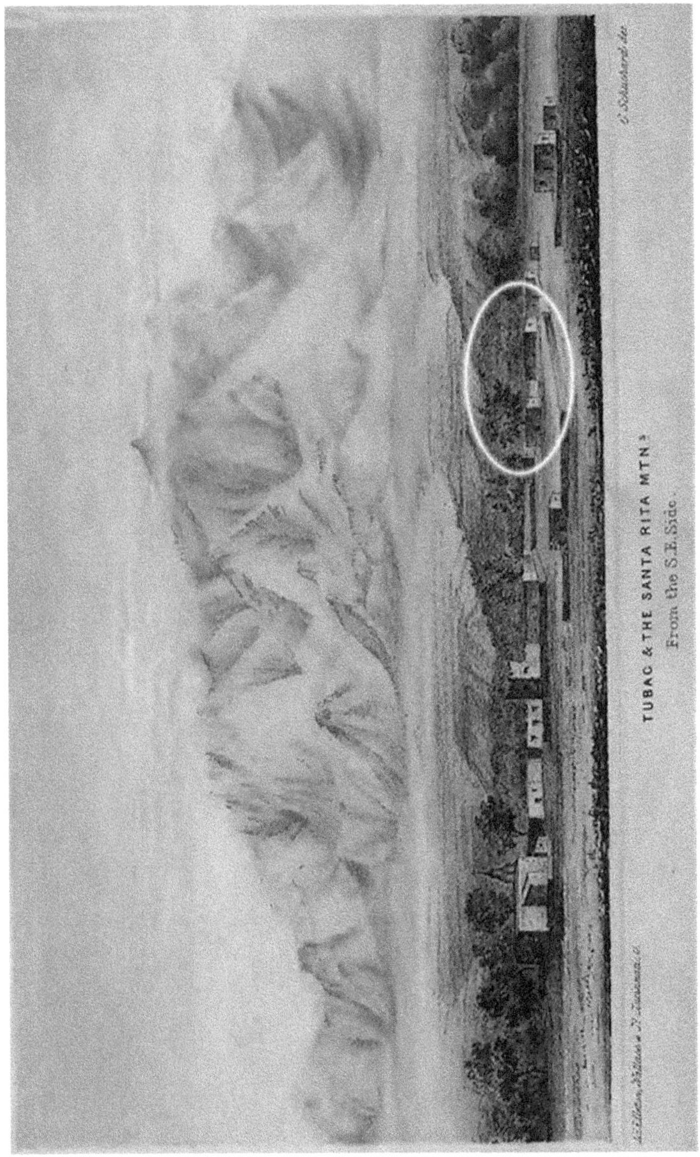

Figure 2.29. The C. Schuchard Engraving of the Tubac & the Santa Rita Mountains is the earliest known image of Arizona's first European privately-owned home, the Otero *Solar*. The *Solar* is highlighted in the engraving to the center of the tree. (Heintzelman, Samuel. *Report of the Sonora Exploring and Mining Co., Made To The Stockholders*. Railroad Record Print. Cincinnati: 1857. Public domain).

[illegible]

CHAPTER THREE
RANCHO DE OTERO

The Otero family of Tubac is most often remembered for its ranch/farm lands one mile north of Tubac. While Rancho de Otero history merits a worthy place in Arizona's history because it is the second parcel of land specified in the Otero Spanish land grant of 1789, Arizona's first European private title to land, it has another significant attribute. It holds the first title for the oldest continuously operated privately-owned ranch in Arizona history, 148 years.

In 1881, United States Deputy Surveyor General George J. Roskruge's survey identified the boundaries of the original Rancho de Otero land grant located one mile north of the townsite of Tubac. *See* Appendix E. His field notes describe the historic property with exacting detail. A review of the Preliminary Survey notes and associated Otero land grant plat completed on April 13, 1881 reveals two houses were located at the Rancho de Otero. The house that belonged to Atanacio Otero, son of land grantee Don Torivio de Otero, was located just south of the existing historic hacienda (ranch house) and marked "Old Ruins" on Roskruge's survey notes. Otero ranch lands south of Atanacio's house located in Section 8 of the Plat extending to Post Mark Otero S.W and Otero S.E. reflect the Martinez land grant's property boundaries. The Martinez land was initially sold by Jose Maria Martinez to Manuel Otero (*see* Chapter One) then subsequently sold to Sabino Otero by Martinez's heir Dario Martinez to avoid having the

Martinez land challenged during Land Court and Private Court of Land Claims proceedings. Roskruge's mention of Atanacio's house informs that Don Torivio de Otero's son Atanacio built a second Otero house at the historic ranch/farming lands at Tubac during Arizona's Spanish era.

Jose Maria Martinez's land grant document reviewed by U.S. Surveyor General John Wasson during the Sabino *et al* petition before the U.S. Surveyor General's land office proceedings reports that Martinez's land boundaries (subsequently the Otero property expansion), was measured from the enclosure of Atanacio Otero's property in April of 1838. According to the 1831 census, both Don Torivio and Atanacio were living together at Tubac.[1] We can only speculate if father and son lived together at the Otero *Solar* in town or the hacienda at the rancho north of town.

North of Atanacio's house ruins was a second house marked by Roskruge as "Old House." [2] This "Old House" was not in ruin. Its location aligns with the present location of the historic building known as the "Hacienda de Otero." This revelation strongly suggests that the current Hacienda de Otero was built on the ruins of the "Old House" as was Spanish custom or that the "Old House" was renovated and is in fact the current Hacienda de Otero. In either case, Roskruge's survey confirms that the "Old House" was built prior to 1881. Some cottonwood trees were identified by Roskruge on both sides of the Santa Cruz River banks and some very old pear trees were growing near the Otero ranch buildings. These old pear trees were likely the fruit trees required to be planted in accordance with the 1789 Spanish land grant mandates. A north running ditch was also evident and the fields were in a "high state of cultivation" used by Sabino Otero.[3] A map of the Rancho de Otero drawn by Jose T. Otero in 1914 (*see* Figure 3.x) suggests the ditch identified by Roskruge was part of the original irrigation system built by Don Torivio as mentioned in the 1789 and 1804/1807 land documents.

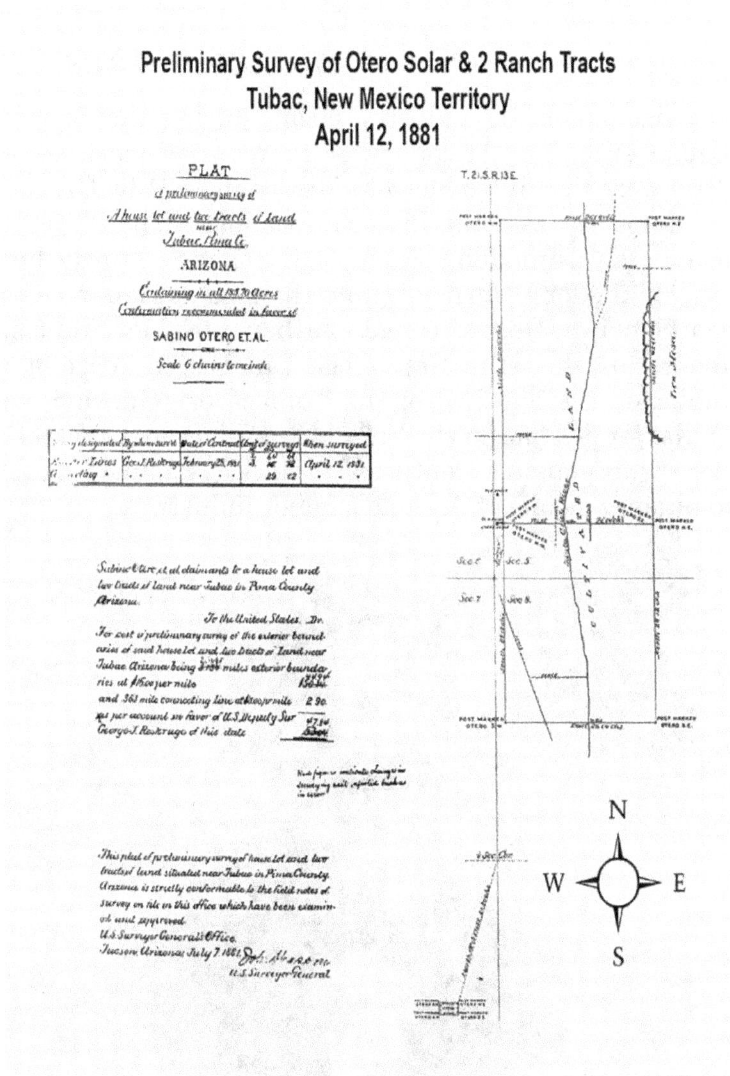

Figure 3.1. The Sabino *et al* land grant sketch by the U.S. Surveyor General's Office at Tucson. Above the intersection of .Sections 6, 5, 7, and 8, is mention of an "Old Ruin Otero House." (Arizona State Library, Archives & Public Records).

RANCHO DE OTERO – THE EARLY YEARS

Arizona's cattle industry began during the Spanish Arizona era when Arizona was known as Pimería Alta.[4] Cattle were first introduced to Mexico in 1521 by Gregorio de Villalobos,[5] then into Pimería Alta in 1540 by Francisco Vásquez de Coronado.[6] Some of Coronado's sturdy herd survived the long journey from California as it roamed the open Sonoran Desert range. Father Eusebio Francisco Kino established the first stock ranches in Arizona at Quiburi on the San Pedro; and Tumacácori, Guevavi, and San Xavier del Bac on the Santa Cruz River around 1697.[7] Over subsequent centuries, stock raising gained prominence as one of Arizona's major industries.

Figure 3.2. Illustration of Sabino Otero, Cattle King of Tubac, by Dorotea Cvijanovic commissioned exclusively for *Terrenos* © 2018 Diana DeLugan. All rights reserved.

Figure 3.3. Illustration of Teofilo Otero, the second Cattle King of Tubac, by Dorotea Cvijanovic commissioned exclusively for *Terrenos* © 2018 Diana DeLugan. All rights reserved.

During the late 19th and early 20th centuries, Sabino and Teofilo Otero were known the Cattle Kings of Tubac. Their vast stock raising operations spanned from Sonora to Casa Grande.[8] Their cattle were sold and distributed throughout the United States and Mexico. It was a family affair. Otero ranch operations were inherited from Sabino and Teofilo's Spanish ancestors: their father Manuel, grandfather Atanacio and great-grandfather Torivio de Otero, Spanish land grantee. The Otero land grant of 1789 confirms that an agricultural ranch operation had been established by 1789. Cattle were introduced to the Rancho de Otero during Spanish times and remained a part of the ranch property until the ranch was sold to private interests in 1937. [9] Modern history mistakenly reports that Sabino Otero was the first to introduce cattle to the Rancho de

Otero. Although Sabino was certainly the most prolific stock raiser of the family during U.S. government rule, the Otero cattle brand was identified by anthropologist James Officer as among the brands of Tubac's first Spanish families.[10]

After Arizona became a U.S. possession subsequent to the 1854 Gadsden Purchase, Tubac was situated within Pima County. In 1899, Santa Cruz County was formed out of the southern portion of Pima County.[11] Like other Tubac stock raisers who moved to Tucson due to unrelenting Apache attack, Sabino Otero became an active participant in stock industry associations in both Pima and Santa Cruz counties. The Arizona Live Stock Ranchmen's Association was one of Pima County's most active organizations. It determined the routes for round-ups and organized rodeos from Tucson to the International U.S. Mexican border. Its members included Sabino Otero, Frank Proctor, and T.D. Hogan.[12] Sabino was also active in the Pima County Cattlemen's' Association who also organized grand cattle round-ups[13] and helped establish commerce guidelines.[14] The Pima County Cattlemen's Association included Manuel Amado, Maish & Driscoll, and Juan Elias. In Santa Cruz County, members of the Santa Cruz Stock Growers' Association included Chas. Alischul, G.W. Atkinson, G.H. Beckwith, James Breen, Juan Elias, Mark Ezekiels, M.L. Martinez, T. Lille Mercer, Sabino Otero, Jas. Owens, A.L. Peck, and Isaac I. Town. Sabino was elected vice-president of the Santa Cruz Stock Growers' Association in 1886.[15] The Rancho de Otero and its vaqueros regularly participated in organized open range roundups while protecting its vast herd.

FINANCIAL IMPACT TO OTERO OPERATIONS

After Tubac and the Rancho de Otero fell under United States governance, Manuel Otero continued the Otero family cattle operation. By the winter of 1876, Tubac and other Santa Cruz Valley ranch enterprises were divided between agriculture and stock raising, the later having a slight edge. Stock men and farmers grew concerned due to the recent lack of rain necessary to sustain their herds and fields. Most ranches kept their cattle rounded up in the evenings. However, free-roaming cattle like that of Sabino Otero and the Maish & Driscoll were reported to be the healthiest.[16] Free-roaming cattle remained visible throughout the Santa Cruz valley in 1877 seven years after Sabino Otero inherited the Otero cattle business after his father Manuel's death. Sabino also had an estimated 1,000 head of cattle and some mares on the Reventon Ranch.[17] Nearby ranches like that of A.C. Benedict and Maish & Driscoll at the Rancho San Ygnacio de Canoa ranch were also in great condition on account that the valley was abundant with grass and bottom land rich.[18]

By the early 1880s, large cattle interests were busy buying land in the Santa Cruz valley to expand their operations. Frederick Maish and Thomas Driscoll received the remaining interests to the Rancho San Ygnacio de Canoa from J.M. Yancey and Anna J. Ortiz de Yancey; and Narcisco Martinez and wife Maria Ana de Martinez on September 15, 1883.[19] Despite the growing competition, the Otero cattle business boomed. In 1884, 12,000 head of Otero cattle were sold for $35,000 to a firm in California in a single transaction.[20] The next year, M.H. Wells of Navajo Springs purchased Otero cattle at a cost of "$11 for each one year old, $16 for twos and $24 for cows with calves."[21] In total, 1,600 cattle were purchased from Otero in the week before the start of the cattle drive in 1885.[22] According to local reports, Otero's sale was a joint venture with Juan Elias under the Wabash Cattle company name.[23] The herd of mostly yearlings and two year olds were on a drive towards Navajo Springs Ranch in Apache County. Driving a herd was not easy. Cattle drivers charged $1.50 per head to drive a herd of 1,500.[24] A total of "seventeen vaqueros, each with three mounts, and two wagons loaded with supplies"[25] were required to complete the job. It took approximately forty days to herd the cattle from Santa Cruz County to Apache County.[26]

In 1885, two transcontinental railways introduced the Arizona cattle industry to new markets.[27] This period marked the beginning of oversight by stock associations. Loss of cattle was at a low. Pima County reported the highest number of cattle at 74,000.[28] The firm of Pusch & Zellweger bought 500 fat steers from "the cattle king of Tubac" in 1887, to add to its growing cattle operations.[29] The Pusch & Zellweger ranch was later known as the "Steam Pump Ranch" in Oro Valley.[30] Although stock raising seemed secure for now, Tubac and the surrounding area began to reduce its agricultural prospects due to lack of rain. The Rancho de Otero was the only farm to plant at Tubac in early 1887.[31] Stock raising peaked at Pima County the following year, which included Santa Cruz county and the Rancho de Otero at the time. Several companies owned massive herds. Maish & Driscoll 23,000 head, W. L. Vail and Associates 20,000 head, and the Land & Hays Company at 15,000 head. Of the private cattle owners, Sabino was Arizona's Cattle King at 7,000 head. Other Santa Cruz valley ranches ranged an average of 500 to 1,500 head of cattle.[32]

Stock interests expanded to locations outside of Arizona. In 1889, Otero and others were shipping cattle to the Wyoming Territory.[33] By 1890, Kansas City and Chicago markets benefitted from cattle sales from Sabino Otero, Maish & Driscoll, Juan Elias, and others from Santa Cruz.[34] Unfortunately, the cattle industry would soon face a significant struggle. The price of cattle significantly decreased from five years prior, bringing $7 for yearlings, $10 for two-year-olds, and $13.75 for three-year-old and up. A bulk of the cattle sales from Santa Cruz valley were headed to Montana.[35] A large Otero cattle transaction occurred when 2,000 head of 2 and 3-year-old cattle were shipped to Kansas City on March 15, 1890.[36]

As the dawn of the 21st century approached, the cattle industry became depressed forcing more local stock owners to sell their herds. Maish & Driscoll, one of southern Arizona's largest stock companies sold 600 head of cattle around the same time that Sabino Otero sent two carloads of cattle headed for consumption at Salinas, California.[37] In 1891, Sabino sold 400 head of cattle to J.L. Powell of Los Angeles, California for $14 a head.[38] Just seven years earlier, two-year-olds were being sold at $16 a head. By October of 1900, the cattle industry suffered a drastic blow. A severe drought gripped the Santa Cruz Valley. Sabino Otero reported during a visit to Nogales that cattle were being shipped out of the county to prevent them from dying.[39]

A LAW-SUIT IN PROGRESS.—This illustrates the Principles and Philosophy of a Law-suit. The two contestants are pulling with all their strength to gain the case, while the lawyer gets all the benefit that is in the trial. The contestants simply hold the cow while the lawyer does the milking.

Figure 3.4. Etching from *The Farmer's Manual*, J.L. Nichols & Co., Naperville. 1900. Illustration depicts how stockmen's' legal struggles only benefit lawyers. (Public domain).

Stock raising was serious business. Vaqueros likely argued that stealing a man's cattle was as serious as stealing a man's wife. Some might even say it was more sacrilegious than absconding with one's wife. In one highly publicized Otero court case, a steer valued at $1.50 was the subject of controversy on full display in the middle of Judge Bethune's courtroom at Tucson. A few weeks prior, the same steer was the issue at controversy in another high-profile case. In the first case, Plaintiff Sabino Otero accused defendant Eugenio Moreno of branding one of Sabino's steer in 1894. Moreno was found guilty[40] and began serving his one-year sentence at the Yuma Territorial Prison as prisoner number 00135 on January 13, 1895.[41] One of Moreno's friends, Ramon Sardina, was apparently dissatisfied with the outcome of Moreno's case. Nearly one year later, Sardina accused Sabino's brother Teofilo Otero with branding a steer that belonged to Sardina. Curiously, the steer at controversy in the Sardina case was the same $1.50 steer at issue in Sabino's case one year before. To prove his innocence, Teofilo had the hefty steer transported into the wood paneled courtroom. The main witness, Defendant's Exhibit A, had its hooves fastened. The steer's coarse hair was shaved off as fifty or so spectators peered on to ponder whose cattle brand was original. No winner prevailed. The case was dismissed because it was simply too difficult to tell one brand from the other. Apparently offended at having been dragged into court, Teofilo Otero immediately charged Ramon Sardina with malicious prosecution.[42] The record is silent on what happened to the charge against Sardina.[43]

In addition to cattle rustling, stock raising profits were negatively impacted by other economic hardships. On July 29, 1876, the Board of Equalization assessed Sabino for an insufficient real estate assessment, an increase of $400 from $600 dollars to $1,000.[44] The assessment was a huge sum in 1876 by today's standards. At the July 1903 meeting of the Board, Sabino was charged additional fees for 4 work horses, 20 range horses, and 30 saddle horses.[45] Other cattle operation assessments occurred on August 13, 1904. Sabino Otero was charged $500 for 25 saddle horses, $8,000 for 800 cattle, and $100 for an additional 4 mules.[46] Then in 1909, the Tucson Board of Equalization assessed Sabino an additional $5,000 for 500 head of range cattle that were previously unassessed.[47] Others with high assessments in the same year were Teresa Amada, $5,000 for 500 head and the Crittenden Cattle Co, $6,000 for 600 head of range cattle.[48] Profits from the cattle business continued to be undercut as the local Board of Equalization regularly charged additional fees for insufficient assessments.

Figure 3.5. Sabino Otero Cattle Brand filed on 9/6/1883. (Photograph by the author of the Arizona Brand Book, No. 1 at the Arizona State Library, Archives & Public Records).

While Sabino tended to his vast herd, his brothers Teofilo and Fernando maintained their own herds which added economic force behind the Otero family name. Extended family members also financially benefitted from family liaisons. Luis Quesse, husband of Maria Manuela Otero de Quesse and brother-in-law to Sabino, managed his own herd while Sabino's nephew Anthony Coenen was a close business associate. Anthony notarized many of the Otero business records, witnessed several land transaction documents, and had Sabino act as statutory agent for the

Coenen & Co. Cattle Company. Arizona's first Cattle Brand Books are replete with Otero family brands and of their close associations.

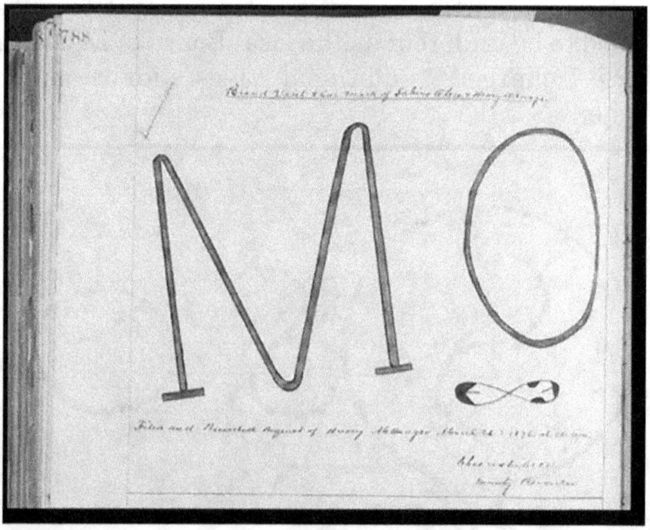

Figure 3.6. Henry Menager and Sabino Otero Cattle Brand filed on 3/26/1896. (Photograph by the author of the AZ Brand Book No. 2 at the Arizona State Library, Archives & Public Records).

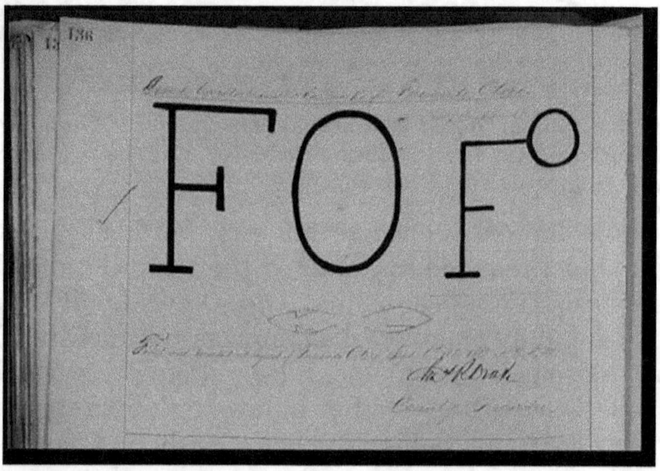

Figure 3.7. Fernando Otero Cattle Brand filed on 9/6/1883. (Photograph by the author of the AZ Brand Book No. 1 at the Arizona State Library, Archives & Public Records).

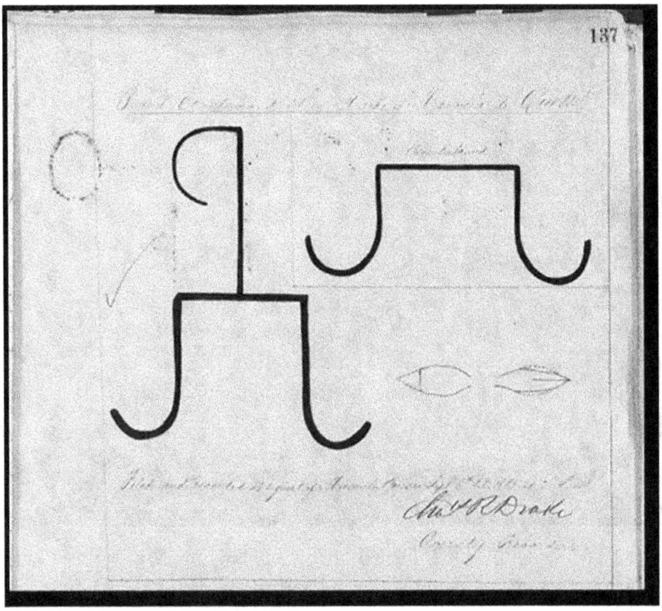

Figure 3.8. Manuela Quesse de Otero Cattle Brand filed on 9/6/1883. (Photograph by the author of the AZ Brand Book No. 1 at the Arizona State Library, Archives & Public Records).

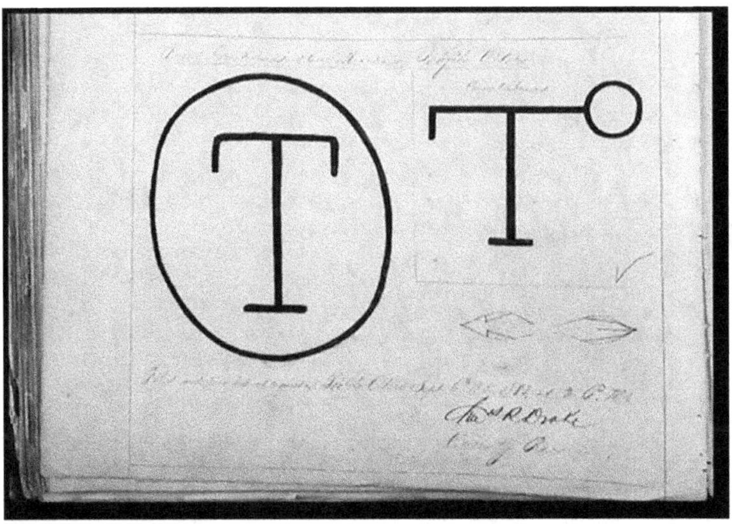

Figure 3.9. Teofilo Otero Cattle Brand filed on 9/6/1883. (Photograph by the author of the AZ Brand Book No. 1 at the Arizona State Library, Archives & Public Records).

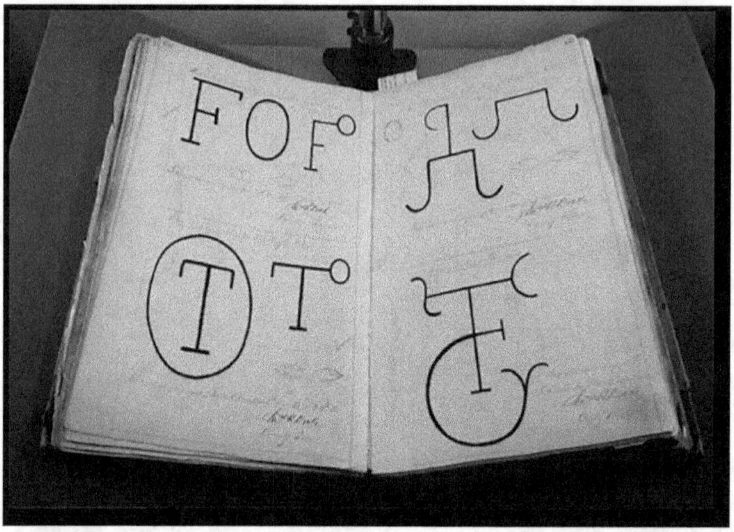

Figure 3.10. On 9/6/1883, Otero siblings Sabino, Manuela, Fernando, and Teofilo, walked into the Livestock Sanitary Board's office to register their individual cattle brands as one united family. It was two in the afternoon. (Photograph by the author of the AZ Brand Book No. 1 at the Arizona State Library, Archives & Public Records).

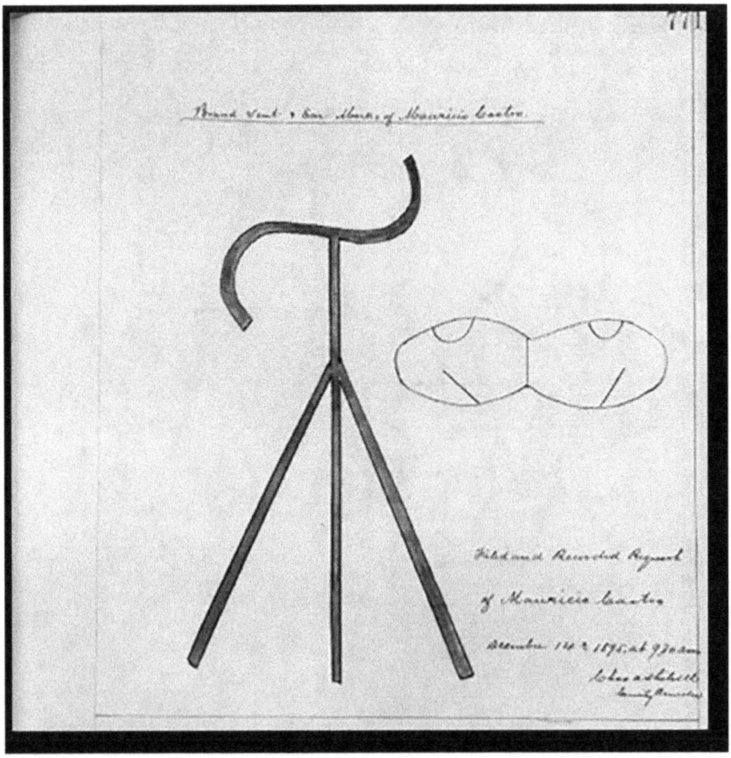

Figure 3.11. Mauricio Castro Cattle Brand filed on 12/14/1895. Castro was the husband of Maria Elena de Jesus Otero, and father of Brijida Castro Coenen, one of the last heirs at law of the Rancho de Otero. (Photograph by the author of the AZ Brand Book No. 2 at the Arizona State Library, Archives & Public Records).

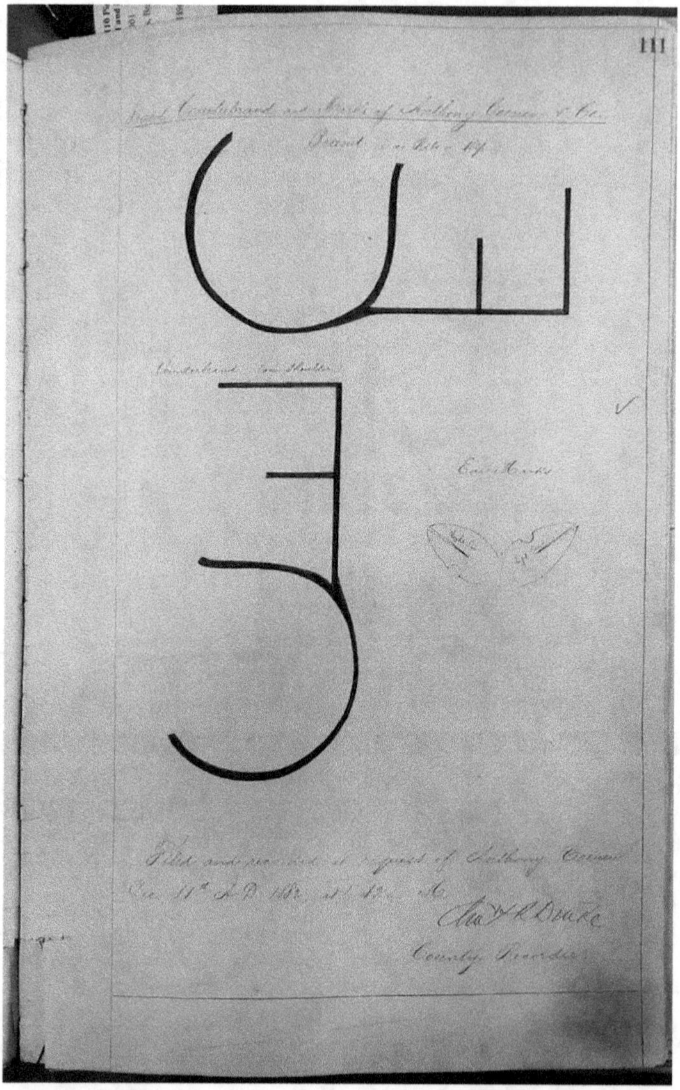

Figure 3.12. Anthony Coenen and Co. Cattle Brand filed on 12/11/1882. Sabino Otero was the statutory agent for Coenen & Co, a business owned by his nephew Anthony. (Photograph by the author of the AZ Brand Book No. 1 at the Arizona State Library, Archives & Public Records).

WESTERN ENGINES DELIVER WET GOODS

Schweitzer Outfits on Development Project at Tubac Get Results

The Schweitzer Machine company reports a busy week in their rengine and pump department. Monday and Tuesda Mr. Schweitzer started plant Number 1 on the development project of Teofilo Otero at Tubac. This

Figure 3.13. Newspaper clipping excerpt regarding Rancho de Otero improvements in 1915. (Arizona Daily Star. Tucson, AZ: 8/15/1915, p.7).

As Otero family cattle were shipped to ranches throughout Arizona, California, Missouri, Wyoming, Montana, and Mexico, ranches at Tubac and the surrounding country suffered due to over-populated ranges and drought.[49] After Sabino Otero's death in 1914, Teofilo sold most of the Rancho de Otero stock which foreshadowed the sale of the Rancho de Otero to private owners. After the cattle industry declined at the start of the 20th century, Teofilo Otero decided to modernize the Rancho de Otero in an effort to expand the ranch's agricultural potential.[50] In 1915, he contracted with the Schweitzer Machine Company to install the first of several wells on the property. The first two wells consisted of a "30 H.P. model

15, Western [oil] engine, and Layne and Bolwer 15-inch high capacity pump" drilled by J.W. Belt.[51] After a total of five water plants were installed, "both Mr. Schweitzer and Mr. Otero enthusiastically assert[ed] that this combination cannot be beat for economy and efficiency."[52] Incidental purchases were also made to keep the ranch in shape. Angel Monreal sold Teofilo Otero 2 horses, 1 mare, 1 mule, 1 wagon, and 2 sets of harness for $250 in 1917.[53]

APACHE DEPREDATIONS

Among the greatest hardships faced by the Otero family to maintain its historic property were Apache depredations. During the Hispanic Arizona era, Apache depredations were widely reported throughout southern Arizona. Tubac and the Rancho de Otero faced constant risk of destruction. Tubac was a small community with much at stake. In the spring of 1859, President James Buchanan told Congress, "The Mexican population at this end of the Territory is very small, not over one hundred and forty men, women, and children at Tubac, and perhaps twice that number at San Zavier (sic) and Tucson."[54] Although Tubac's population dwindled to approximately 140 citizens, Manuel Otero bravely continued to farm the land and raise cattle while fending off Apache attack. Worried citizens increased their complaints and cried out to the government for help.

In 1871, the Territory of Arizona Legislature held a series of hearings to discover the breadth of life and property loss. The hearings revealed that death, theft, and destruction of property was commonplace. Deposition testimony taken at the legislative hearings revealed that the Rancho de Otero was attacked by Apaches in June of 1869. Five head of cattle were stolen and a young ranch hand, just a boy, was murdered during the attack.[55] Indian depredations reached their height during 1869 and 1870. During the summer of 1870 another Otero property known as the Palo Parado was robbed of four horses and numerous sacks of barley.[56] In October of 1870, Apache Indians renewed their attack on the Rancho de Otero. A second young boy was murdered by the Apaches while another one was injured. Two horses were also taken.[57] Similar loss of life and property was suffered by other Tubac citizens as southern Arizona was gripped with fear, among them was Louis Quesse, Manuela Otero de Quesse's husband.

LOUIS QUESSE, *sworn:* Has resided in Arizona fourteen years; occupation, blacksmith. That in January, 1869, the Apache Indians captured from his rancho, near Tubac, two horses and eight head of cattle. That about January 30th, 1869, the same Indians killed four head belonging to witness. That about the 27th of February, 1869, the same Indians attacked his cattle corral, wounding two Papago Indians and capturing thirty-three head of cattle. That August 15th, 1869, the same Indians captured eight horses and two mules from his rancho. That in the month of October, 1869, the same Indians captured nine head of cattle. That in January, 1870, the same Indians captured eleven head of cattle. That in April, 1870, they captured four head of cattle. That in October, 1870, they attacked his herder, wounding him severely, capturing one horse, one gun, and fifteen head of cattle. That February 6th, 1870, they killed four head of cattle near his house. That his total loss by Apache Indians, during the years 1869 and 1870, amounts to $3,655.

That in the town of Tubac the citizens are afraid to appear on the streets after dark, on account of Indians.

Figure 3.14. Testimony excerpt from *Memorial and Affidavits Showing Outrages Perpetrated by the Apache Indians, in the Territory of Arizona, during the Years 1869 and 1870.*, Legislature of the Territory of Arizona, San Francisco: 1871, p.24. (Public domain).

During this same period, the road connecting Tubac to Tucson was treacherous. Maintaining two residences in Tubac and Tucson made long travel seem endless across hazardous desert roads. One traveler reported "I have made three trips over Arizona, and twice without escort; but the "most uneasy" ninety-two miles I ever made, was from Tucson to Tubac and return in 1867. There was hardly a day during that year that there were not Indian atrocities of some kind."[58] The only protection Tubac had in 1867 was a small cavalry under the command of Lieutenant Colonel McGarry. We are left to speculate what drove McGarry to commit suicide at the Occidental Hotel in 1879.[59]

On August 8, 1872, Apaches attacked Otero staff and property yet again. One of the Otero ranch hands was grazing cattle just within the Tucson town limits. The ranch hand became suspicious when he saw the horses act abnormally. As he headed over to investigate, an Apache bullet pierced the Otero ranch hand's left arm breaking a bone. The Apaches fled stealing four horses.[60]

According to the *Report of the Acting Governor of Arizona Made to the Secretary of the Interior for the year 1881,* in the years preceding 1874, large herds of cattle grazed on the open range as territorial citizens' feared constant attack by marauding Apache.[61] Territorial Governor F. A. Tritle's report of 1883 states that up to 1874, the year when Native Americans were placed on reservations:

> *One of the greatest drawbacks to Arizona's prosperity had been the hostile Apaches, who for years kept up a murderous warfare against the pioneers who opened this land to settlement and civilization.*
>
> *To enumerate the many atrocities they have committed since the settlement of this Territory of Arizona would fill a volume. Up to the year 1874 they terrorized the entire Territory, kept out immigration and capital, and had life and property virtually at their mercy...But the raids of the last two years have rudely awakened them from their dream of security.*[62]

Reports of continued hostile attacks upon local residents and miners rumbled across the undulating desert during 1879 and burdened the hearts of Tubac's dwindling citizens. "Tubac is even now a straggling cluster of ruins, which is being gradually leveled with the surrounding adobe through the influence of the elements," said one report.[63] Charles "Charly" Poston recorded the 1880 United States census for Tubac. Of the sixty-two reported souls, one-third were children under eighteen years of age. Seventeen-year-old Teofilo Otero was among the twenty-one children.[64] Tubac and the surrounding communities did their utmost to protect life and property, but at times it simply was not enough.

By the late 1890s, Apache depredations waned. But, trouble continued as Papago encroachment on local ranches increased. A general call to organize against the Papagos was encouraged by local newspapers in 1896, "The herds have been almost the sole support of those Indians for years, and cattlemen have suffered losses running up into the thousands...Sabino Otero, whose range is next nearest the Papago country, will probably move his herds away."[65] Pima county cattlemen responded to the threat of Papago encroachment. On September 2, 1896, thirty cattlemen met in a Pima county district courtroom. After discussing the Indian threat to local ranches, they formally organized to establish a system of patrol to capture cattle thieves and bring them to justice. C.W. Wright was President, W. J. Ross; treasurer, and Sabino Otero were among the executive committee. The cattlemen's organization agreed to fund the security patrol by imposing a levy upon stockowners based on the size of each herd in need of protection. All cattlemen in attendance agreed unanimously and signed the agreement. The men decided that the patrol system should be offered to any interested cattlemen not in attendance.

While Sabino was busy establishing protection for other Pima county cattlemen, the Rancho de Otero was attacked once again. One March evening in 1898 while the Oteros were away, approximately $500 worth of goods from a storeroom and a wagon and team of horses were stolen. No injuries were reported. Thieves escaped detection by wearing gunny sacks on their feet. Given the nature of the crime local press suspected the theft was made by someone familiar with the ranch premises.[66] Nothing deterred Sabino Otero's commitment to Tubac and its citizens. In

November of the same year he returned to Tubac to administer local elections.[67]

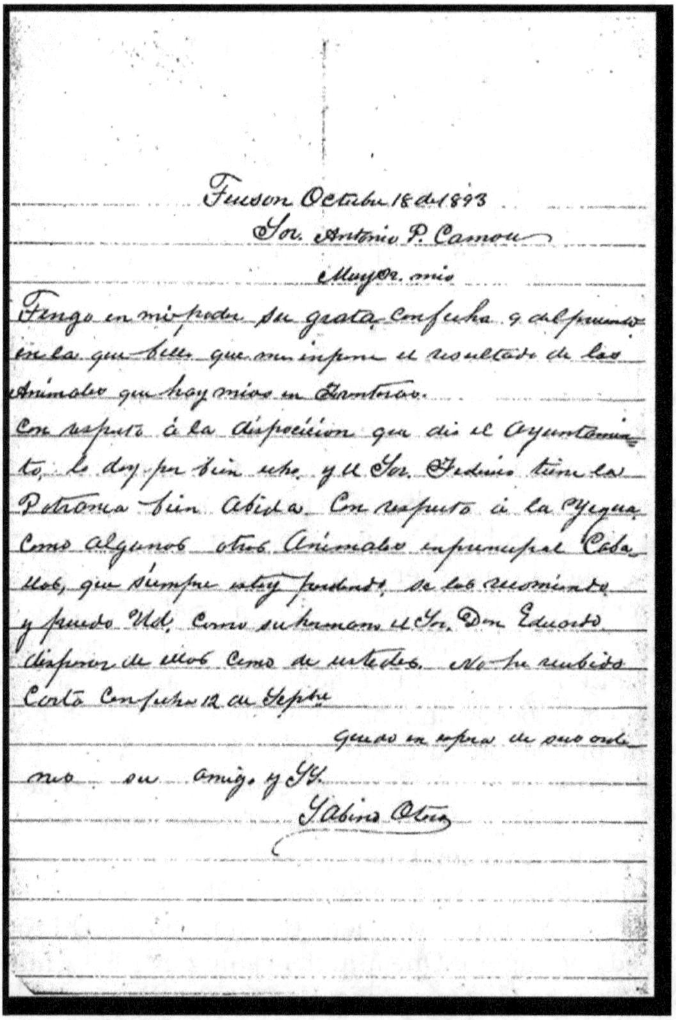

Tucson Octubre 18 de 1893
Sor. Antonio P. Camou
Muy Sr. mio
Tengo en mi poder su grata con fecha 9 del presente en la que bello que me impone el resultado de los Animales que hay mios en Fronteras.
Con respeto à la disposicion que dio el Ayuntamiento, lo doy por bien echo, y el Sor. Federico tiene la Patrona bien abida. Con respeto à la Yegua como algunos otros Animales en principal Caballos, que siempre estoy perdiendo, se los recomiendo y puede Ud. como su hermano el Sor. Don Eduardo disponer de ellos como de ustedes. No he recibido Carta con fecha 12 de Septbre
Quedo en espera de sus ordenes su amigo y S.S.
Sabino Otero

Figure 3.15. 1893 Spanish language letter from Sabino Otero to Antonio P. Camo regarding some animals. This is one of the only known letters in Sabino Otero's own handwriting. (Gift of Eduardo Robinson, Nogales, AZ to the author).

RANCHO DE OTERO: THE FINAL YEARS

At the turn of the 20th century, the Otero family faced increased personal struggles. Lawsuits became more commonplace which resulted in certain necessary expenses to protect the family's ranch and real estate interests. Court records reveal a family torn by desire to be recognized as a legitimate family relation or for financial gain. To further complicate matters, the cattle industry had peaked and began its steady decline due to drought and the gradual fencing in of the open range. Innovative ways to use the Rancho de Otero became necessary to maintain it as a viable agricultural farm. Natural resources were needed now more than ever.

Sacramento Granillo - Water Challenge

Eighty-seven years after Don Torivio de Otero successfully won a squatter challenge after three men occupied a portion of his cultivated land and usurped his irrigation system for their own personal use, Don Torivio's descendants issued a Complaint against a Tubac neighbor after water was being illegally diverted from the Rancho de Otero. Plaintiffs Sabino and brother Teofilo alleged that neighbor and defendant Sacramento Granillo[68] wrongfully and unlawfully placed a dam in the Santa Cruz River about 450 yards above the Otero's dam. Granillo said he would never remove the structure which prevented the river from flowing into the Otero's river channel to irrigate their land where they had been planting "wheat, barley, corn, alfalfa and vegetables" for more than twenty years.[69] C.W. Wright, Attorney for Granillo, filed a demurrer and denied all allegations stated in the Otero's moving papers.[70] In essence, Defendant through his attorney objected to the legal sufficiency of the charge. The presiding judge disagreed.

On April 19, 1892, Judge Richard E. Sloan, In the District Court of the First Judicial District of the Territory of Arizona, Pima County issued an Injunction to stop Defendant Granillo's actions. The Order prohibited Granillo or his agents, servants, and others acting through him from:

> taking, on in any way or manner interfering with the waters of the said Santa Cruz river, at any place, or, said river above the cultivated fields of the plaintiffs, in such manner as shall in any way or to any extent prevent the free and unobstructed flow of the waters of said river into the irrigating ditch of the plaintiffs, to the extent that the growing crops and trees now planted and of water thus commanded to be permitted to flow into the said ditch of the plaintiffs shall be the quantity that shall be necessary to irrigate said crops of the plaintiffs in a prudent and husband like manner.[71]

The Court then issued a restraining order against Polonio Valdez on December 10, 1892 who was an agent of Granillo, but the Court's orders fell on deaf ears. Vital waters from the Santa Cruz River continued to be diverted. In January of 1893, the Oteros discovered that Polonio Valdez and Rosario Brena, acting on Granillo's behalf, knowingly continued to divert the water from the Rancho de Otero even after they were shown a copy of the December 10th court order enjoining such actions.

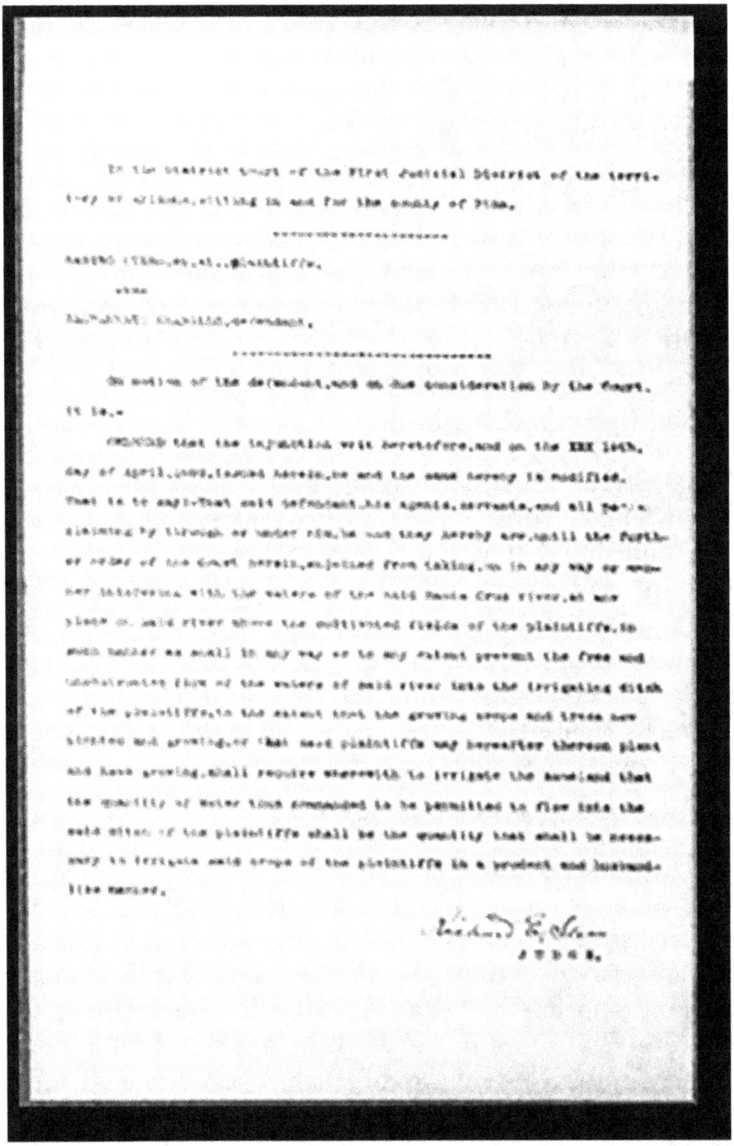

In the District Court of the First Judicial District of the Territory of Arizona, sitting in and for the County of Pima.

Sabino Otero, et al., Plaintiffs,

vs.

Sacramento Granillo, Defendant.

On motion of the defendant, and on due consideration by the Court, it is,-

ORDERED that the injunction writ heretofore, and on the [illegible] 16th day of April, 1892, issued herein, be and the same hereby is modified. That is to say:- That said defendant, his agents, servants, and all persons claiming by through or under him, be and they hereby are, until the further order of the Court herein, enjoined from taking, or in any way or manner interfering with the waters of the said Santa Cruz River, at any place on said river above the cultivated fields of the plaintiffs, in such manner as shall in any way or to any extent prevent the free and unobstructed flow of the waters of said river into the irrigating ditch of the plaintiffs, to the extent that the growing crops and trees now planted and growing, or that said plaintiffs may hereafter thereon plant and have growing, shall require wherewith to irrigate the same; and that the quantity of water thus commanded to be permitted to flow into the said ditch of the plaintiffs shall be the quantity that shall be necessary to irrigate said crops of the plaintiffs in a prudent and husband-like manner.

Richard E. Sloan

JUDGE.

Figure 3.16. Copy of Territory of Arizona District Court Judge Richard E. Sloan's Injunction to stop Sacramento Granillo, his agents, and assigns from obstructing the flow of water from the Santa Cruz River to the Otero farm lands at Tubac. Order is dated 4/19/1892. (Public domain).

The Oteros were forced to return to court for a permanent legal remedy. On February 8, 1893, Teofilo Otero submitted a sworn deposition asking Valdez and Brena appear for contempt of court.[72] The next day, the Court issued notice for Polonio Valdez to appear for a contempt hearing.[73] Although the existing case file omits detail regarding the final outcome of the Valdez contempt hearing, the court file contains a piece of evidence that likely persuaded the Judge to previously rule in favor of the Otero brothers' superior water rights. A transcript copy of the Otero family's 1789 Spanish land grant provided by the Office of the Surveyor General on December 6, 1892 was submitted to the court on the petitioners' behalf. The 1789 Otero Spanish land grant included water, acknowledged water was necessary for irrigation of Otero's land, and noted that land grantee Don Torivio de Otero built an irrigation system to provide for his crops. Less than 30 days after the Granillo/Valdez water encroachment case was heard, the Otero family removed the Rancho de Otero claim from the Court of Private Land Claims to secure their land and water rights under United States laws by procuring a Land Patent.

Territory vs. Otero & Otero vs. Otero

The case of Anna Brown Otero versus Teofilo Otero involves a request to apportion the Rancho de Otero property so that Anna could take her share of the land as Teofilo's ex-wife. Ana alleged she and Teofilo had an intimate relationship that resulted in the birth of four children. She swore out a warrant against Teofilo before United States Commissioner Richey after she allegedly caught him in the act of adultery with a Tucson woman named Pilar Cota.[74] On October 25, 1910, the grand jury indicted Teofilo for an alleged violation of the Edmunds Act,[75] an act initially created as a Mormon ban on polygamy.[76] Teofilo entered a plea of not guilty on October 28, 1910.[77] The case was eventually dropped on October 23, 1911.[78]

After the federal case ended, Anna filed a Complaint against Teofilo at the District Court, First Judicial District for the County of Pima, Territory of Arizona on November 19, 1910. Through her attorneys W.H. Sawtelle and Edwin F. Jones, Ana claimed she and Teofilo were legally married pursuant to an Arizona Territorial statute of 1901.[79] Title 45, Chapter 1, Paragraph 3098, Section 12 of the Revised Statutes of the Arizona Territory states:

> All persons who at any time heretofore have lived together as husband and wife for the period of one year or more, and who shall continue to live together for the period of one year from and after the time this chapter takes effect, or until one of the parties shall die, if death occurs before the expiration of one year after this chapter takes effect, shall be considered as having legally married, and the children heretofore or hereafter born of such cohabitations are declared legitimate.

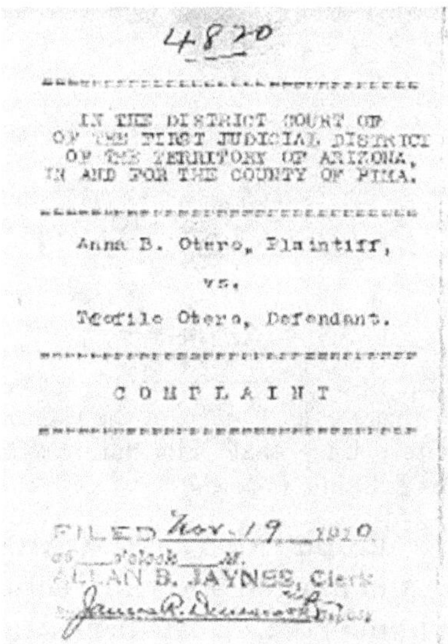
4820

IN THE DISTRICT COURT OF
OF THE FIRST JUDICIAL DISTRICT
OF THE TERRITORY OF ARIZONA,
IN AND FOR THE COUNTY OF PIMA.

Anna B. Otero, Plaintiff,

vs.

Teofilo Otero, Defendant.

COMPLAINT

FILED Nov. 19 1910
at ___ o'clock ___ M.
ALLAN B. JAYNES, Clerk

Figure 3.17. Docket information in the Case 4820 of Anna B. Otero vs. Teofilo Otero. File date 11/19/1910. (Arizona State Library, Archives & Public Records).

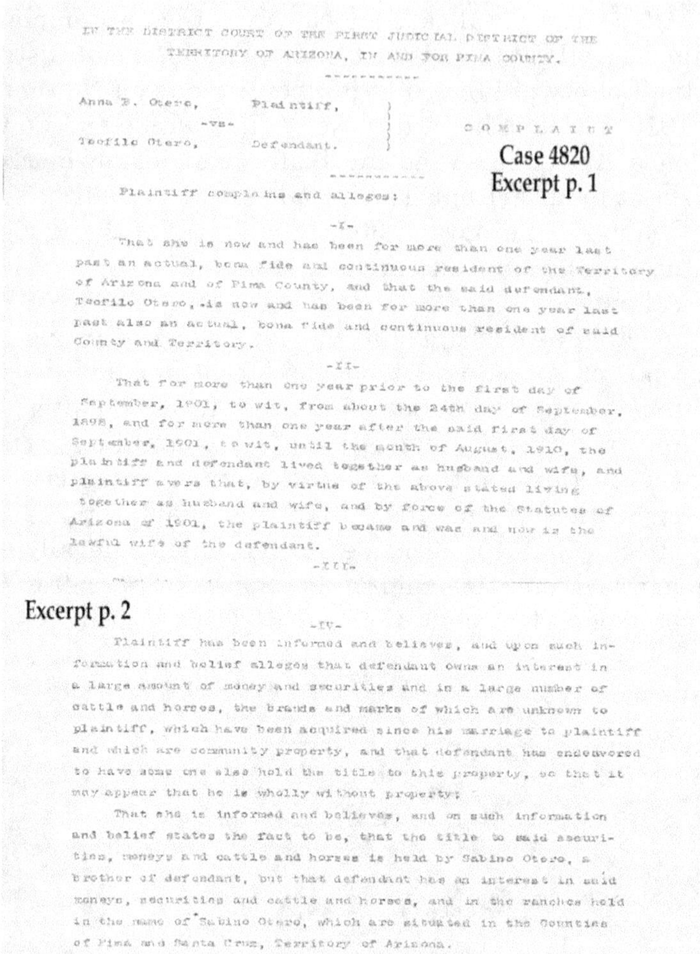

IN THE DISTRICT COURT OF THE FIRST JUDICIAL DISTRICT OF THE TERRITORY OF ARIZONA, IN AND FOR PIMA COUNTY.

Anna B. Otero, Plaintiff,)
-vs-) C O M P L A I N T
Teofilo Otero, Defendant.)

Case 4820
Excerpt p. 1

Plaintiff complains and alleges:

-I-

That she is now and has been for more than one year last past an actual, bona fide and continuous resident of the Territory of Arizona and of Pima County, and that the said defendant, Teofilo Otero, is now and has been for more than one year last past also an actual, bona fide and continuous resident of said County and Territory.

-II-

That for more than one year prior to the first day of September, 1901, to wit, from about the 24th day of September, 1898, and for more than one year after the said first day of September, 1901, to wit, until the month of August, 1910, the plaintiff and defendant lived together as husband and wife, and plaintiff avers that, by virtue of the above stated living together as husband and wife, and by force of the Statutes of Arizona of 1901, the plaintiff became and was and now is the lawful wife of the defendant.

-III-

Excerpt p. 2

-IV-

Plaintiff has been informed and believes, and upon such information and belief alleges that defendant owns an interest in a large amount of money and securities and in a large number of cattle and horses, the brands and marks of which are unknown to plaintiff, which have been acquired since his marriage to plaintiff and which are community property, and that defendant has endeavored to have some one else hold the title to this property, so that it may appear that he is wholly without property;

That she is informed and believes, and on such information and belief states the fact to be, that the title to said securities, moneys and cattle and horses is held by Sabino Otero, a brother of defendant, but that defendant has an interest in said moneys, securities and cattle and horses, and in the ranches held in the name of Sabino Otero, which are situated in the Counties of Pima and Santa Cruz, Territory of Arizona.

Figure 3.18. Excerpts from page 1 and 2 of the Complaint from Anna B. Otero vs. Teofilo Otero Case 4820. File date 11/19/1910. (Arizona State Library, Archives & Public Records).

Relying on paragraph 3098 of the Arizona Revised Statutes of 1901, Anna alleged she and Teofilo Otero lived together from September 24, 1898 until August of 1910, fulfilling the requisite time required under the statute for cohabitation.[80] As common-law wife, she demanded Teofilo Otero pay for child support and maintenance of two living children, Eduardo and Anna, as well as alimony. The

Complaint further claims Teofilo hid all of his assets by giving them to his older brother Sabino Otero and asked the Court to order Sabino to provide an accounting of the Rancho de Otero estate so that assets could be partitioned to give Ana her rightful share as common-law wife. [81]

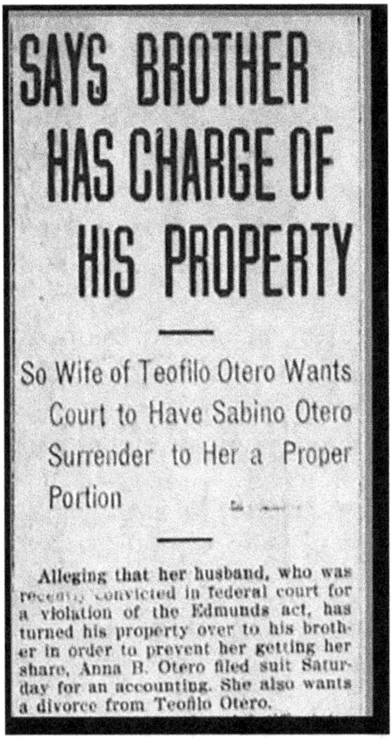

SAYS BROTHER HAS CHARGE OF HIS PROPERTY

So Wife of Teofilo Otero Wants Court to Have Sabino Otero Surrender to Her a Proper Portion

Alleging that her husband, who was recently convicted in federal court for a violation of the Edmunds act, has turned his property over to his brother in order to prevent her getting her share, Anna B. Otero filed suit Saturday for an accounting. She also wants a divorce from Teofilo Otero.

Figure 3.19. News clipping excerpt regarding the Anna B. Otero divorce case against Teofilo Otero in which she alleges his brother Sabino Otero is hiding Teofilo's assets. (Arizona Daily Star. Tucson: 11/20/1910, p.5).

On December 17, 1910, Teofilo Otero filed a Demurrer and Answer through his attorneys Frank Hereford and Frank Curley denying he cohabitated with Anna Brown Otero or that she was his lawful wife at any time. Then on May 16, 1911, an Amended Demurrer and Answer was filed followed by a Second Amended Demurrer and Answer on May 26, 1911, declaring any attempted marriage to be null and void due to anti-miscegenation. Anti-miscegenation laws enforce racial segregation by criminalizing interracial marriage or sex. Section III of the Second Amended Demurrer and Answer stated:

> Further answering, this defendant alleges that plaintiff's father was a negro and that plaintiff is of Caucasian blood, defendant's parents being Caucasian, and that any attempted marriage between plaintiff and defendant, as alleged in plaintiff's complaint, is and was in violation of Paragraph 3092 of the Revised Statutes of Arizona of 1901, and is and was at all times set out in plaintiff's complaint null and void.[82]

An unfortunate reflection of Arizona's cultural norms at the turn of the 20th century, Paragraph 3092 (Sec.6) of the Arizona Revised Statutes of 1901 states, "All marriages of persons of Caucasian blood, or their descendants with negroes, Mongolians or Indians, and their descendants, shall be null and void."[83] Anna's lawyers quickly responded with a Constitutional argument alleging that paragraph 3092 of the Revised Statutes of Arizona was discriminatory.[84] Teofilo's lawyers argued that since the territorial legislature forbade intermarriage of individuals of Caucasian and Negro[85] blood, the court was prohibited from inquiring into the marriage law because the United States Constitution did not bar states from passing laws related to marriage contracts.[86]

The case of Otero v. Otero raises an important question for many of the Otero family descendants and provides unique insight into Arizona's pre-statehood mores. Why did Otero brothers Sabino, Fernando, and Teofilo Otero all have children out-of-wedlock, yet none of the brothers married? We may never know if maintaining racial purity was truly the motivating factor for the Otero brothers, but such motivation is suspect. Otero oral family history reports that sibling Maria Elena de Jesus Otero Castro was given an ultimatum to leave her Mexican husband Mauricio Castro or be disowned by the family. Since interracial marriages were prohibited by legislative statute and heartily rejected by territorial societal norms, it may shed some light why the Otero brothers remained lifelong bachelors. Anna Brown Otero lost her case, but she lived long enough to revisit the issue another day.

Teofilo's Federal Charges

Although Teofilo Otero achieved independent recognition as an accomplished cattleman and farmer during his lifetime, history has mostly remembered him for his exploits living the fast life. Custom's officials placed him under federal arrest on April 24, 1915. The *El Paso Herald* reported Teofilo's arrest as newsworthy given he was "one of the richest men in Arizona," noting mescal, cologne, and cigars were found in his automobile as he crossed the international border at Nogales, AZ. [87] Such contraband, though miniscule by today's standards, was perceived significant in pre-prohibition Arizona. Although he was released on his own recognizance, his automobile was confiscated.[88] Teofilo pleaded not guilty to the charges on May 8, 1915.[89] No information was located to advise how the federal case ended, but we suspect the charges were dropped as no criminal conviction records have been located.

Sabino Otero's Death and the Manuel Otero vs. Teofilo Otero Case

Sabino Otero had been in declining health for several months until he lost his battle on January 22, 1914. He was 72-years-old.[90] Sabino's funeral was held at San Augustin Cathedral on January 24, 1914 promptly followed by his internment at Holy Hope Cemetery. Although Sabino lived a full and fruitful life, some obituaries and articles about his life and death published misinformation that continues to cause confusion.[91]

Teofilo Otero filed papers as Executor without bond for the estate of Sabino Otero deceased and the matter was heard on February 17, 1914 at the Tucson Court House.[92] Sabino's Last Will and Testament provided a one-third interest to the Otero land grant to his brother Teofilo and two nieces Ana Maria Comadurán Coenen and Brijida Coenen including other bequeaths of land and cash to close family and friends.[93]

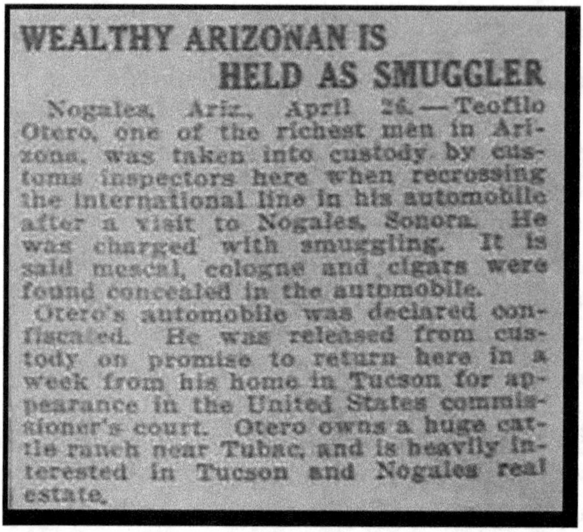
WEALTHY ARIZONAN IS HELD AS SMUGGLER

Nogales, Ariz., April 26.—Teofilo Otero, one of the richest men in Arizona, was taken into custody by customs inspectors here when recrossing the international line in his automobile after a visit to Nogales, Sonora. He was charged with smuggling. It is said mescal, cologne and cigars were found concealed in the automobile.

Otero's automobile was declared confiscated. He was released from custody on promise to return here in a week from his home in Tucson for appearance in the United States commissioner's court. Otero owns a huge cattle ranch near Tubac, and is heavily interested in Tucson and Nogales real estate.

Figure 3.20. Newspaper clipping *Wealthy Arizonan is Held as Smuggler.* (El Paso Herald. El Paso: 4/26/1915).

A bequeath of $2,500.00 to Sabino's son Manuel Otero in Sabino Otero's Last Will and Testament proved controversial.[94] Sabino's Last Will and Testament referred to each family member with terms of endearment calling each his "beloved," all except his son Manuel. In addition, his son would receive nothing if he contested the gift:

> I give and bequeath to Manuel Otero, the sum of Twenty-five Hundred Dollars ($2,500.00), provided however, that should the said Manuel Otero, legatee hereinabove named and mentioned, controvert any of the provisions herein contained or attack the validity of this will or any part or portion thereof in any court of law or equity, the bequest hereinbefore made to the said Manuel Otero shall cease and be void to all intents and purposes as though same had not be given or made.[95]

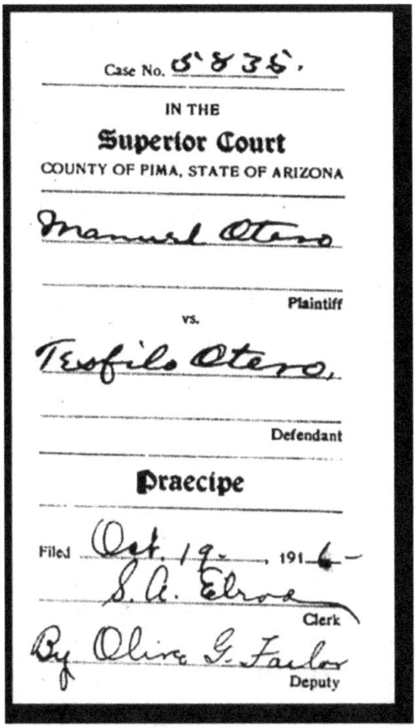

Case No. 5835.

IN THE

Superior Court

COUNTY OF PIMA, STATE OF ARIZONA

Manuel Otero

Plaintiff

vs.

Teofilo Otero.

Defendant

Praecipe

Filed Oct. 19, 1916

S. A. Elrod

Clerk

By Olive G. Taylor

Deputy

Figure 3.21. Docket information for Case 5835 Manuel Otero vs. Teofilo Otero in the Superior Court County of Pima, State of Arizona dated 10/19/1916. (Public domain).

More than two years after Sabino Otero's death, Manuel's inheritance became the issue at controversy in the case of *Manuel Otero vs Teofilo Otero*. The Complaint was subscribed and sworn by Manuel Otero on March 11, 1916 and alleged:

- In life, Sabino acknowledged and held out Manuel as Sabino's legitimate son and they lived together for many years[96]
- Sabino was mentally and physically incompetent to execute his Last Will and Testament
- Sabino was induced by Manuel's uncle Teofilo to sign a new will on January 15th of 1914[97] to preclude Manuel from being the sole heir-at-

law of Sabino's estate as his only son while keeping Manuel away from Sabino's bedside despite Sabino's request to see his son

- While Sabino was mentally and physically competent before his death, he executed a prior will that bequeathed Manuel the bulk of Sabino's estate
- Teofilo engaged in seduction and rape and sired illegitimate children that would have incensed Sabino to the point of disinheriting his brother Teofilo
- Teofilo made a deal with Manuel to pay him $50,000.00 in exchange for Manuel's agreement not to contest Sabino's Last Will and Testament
- Teofilo made excuses to Manuel for late payment to cause the statute of limitations to run precluding Manuel from contesting Sabino's Last Will and Testament
- Manuel asked that Teofilo be compelled to issue payment according to the strict terms of their mutual agreement[98]

Teofilo filed a Demurrer and Answer to the Complaint on March 6, 1916. A "demurrer" is a legal term for the plea to dismiss a lawsuit on the grounds that even if the statements of the opposing party are true, the claims are defective or insufficient.[99] In the filing, Teofilo denied all the allegations including that Manuel was Sabino's son or that Sabino's will was defective having been signed under mental or physical duress. Teofilo asserted he first heard of any alleged contract between him and Manuel on March 8, 1916 when Manuel's attorney John B. Wright demanded payment of $50,000.00 or advised he would file Manuel's Complaint. Teofilo further argued that Manuel's Complaint was "without any consideration of any kind, and is void" since Manuel accepted Sabino's bequeath of $2,500.00.[100]

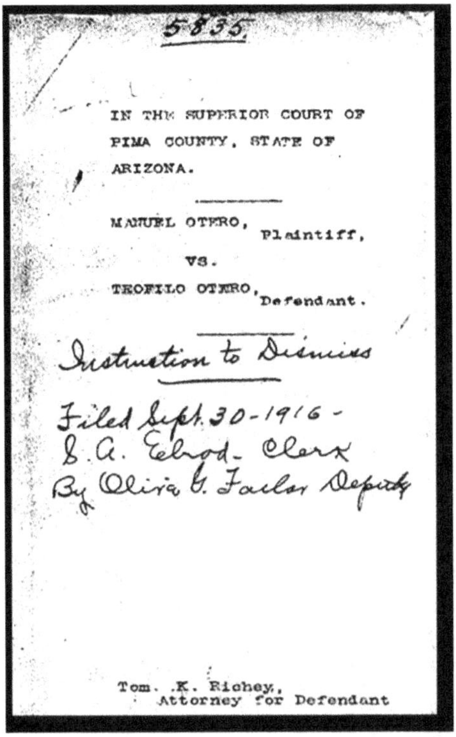

5835

IN THE SUPERIOR COURT OF
PIMA COUNTY, STATE OF
ARIZONA.

MANUEL OTERO,
Plaintiff,
vs.
TEOFILO OTERO,
Defendant.

Instruction to Dismiss

Filed Sept. 30-1916 -
S. A. Elrod - Clerk
By Olivia G. Fowler Deputy

Tom. K. Richey,
Attorney for Defendant

Figure 3.22. Docket information for Case 5835 Manuel Otero vs. Teofilo Otero in the Superior Court County of Pima, State of Arizona. Instruction to Dismiss filed 9/30/1916. (Public domain).

The Court ruled in favor of Teofilo and an instruction to Dismiss was filed in Case No. 5835 on September 30, 1916. A successful claim may have made Manuel Otero the sole owner of the Rancho de Otero. Instead, Teofilo successfully defended the case against him and retained the historic Otero land grant property for another two decades.

Teofilo Otero vs. Jose Otero

As Teofilo Otero was busy defending his one-third ownership rights of the Rancho de Otero in the *Manuel Otero vs Teofilo Otero* case, he was simultaneously engaged in another court battle where ranch profits were at issue. Jose T. Otero was a relative of Teofilo Otero from the Otero family of Sonora, Mexico and an accomplished agriculturalist in his own right. Jose arrived with his family at the Rancho de Otero in Tubac a refugees during the Mexican Revolution of 1910-20. Both men agreed Jose would farm the land while Teofilo would financially back the costs. Teofilo would recoup his costs with proceeds from each harvest. A non-transferrable agreement for a duration of four years was signed on January 20, 1916 by Teofilo Otero, Ana Maria Coenen, and Jose T. Otero that provided in part:

- Teofilo was to provide all water necessary for irrigating the land from the five pumping plants on his ranch to irrigate alfalfa, except in the event of dry wells, unavoidable accidents, or superior force; Jose T. was to pay fifty cents per pumping hour for the water used in irrigation;
- Teofilo reserved the right to employ someone to oversee the planting of alfalfa and to cancel the contract in the event of waste, carelessness, or failure to adequately manage the crops in a proper or economical manner;
- Teofilo retained the sole privilege to sell the harvested products to recoup the cost of principle and interests due him from lending Jose money secured by properly executed promissory notes, and agreed to pay Jose any excess from the product sales; and
- Jose was responsible for the labor to level, prepare and plant alfalfa; and maintain the land.[101]

Due to unknown circumstances, Jose was absent from the Rancho de Otero for an extended period of time. During

Jose's absence, Teofilo lodged formal Complaint No. 5904 in the Superior Court at Tucson, for the County of Pima on August 12, 1916 before M.S. Brown, Deputy Clerk to recover his financial losses in light of Jose's absence.[102] During the course of the business relationship, Jose executed numerous promissory notes in favor of Teofilo Otero for a total of $10,149.41 with interest between January to July of 1916,[103] an estimated value of $227,929.68 in 2017.[104]

Defendant Jose T. Otero Answered Teofilo's Complaint and filed a Counterclaim that alleged Jose purchased a large amount of tools, equipment, and livestock; he prepared and planted 100 acres of alfalfa, constructed numerous ditches and canals in a proper and useful manner. He further claimed that Teofilo filed the initial Complaint in an attempt to defraud Jose of his money, work, and labor; and that Teofilo withheld financing from Jose to make the planting and cultivation of alfalfa possible. Through his attorney, Teofilo replied and alleged that only 70 acres were planted, purchases were extravagant, and any ditches and canals were done improperly or carelessly. He also denied that financing was improperly withheld. In support of his reply, Teofilo produced numerous promissory demand notes executed by Jose.[105] Repayment from Jose was secured by his financial interests in Sonora. Teofilo was victorious in his action.

In the Counter-claim, the jury also rendered a verdict for Jose T. Otero for thirteen thousand one hundred twenty four dollars and ninety three cents ($13,124.93). On August 6, 1917, the Superior Court granted Teofilo's Motion for a New Trial that contested the jury verdict in favor of Jose. The Motion for New Trial was appealed to the Arizona Supreme Court at Pima County in Case No. 1630. Oral arguments were set for January 23, 1918.[106] On May 20, 1919, Arizona Supreme Court Justice D.L. Cunningham issued a Mandate affirming the lower court's verdict for a new trial in favor of Teofilo. Jose's appeal failed after his attorneys neglected to file a mandatory Abstract of the record and briefs by the specified March 10, 1919 deadline.[107]

The Teofilo Otero v. Jose Otero case provides us with a fascinating piece of ranch history. Within the forgotten court case file is a fragile, browning, torn piece of paper. It is a folded, faded hand-drawn map likely presented as evidence at trial. Written primarily in Spanish, it was apparently created by Jose Otero. (See Figure 3.24). In addition to identifying the Hacienda de Otero, the map reveals the 1916 agricultural plan of the Rancho de Otero. Four houses are represented on the map: two west and one east of the old canal, both located west of the Santa Cruz River; and one southeast of the river. A small road heads south from the Hacienda de Otero to the first house located east of the hacienda, then proceeds east over the Santa Cruz River winding towards the railroad track. The "Old Canal," presumably the original canal mentioned in the 1789 and 1804/1807 Spanish land documents built by Don Torivio de Otero land grantee, appears to diverge on both sides of the Hacienda de Otero. Land located east of the Santa Cruz River was used for corn during the summer months. Beans and alfalfa were also planted east of the river. A thicket of mesquite trees intersects the Old Canal and the Santa Cruz River. Farm land described partitions for agriculture and future planting. The Jose T. Otero illustration of Rancho de Otero reads like a time capsule informing how the Otero ranch operated while Arizona became a new state.

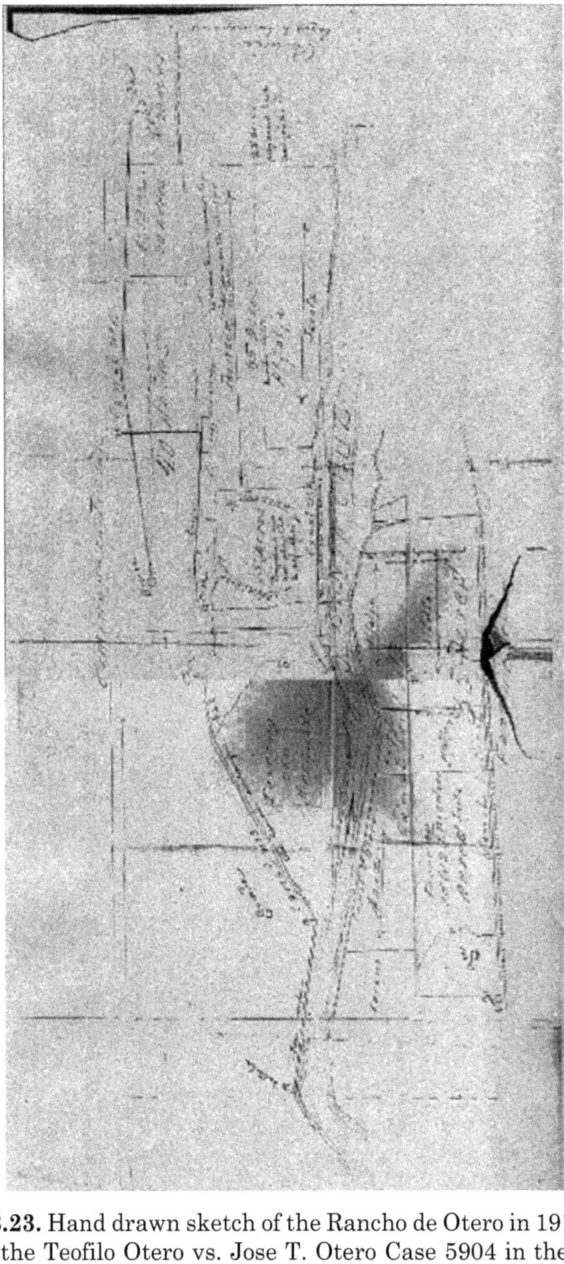

Figure 3.23. Hand drawn sketch of the Rancho de Otero in 1916 by Jose Otero in the Teofilo Otero vs. Jose T. Otero Case 5904 in the Superior Court for Pima County, AZ. (Arizona State Library, Archives & Public Records).

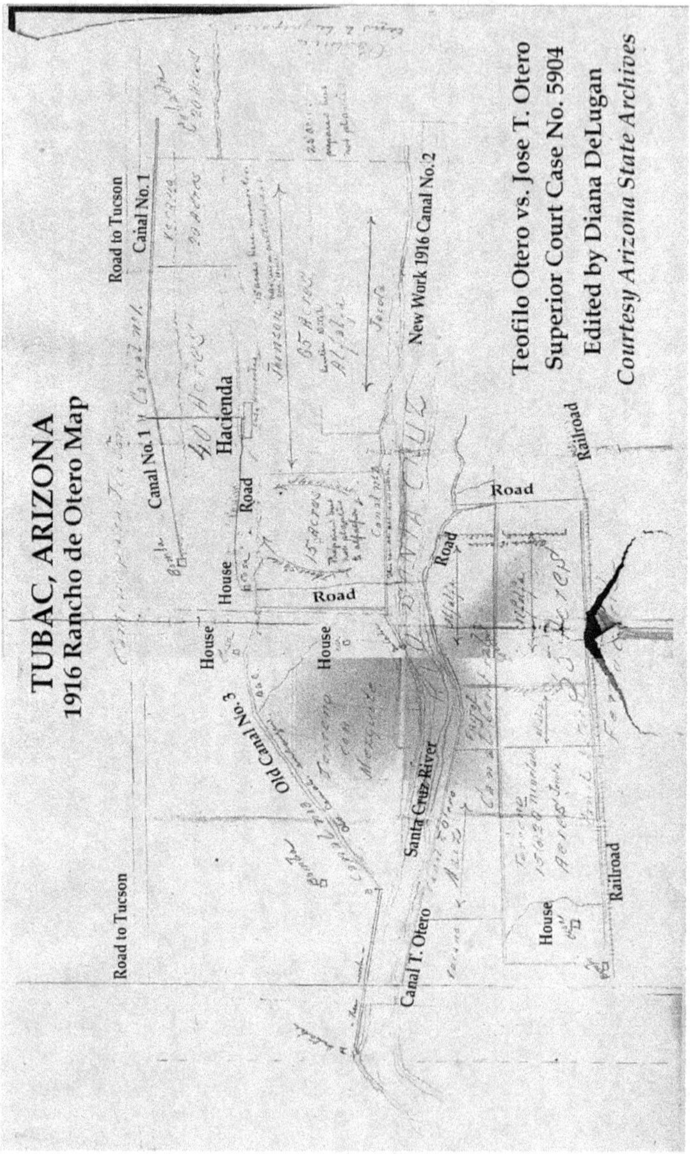

Figure 3.24. Hand drawn sketch by Jose T. Otero in 1916. (Edited by the author).

Revolutionary Activities Suspected

Jose T. Otero was not only an accomplished agriculturalist, he was also widely known as Jose Tiburcio Otero, son of a famous military and former governor of Sonora, owner of the Hacienda de "Juapateco" and the "Anita Copper Mine," at Huatabampo within the district of Alamos in Sonora, Mexico.[108] Jose T. Otero's absence was not only noticed at Tubac, it was noticed by the Agency. The "Agency" later known as the Federal Bureau of Investigation (FBI) investigated known and perceived threats to the United States. During the Mexican Revolution of 1910-1920, surveillance resulted in *The Mexican Files.*

Numerous reports in *The Mexican Files* linked Jose Tiburcio Otero to Mexican revolutionary activities. Juan Ortiz of Tucson was an informant for the" Agency." On July 6, 1916, Ortiz was at the French Restaurant at Tucson in Meyer Street. While there, he ran into several men including Jose Tiburcio Otero, who professed that "contending parties in Mexico will never arrive at an agreement with [Venustiano] Carranza,[109] and much less his men."[110] Ortiz further reported that Jose Tiburcio Otero disclosed that his family at Alamos was aware of a pending massacre of sixty individuals in the Mayo region of Sonora, Mexico in July of 1916.[111]

William Neunhoffer, an agent of the "Agency," reported that prisoners at the County Jail connected then Jose Tiburcio Otero and his nephew (Teofilo) with the Barron movement. Allegedly, 200 rifles and 40,000 rounds of ammunition had been shipped to the Rancho de Otero at Tubac from Miguel Tariba & Son, San Francisco for use in the Barron movement,[112] opposition to Venustiano Carranza. Neunhoffer interrogated a man called Yzurieta about the alleged Otero-Mexican Revolution connection. Yzurieta admitted he knew the Oteros and suspected that General Luis Medina Barrón intended to secure arms and ammunition from the Oteros for use in an expedition at

Arivaca.[113] After General Santiago Rivero's release from jail on July 28, 1916, Rivero reported the Oteros were custodians for the Nogales arms and ammunition which were likely hidden at the Rancho de Otero.[114]

Another "Agency" report claimed that the Otero brothers received direct orders from revolutionary actor Jose Maria Maytorena. A former colonel in the Maytorena army, Francisco Cardenas was a farmer at Tubac during 1916. Cardenas was interviewed by Neunhoffer and reported that all the visitors at the Rancho de Otero left, save one man.[115] By August of 1916, Cardenas reported that there had been no recent activity at the Rancho de Otero or strangers. Only one of "the Otero boys" was present at the ranch busy with farming activities.[116] It is unknown if Cardenas referred to Ysidro or Ricardo Otero, sons of Teofilo Otero given that he referred to the Oteros as "boys" and both were known to have worked on the Rancho de Otero while Teofilo was a 53-year-old man when the report was given.

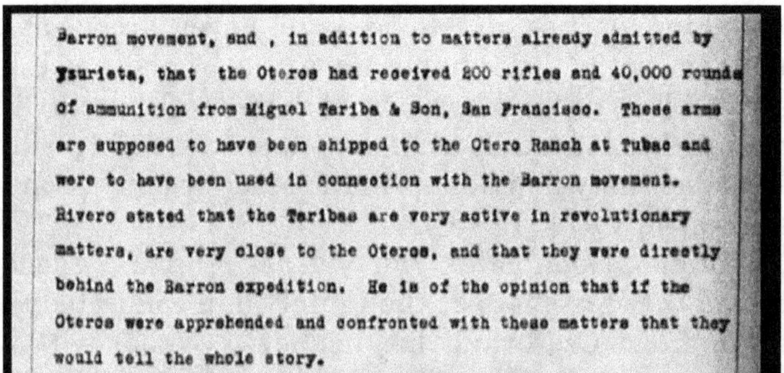

Barron movement, and , in addition to matters already admitted by Ysurieta, that the Oteros had received 200 rifles and 40,000 rounds of ammunition from Miguel Tariba & Son, San Francisco. These arms are supposed to have been shipped to the Otero Ranch at Tubac and were to have been used in connection with the Barron movement. Rivero stated that the Taribas are very active in revolutionary matters, are very close to the Oteros, and that they were directly behind the Barron expedition. He is of the opinion that if the Oteros were apprehended and confronted with these matters that they would tell the whole story.

Figure 3.25. Excerpt from 7/28/1916 FBI report alleging Rancho de Otero at Tubac may be storing ammunition for the Mexican Revolution of 1910-1920. (Public domain).

During the 1990's, Otero descendant Anna Maldonado Fimbres was interviewed as part of the "Voices of the Valley" Tubac Historical Society Oral History Project. She recalled when Jose Tiburcio Otero came to the Rancho de Otero:

> They came and asked, actually, if they could stay there. So my uncle [Teofilo] of course did. What he did then, he rented them half of the house. They added a place, a kitchen, because they had their own cook, you see. Every Saturday, there used to be a little line of fellows – because other people came too, also...from Mexico. Being such a big farm and all, Teofilo subsidized them. They wanted to farm. Some of them are still in Huatabampo. They established that farming area there, south of Navajoa. They did pretty well. I remember that they added more clear land at that time. They stayed there until President Obregon came into office in Mexico, which was in 1921, and he [Teofilo] was invited to the presidential inaugural.[117]

Fimbres reminisced saying that Teofilo was treated like royalty at President Obregon's inauguration at Mexico City attending parties and banquets. After Obregon became president, the Otero relatives from Sonora left the Rancho de Otero at Tubac and returned home to Sonora.[118]

During the Mexican Revolution of 1910-1920, Teofilo gained full ownership of the Rancho de Otero at Tubac after his brother Sabino's death in 1914. Accompanied by his niece, Ana Maria Comadurán Coenen, they moved back to Tubac from Tucson into the newly remodeled Hacienda de Otero.[119] Ana Maria emerged as a community leader spearheading efforts to build Saint Anne's Church at Tubac. She also hosted the annual *fiestas* at Tubac.[120] Ana Maria and Teofilo managed to keep the Rancho de Otero viable as an agricultural farm. In 1918, Teofilo received local acclaim by the local chamber of commerce for harvesting a 51-pound watermelon, "one of the largest melons on record in Pima county."[121] Despite occupational success, Teofilo's personal challenges seemed endless.

Teofilo Otero & Francisco Rojas vs. Hector Soto & Carmen Soto Gonzales

Teofilo also discovered that being a wealthy rancher came with other unexpected risks. It started out like any usual Sunday day, time for rest and relaxation. Francisco Rojas, a Rancho de Otero ranch hand, decided to set out for a short trip to Nogales around 5:00 pm, July 25, 1926. [122] Francisco who was accompanied by two friends borrowed a truck from his boss Teofilo Otero without permission.[123] The truck unexpectedly broke down about 10 miles north of Nogales, AZ. Francisco received a tow from another car after fastening the truck with some heavy wire then continued southbound towards Nogales. At the same time, a motorcycle driven by a driver with a passenger attempted to pass the two vehicles. In the process, motorcyclist Hector Soto, a minor, broke his leg when the two vehicles collided.

Carmen Soto Gonzales, Soto's guardian ad litem[124] filed a Complaint against Rojas the driver and Teofilo Otero, the truck owner. Shortly after the accident, Rojas wrote a statement that revealed he was driving for company business at the time of the accident. During trial, Rojas recanted his previous statement and testified he borrowed his boss's truck exclusively for a personal trip. Rojas' two companions testified at trial and confirmed the Nogales excursion was only for pleasure. The jury discounted the defense's court testimony and rendered a verdict in favor of plaintiff Soto.

Teofilo Otero and Francisco Rojas appealed the verdict against them to the Arizona Supreme Court. Oral arguments were held on April 21, 1928 at the Arizona Supreme Court in the case of Otero & Rojas vs Soto.[125] The high court ruled that evidence that Rojas was driving Teofilo's truck was not conclusive proof that Rojas was acting as Teofilo's agent when he collided with and injured motorcyclist Soto. Second, the trial jury was not at liberty to arbitrarily reject Rojas' passengers' uncontradicted testimony. Although the prior written statement issued by

Rojas that said he took Teofilo's truck in for repairs served to impeach his trial testimony, there was no evidence to impeach the testimony of the passengers. Thus, the Arizona Supreme Court affirmed the verdict against Rojas the driver and reversed the lower court's ruling against Teofilo. The case was remanded back to the trial court with instructions to enter a judgment in favor of Teofilo.

Rancho de Otero Final Transfer of Title and the Leonardo Moreno Trustee Probate Challenges

Otero land grant history reveals that the final parcel of the 1789 Spanish land grant, known as the Rancho de Otero, left the family's real estate holdings when Teofilo Otero sold the ranch property at Tubac to M. Addison Pelletier, an eastern woman on March 31, 1937. Four years later, Teofilo Otero died on May 15, 1941 at 7:22 a.m. at the same home he was born in, 219 South Main, Tucson, AZ. Like his siblings, Teofilo was buried at Holy Hope Cemetery at Tucson on May 17, 1941.[126] Teofilo's death, ushered in the second major intra-family conflict, two separate probate challenges to his Last Will and Testament.

On July 15, 1941, Leonor Capan (Kaphan) Otero and her son Ysidro Otero filed a Complaint for Declaratory Judgment in Case No. 21094 against Leonardo Moreno, Executor of the Estate of Teofilo Otero, and Teofilo's heirs-at-law in the Superior Court of Pima County, AZ. The Complaint alleged Leonor was the surviving widow of Teofilo entitled to an undivided one-half interest of Teofilo's estate, and Ysidro alleged he was Teofilo's sole heir-at-law and surviving son. They challenged Teofilo's Last Will and Testament in primary part stating the creation and administration of any trust and the terms of the will are so vague, the will should be considered null and void. Further, if the will is null and void, Ysidro Otero is entitled to all of Teofilo's estate except for the one-half community interest which should cede to his mother Leonor.[127]

Defendant Leonardo Moreno responded to the Complaint on September 6, 1941 through his attorneys Darnell, Pattee & Robertson. He denied the allegations and argued that the distribution of Teofilo's estate could only be challenged if he died intestate, without a will. The denial stated since a will was properly executed and Ysidro was intentionally omitted, his legal challenge should be dismissed.[128] On the same day, a motion to dismiss Ysidro Otero's claim was filed by attorneys for the heirs at law: Ana Maria Coenen (Comadurán), Anita C. Maldonado, Brijida Coenen, Melania C. Sanchez, Sophia Polanco, Mercedes Madril, Jose Sanchez, Ymelda Coenen, and Miguel Sanchez.[129]

Figure 3.26. Illustration of Ysidro Otero, son of Teofilo Otero and Leonor Kaphan (Capan) by Dorotea Cvijanovic commissioned exclusively for *Terrenos* © 2018 Diana DeLugan. All rights reserved.

Deposition testimony was held in the Leonor Capan Otero and Ysidro Otero case highlighted by the deposition of Ana Maria Coenen held on Friday, October 17, 1941 at the Otero family home at 219 South Main Street, Tucson, AZ. Sam Hughes was duly sworn as the Spanish language interpreter.[130] Ana Maria testified she lived with her uncle Teofilo Otero in their home except when they traveled back to Tubac. She learned about Ysidro several months after Sabino died and knew Leonor, her parents, and siblings when they moved near the Reventon Ranch while Ana Maria was living there with family.[131] Ana Maria denied Ysidro was the son of Teofilo and revealed a second son named Ricardo existed through the union of Teofilo and Leonor. Ana Maria qualified her testimony saying she also heard Ricardo was actually the son of another man by the surname Gutierrez and denied knowing that Ricardo was baptized with the last name Otero.[132]

Figure 3.27. Illustration of Ana Maria Comadurán Coenen by Dorotea Cvijanovic commissioned exclusively for *Terrenos* © 2018 Diana DeLugan. All rights reserved. Ana Maria was one of the namesakes for Saint Anne's Church at Tubac.

While the Leonor Capan Otero and Ysidro Otero challenge was pending, a second family issued a claim against Executor Moreno for legal rights as the common-law wife and children of Teofilo Otero. Claimants were Anna Brown Otero and her children Ana Otero Provencio and Edward Otero.[133] Unfortunately, Anna Brown Otero's individual claim was dismissed and effectively barred because it was the same claim she lost in the 1911 *Otero vs Otero* case wherein she claimed to be Teofilo's common-law wife.

The Court acknowledged that if the Otero & Otero claim proceeded, and if claimants could show their relationship to Teofilo, it might defeat the will. As to the Provencio Otero & Otero claim, the Court was informed that the claim was being brought on a theory of adoption. If proven, it too might defeat Teofilo's will dispossessing the named heirs-at-law. Leonardo Moreno testified to the Court that the cost of defending both probate challenges would be costly and time consuming during which any payments to designated heirs must be suspended until both cases could be resolved.[134]

Figure 3.28. Illustration of Eduardo Otero, son of Teofilo Otero and Anna Brown Otero by Dorotea Cvijanovic commissioned exclusively for *Terrenos* © 2018 Diana DeLugan. All rights reserved.

The remaining challengers to Teofilo's estate and Executor Moreno asked the Court to approve a compromised settlement where the heirs-at-law would agree to pay a $5,000.00 settlement to Leonor Capan as Teofilo Otero's common-law-wife and $5,000.00 to be divided between sons Ysidro and Ricardo Otero as Teofilo's children. An additional $5,000.00 was allotted to be divided between Ana O. Provencio and her brother Eduardo Otero for their claim as Teofilo's children.[135]

On March 31, 1942, Executor Moreno testified first. Ysidro Otero testified next. The Court questioned the validity of a Deed and Assignment document signed by Ysidro's mother Leonor Capan Otero where she assigned all her rights to her claim against Executor Moreno to Ysidro. Then Ysidro was asked about a Deed and Assignment signed by his brother Ricardo Otero.[136] The Court resumed later the same afternoon and held a further direct examination of Ysidro Otero. It inquired if Ysidro's mother knew what she was signing. Ysidro said yes, he said he explained the contents of the Deed and Assignment to her. The Court asked about Ricardo Otero. Ysidro testified that Ricardo was his brother and that since Ricardo gave him power of attorney to act on his behalf as did their mother, and Ysidro personally explained to both what they were signing, they knew what they were signing.[137] The compromised settlement between the parties was signed by the presiding judge on March 31, 1942[138] ending all claims against Executor Leonard Moreno and the Estate of Teofilo Otero.

Figure 3.29. Illustration of Ricardo Otero, son of Teofilo Otero and Leonor Kaphan de Otero by Dorotea Cvijanovic commissioned exclusively for *Terrenos*

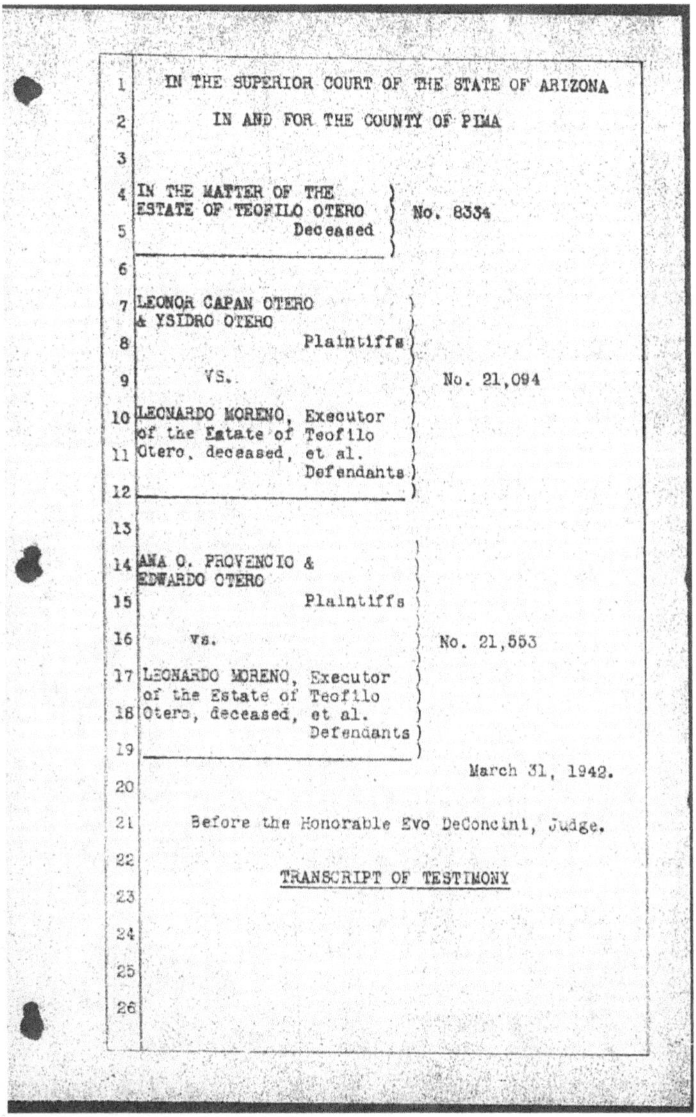

IN THE SUPERIOR COURT OF THE STATE OF ARIZONA
IN AND FOR THE COUNTY OF PIMA

IN THE MATTER OF THE ESTATE OF TEOFILO OTERO Deceased) No. 8334

LEONOR CAPAN OTERO & YSIDRO OTERO Plaintiffs
vs.) No. 21,094
LEONARDO MORENO, Executor of the Estate of Teofilo Otero, deceased, et al. Defendants

ANA O. PROVENCIO & EDWARDO OTERO Plaintiffs
vs.) No. 21,553
LEONARDO MORENO, Executor of the Estate of Teofilo Otero, deceased, et al. Defendants

March 31, 1942.

Before the Honorable Evo DeConcini, Judge.

TRANSCRIPT OF TESTIMONY

Figure. 3.30. The two probate challenges by the Capan Otero Case No. 21,094 and Brown Otero families, later Case No. 21,553, were eventually consolidated and compromised. This resulted in a settlement for all of the Plaintiffs, excluding Anna Brown Otero, as she previously alleged the claim as Teofilo's common-law wife and lost. Cases filed at the Superior Court for Pima County, AZ. (Arizona State Library, Archives & Public Records).

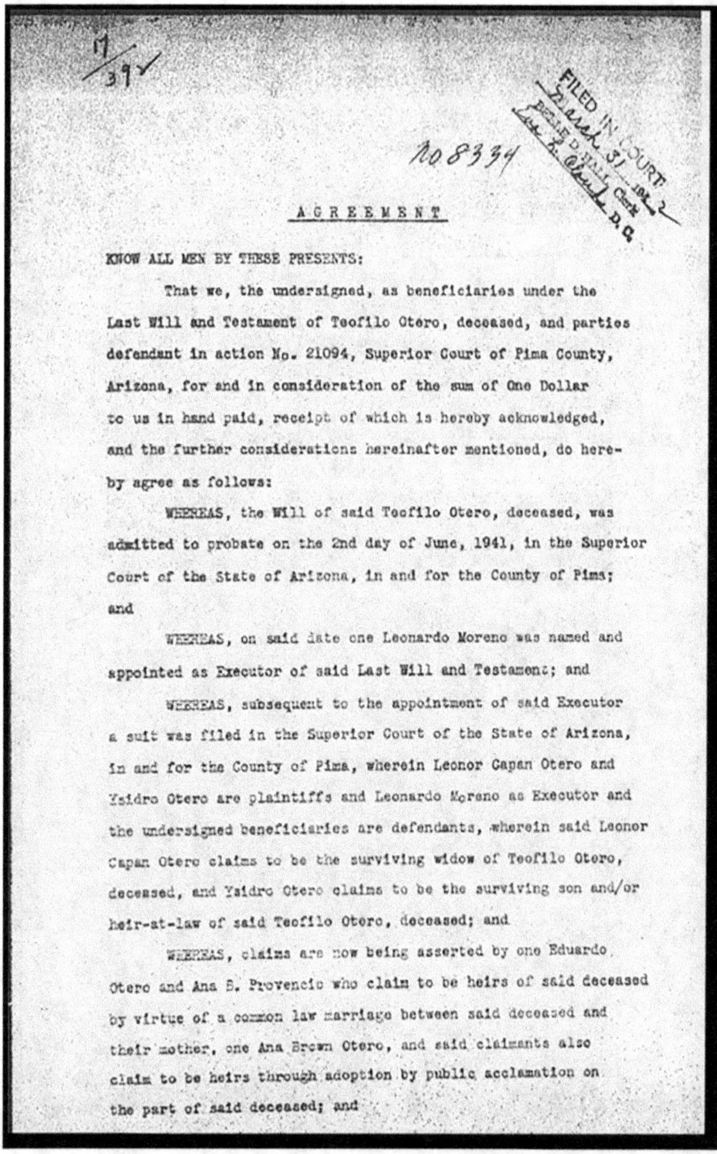

FILED IN COURT

no 8334

A G R E E M E N T

KNOW ALL MEN BY THESE PRESENTS:

That we, the undersigned, as beneficiaries under the Last Will and Testament of Teofilo Otero, deceased, and parties defendant in action No. 21094, Superior Court of Pima County, Arizona, for and in consideration of the sum of One Dollar to us in hand paid, receipt of which is hereby acknowledged, and the further considerations hereinafter mentioned, do hereby agree as follows:

WHEREAS, the Will of said Teofilo Otero, deceased, was admitted to probate on the 2nd day of June, 1941, in the Superior Court of the State of Arizona, in and for the County of Pima; and

WHEREAS, on said date one Leonardo Moreno was named and appointed as Executor of said Last Will and Testament; and

WHEREAS, subsequent to the appointment of said Executor a suit was filed in the Superior Court of the State of Arizona, in and for the County of Pima, wherein Leonor Capan Otero and Ysidro Otero are plaintiffs and Leonardo Moreno as Executor and the undersigned beneficiaries are defendants, wherein said Leonor Capan Otero claims to be the surviving widow of Teofilo Otero, deceased, and Ysidro Otero claims to be the surviving son and/or heir-at-law of said Teofilo Otero, deceased; and

WHEREAS, claims are now being asserted by one Eduardo Otero and Ana B. Provencio who claim to be heirs of said deceased by virtue of a common law marriage between said deceased and their mother, one Ana Brown Otero, and said claimants also claim to be heirs through adoption by public acclamation on the part of said deceased; and

Figure 3.31. Page 1 of Agreement to Settle Actions between Leonardo Moreno and Leonor Capan Otero for her claim as common-law wife of Teofilo Otero and brothers Ysidro and Ricardo Capan Otero for their claims as natural children of Teofilo Otero; and to settle the claim of Ana B. Provencio and Eduardo Otero. Compromised filed 3/31/1942. (Arizona State Library, Archives & Public Records).

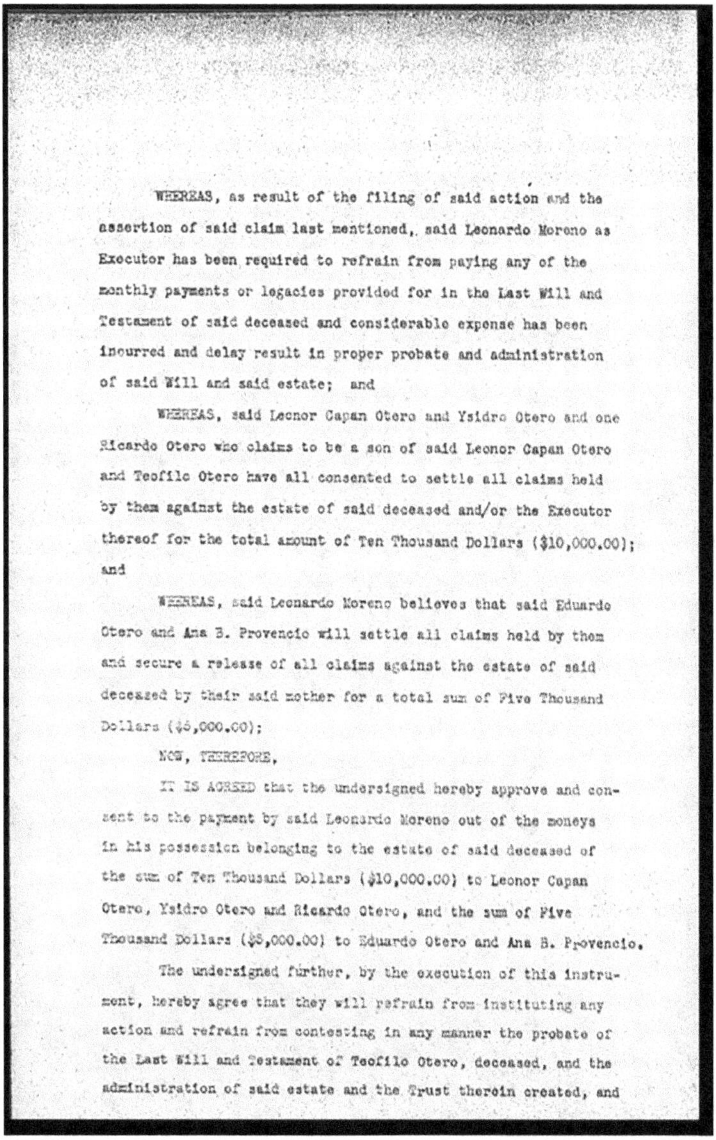

WHEREAS, as result of the filing of said action and the assertion of said claim last mentioned, said Leonardo Moreno as Executor has been required to refrain from paying any of the monthly payments or legacies provided for in the Last Will and Testament of said deceased and considerable expense has been incurred and delay result in proper probate and administration of said Will and said estate; and

WHEREAS, said Leonor Capan Otero and Ysidro Otero and one Ricardo Otero who claims to be a son of said Leonor Capan Otero and Teofilo Otero have all consented to settle all claims held by them against the estate of said deceased and/or the Executor thereof for the total amount of Ten Thousand Dollars ($10,000.00); and

WHEREAS, said Leonardo Moreno believes that said Eduardo Otero and Ana B. Provencio will settle all claims held by them and secure a release of all claims against the estate of said deceased by their said mother for a total sum of Five Thousand Dollars ($5,000.00);

NOW, THEREFORE,

IT IS AGREED that the undersigned hereby approve and consent to the payment by said Leonardo Moreno out of the moneys in his possession belonging to the estate of said deceased of the sum of Ten Thousand Dollars ($10,000.00) to Leonor Capan Otero, Ysidro Otero and Ricardo Otero, and the sum of Five Thousand Dollars ($5,000.00) to Eduardo Otero and Ana B. Provencio.

The undersigned further, by the execution of this instrument, hereby agree that they will refrain from instituting any action and refrain from contesting in any manner the probate of the Last Will and Testament of Teofilo Otero, deceased, and the administration of said estate and the Trust therein created, and

Figure 3.32. Page 2 of Agreement to Settle Actions between Leonardo Moreno and Leonor Capan Otero for her claim as common-law wife of Teofilo Otero and brothers Ysidro and Ricardo Capan Otero for their claims as natural children of Teofilo Otero; and to settle the claim of Ana B. Provencio and Eduardo Otero. Compromised filed 3/31/1942. (Arizona State Library, Archives & Public Records).

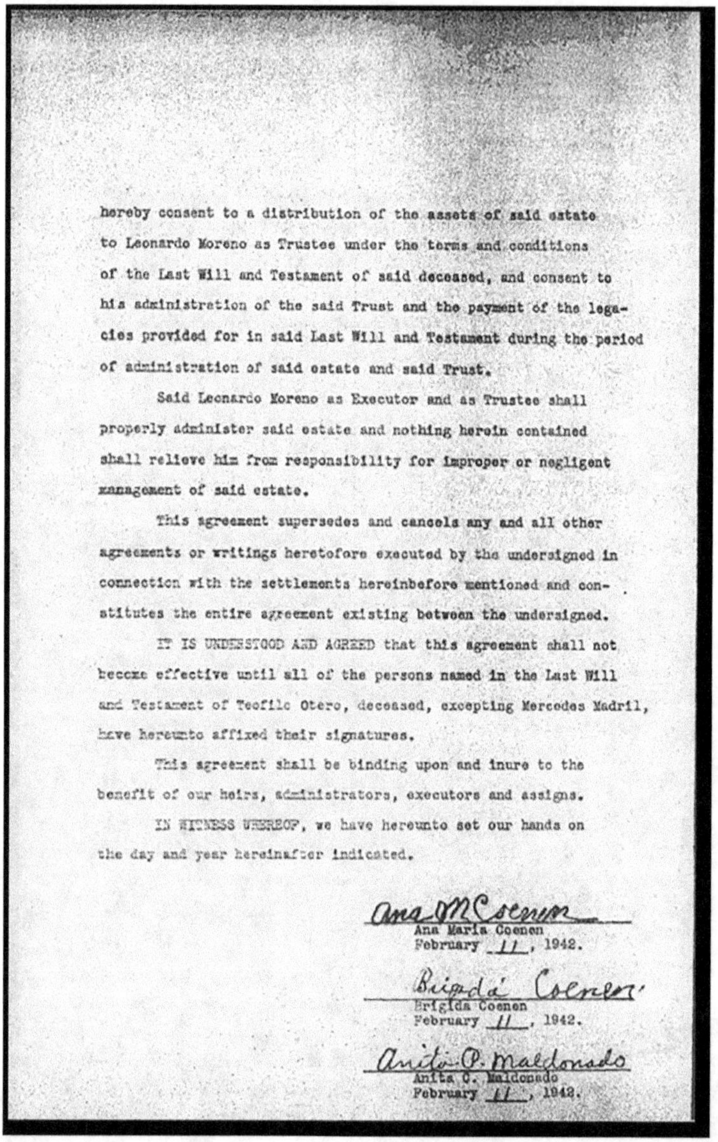

hereby consent to a distribution of the assets of said estate to Leonardo Moreno as Trustee under the terms and conditions of the Last Will and Testament of said deceased, and consent to his administration of the said Trust and the payment of the legacies provided for in said Last Will and Testament during the period of administration of said estate and said Trust.

Said Leonardo Moreno as Executor and as Trustee shall properly administer said estate and nothing herein contained shall relieve him from responsibility for improper or negligent management of said estate.

This agreement supersedes and cancels any and all other agreements or writings heretofore executed by the undersigned in connection with the settlements hereinbefore mentioned and constitutes the entire agreement existing between the undersigned.

IT IS UNDERSTOOD AND AGREED that this agreement shall not become effective until all of the persons named in the Last Will and Testament of Teofilo Otero, deceased, excepting Mercedes Madril, have hereunto affixed their signatures.

This agreement shall be binding upon and inure to the benefit of our heirs, administrators, executors and assigns.

IN WITNESS WHEREOF, we have hereunto set our hands on the day and year hereinafter indicated.

Ana M Coenen
Ana Maria Coenen
February 11, 1942.

Brigda Coenen
Brigida Coenen
February 11, 1942.

Anita O. Maldonado
Anita O. Maldonado
February 11, 1942.

Figure 3.33. Page 3 of Agreement to Settle Actions between Leonardo Moreno and Leonor Capan Otero for her claim as common-law wife of Teofilo Otero and brothers Ysidro and Ricardo Capan Otero for their claims as natural children of Teofilo Otero; and to settle the claim of Ana B. Provencio and Eduardo Otero. Compromised filed 3/31/1942. (Arizona State Library, Archives & Public Records).

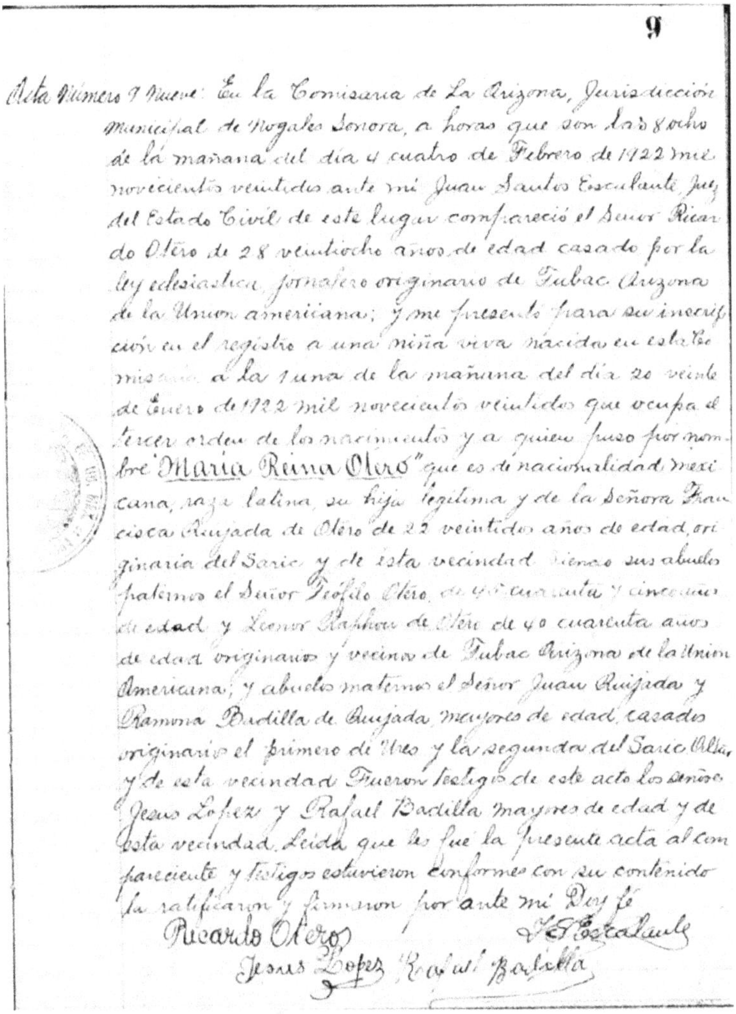

9

Acta Número 9 Nueve: En la Comisaría de La Arizona, Jurisdicción Municipal de Nogales Sonora, a horas que son las 8 ocho de la mañana del día 4 cuatro de Febrero de 1922 mil novecientos veintidós ante mí Juan Santos Escalante Juez del Estado Civil de este lugar compareció el Señor Ricardo Otero de 28 veintiocho años de edad casado por la ley eclesiástica, jornalero originario de Tubac Arizona de la Unión americana; y me presentó para su inscripción en el registro a una niña viva nacida en esta misma a la 1 una de la mañana del día 20 veinte de Enero de 1922 mil novecientos veintidós que ocupa el tercer orden de los nacimientos y a quien puso por nombre "María Reina Otero" que es de nacionalidad mexicana, raza latina, su hija legítima y de la Señora Francisca Quijada de Otero de 22 veintidós años de edad, originaria del Sáric y de esta vecindad. Siendo sus abuelos paternos el Señor Teófilo Otero de 45 cuarenta y cinco años de edad y Leonor Kaphan de Otero de 40 cuarenta años de edad originarios y vecinos de Tubac Arizona de la Unión Americana; y abuelos maternos el Señor Juan Quijada y Ramona Badilla de Quijada, mayores de edad, casados originarios el primero de Ures y la segunda del Sáric Alta, y de esta vecindad. Fueron testigos de este acto los señores Jesús López y Rafael Badilla mayores de edad y de esta vecindad. Leída que les fué la presente acta al compareciente y testigos estuvieron conformes con su contenido la ratificaron y firmaron por ante mí. Doy fe.

Ricardo Oteros — J S Escalante

Jesus Lopez — Rafael Badilla

Figure 3.34. Teofilo's son Ricardo Otero was deprived of his day in court to assert a claim against the Teofilo Otero Probate Estate as Teofilo's natural son. The birth registration of Ricardo's daughter Maria Reina Otero reflect Teofilo Otero and Leonor Kaphan de Otero as Maria Reina's paternal grandparents. The records is dated 2/4/1922 and precedes Teofilo Otero's death and probate controversies. (Sonoran Civil Birth Register, Public domain).

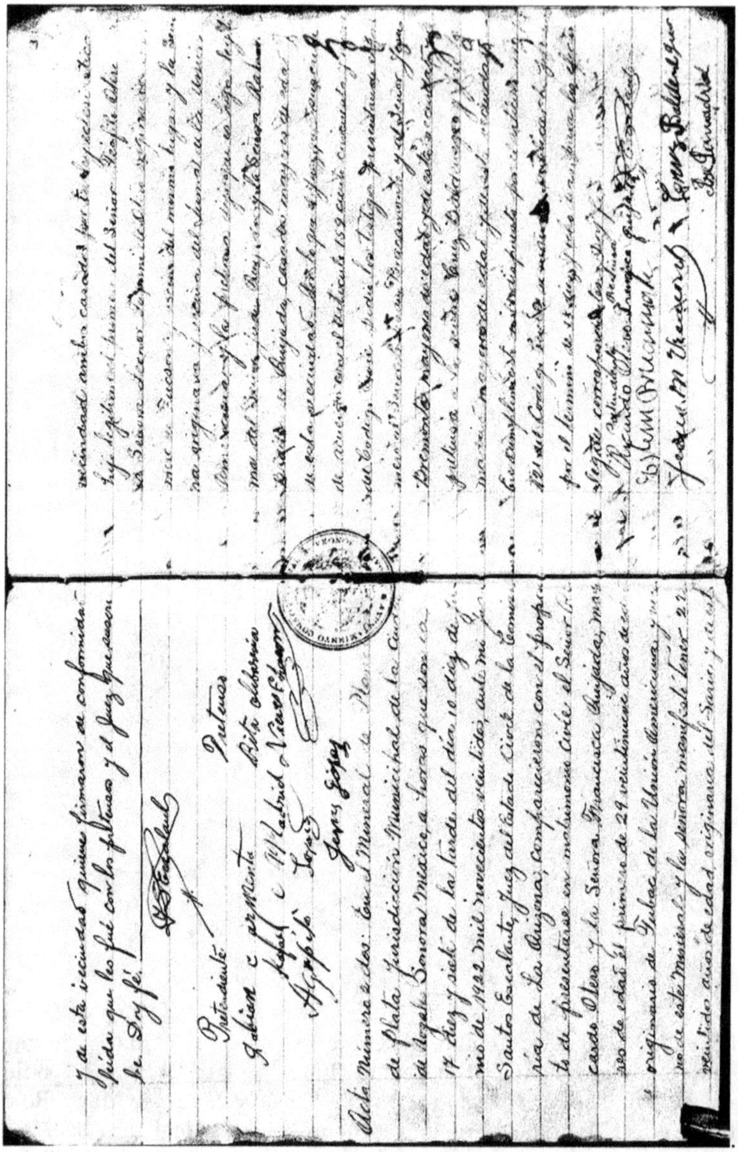

Figure 3.35. Ricardo Otero and Francisca Quijada's Mexican marriage registry at the Mining Town of Plancha de Plata, a municipality of the City of Nogales, Sonora, Mexico reports that Ricardo was the legitimate son of Teofilo Otero and Leonor Kaphan. (Sonoran Civil Marriage Register, 6/10/1922. Public domain).

The Deed and Release documents received by the Court that released the claims of Leonor Capan Otero and Ricardo Otero in favor of Ysidro Otero in exchange for $10.00 each are questionable. Ysidro visited Ricardo when he was ill, just a few short years before Ricardo's death. The release document signed by Ricardo were in English but Ricardo only spoke Spanish. Ricardo told family members Ysidro told him to sign a paper to protect his legal rights as Teofilo's son. Ysidro told his brother he would appear in court to protect Ricardo's legal rights in his absence. Instead, Ysidro had Ricardo sign a Release that granted Ricardo's share of any settlement to Ysidro in exchange for ten dollars. The Court never knew that Ricardo Otero was never fully informed of his legal rights due to a known language barrier or other essential omissions.

When Ricardo discovered this inequity, he told family he harbored no resentment or anger towards his brother Ysidro as he could not be angry about a settlement he never had in the first place.[139] Ricardo Otero died on March 20, 1946.

By the time all lawsuits against the Estate of Teofilo Otero were settled against the Otero family heirs-at-law, the Otero land grant properties were owned by outside private interests. Teofilo's heirs-at-law received monthly distributions until the money from his estate was fully distributed. The estate value included approximately $85,000 in cash, $53,000 in securities and other personal property, and approximately 20 city lots in Tucson.[140] Even though the historic land grant property was no longer owned by the Otero family, the *Terrenos* (lands) still remain an important memory of Arizona ranching and farming history. When you visit *Terrenos* once owned by the Otero family of Tubac, located at the town of Tubac and at the Tubac Golf Resort & Spa, remember that the Otero Spanish land grant of 1789 played a significant role in Arizona's history.

CHAPTER FOUR
RANCHO DE OTERO LEGACY

Ancient records preserved at the United States National Archives confirm that the Otero Spanish land grant property was the first documented privately-owned property in Arizona's history and among the longest held ranch operations in Arizona spanning from 1789 to 1937. Don Torivio de Otero passed down the ranch property at Tubac to his son Atanacio, from Atanacio to his son Manuel, then Sabino Otero assumed control beginning 1870. After Sabino's death in 1914, the Rancho de Otero was bequeathed to Sabino's sole surviving sibling, his youngest brother Teofilo Otero, and Teofilo's nieces Ana Maria Comadurán Coenen and Brijida Coenen. Each had an equal one-third interest in the Rancho de Otero at Tubac. Brijida issued a Bargain and Sale Deed for her one-third interest to Teofilo on February 24, 1915 for a consideration of $10.00.[1] Ana Maria also deeded her one-third interest of the ranch to Teofilo on January 31, 1918 for a consideration of $10.00.[2] Thus, Teofilo Otero became the final and sole direct heir-at-law of the Otero Spanish land grant known as Rancho de Otero.

Once a quaint private family ranch, the Otero land grant property was used for agricultural and stock raising pursuits that spanned from the 18th to 20th centuries despite drought, Apache depredations, and numerous court battles. The Hacienda de Otero, once the Otero family's ranch home, was primarily used as the Otero family's ranch operations headquarters. The Hacienda or as locals affectionately call it "The Otero" is the iconic symbol that encapsulates Arizona's Spanish land grant history.

Figure 4.1. The Hacienda de Otero at the Tubac Golf Resort & Spa known fondly by locals as simply "The Otero." (Photograph by the author) .

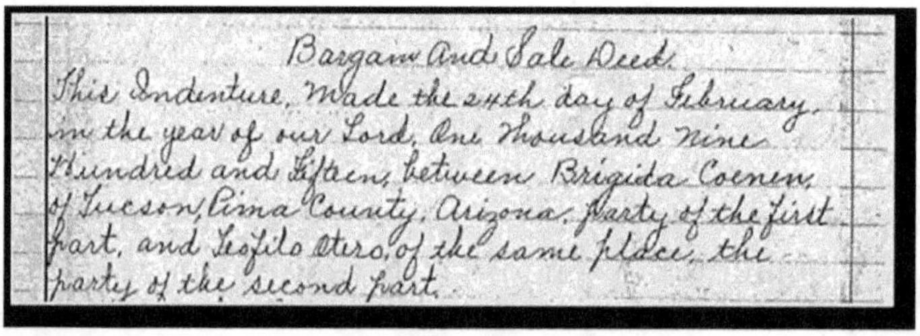

Bargain And Sale Deed.
This Indenture, Made the 24th day of February, in the year of our Lord, One Thousand Nine Hundred and Fifteen, between Brigida Coenen, of Tucson, Pima County, Arizona, party of the first part, and Teofilo Otero, of the same place, the party of the second part.

Figure 4.2. Excerpt of the Bargain and Sale Deed between niece Brijida Coenen and her uncle Teofilo Otero for her one-third interest of the Rancho de Otero on 2/24/1915. Book 8: 148. (Santa Cruz County Recorder's Office).

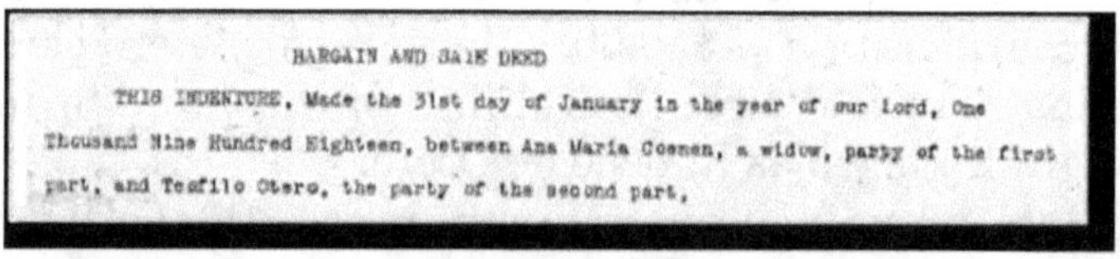

BARGAIN AND SALE DEED

THIS INDENTURE, Made the 31st day of January in the year of our Lord, One Thousand Nine Hundred Eighteen, between Ana Maria Coenen, a widow, party of the first part, and Teofilo Otero, the party of the second part,

Figure 4.3. Excerpt of the Bargain and Sale Deed between niece Ana Maria Coenen and her uncle Teofilo Otero for her one-third interest of the Rancho de Otero on 1/31/1918. Book 10: 285. (Santa Cruz County Recorder's Office).

Figure 4.4. Ana Maria Comadurán Coenen (left) and Brijida Castro Coenen (right). Each owned a one-third interest in the historic Rancho de Otero. (Courtesy Martha Desoto Green).

The Otero is also a focal point for the Tubac Golf Resort & Spa (TGRS), a member of the Historic Hotels of America. TGRS is owned by the Ron Allred family and now includes a 27-course championship golf course.[3] Of the several twentieth century owners of the Otero land grant property, a few are notable. They include a Hollywood celebrity, an aviation pioneer, and one visionary pioneer of modern Tubac. Upon each subsequent change of title, owners of the Rancho de Otero continued to celebrate its history as Arizona's first European title to land. This tradition exists today.

ADDISON PELLETIER

M. Addison Pelletier was the first non-Otero family member to own the Otero Spanish land grant property. Pelletier, an unmarried woman, purchased the land under a warranty deed from Teofilo Otero on March 31, 1937. Consideration paid was ten dollars. Property in this single transaction included land in two townships.[4] These first two properties were located at Township 20 South, Range 13 East, north of Tubac headed towards Amado, Arizona:

> The Southeast (SE¼) quarter of Section 31, Township 20 South, Range 13 East.
>
> The Southwest (SW¼) quarter of Section 32, Township 20 South, Range 13 East.

The remaining properties in this land transaction were located at Township 21 South, Range 13 East. The location of this additional property is the current day site of the Tubac Golf Resort & Spa and the Tubac town site:

> The whole west (W½) half of Section 5, Township 21, Range 13 East including Lots 3-19.
>
> The Southwest (SW¼) quarter of the Southeast (SE¼) of Section 5, Township 21 South, Range 13 East.
>
> Lots 1, 2, 6 and 7 and the Southeast quarter of the Northwest (SE¼ NW¼) quarter, and the South

half of the Northeast (S½ NE¼) quarter and the east half of the Southwest (E½SW¼) and the Southeast (SE¼) quarter of section 6, Township 21 South, Range13 East.

The Northeast quarter of the Northwest (NE¼NW¼) quarter and the Northwest quarter of the Northeast (NW¼NE¼) quarter of Section 7, Township 21 South, Range 13 East.

Lots 2 (sometimes described as the fractional Northeast quarter of the Northwest (NE¼NW¼) quarter, and all of lots 3-9 of Section 8, Township 21 South, Range 13 East; otherwise described as the whole of the Northwest (NW¼) quarter of Section 8.

The North ½ of the Southwest (N½SW¼) quarter, and the Northwest quarter of the Northeast (NW¼NE¼), and the Northeast quarter of the Southwest quarter of the Northeast (NE½SW½NE¼) quarter of Section 8, Township 21 South, Range 13 East.

All listed properties were according to the Gila and Salt River Meridian.

Land purchased by Pelletier included all the ditches and ditch rights, tanks, pumps, and pumping equipment, water and water rights, and sufficient water from the Santa Cruz River to irrigate not less than 90 acres of land.[5] On April 15, 1937, M. Allison Pelletier entered into a Bargain and Sale Deed with the Hacienda de Otero, Inc. to perfect her purchase of the Rancho de Otero property. She paid ten ($10.00) dollars for and in consideration subject, in pertinent part, to "secure an indebtedness of $25,000.00" for the mortgage by Pelletier to Teofilo Otero on March 31, 1937.[6]

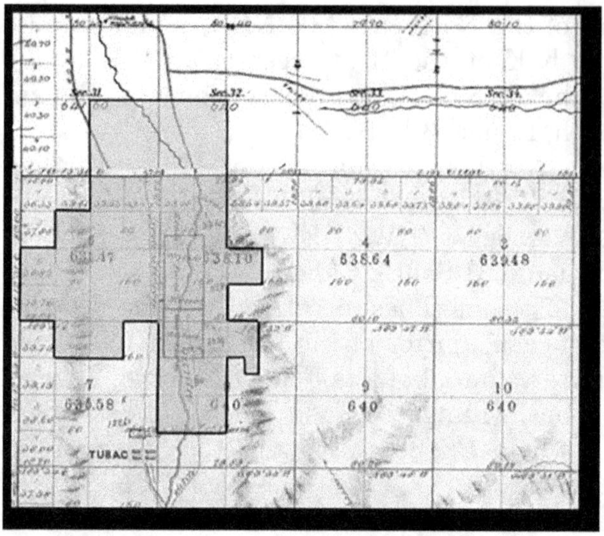

Figure 4.5. Above composite map of Townships 20 and 21 at Range 13 East Gila and Salt River Meridian shows the land expansion of the Rancho de Otero by Teofilo Otero that was sold to Addison Pelletier represented by the shaded area. The original land grant boundaries of both the Torivio de Otero and Jose Maria Martinez land grant addition are visible within the shaded area. (U.S. Bureau of Land Management. Edited by the author).

All land parcels sold by Teofilo Otero to M. Addison Pelletier totaled 1,530 acres. In Township 20 South, Range 13 East, 320 acres were sold. An additional 1,210 acres located in Township 21 South, Range 13 East. [7]

WIRT G. BOWMAN

Wirt G. Bowman, retired United States Customs Collector,[8] purchased the historic Otero Ranch in 1940 to use as his private residence for his family. His daughter Georgia fondly recalls how her father enjoyed giving his friends tours of the property and how "lovely" the porch was at the Hacienda de Otero.[9] Cognizant of the historical value of the old Otero land grant, Wirt meticulously caused a map to be drawn of the Hacienda de Otero property.

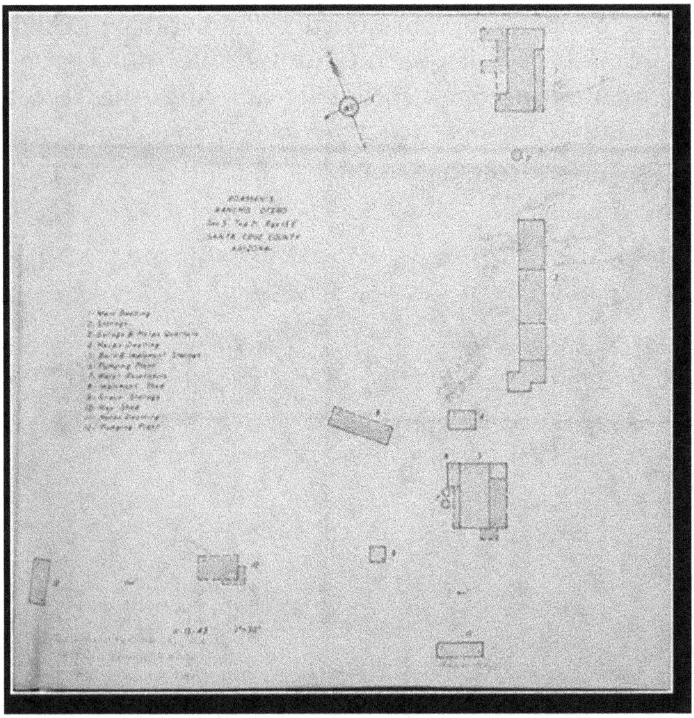

Figure 4.6. Black and white rendition of a colored map drawn by Wirt Bowman that identifies the original Otero family structures. The Hacienda, Foreman's Quarters, Barn and Silos are among the structures original to the land. (Courtesy John Shankle).

Tan structures on the map indicate original structures built by the Otero family from 1890-1908. Yellow structures indicated open areas with roofs, like the Hacienda de Otero porches. Structures colored in Pink were built by Wirt during the 1940s. It is an amazing map that gives us with a visual image of how the Hacienda de Otero looked when owned by the Otero family.

The Hacienda proper was a long dwelling that had an open front and back porch. Modern visitors to Tubac can use the Hacienda as a Meeting Room or as the only stand-alone suite on the Tubac Golf Resort & Spa (TGRS) grounds known now as the "Otero Suite." Existing TGRS executive offices were once the residence of the Otero family's foreman, servant quarters, and stables. Although the foreman/servant quarters and stables appear on the Bowman map as one contiguous building, the structure was actually four separate structures with adjoining walls.

Figure 4.7. Hacienda de Otero Porch circa 1940s. (Courtesy Georgia Bowman Allen).

The porch's arched walkways remain a focal point of TGRS's existing architectural design. Mr. Bowman used the same building as guest rooms and servant quarters. A portion of this building has since been transformed into the TGRS's Stables Ranch Grille, where visitors can enjoy breakfast, lunch, and dinner.

Figure 4.8. Wirt Bowman (wearing the hat) pauses to give his friends a tour of the property. This was one of his favorite past times. The group is located south of the Hacienda de Otero circa 1940s. The tree to the right of the party is still growing strong in 2018. (Courtesy Georgia Bowman Allen).

Figure 4.9. Wirt Bowman (wearing the hat) giving a tour of the historic Otero land grant property circa 1940s. The white building is the Otero Foreman's Quarters, the barn and silos are visible towards the back right. (Courtesy Georgia Bowman Allen).

A barn and supplemental storage was built by the Oteros adjacent to two 50 foot grain silos. Presumably, Wirt Bowman also used it to care for his animals as did subsequent owners like Joanna Fay Shankle Davis. Over the past century, the barn and storage were enclosed. Today, the building houses Dennis and Lorraine Rowden's store Pancho's Resource & Design.[10] Wirt Bowman sold the Hacienda de Otero to manufacturing magnate G.L. Elliot of Springfield, Ohio in February of 1946.[11]

G.L. ELLIOTT

During the 1940's, the Rancho de Otero property was one of the largest ranches in southern Arizona. On January 3, 1948, the Hacienda Otero Ranch was advertised for sale at a replacement cost of $160,000 with a main house, servant and foreman's accommodations, barns, corrals, an estimated 675 acres with irrigation, and domestic wells. L.A. Romine was the property realtor.[12] One month later, the Hacienda de Otero was advertised by Ranch Grace & Grace Realtors who increased the price of the historic property to $165,000. The advertisement informed that the property consisted of 2,000 acres, 200 acres of which are irrigated and an additional 150 acres [that] can be irrigated."[13] Property features not previously mentioned in the January 3rd ad included a library, butler's pantry, steam heat, loading chutes, and grain and tack rooms.[14]

On February 27, 1946, Wirt G. Bowman and Teresa V. Bowman sold the property to Gilbert Leyden Elliott and Pearl R. Elliott, husband and wife. The real estate transaction was memorialized in a Bargain and Sale Deed that listed a consideration payment of ten ($10.00) dollars with an undisclosed mortgage amount.[15] Elliott was the head of G.L. Elliot Company, an electrical manufacturing company at Jeannette, PA.[16] The Tucson Daily Citizen reported that the transaction included "a luxurious ranch house built by M. Adison Pelletier, former owner of the ranch."[17] This report is misleading. The Hacienda de Otero located on the Rancho de Otero property was already built when Ms. Pelletier purchased the property. However, Ms. Pelletier should possibly be credited for many upgrades. At the time of the Elliott's purchase, Mr. and Mrs. Ken Holbrook were residing at the Otero ranch and they had plans to relocate to Tucson.[18]

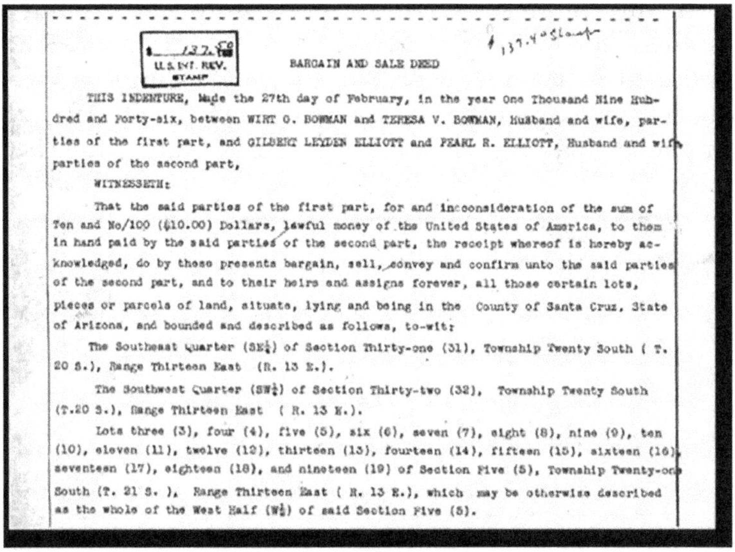
$ 137.50
U.S. INT. REV. STAMP

BARGAIN AND SALE DEED

THIS INDENTURE, Made the 27th day of February, in the year One Thousand Nine Hundred and Forty-six, between WIRT G. BOWMAN and TERESA V. BOWMAN, Husband and wife, parties of the first part, and GILBERT LEYDEN ELLIOTT and PEARL R. ELLIOTT, Husband and wife, parties of the second part,

WITNESSETH:

That the said parties of the first part, for and in consideration of the sum of Ten and No/100 ($10.00) Dollars, lawful money of the United States of America, to them in hand paid by the said parties of the second part, the receipt whereof is hereby acknowledged, do by these presents bargain, sell, convey and confirm unto the said parties of the second part, and to their heirs and assigns forever, all those certain lots, pieces or parcels of land, situate, lying and being in the County of Santa Cruz, State of Arizona, and bounded and described as follows, to-wit:

The Southeast Quarter (SE¼) of Section Thirty-one (31), Township Twenty South (T. 20 S.), Range Thirteen East (R. 13 E.).

The Southwest Quarter (SW¼) of Section Thirty-two (32), Township Twenty South (T.20 S.), Range Thirteen East (R. 13 E.).

Lots three (3), four (4), five (5), six (6), seven (7), eight (8), nine (9), ten (10), eleven (11), twelve (12), thirteen (13), fourteen (14), fifteen (15), sixteen (16), seventeen (17), eighteen (18), and nineteen (19) of Section Five (5), Township Twenty-one South (T. 21 S.), Range Thirteen East (R. 13 E.), which may be otherwise described as the whole of the West Half (W½) of said Section Five (5).

Figure 4.10. Excerpt of the Bargain and Sale Deed between Wirt G. and Teresa V. Bowman and Gilbert Leyden and Pearl R. Elliott for the sale of the Rancho de Otero. Book 28: 238. (Santa Cruz County Recorder's Office).

JOANNA FAY (SHANKLE) DAVIS

Johnna Fay Shankle Davis was among the most notable owners of the Rancho de Otero. A highly respected aviatrix and the mother of four children,[19] Davis purchased the historic Hacienda de Otero from G.L. Elliott for a mortgage of $134,000 on July 12, 1948. Prior to this purchase, Joanna Fay purchased the Pajaritos Migratorios or P.M. ranch from Thomas Casanegas[20] which adjoins the Rancho de Otero.[21]

C.E. "Dutch" Shankle taught his wife Joanna Fay to fly. She had the distinction of being the "first woman to fly solo from Boston to Miami" and was also a race pilot.[22] Joanna, self-identified as "Joan" on her Pilot's Identification Card.[23] Johnna Fay and her husband C.E. "Dutch" Shankle moved to Tubac, Arizona in the 1930's and built the PM[24] Ranch. The PM Ranch was the first ranch immediately north of the Otero ranch and it contained an airfield to house their "Stearman J-5 and Lockheed Sirius" planes.[25] The PM was sold after World War II started and the couple moved back east. After the war ended, Joan returned to Arizona and bought the Otero Ranch.[26]

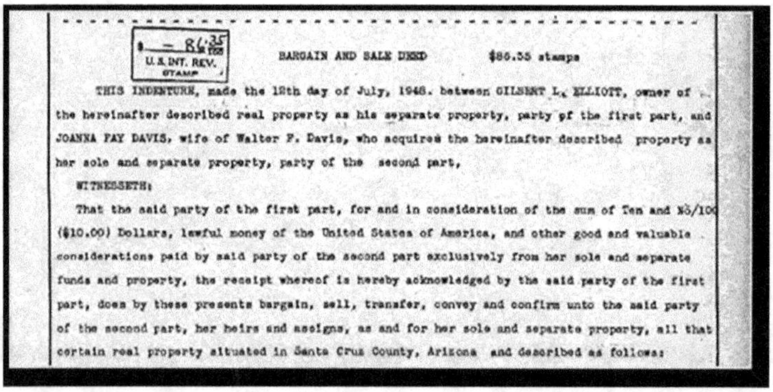
$ — 86.35
U.S. INT. REV. STAMP

BARGAIN AND SALE DEED $86.35 stamps

THIS INDENTURE, made the 12th day of July, 1948. between GILBERT L. ELLIOTT, owner of the hereinafter described real property as his separate property, party of the first part, and JOANNA FAY DAVIS, wife of Walter F. Davis, who acquires the hereinafter described property as her sole and separate property, party of the second part,

WITNESSETH:

That the said party of the first part, for and in consideration of the sum of Ten and No/100 ($10.00) Dollars, lawful money of the United States of America, and other good and valuable considerations paid by said party of the second part exclusively from her sole and separate funds and property, the receipt whereof is hereby acknowledged by the said party of the first part, does by these presents bargain, sell, transfer, convey and confirm unto the said party of the second part, her heirs and assigns, as and for her sole and separate property, all that certain real property situated in Santa Cruz County, Arizona and described as follows:

Figure 4.11. Excerpt of the Bargain and Sale Deed between Gilbert Leyden and Pearl R. Elliott and Joanna Fay Davis for the sale of the Rancho de Otero as her sole and separate property. Book 30: 54. (Santa Cruz County Recorder's Office).

Joan's second marriage with Mr. G.W. Davis was a contentious relationship that resulted in a highly-publicized court battle.[27] While at the Rancho de Otero, she lived with her son John Shankle who expressed fond memories living at the Rancho de Otero and sorrowed that the Hacienda was eventually turned into a resort. The following photographs provided by John Shankle give us an intimate insight into the Rancho de Otero during the latter part of the 1940s through the early 1950s. Like the Otero Family, Joanna Fay used the historic property as a stock ranch a mere 11 years after it was sold by Teofilo Otero to non-family private interests. Johnna Fay and C.E. "Dutch" Shankle were "inducted into the Arizona Aviation Hall of Fame on April 17, 1999."[28]

Figure 4.12. Joan flying NC13W. (Courtesy John Shankle).[29]

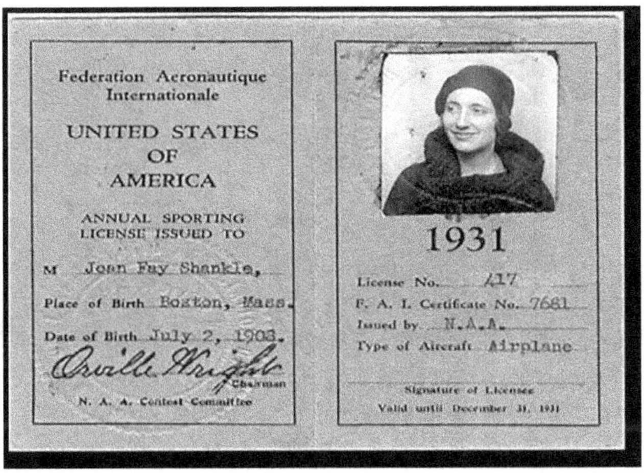

Federation Aeronautique Internationale

UNITED STATES OF AMERICA

ANNUAL SPORTING LICENSE ISSUED TO

M Joan Fay Shankle,

Place of Birth Boston, Mass.

Date of Birth July 2, 1903.

Orville Wright Chairman

N. A. A. Contest Committee

1931

License No. 417

F. A. I. Certificate No. 7681

Issued by N.A.A.

Type of Aircraft Airplane

Signature of Licensee

Valid until December 31, 1931

Figure 4.13. John Fay Shankle's Federation Aeronautique Internationale License, 1931. (Courtesy John Shankle).

Figure 4.14. Hacienda de Otero facing west. (Courtesy John Shankle).

Figure 4.15. Wide view of the Hacienda de Otero facing west. The Foreman's Quarters, barn and silos are to the far right. (Courtesy John Shankle).

Figure 4.16. Shankle family living room now used as Executive Meeting Rooms by the Tubac Golf Resort & Spa. (Courtesy John Shankle).

Figure 4.17. Shankle's family dining room now used as part of the Executive Meeting Room facility by the Tubac Golf Resort & Spa. (Courtesy John Shankle).

Figure 4.18. Shankle barn originally built by the Otero family. It was eventually redesigned and is now Pancho's Resource & Design at the Tubac Golf Resort & Spa. (Courtesy John Shankle).

Figure 4.19. Foreman's Quarters was an original structure built by the Otero family. The arched areas are now part of dining and shopping facilities at the Tubac Golf Resort & Spa. (Courtesy John Shankle).

Figure 4.20. Cattle at the Rancho de Otero owned by Joanna Fay Shankle. (Courtesy John Shankle).

WILLIAM MORROW, CHAIRMAN OF THE BOARD BING CROSBY, AND THE BIRTH OF THE TUBAC VALLEY COUNTRY CLUB

The sleepy community of Tubac was abruptly awakened by the arrival of William C. Morrow, a native of Willcox. In 1958, Morrow purchased the 2,000-acre Rancho de Otero for $170,000.[30] Former developer of the Morrow's Nut Houses chain, Morrow applied his entrepreneurial skills laying the foundation for modern Tubac. He created plans to build 1,000 Spanish style homes on the old Otero land grant property and a 150-acre industrial park northwest of old Tubac.[31] He invested more than a million dollars at Tubac from 1958 to 1960.[32]

Morrow, owner of the Otero Ranch, sold the property to the group of prominent investors that soon established the Tubac Valley Country Club (TVCC).[33] The charter member roster included Dick Baker, Keith Brown, Charles Crary, Chester Crebbs, Howard Cursey, Charles Day, Richard Ensign, Bill Golberg, Kenneth Herman, William

C. Scott, and Will Rogers, Jr.[34] Rogers presided as Tubac's unofficial mayor and owned the only two-story home at Tubac.[35] Another promoter was Arizona State Senator Neilson Brown, and Robert F. Lawrence of Tucson, past president of the American Society of Golf Course Architects was hired to lay out the course.[36]

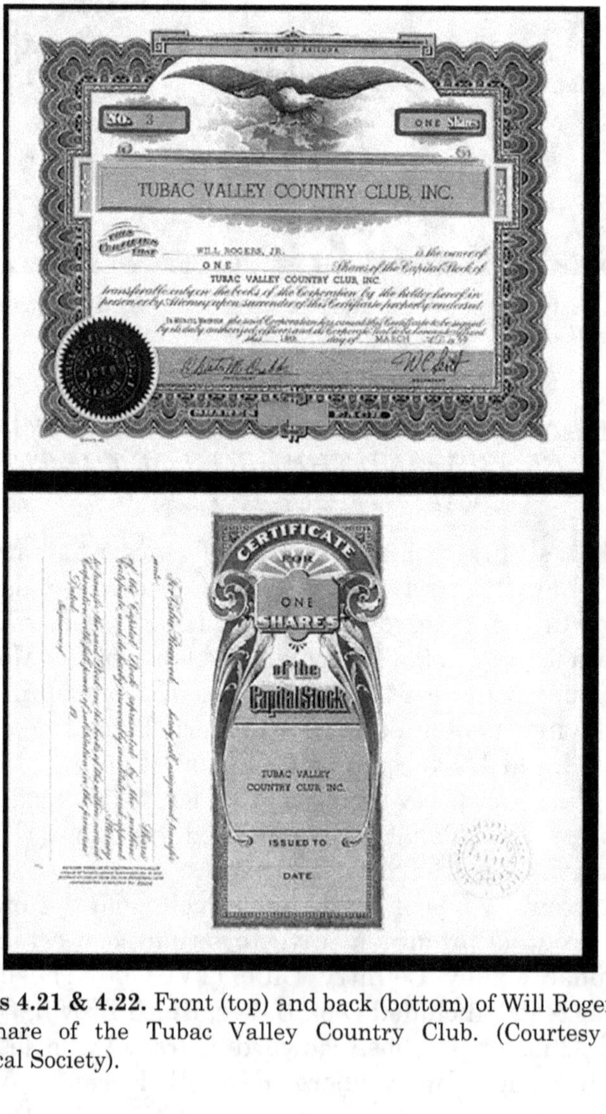

Figures 4.21 & 4.22. Front (top) and back (bottom) of Will Rogers, Jr.'s One Share of the Tubac Valley Country Club. (Courtesy Tubac Historical Society).

Figure 4.23. Illustration of Bing Crosby by Dorotea Cvijanovic commissioned exclusively for *Terrenos* © 2018 Diana DeLugan. All rights reserved. Not only was Bing Crosby the Chairman of the Board for the Tubac Valley Country Club, his son Harry L. Crosby also purchased resort property at the Tubac resort.

Legendary crooner and Hollywood star Bing Crosby became a charter member of the Tubac Valley Country Club on May 10, 1959. Mr. Crosby purchased 170 acres of Otero Ranch cotton land from William Morrow.[37] On June 8, 1959, Crosby was elected as the TVCC's first Chairman of the Board. During TVCC's first meeting, the country club consisted of 640 acres under development.[38] On October 23, 1959, Bing Crosby took a lease with option to buy an additional 800 acres of land near the Tubac golf course. This land deal adds to the 135 acres Crosby purchased east of Tubac in 1958.[39] Crosby was an active member of the Tubac community and became a member of the Tubac Chamber of Commerce in March of 1960.

Tubac Valley Country Club announced it would open in September of 1960 much to the excitement of local residents. Country club memberships sold for $5,000 each, which included three-acre lots for each owner.[40] The historic Hacienda de Otero was projected to be "refurbished into a clubhouse" along with the construction of an "18-hole championship golf course"[41] designed by Red Lawrence of Florida.[42] The property also included 12 ladies' tees, with plans to build a new clubhouse and three-decked Gazebo.[43] When the country club informally announced it planned to open the weekend of November 26 and 27, 1960, the Hacienda de Otero was being used to conduct business for the Tubac Valley Country Club. A formal opening was scheduled for early 1961.[44] The country club's main features included:

> The longest fairways in the area, the par 5, 603-yard 7th and 575-yard, par five, 16th.
> The largest and most undulated greens in the area, including a five-level, 10,000 foot 18th.
> A river, the Santa Cruz, running through its middle.[45]

The first tee shot at the TVCC was held on Thanksgiving Day of 1960. Some reports indicate that initial business growth was slow. Others claimed that the country club was a flop. But it was golfing pros with a discerning eye that considered the then-existing golf course on the historic Otero land grant property to be a "diamond in the rough,"[46] attracting golf legends like Arnold Palmer, Mike Souchak,[47] Lionel Hebert, and Al Watrous.[48] A new general manager and partner Tucson native Bill Gahlberg took control of the club in 1963. Territorial design casitas were built under his leadership which helped increase interest in the property.[49]

Just one year before the country club was established, Arizona's first state park was established in Tubac.[50] A short video presentation about Tubac narrated by Will Rogers, Jr., Tubac's then-unofficial mayor and founding member of the country club, can be viewed at the Tubac Presidio State Park and Museum.

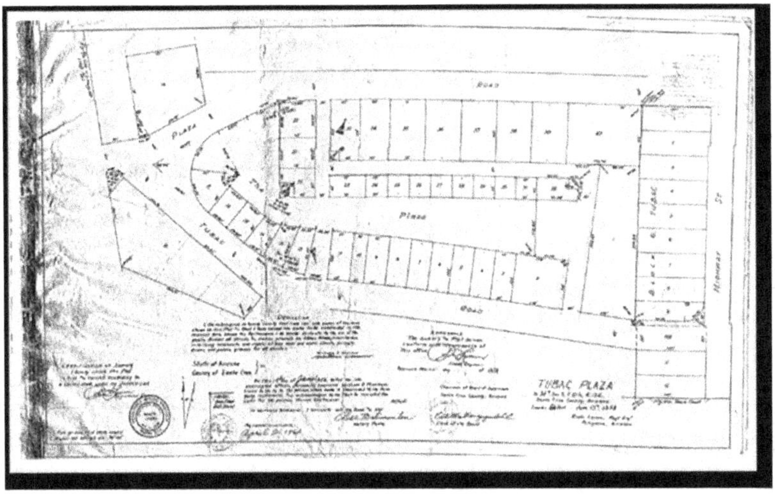

Figure 4.24. William Morrow dedicated the Tubac Plaza to the township of Tubac on 6/15/1958. The donated land resulted in the commercial expansion of the Village of Tubac and its south east corner abuts the Tubac Presidio State Park grounds. (Courtesy Santa Cruz County Recorder).

HARRY C. POLLOCK AND A MEETING OF TWO PRESIDENTS

Harry C. Pollock, formally of Cleveland, Ohio purchased the Otero land grant property then known as the Tubac Valley Country Club for an undisclosed sum. [51] He was a retired U.S. Marine captain[52] from Cleveland, Ohio, and "one of the 44 partners who previously owned Tubac Valley Resorts."[53] Although the sale of the Tubac Valley Country Club was not disclosed to the public for over a week, Pollock gained formal control of the property on June 1, 1969. He brought with him a wealth of experience as the former secretary of the Cleveland District Golf Association. Under Pollock's stewardship, he remodeled the Hacienda de Otero, built a new golf and tennis pro shop and planned another nine-hole golf course. Pollock also initiated negotiations for a portion of Bill Crosby's 140 acres at Tubac.[54]

Figure 4.25. President Gerald Ford at the Hacienda de Otero part of the Tubac Valley Country Club on 10/21/1974. (Courtesy President Ford Library).

Figure 4.26. President Gerald Ford meeting with Mexican President Echeverria at the historic Rancho de Otero known as Tubac Valley Country Club. (Courtesy President Ford Library).

On October 21, 1974, historic Otero hacienda owner Harry Pollock hosted a widely anticipated visit by President Gerald Ford and Mexican President Luis

Echeverria at the historic Hacienda de Otero upon return from a presidential meeting at Magdalena, Sonora, Mexico. In the days preceding the historic presidential visit to Tubac, Pollock reported that Secret Service agents had contacted him at least three separate times.[55] The presidents of both countries and U.S. Secretary of State Henry A. Kissinger sat at the head table inside the Hacienda de Otero dining room to enjoy a buffet luncheon. The room held a walnut table and candelabra from Guadalajara.[56] The beehive fireplace and exposed cedar beams mentioned in news reports appear to be original to the Otero building based on prior owner's reports. After the meal, President Ford strolled over to the cocktail lounge for a refreshment. The presidential party left Tubac and the Hacienda de Otero and returned to Davis-Monthan Air Force Base after a fifteen-minute chopper ride from Tubac.[57] Upon arrival at the air force base, President Ford elicited a "hearty laugh from the audience" after mispronouncing *hasta luego*. It came out "hasta loo-eee-go" and said, "Us Michiganders have a little trouble..."[58]

ALLRED

Although the Rancho de Otero experienced multiple changes in ownership after Teofilo Otero sold the land to private interests, the historic property has always remained an integral part of the township of Tubac. Tubac Golf Resort & Spa (TGRS) is under the current stewardship of Ron Allred, former developer of Colorado's Telluride Ski & Golf Co. and the Rancho Mañana Golf Club in Cave Creek, Arizona. Allred organized a group of silent investors to purchase TGRS for $7.28 million[59] under the name of Tubac Management Co., L.L.C., established as an Arizona business entity on August 8, 2002. Its current managing members are Tubac Allred, LLC and Allred Capital LLLP.[60] Ron Allred is the sole member of Tubac Allred, LLC[61] while Allred Capital LLLP is owned by Dann

Holdings, Inc. under the management of Ronald D. Allred, President and Michael D. Allred, Vice-President.[62]

After Allred and his silent investors purchased the property in 2002 from a family-held interest that owned the property since 1988,[63] TGRS received a $40 million renovation including 52 new hacienda suites, a replica of a 1700's mission, and added 9-holes to the 18-hole championship golf course [64] The Hacienda de Otero Suite is scheduled to undergo an upgrade in 2018.

Figure 4.27. Historic Hacienda de Otero Suite at the Tubac Golf Resort & Spa 2017. The Hacienda is the former ranch home of the Otero family. (Photograph by the author).

Figure 4.28. Arch at the Tubac Golf Resort & Spa reads "Otero Ranch Est. 1789 Where The History Lives On. (Photograph by the author).

TGRS' management and staff ensure that visitors learn about its designation as a "Historic Hotel of America." The *Historic Hotels of America* website reports it "is the official program of the National Trust for Historic Preservation for recognizing and celebrating the finest Historic Hotels...[who] faithfully maintained their authenticity, sense of place, and architectural integrity."[65] The Otero family legacy at TGRS is preserved, in part, by the Hacienda de Otero building, which is the only stand-alone suite on the property. It was once the ranch home of the Otero family of Tubac and is likely be the then-existing building referenced in Arizona Assistant Surveyor General Roskruge's 1881 Field Notes. The Otero land grant is also referenced in Guest Room Booklets while menus and décor at the Stables Ranch Grille & Patios also celebrate the family. An interesting display of some of the Otero cattle brands are on exhibit at the restaurant's bar. History often links the Otero name to stock raising. Cattle graze on the

TGRS property as a visual reminder that the land was once a vibrant stock ranch owned by the Otero family.

Although some misinformation about the Otero family is promoted within TGRS's printed and online communications, it can easily be attributed to misinformation passed down for more than a century by other writers and historians.

Figure 4.29. Calf at the Tubac Golf Resort & Spa. (Photograph by the author).

MOVIE CREDITS

In addition to hosting presidents, Hollywood celebrities, and a famous aviatrix, the historic Otero Ranch property also gained fame for its use as a Hollywood movie filming location. During the mid-1950s, the Otero Ranch Stables was briefly used as a backdrop in the film *Strange Lady in Town* starring Greer Garson.[66] The movie was released on April 12, 1955 and ran 112 minutes.[67]

Figure 4.30. The Tin Cup Hole at the Tubac Golf Resort & Spa memorializes the movie of the same name that was filmed at the resort. (Photograph by the author).

On August 16, 1996, the movie *Tin Cup* starring Kevin Costner and directed by Ron Shelton was released.[68] The first two-halves of the romantic golf film were recorded on location at the Otero Ranch. Filming took approximately two weeks.[69] In the movie, Tin Cup caddy for the "handsome-but-evil- Don Johnson," play the "first U.S. Open qualifying round at this charming golf resort. Also, post-qualifying 19th hold exteriors were shot outside the resort's Otero Suite [Hacienda de Otero]."[70] In addition, the Hacienda de Otero was used as the film's "Cottonwood Country Club's 19th hole and the archway entrance [was] visible from I-19."[71] Then Tubac Golf Resort co-owner Al Kaufman reported that the cast and crew of *Tin Cup* "were as pleasant, courteous and professional as could be. There wasn't even a gum wrapper left on this place."[72]

It is evident that the rich and proud history of the Otero family lives on at the Rancho de Otero. One constant between each subsequent owner of the historic Otero Land Grant lands is that they celebrated the land's history as a farm and cattle ranch. They celebrated the land's designation as Arizona's first European title to private land that was granted to Don Torivio de Otero on January 10, 1789 in a small ceremony at the Tubac Spanish Presidio. Otero family descendants, indeed any visitor, can walk the same land that witnessed the passage of Spanish, Mexican, and Territorial governments. At Rancho de Otero, the very land is the embodiment of Arizona's pioneer history.

CHAPTER FIVE
BABOQUIVARI AND OTHER *TERRENOS*

Rancho de Otero at Tubac was a successful business operation. Its financial prosperity permitted the Otero family to expand its real estate holdings. One parcel of land near Tucson, Arizona is legendary: Sabino Canyon. Nestled within the Santa Catalina Ranger District at the Coronado National Forest, Sabino Canyon was allegedly named after Arizona pioneer Sabino Otero of the Tubac land grant family because he grazed his livestock there during the late nineteenth century.[1] Some argue, many pioneer cattle ranchers in southern Arizona grazed livestock on the open range, not just Sabino Otero.[2] That fact is true. A competing urban legend published on December 15, 1883 in the *Arizona Weekly Citizen* of Tucson suggests Sabino Canyon was actually named after a "bright flannel red" bluff located one side of the controversial canyon. The story says the red bluff is a group of bewitched Apache maidens who were transformed into granite because they longed for "the pretty red skirts and the charming hose of the white men's daughters."[3] No one verifiable source has been located to discover the origin of Sabino Canyon's name. Nonetheless, there is a second, less familiar Sabino Canyon that was indeed named after local rancher Sabino Otero. It is located at the rugged Baboquivari Mountains within the Altar Valley Conservation Area.

Figure 5.1. Etching of the Baboquivari Mountains. (John Ross Browne from *Adventures in the Apache Country*. Public domain).[4]

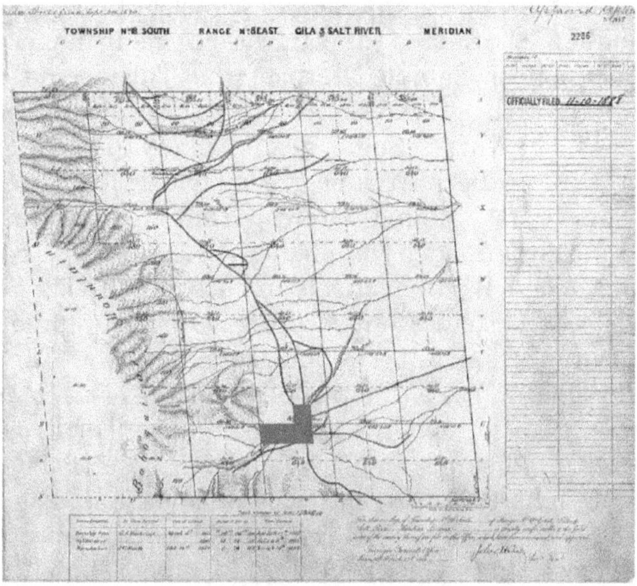

Figure 5.2. Plat of Township No. 18 South Range 8 East Gila & Salt River Meridian filed 11/10/1888 includes the Baboquivari Mountains. The shaded area depicts the Sabino Otero Homestead. (U.S. Bureau of Land Management. Edited by the author).

Located fifty miles southwest of Tucson within the 10,000-acre Elkhorn Ranch lies a historic parcel of 160 acres that was homesteaded by Sabino Otero in 1892 pursuant to the 1862 Homestead Act. In addition to Otero ranches at San Vicente[5] and Santa Rosa (currently known as Santa Rosa Schuck on the Tohono O'odham reservation),[6] Sabino improved the Baboquivari land and used it as a livestock water station. A homestead application for the Baboquivari land was filed on August 8, 1892 at the Tucson Land Office. The next day, Land Office Registrar Herbert Brown issued the first Notice for Publication in *The Arizona Citizen* newspaper. The Notice was subsequently published for thirty (30) consecutive days[7] which stated final proof in support of Otero's homestead claim No. 1302 would be made on September 10th of the same year.[8] Sabino Otero likely entered the Baboquivari mountain range with the intent to homestead land around 1884 to initiate required homestead improvements. Records reflect he was well established at the Baboquivari ranch by August 1, 1886. By that date, approximately twelve (12) acres had been cultivated for one year and Sabino further reported that the unincorporated land was primarily intended for grazing.[9]

Improvements on the land included a single adobe house with four rooms and a shingle roof, one lumber house, three wells/water tanks, one stable, four corrals, ten fenced acres and a reservoir with an estimated value of $7,000.00.[10] On September 10, 1889, written affidavits were taken at the Tucson Land Office from Sabino Otero, Raimundo Vasquez, and George Martin, all residents of Tucson, Arizona in support of Otero's homestead application. On the same day, Sabino executed the Final Affidavit required of homestead claimants that affirmed everything contained in his Homestead Application was true. He also attested that he was a natural born citizen of the United States, and that no known minerals existed on the Baboquivari land.

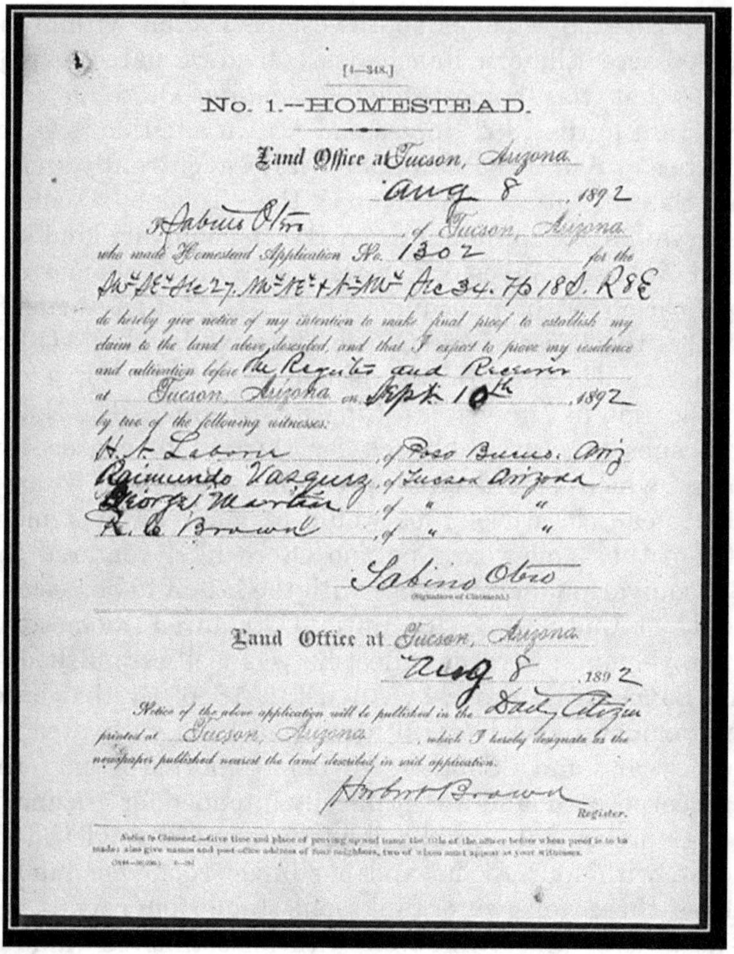

[4—348.]

No. 1.—HOMESTEAD.

Land Office at Tucson, Arizona

Aug 8, 1892

I Sabino Otero of Tucson, Arizona

who made Homestead Application No. 1302 for the

SW¼ SE¼ Sec 27. NW¼ NE¼ + N½ NW¼ Sec 34. Tp 18 S. R 8 E

do hereby give notice of my intention to make final proof to establish my claim to the land above described, and that I expect to prove my residence and cultivation before the Register and Receiver

at Tucson, Arizona on Sept. 10th, 1892

by two of the following witnesses:

H. A. Laborn, of Poso Bueno. Ariz

Raimundo Vasquez, of Tucson Arizona

George Martin, of " "

R. C. Brown, of " "

Sabino Otero
(Signature of Claimant.)

Land Office at Tucson, Arizona

Aug 8, 1892

Notice of the above application will be published in the Daily Citizen printed at Tucson, Arizona, which I hereby designate as the newspaper published nearest the land described in said application.

Herbert Brown
Register.

Notice to Claimant.—Give time and place of proving up and name the title of the officer before whom proof is to be made; also give names and post-office address of four neighbors, two of whom must appear as your witnesses.

Figure 5.3. Sabino Otero Notice of Homestead Application filed 8/8/1892. (U.S. Bureau of Land Management).

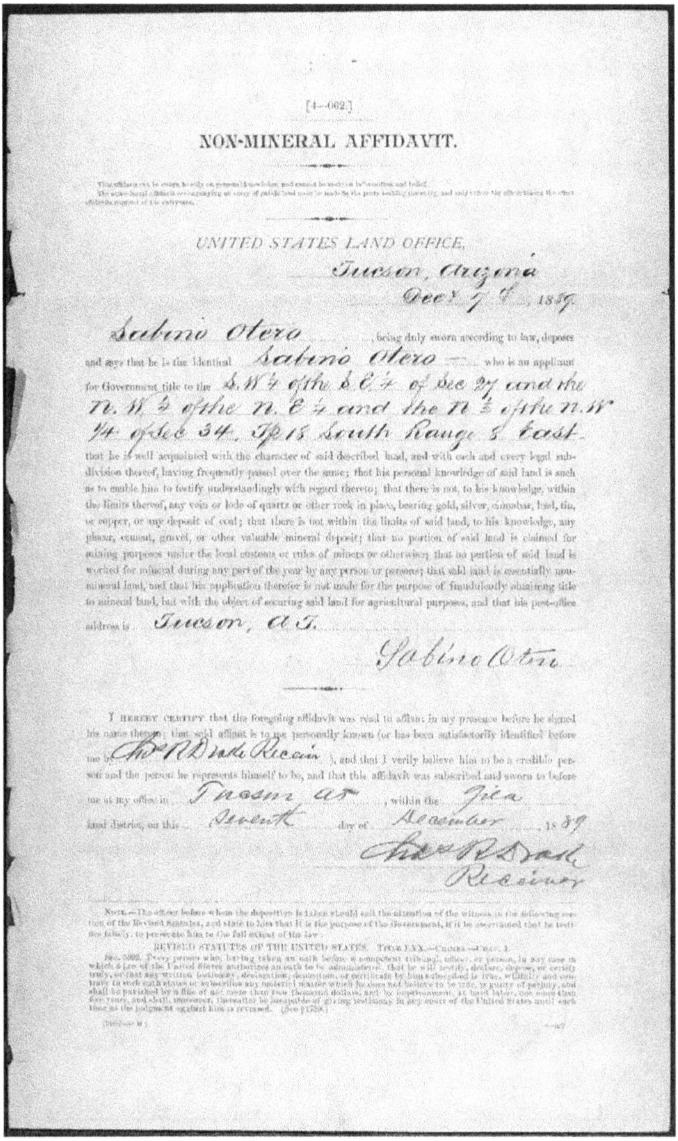

[4—062.]

NON-MINERAL AFFIDAVIT.

UNITED STATES LAND OFFICE,

Tucson, Arizona

Decr 7th, 1889.

Sabino Otero, being duly sworn according to law, deposes and says that he is the identical Sabino Otero who is an applicant for Government title to the S.W ¼ of the S.E ¼ of Sec 27 and the N.W ¼ of the N.E ¼ and the N ½ of the N.W ¼ of Sec 34. Tp 18 South Range 8 East that he is well acquainted with the character of said described land, and with each and every legal subdivision thereof, having frequently passed over the same; that his personal knowledge of said land is such as to enable him to testify understandingly with regard thereto; that there is not, to his knowledge, within the limits thereof, any vein or lode of quartz or other rock in place, bearing gold, silver, cinnabar, lead, tin, or copper, or any deposit of coal; that there is not within the limits of said land, to his knowledge, any placer, cement, gravel, or other valuable mineral deposit; that no portion of said land is claimed for mining purposes under the local customs or rules of miners or otherwise; that no portion of said land is worked for mineral during any part of the year by any person or persons; that said land is essentially non-mineral land, and that his application therefor is not made for the purpose of fraudulently obtaining title to mineral land, but with the object of securing said land for agricultural purposes, and that his post-office address is Tucson, A.T.

Sabino Otero

I HEREBY CERTIFY that the foregoing affidavit was read to affiant in my presence before he signed his name thereto; that said affiant is to me personally known (or has been satisfactorily identified before me by Chas R Drake Receiver), and that I verily believe him to be a credible person and the person he represents himself to be, and that this affidavit was subscribed and sworn to before me at my office in Tucson AT, within the Gila land district, on this Seventh day of December, 1889

Chas R Drake
Receiver

NOTE.—The officer before whom the deposition is taken should call the attention of the witness to the following section of the Revised Statutes, and state to him that it is the purpose of the Government, if it be ascertained that he testifies falsely, to prosecute him to the full extent of the law.

REVISED STATUTES OF THE UNITED STATES.

Figure 5.4. Sabino Otero Non-Mineral Affidavit filed 12/7/1889. (U.S. Bureau of Land Management).

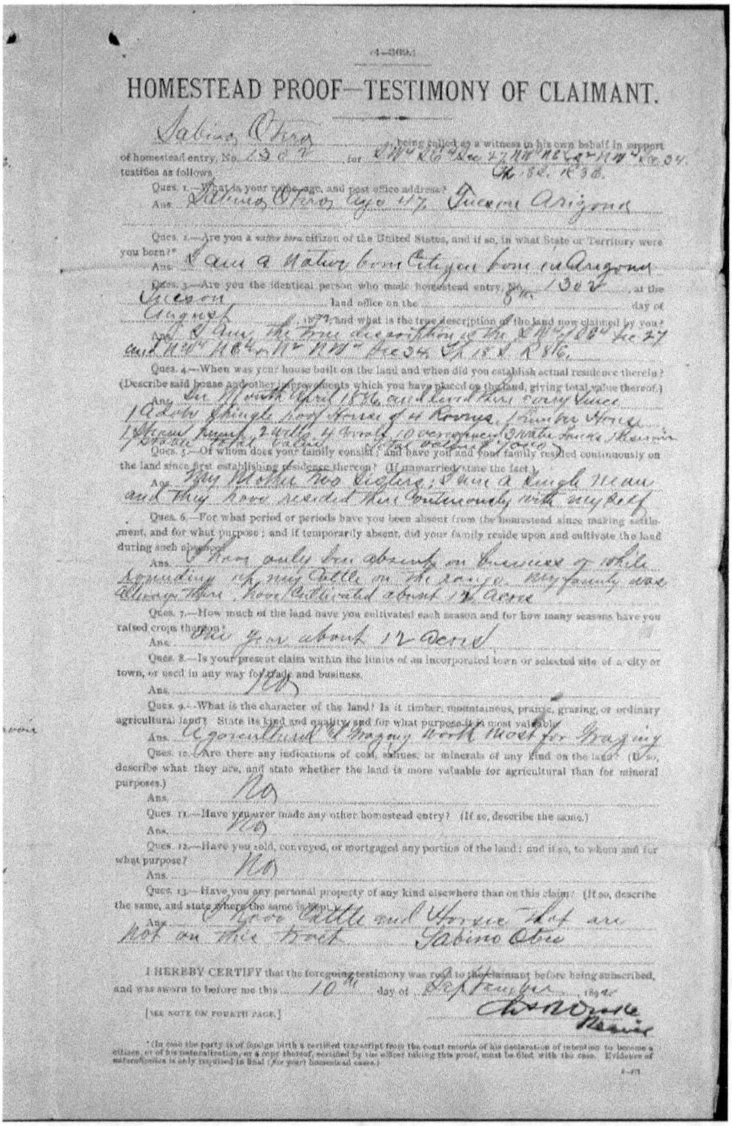

4-369.

HOMESTEAD PROOF—TESTIMONY OF CLAIMANT.

Sabino Otero being called as a witness in his own behalf in support of homestead entry, No. 1302 for SW¼ NE¼ Sec 27 NW¼ NE¼ & NW¼ NW¼ Sec 34. Tp. 18. R 8E. testifies as follows:

Ques. 1.—What is your name, age, and post office address?
Ans. Sabino Otero Age 47 Tucson Arizona

Ques. 2.—Are you a native born citizen of the United States, and if so, in what State or Territory were you born?
Ans. I am a Native born Citizen born in Arizona

Ques. 3.—Are you the identical person who made homestead entry, No. 1302, at the Tucson land office on the 6 day of August 1892, and what is the true description of the land now claimed by you?
Ans. I am, the true description is the SW¼ NE¼ Sec 27 and NW¼ NE¼ & NW¼ NW¼ Sec 34 Tp 18 S. R 8 E.

Ques. 4.—When was your house built on the land and when did you establish actual residence thereon? (Describe said house and other improvements which you have placed on the land, giving total value thereof.)
Ans. In Month April 1886, and lived there ever since. 1 Adobe Shingle roof House of 4 Rooms, 1 Lumber House, 1 Steam pump, 2 wells, 4 corrals, 10 acres fenced, 3 Water tanks ... Total value $ ...

Ques. 5.—Of whom does your family consist; and have you and your family resided continuously on the land since first establishing residence thereon? (If unmarried, state the fact.)
Ans. My Mother two Sisters; I am a Single man and they have resided there continuously with myself

Ques. 6.—For what period or periods have you been absent from the homestead since making settlement, and for what purpose; and if temporarily absent, did your family reside upon and cultivate the land during such absence?
Ans. I have only been absent on business or while rounding up my cattle on the range. My family was always there. Have cultivated about 12 acres

Ques. 7.—How much of the land have you cultivated each season and for how many seasons have you raised crops thereon?
Ans. One year about 12 acres

Ques. 8.—Is your present claim within the limits of an incorporated town or selected site of a city or town, or used in any way for trade and business?
Ans. No

Ques. 9.—What is the character of the land? Is it timber, mountainous, prairie, grazing, or ordinary agricultural land? State its kind and quality, and for what purpose it is most valuable.
Ans. Agricultural & Grazing Worth most for Grazing

Ques. 10.—Are there any indications of coal, salines, or minerals of any kind on the land? (If so, describe what they are, and state whether the land is more valuable for agricultural than for mineral purposes.)
Ans. No

Ques. 11.—Have you ever made any other homestead entry? (If so, describe the same.)
Ans. No

Ques. 12.—Have you sold, conveyed, or mortgaged any portion of the land; and if so, to whom and for what purpose?
Ans. No

Ques. 13.—Have you any personal property of any kind elsewhere than on this claim? (If so, describe the same, and state where the same is kept.)
Ans. I have Cattle and Horses that are not on this tract

Sabino Otero

I HEREBY CERTIFY that the foregoing testimony was read to the claimant before being subscribed, and was sworn to before me this 10th day of September 1892.

[SEE NOTE ON FOURTH PAGE.]

[signature] Register

* (In case the party is of foreign birth a certified transcript from the court records of his declaration of intention to become a citizen, or of his naturalization, or a copy thereof, certified by the officer taking this proof, must be filed with the case. Evidence of naturalization is only required in final (five year) homestead cases.)

Figure 5.5. Sabino Otero Homestead Proof – Testimony of Claimant filed 9/10/1892. Affidavit informs other cattle and horses were maintained outside of Baboquivari. (U.S. Bureau of Land Management).

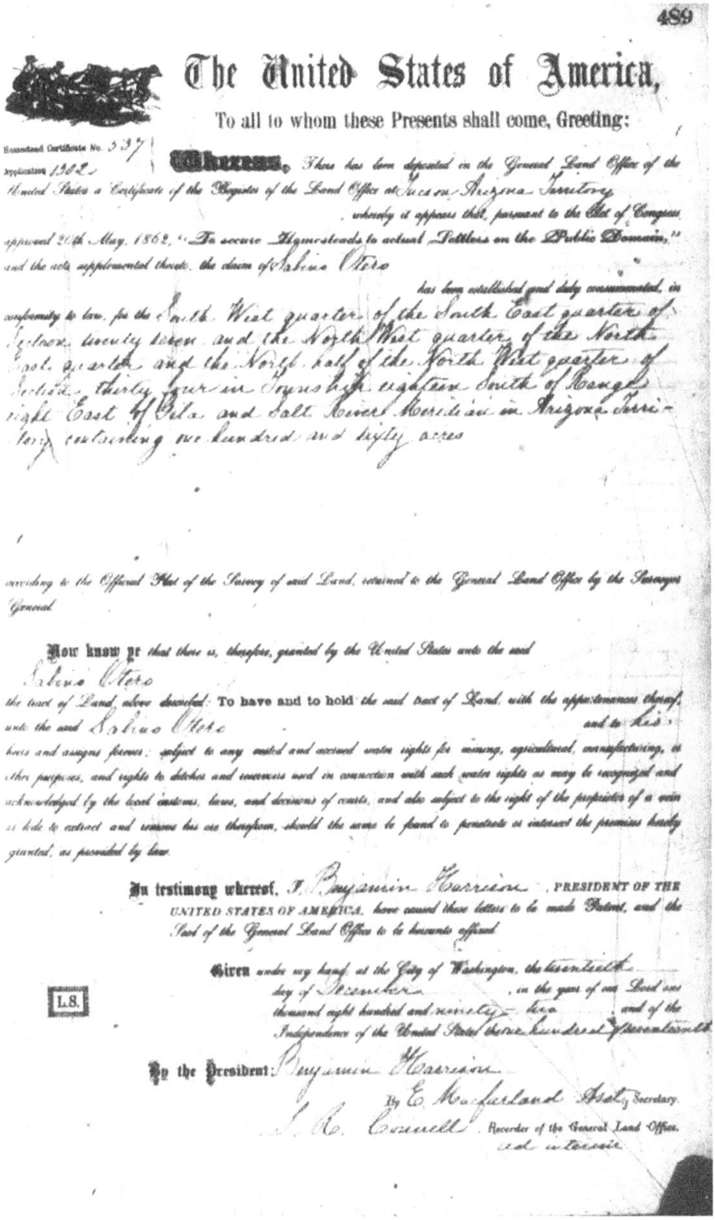
489

The United States of America,

To all to whom these Presents shall come, Greeting:

Homestead Certificate No. 537

Application 1302

Whereas, There has been deposited in the General Land Office of the United States a Certificate of the Register of the Land Office at Tucson Arizona Territory, whereby it appears that, pursuant to the Act of Congress approved 20th May, 1862, "To secure Homesteads to actual Settlers on the Public Domain," and the acts supplemental thereto, the claim of Sabino Otero has been established and duly consummated, in conformity to law, for the South West quarter of the South East quarter of Section twenty seven and the North West quarter of the North East quarter and the North half of the North West quarter of Section thirty four in Township eighteen South of Range eight East of Gila and Salt River Meridian in Arizona Territory containing one hundred and sixty acres

according to the Official Plat of the Survey of said Land, returned to the General Land Office by the Surveyor General.

Now know ye that there is, therefore, granted by the United States unto the said Sabino Otero the tract of Land above described: To have and to hold the said tract of Land, with the appurtenances thereof, unto the said Sabino Otero and to his heirs and assigns forever; subject to any vested and accrued water rights for mining, agricultural, manufacturing, or other purposes, and rights to ditches and reservoirs used in connection with such water rights as may be recognized and acknowledged by the local customs, laws, and decisions of courts, and also subject to the right of the proprietor of a vein or lode to extract and remove his ore therefrom, should the same be found to penetrate or intersect the premises hereby granted, as provided by law.

In testimony whereof, I, Benjamin Harrison, PRESIDENT OF THE UNITED STATES OF AMERICA, have caused these letters to be made Patent, and the Seal of the General Land Office to be hereunto affixed.

Given under my hand, at the City of Washington, the twentieth day of December, in the year of our Lord one thousand eight hundred and ninety-two, and of the Independence of the United States the one hundred and seventeenth.

L.S.

By the President: Benjamin Harrison

By E. McFarland Asst. Secretary.

I. R. Connell Recorder of the General Land Office. ad interim

Figure 5.6. Sabino Otero Homestead Certificate No. 537, signed by E. McFarland, Assistant Secretary for President Benjamin Harrison on 12/20/1892. (U.S. Bureau of Land Management).

Before any homestead application could be perfected, a surveyor had to measure the land. Sabino's homestead at Baboquivari was no exception. Township lines were initially surveyed by U.S. Surveyor J.C. Smith from November 10 to 14, 1884. The Township lines and subdivisions were subsequently re-surveyed by George J. Roskruge from September 20 to 27, and Oct 5 to 9, 1886. The surveyor's plat was filed in the Land Office on March 27, 1888 by U.S. Surveyor General John Hise and recorded in the Land Office on March 27, 1888. Upon close inspection of the surveyors' plat, then existing landmarks were noted. Leon's Gulch was located in Section 3 and 4, not far from the house and as was a well that belonged to Leon in Section 5. A house and corral owned by Redondo was noted in the Northeast quarter (¼) of Section 17. South of Redondo was the Contreras house, well and corral located in the Southwest quarter (¼) of Section 21. Continuing south in the path of seasonal cattle roundups was Otero Gulch that traversed Sections 27, 33 and 34. Further down in the Southeast quarter ¼ of Section 27 was the Sabino Otero house and corral.

Three months later on December 7, 1889, Sabino Otero formally filed the Final Homestead application number 1302 at the Tucson Land Office which was certified by Herbert Brown, Register of the Land Office. The requisite sixteen-dollar fee was paid to Receiver Chas Drake[11] and the application formally filed on December 17, 1889. The one hundred and sixty acres (160) requested were for the Southwest quarter (¼) of Southeast (¼) Section twenty-seven (27) and Northwest quarter (¼) of Northeast quarter (¼) and North half (½) of Northwest quarter (¼) of Section Thirty-Four (34) of Township 18 South Range 8 East of the Gila and Salt River Meridian.

The homestead application was granted under the authority of Section No. 2290, U.S. Revised Statutes.[12] Three years later, Sabino Otero Homestead Certificate Number 537 was issued on December 20, 1892, signed by E. McFarland, Assistant Secretary for President Benjamin Harrison to confirm Sabino Otero's ownership of the homesteaded lands at the Baboquivari Mountains.[13]

ELKHORN RANCH AND THE FAMILIA BALLESTEROS

The Sabino Otero Affidavit in support of his Homestead Application reported several improvements to the land at Baboquivari, including an adobe house, a dam and four corrals. According to the Elkhorn Ranch website, the ranch is located at the site of the historic Otero homestead at Baboquivari. This asserted fact was independently confirmed after United States Bureau of Land Management (BLM) plats were obtained. Research efforts were taken to determine if any structures or artifacts survived at the Sabino Otero Baboquivari homestead. Elkhorn Ranch at Baboquivari is currently under the stewardship of Charley and Mary Miller and Tom and Anne Miller, third generation Millers, who run the dude ranch with a careful eye towards conservation.[14] Mary Miller proprietor of Elkhorn Ranch was contacted in September of 2016. After introductions were exchanged and a brief telephone conversation regarding Otero family land research efforts, Mary generously extended an invitation to visit Elkhorn Ranch and discuss the Altar Valley's rich ranching history and its connection to the Otero family. A date was set. An important chapter of Otero land history was about to reveal itself.

Available records reported Jim Converse of the Tanque Verde Ranch helped Ernest and Grace Miller locate the Fresnal Ranch School location during the spring of 1946.[15] The Millers purchased the Elkhorn Ranch as a winter complement to their Elkhorn Ranch operation in Montana.[16] The original Elkhorn Ranch was established in Montana in 1922.[17] Located at an altitude of 3,700 feet at the mouth of Sabino Canyon, the 10,000 acre Arizona Elkhorn Ranch celebrates its rich legacy from two historic properties: the Peters' Fresnal Ranch School and Sabino Otero homestead. With a better understanding of the Otero/Elkhorn connection, it was soon time to visit Elkhorn. Following is a recap of this memorable visit:

With research partner Philip Halpenny at the wheel, we drove across the often-bumpy dirt road towards Elkhorn Ranch. We exchanged independent research findings about the ranch property in rapid-fire. My heart raced with anticipation. As I gazed out the passenger window inhaling the breathtaking 360-degree view of the desert land, Philip insightfully shared, "it remains virtually in the same condition as when your ancestors lived and ranched on the land." Multi-colored overgrown brush adjacent dusty horse trails scattered across the desert to unknown destinations.

Eventually we arrived at Elkhorn Ranch. As we drove through the mesquite-fenced entrance of the ranch, we were unaware of the area's historic significance. As Philip parked his truck near the Elkhorn Ranch office, Mary Miller's welcoming smile greeted us. After a short walk to the Elkhorn office and pleasantries were exchanged, we soon discovered that Elkhorn lacked copies of the Otero homestead land documents. We were honored to provide copies of the Sabino Otero homestead land records for Elkhorn Ranch use. During that brief moment in time, history formally bound the Otero and Miller families forever based on our mutual ties to the land.

After we discussed Otero land improvements listed on the Sabino homestead application, Mary offered to lead us to one of the greatest remaining artifacts of the old Sabino Otero homestead – a dam. This was the first major discovery at Baboquivari. As we followed Mary's upbeat stride past the mesquite-fenced trail, I recalled that the reservoir built by Sabino Otero was noticeably absent from BLM's 1888 U.S. Surveyor's plat. Previous Otero land research revealed an 1891 news article that reported Sabino Otero built a dam located eight miles above Poso Bueno in a large canyon known as Sabino Canyon. This rock and sediment dam served Sabino's ranch operations for at least six years beginning 1884. Over time, the center of the dam weakened and washed away during the fall of 1890. The reservoir was replaced by an engine and well adequate to furnish abundant water to Otero ranch operations at Baboquivari.[18]

We arrived at the site of the dam. Nothing could have prepared us for what we saw. This 132-year-old dam was virtually in the same condition as when its center broke in 1890, both ends of its supporting walls intact. Large rocks that once retained massive volumes of water were scattered across the gulch. Remaining debris looked as if the dam had just busted. Otero land research, news articles, maps, plats, Philip's expertise as a retired hydrologist, and Mary's knowledge of local oral history converged as we gazed upon the engineering marvel. As Philip stood atop the 1880s Otero dam, he deemed the dam a significant Arizona discovery because it dwarfed other known contemporaneously-built man-made dams. The average dam size during the 1880s was four to five feet in height. Due to its composition and size, Philip speculated that Sabino must have hired an engineer to build the dam.

Figure 5.7. Trail at Elkhorn Ranch on the section once known as the Sabino Otero Homestead at Baboquivari. Trail leads to the Sabino Otero Dam. (Photograph by the author).

Figure 5.8. Corrals at the Elkhorn Ranch built in the same fashion as corrals during the Spanish and Mexican Arizona eras. (Photograph by the author).

Figure 5.9. Sabino Otero Dam at Baboquivari. Philip Halpenny, historian and retired hydrologist, stands on the top of the dam. The dam is approximately three feet wide and 130 feet across. It remains in near identical condition as when the dam washed out in 1890. A large monument, it can be seen from Google Earth. (Photograph by the author).

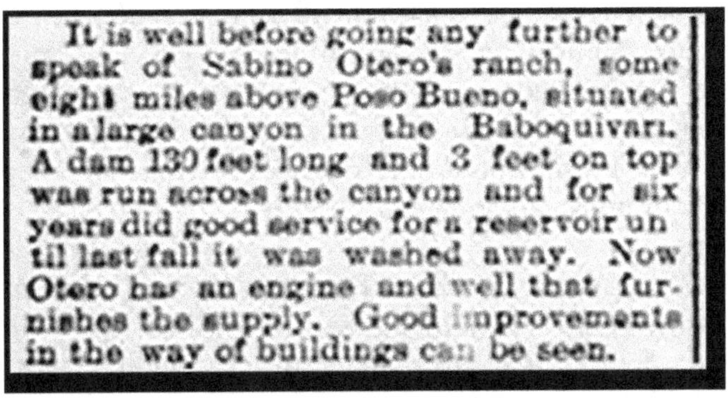

It is well before going any further to speak of Sabino Otero's ranch, some eight miles above Poso Bueno, situated in a large canyon in the Baboquivari. A dam 130 feet long and 3 feet on top was run across the canyon and for six years did good service for a reservoir until last fall it was washed away. Now Otero has an engine and well that furnishes the supply. Good improvements in the way of buildings can be seen.

Figure 5.10. Newspaper clipping describes the Otero dam at Baboquivari from *Arizona Weekly Citizen*. Tucson: 7/4/1891. (Public domain).

Before we left Elkhorn Ranch, Mary Miller shared one more important piece of information that soon led to a second major discovery. In Mary's cell phone was a photograph of Jorge Castillo Ballesteros, father of Tucsonense David Ballesteros. She said that David and his family may have once lived in Sabino's adobe house at Baboquivari. She suggested we follow up with him to discover what he might know about the property. As I clutched the paper with David's phone number in my hands, my heart raced with nervous excitement. When I phoned him that weekend, I could not have imagined what information this new contact would soon provide.

A deep male voice with seasoned cowboy charm answered my call. It was David Jesus Valles Ballesteros. I introduced myself and we discussed the nature of my research. David was open to meeting with me in person after I shared that I received his phone number from Mary Miller of Elkhorn Ranch. It was obvious that David maintains a true personal, well-established relationship with the Miller family. He said that when Ernest and Grace Miller purchased Elkhorn Ranch in 1946, the Sabino Otero house and corrals were intact. He provided me with a brief verbal sketch of his family's connection to the Miller/Otero land.[19] Having confirmed there was more to learn from David about the historic Otero ranch property at Baboquivari, a date was quickly set for a face-to-face meeting.

On September 17, 2016, Philip Halpenny, my husband James and I set out to meet with David Ballesteros at the Famous Sam's Restaurant & Bar located at Grant and Silverbell, Tucson. Our small research group entered the establishment. As cowboy guitar music played in the background, we noticed a dark-skinned mustached man standing across the room wearing a western shirt, dark-blue Levis and a shiny belt buckle. He clasped some papers near his chest as his sparkling green eyes peered at us from beneath his beige wide-brimmed cowboy hat. Immediately, we sensed it was David.

Figure 5.11. Dionicio Martinez Ballesteros (on horseback) and son Angel Castillo Ballesteros (standing far left by fence wearing a black hat) at the corrals once owned by Sabino Otero. (Courtesy of David Jesus Valles Ballesteros).

After the men shook hands and I grabbed a quick hug, we sat down at a smallish table, ordered drinks and the conversation rushed forward like a steer jumping out of a shoot at rodeo. David shared that his grandfather, father and uncle were trusted local ranch hands hired by Ernest and Grace Miller to help round up cattle on the newly purchased Elkhorn Ranch.[20] His grandfather Dionicio Martinez Ballesteros and his wife Virginia Castillo Ballesteros emigrated from Mexico in 1915 when their son Jorge was an infant.[21] Dionicio, known to the U.S. federal authorities as a Villista,[22] passed down his knowledge of being a vaquero to his sons according to Mexican tradition. Having conducted some research on David's family in anticipation of our meeting, I gave him copies of documents that substantiated his family's oral history about his grandfather's interesting past as a Villista.

David continued, in 1930 Dionicio and sons Jorge and Rafael Castillo Ballesteros worked for the John F. King's Anvil Ranch while the Ballesteros family was living at Mr. Steven's Ranch. In 1935, Jorge married Esperanza Valles. By 1943, Jorge, Esperanza and their children moved to King's Redondo Ranch as Jorge continued to work for John King. Finally, in 1946, Jorge and his family moved into the historic Sabino Otero adobe house at Baboquivari, then-owned by Brian Peters as part of the Fresnal Ranch School for Boys. As David conveyed his deeply personal story, he shared treasured family photographs with us. One by one, each photo added depth to David's story connecting names to the faces. David Ballesteros' assistance was highly important to the *Terrenos* research. His first-hand knowledge and prized images verified the existence of the Otero house, the second significant discovery at Baboquivari.

Figure 5.12. Jorge Castillo Ballesteros at the Elkhorn Ranch property circa 1940s. (Courtesy David Jesus Valles Ballesteros).

A month after we first met David in person at Tucson, David Ballesteros and Mary Miller arranged for a follow up meeting at the Elkhorn Ranch. John King, his lovely wife Pat (owners of the Anvil Ranch), Charley and Mary Miller, Philip Halpenny, and my husband James and I attended. We spent an enjoyable afternoon discussing 19th and 20th century history of Altar Valley, the Sabino Otero homestead, among other topics related to ranching. During the conversation, John King and Charley Miller shared local oral history which suggests Tucsonense Pepe Ronstadt purchased the Otero Baboquivari site from Sabino Otero.

Figure 5.13. Occupants of the Sabino Otero house at Baboquivari circa 1940s: (front row) David Jesus Valles Ballesteros and Ernesto Valles Ballesteros (back row) Esperanza Valles Ballesteros and husband Jorge Castillo Ballesteros. Ballesteros children not in photo were George Jr., Herminia, Armida, Olivia and Grace. (Courtesy David Jesus Valles Ballesteros).

After the delightful conversation wrapped up, it was almost time to leave. Before our departure from Elkhorn Ranch, Charley and Mary met us at the mesquite fences that we passed on our way into the ranch. Recalling that U.S. Bureau of Land Management records reflect that the Otero Corrals were immediately located adjacent to the Otero house and Gulch. Charley confirmed that the lower corrals located at the entrance of Elkhorn Ranch were once the Otero corrals. *See* Figure 5.8. This was the third major discovery at Elkhorn. Philip, whose current work includes study of Spanish colonial history, explained that the fencing is reminiscent of colonial Spanish fencing where posts were used to buttress intertwined mesquite branches. This style of fencing at the historic Otero homesteaded land was a tradition likely passed down from Sabino's Spanish ancestors who lived at Tubac in 1789.[23]

Figure 5.14. This is the only known image that exists of the Sabino Otero house at Baboquivari. Pictured is Jorge Castillo Ballesteros circa 1940s in front of the Otero house. The house was demolished after it was no longer habitable. (Courtesy David Jesus Valles Ballesteros).

Remnants of the Otero corrals remain but have been reinforced by subsequent property owners. Before David Ballesteros left the group, he explained that his family helped improve the lower corrals. The Ballesteros and other vaqueros built a watering trough for the Miller family's ranch needs. Charley Miller pointed out the names of several vaqueros visibly etched in concrete at the trough. Charley then guided us through another fenced-in area at the lower corral. We followed a well-established horse trail to the location of the historic Sabino Otero adobe house. Charley recalled that the Otero house was still intact when he was a teenager. It had become infested with bees after the Ballesteros family had moved out of the home. In addition to the bees, the roof fell in on the house.

As a vibrant dude ranch with a trail adjacent the dilapidated Otero house, the Miller's became concerned that the bees would bother or attack horseback riders. With the house simply too deteriorated to refurbish, the Miller family made the wise decision to tear down the structure. All that remains of the Otero house are broken pieces of the house's foundation. For a brief moment, I stood with Charley on the largest section of the Otero house foundation ruins and felt deeply grateful that this artifact remains to remind others that the Otero family once lived, ranched and thrived at Baboquivari.

Figure 5.15. Third generation Elkhorn Ranch owner Charles Miller standing on the Sabino Otero house ruins. The Otero house fell into disrepair. The house roof had fallen in and the structure subsequently infested by bees. The house was ultimately demolished by the Miller family to protect its visiting horseback riders from injury. (Photograph by the author).

Elkhorn Ranch at Baboquivari proved to be an important part of Otero land history. Among the most treasured images shared by David Ballesteros (now affectionately known as Pancho because of his grandfather's ties to Pancho Villa) is the only known image of the historic Otero adobe house at Baboquivari. See Figure 5.14. With David's gracious permission, it is shared here with the public for the first time. In the image, his father Jorge Castillo Ballesteros is on horseback located immediately in front of the Sabino Otero house built in the 1880s. A siding addition subsequently added appears in the image. Like Charley and Mary Miller of Elkhorn Ranch, the Ballesteros family are forever linked to the Otero family because of their mutual ties to a *terreno* once owned by the Oteros. For history's sake, I am thankful that the Otero dam, corrals, and foundation of the Otero adobe home remain preserved at Elkhorn Ranch.

Of all the historic Otero family properties, the Elkhorn Ranch singularly conserves its dude ranch lands in virtually the same condition as it would have been when Sabino Otero lived and ranched on the land. Although the Otero house has been demolished and the massive man-made dam washed away, those ruins remind us of the Otero cattle operations that once thrived at Baboquivari. Now, when you look across the canyon and rolling hills, you can almost imagine the ghostly images herds of cattle roaming freely across the Altar Valley range.

REVENTON ~ AGUA LINDA FARM

Another historic ranch with a connection to the Otero family is an early Spanish land grant called El Reventon,[24] known today, in part, as the Agua Linda Farm, a wedding and special events venue and La Esperanza ranch in Amado, AZ. Reventon was originally known as "El Reventon de los Patos,"[25] translated loosely to "where the ducks explode." Carlos Ronstadt purchased the ranch from the estate of Teofilo Otero in July of 1949 for the bargain price of just over $100,000.00. Ronstadt farmed about 400 acres.[26] The ranch's past reminds us of Arizona's Civil War history and explains why Clara Martinez Otero likely refrained from her valid claim as primary heir-at-law of the Otero Land Grant after her husband Manuel Otero died in 1870.

Shortly after Arizona became a possession of the United States by virtue of the Gadsden Purchase, a Michigan native named Elias Brevoort purchased El Reventon Ranch in March of 1859.[27] He built a palatial adobe house, large corral and garden that cost him a hefty investment of sixteen thousand dollars.[28] It is estimated that Brevoort had at least one thousand head of cattle, in addition to hogs and sheep.[29] El Reventon is located on the lower Santa Cruz River approximately eight miles north of Tubac in present-day Amado. Brevoort was a colorful man. He was the first sutler[30] at Fort Buchanan in 1856, author of *New Mexico,*[31] part-owner of the Patagonia/Mowry Mine, and an alleged Confederate spy. During the late 1850's, Brevoort was sent on a mission into Mexico to retrieve some wagons and teams for the United States Government, but he never returned to the ranch.[32] As southern Arizona became hotly contested during the American Civil War, the abandoned Reventon Ranch became "Camp El Reventon" and was used as a fort by the California Volunteers from July-August, 1862 and in April of 1864.[33]

Growing negative sentiment against Confederate sympathizers caused United States District Attorney Almon Gage, Esq. for the Arizona Territory to initiate six individual lawsuits at the First Judicial District Court of Pima County between May and June, 1864 under Sec. 3, Art. 3. of the U.S. Constitution that says, "Congress shall have power to declare the punishment of treason, but no attainder of treason shall work corruption of blood or forfeiture, except during the life of the person attained."[34]

Figure 5.16. Maria Manuela de Quesse (left), Maria Clara Martinez de Otero (center), Gabriela Otero known as Sister Clara Otero (right). (Arizona Historical Society Image 42936).

In this instance, the lawsuits were intended to confiscate the property of individuals alleged to have engaged in war against the United States. The defendants were Charles Lauer, F.A. Neville, Alfred Frear, Granville H. Oury, Palatine Robinson and Elias Brevoort for his El Reventon Ranch. Through a series of misfortunes including the loss of Gage's "carpet bag" that held the important papers and briefs in the case which was carried away and swallowed up by the swollen Salt River, District Attorney Gage was unable to serve the defendants. On July 4, 1868, President Andrew Johnson granted a full pardon and amnesty for all persons and the full restoration of rights of Confederate enemies.[35] Brevoort never returned to Amado to reclaim El Reventon. A squatter known as "old Jimmy Caruthers" soon began cultivating the El Reventon fields and yielded crops of corn and wheat. Eventually, marauding Apaches stole his stock and broke him financially leaving the ranch abandoned yet again.[36]

As El Reventon Ranch slowly fell into further disrepair, the Otero family was busy expanding its land holdings. This brings us to a curious point of history. Otero family history failed to explain why the Otero siblings petitioned for the Otero Land Grant of 1789 to the exclusion of their living mother. As the widow of Manuel Otero, last heir-at-law of the Otero land grant, she had standing to petition for the lands at Tubac. However, historic documents reveal that Maria Clara Martinez Otero had acquired an ample ranch of her own, El Reventon, which Clara, her daughter Manuela Otero de Quesse, and granddaughter Ana Maria Comadurán took possession of in 1875.[37] This is one of the only ranches at that time run by women.

While the Otero petition was pending before the General Land Office of the Territory of Arizona and subsequently the Court of Private Land Claims, Clara Martinez Otero filed Homestead Application Number 1374 for land that included the abandoned El Reventon Ranch. Clara's application was claimed under the 1862 Homestead Act and consisted of, "Lot numbered four of Section seven and the Lots numbered one, two and three of Section Eighteen in Township Twenty-South of Range Thirteen East of Gila and Salt River Meridian in Arizona Territory, containing one hundred and sixty acres and fifty-two hundredths of an acre."[38] The U.S. Bureau of Land Management plat reflects that Clara's claim to El

Reventon is located off the frontage road in Amado where the Agua Linda Farm is located today.

Clara Otero passed away after her federal land patent was finalized in 1896 by President Grover Cleveland but before January 1899 when Sabino Otero issued a final notice as the administrator of Clara M. Otero's estate. Her death prior to January 1899 explains why the building on Clara's homestead was identified as the Sabino Otero house when Township 20 at Amado was resurveyed in 1901 by land office surveyor Philip Contzen.[39] Sabino acquired the Reventon Ranch after his mother's death to the exclusion of his siblings. After Sabino's death, his brother Teofilo inherited the land under section VII of Sabino Otero's Last Will and Testament saying:

> I give, devise and bequeath to my beloved brother, Teofilo Otero, all the rest, residue and remainder of my property, of every kind, character, nature and description wherever same may be situate, of which I shall die seized and possessed, and to which I shall be entitled at the time of my decease.[40]

El Reventon Ranch was listed and properly identified in the real estate holdings of the estate of Sabino Otero appraised by George W. Atkinson, Fred Ronstadt, and Carlos C. Jacome.[41] The Reventon property remained in Teofilo Otero's possession and he expanded the land from his mother's original 160 acre homestead to approximately 1,572.45 acres according to Teofilo Otero's Last Will and Testament that describes El Reventon's boundaries and the Southern Pacific's right-of-way through Sections 13, 24 and 30 at Amado.[42]

Figure 5.17. A young Ana Maria Comadurán. She helped her grandmother Maria Clara Martinez run the Reventon Ranch. Image taken by H. Buehman, Landscape and General Photographer of Tucson, AZ. (Courtesy Teresa Anita Coenen Seaman).

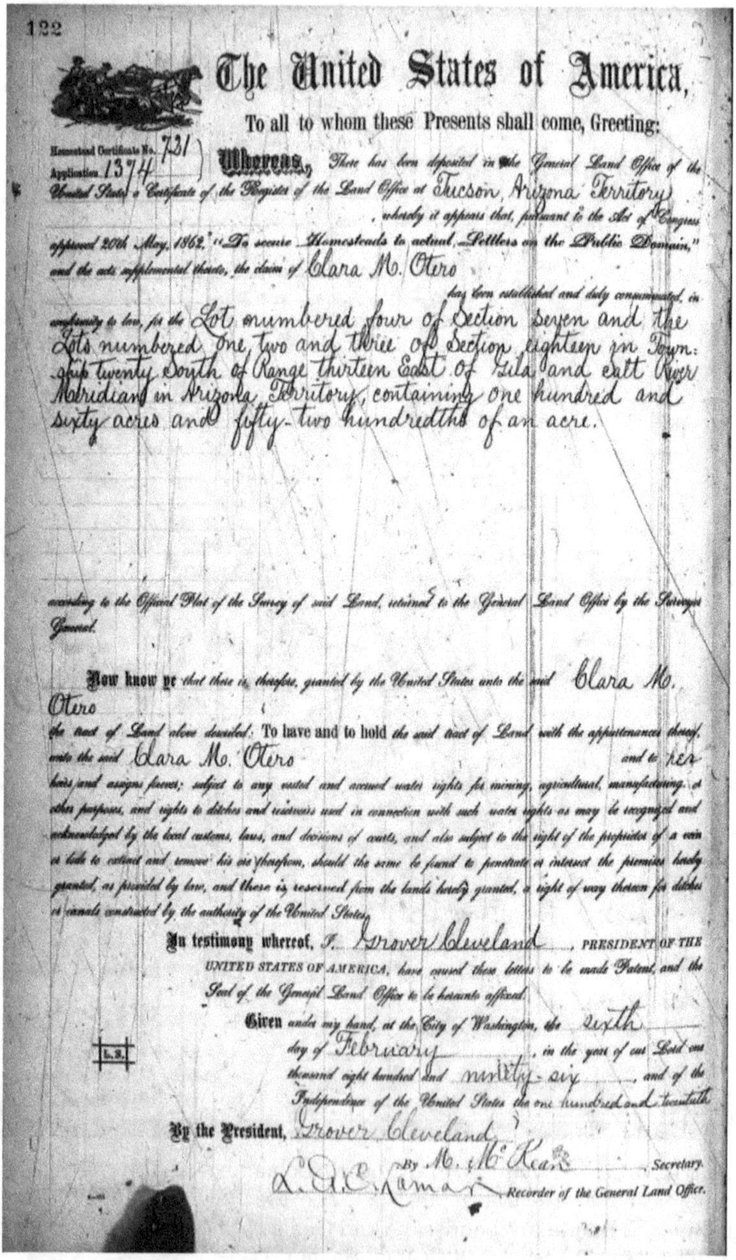

132

The United States of America,

To all to whom these Presents shall come, Greeting:

Homestead Certificate No. 731
Application 1374

Whereas, There has been deposited in the General Land Office of the United States a Certificate of the Register of the Land Office at Tucson, Arizona Territory, whereby it appears that, pursuant to the Act of Congress approved 20th May, 1862, "To secure Homesteads to actual Settlers on the Public Domain," and the acts supplemental thereto, the claim of Clara M. Otero has been established and duly consummated, in conformity to law, for the Lot numbered four of Section seven and the Lots numbered One, two and three of Section eighteen in Township twenty South of Range thirteen East of Gila and Salt River Meridian in Arizona Territory, containing One hundred and sixty acres and fifty-two hundredths of an acre.

according to the Official Plat of the Survey of said Land, returned to the General Land Office by the Surveyor General.

Now know ye that there is, therefore, granted by the United States unto the said Clara M. Otero the tract of Land above described; To have and to hold the said tract of Land with the appurtenances thereof, unto the said Clara M. Otero and to her heirs and assigns forever; subject to any vested and accrued water rights for mining, agricultural, manufacturing, or other purposes, and rights to ditches and reservoirs used in connection with such water rights as may be recognized and acknowledged by the local customs, laws, and decisions of courts, and also subject to the right of the proprietor of a vein or lode to extract and remove his ore therefrom, should the same be found to penetrate or intersect the premises hereby granted, as provided by law, and there is reserved from the lands hereby granted, a right of way thereon for ditches or canals constructed by the authority of the United States.

In testimony whereof, I, Grover Cleveland, PRESIDENT OF THE UNITED STATES OF AMERICA, have caused these letters to be made Patent, and the Seal of the General Land Office to be hereunto affixed.

Given under my hand, at the City of Washington, the sixth day of February, in the year of our Lord one thousand eight hundred and ninety-six, and of the Independence of the United States the one hundred and twentieth.

L.S.

By the President, Grover Cleveland.

By M. McKean, Secretary.

L. Q. C. Lamar, Recorder of the General Land Office.

Figure. 5.18. AZ Patent 321573. Clara Martinez for her homestead of Reventon Ranch. (U.S. Bureau of Land Management).

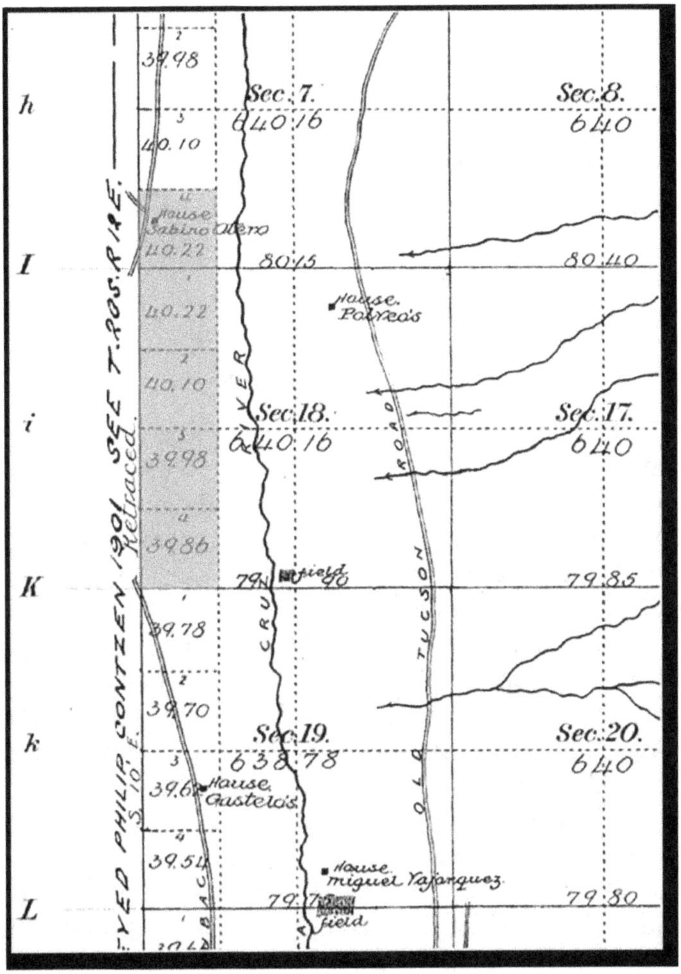

Figure 5.19. Plat of the Maria Clara Martinez Otero lands at Reventon. (U.S. Bureau of Land Management. Edited by Philip Halpenny).

History also suggests that the Ronstadt family of Tucson became an unintended beneficiary of the Sabino and Teofilo Otero estates as it was somehow able to purchase El Reventon, the Baboquivari Ranch, and other Otero real estate at bargain basement prices. Carlos Ronstadt sold a portion of El Reventon known then as the Agua Linda Farm to the Arthur Lowe in 1955. Lowe's family has since retained ownership of Agua Linda Farm under the stewardship of Regina Lowe and her son Steward and his wife Laurel.[43] Although El Reventon and The Agua Linda Farms are memorialized as the sprawling ranch once owned by Carlos Ronstadt for six years, history reminds that Reventon was the final home of Otero family matriarch Clara Martinez Otero and a real estate holding of the Otero land grant family for nearly three-quarters of a century.[44]

MÁS TERRENOS

In addition to the Baboquivari homestead and El Reventon Ranch, Sabino Otero held other real estate interests. In August of 1877, Sabino filed a claim of 640 acres under the Desert Land Act in Pima County.[45] In April of 1884, he located the Callahan's mill site at the Pajarito Mountains,[46] a small mountain range at the Tumacácori Highlands at southwest Santa Cruz County, AZ close to the international border between Mexico and the USA.[47] Later the same year, Sabino purchased the San Antonio Mine, San Antonio Mill Site at Baboquivari Mountains near Tucson, AZ, and the Aliso Mill Site. At the same time, he also acquired Lot 28 ½ feet by 200 feet on Main Street at Nogales, AZ for $500.00 from L. Ephraim.[48] In 1891, Sabino acquired a prestigious lot located on Meyer Street on the corner near the Palace Hotel for $3,000.00, then-occupied by a Chinese grocery.[49]

Rancho de Otero's prosperity allowed the Otero family to gain economic influence by purchasing real estate throughout Southern Arizona until Teofilo Otero's death in 1941. The following non-exclusive list of properties reflects additional *terrenos* previously owned by the Otero family of Tubac. Parties to the transactions are listed along with any available property descriptions.

November 15, 1902. Mining Location.[50]
Sabino Otero.
Puerto Mill Site. Claims 466 ½ feet square located about 4 miles in a northerly direction from the town of Tubac on the trail which leads from Tubac to Arivaca and is about 2 miles in a northerly direction from the Aliso mining claim.

February 6, 1906. Homestead Land Patent.
Lot 4 of Section 7 and Lots 1, 2 and 3

April 9, 1912. Bargain and Sale Deed.[51]
Santiago R. Gastelum, Carmen Gastelum, Librada Gastelum, A.C. Kingsley, Martha Kingsley, Leon C. Gastelum, Anna Maria Gastelum, Guadalupe Gastelum, Jose Gastelum, Dolores Gastelum, Nicolas Gastelum, Manuela Gastelum, Ygnacio Gastelum, Tomas Gastelum of Pima and Santa Cruz counties to Sabino Otero.
All that portion of Section 7 Township 20 South, Range 13 East, commencing at the Southwest corner of the Northeast quarter of the Southwest (NE¼SW¼) quarter of Section 7 in Township 20 South, Range 13 East, and running East 5 chains; then North 20 chains; then West 5 Chains; then South 20 chains to the place of beginning, and containing 10 acres.

June 4, 1909. Bargain and Sale Deed.[52]
Peter G. Smith to Sabino Otero.
The East one-half of the Northwest (E½NW¼) quarter, the northeast quarter of the Southwest (NE¼SW¼) quarter, and the Northwest quarter of the Northeast (NW¼NE¼) quarter of Section 18 in Township 20 South, Range 13 East.

December 27, 1909. Bargain and Sale Deed.[53]
Manuel Otero and Angela de Otero to Sabino Otero.
All of lots 4 and the Southeast quarter of the Southwest (SE¼SW¼) of Section 18 and lot 1 and the Northeast quarter of the Northwest (NE¼NW¼) quarter section of Section 19 in Township 20 South, Range 13 East.

November 11, 1915. Quit-Claim Deed.[54]
John Yatze and Josefa Yatze to Teofilo Otero.
All of lots 15, 16, 17, 18 and 19 of Section 5 and all of lots 6 and 7 of Section 8 in Township 21 South, Range 13 East.

January 15, 1917. Bargain and Sale Deed.[55]
Jose Olivas and Josefa Olivas to Teofilo Otero.
All of Southwest (SW¼) quarter of Section 32 in Township 20, Range 13 East containing 160 acres excluding strip of land 300 feet wide, lying 150 on west side of and 150 feet wide on east side of the surveyed center line of the Tucson & Nogales Railroad across the Southwest (SW¼) quarter of Section 32.

June 27, 1918. Quit-Claim Deed.[56]
Adolfo Alcantar and Guadalupe Solaris de Alcantar to Teofilo Otero.
All of Lot 4 Section 5 in Township 21 South, Range 13 East containing 39.48 acres.

August 17, 1918. Warranty Deed.[57]
Rudolph Bachman and Dolores Bachman to Teofilo Otero.
Lots 3 and 4 of Section 13 and lots 1 and 2 of Section 24 in Township 20, Range 13 East.

December 23, 1918. Bargain and Sale Deed.[58]
W.A. O'Conner (Judge of the Superior Court of Arizona and ex-officio Trustee of the Townsite of Tubac land patent) to Teofilo Otero.
Lots 19, 25, 26 in Block 7 and all of lot 32 in Block 7, lying north of the north boundary line of Baca Float No. 3 as delineated on Glore map of 7/6/1916.

August 28, 1919. Bargain and Sale Deed.[59]
Manuel Rodriguez and Rosario de Rodriguez to Teofilo Otero.
Lot 2 Section 30 in Township 20 South, Range 13 East.

January 28, 1921. Bargain and Sale Deed.[60]
Bibiano O. Gastelum and Josefa A. de Gastelum to Teofilo Otero.
Southhalf of the southeast (S½SE¼) quarter, and the Northwest quarter of the southeast (NW¼SE¼) quarter of section 18 in Township 20 South, Range 13 East, containing 160 acres.

March 11, 1921. Quit Claim Deed.[61]
Francisca Allen and John D. Allen of Tucson to Teofilo Otero.
Southeast (SE¼) quarter of Section 31 and that part of the west half of the Southwest (W½SW¼) quarter of Section 32; Township 20 South, Range 13 East.

June 27, 1921. Bargain and Sale Deed.[62]
N.A. Gonzales and Maria S. Gonzales to Teofilo Otero.
All of lots 3, 5 and 6 in Section 5 of Township 21; Range 13 East; containing 140 acres being the same property conveyed by P.C. Brena and Concha Brena to N.A. Gonzales under unrecorded deed of 6/27/1921.

July 11, 1921. Bargain and Sale Deed.[63]
Mariana Campas and Domitilla Campas to Teofilo Otero.
Southwest quarter of the Southeast (SW¼SE¼) quarter of Section 5 and the fractional northeast quarter of the Northwest (NE¼NW¼) quarter of Township 21 South, Range 13 East; containing 66.39 acres together with any water and water rights, ditch and ditch rights.

May 5, 1924. Bargain and Sale Deed.[64]
Jose Salcido and Carlota K. Salcido of Tucson to Teofilo Otero.
South one-half of the Southeast (S½SE¼) quarter Section 19 and the North one-half of the Northeast (N½NE¼) quarter of Section 30 in Township 20 South, Range 13 East, containing 160 acres.

December 10, 1924. Warranty Deed.[65]
Dennis P. Gleason of Tucson to Teofilo Otero.
Northwest quarter of the Northeast (NW¼NE¼) quarter and the Northeast quarter of the Southwest quarter of the Northeast (NE¼SW¼NE¼) quarter of Section 8, Township 21 South, Range 13 East.

March 12, 1925. Bargain and Sale Deed.[66]
Lots 3 and 4 Section 12 and Lots 1 and 2 of Section 13; Township 20 South, Range 12 East; consisting of 146 acres and 160 acres.

March 25, 1925. Bargain and Sale Deed.[67]
Daniel Castro and Ruecinda Castro (location unknown) to Teofilo Otero.
Lots 3 and 4 of Section 24 in Township 20 South, Range 12 East.

August 21, 1925. Bargain and Sale Deed.[68]
Byril A. Parrish and Pastora G. de Parrish to Teofilo Otero.
Southwest quarter of the Southeast (SW¼SE¼) quarter and the Southeast quarter of the Southwest (SE¼SW¼) quarter of Section 6 and the Northwest quarter of the Northeast (NW¼NE¼) quarter and the Northeast quarter of the Northwest (NE¼NW¼) quarter of Section 7; Township 21 South; Range 13 East.

December 8, 1925 Bargain and Sale Deed.[69]
Byril A. Parrish and Pastora G. de Otero to Teofilo Otero.
Lots 5 and 7 and the Northeast quarter of the Southwest (NE¼SW¼) quarter and the Northwest quarter of the Southeast (NW¼SE¼) of section 6; Township 21 South, Range 13 East.

June 18, 1926. Bargain and Sale Deed.[70]
Daniel Castro and Ruecinda Castro to Teofilo Otero.
North half of the Southeast (N½SE¼) quarter of Section 19; Township 20 South, Range 13 East.

February 27, 1927. Bargain and Sale Deed.[71]
Asa A. Crenshaw of Tucson to Teofilo Otero.
Southeast (SE¼) quarter of Section 31 and that part of the West half of the Southwest (W½SW¼) quarter of Section 32; Township 20 South, Range 13 East.

January 29, 1929. Quit Claim Deed.[72]
Francisca Allen, widow, of Tucson to Teofilo Otero.
Lots 1 and 2, the Southeast quarter of the Northwest quarter (SE¼NW¼) and the Southwest quarter of the Northeast (SW¼NE¼) quarter of Section 6; Township 21 South, Range 13 East.

January 29, 1929. Bargain and Sale Deed.[73]
Pinkney R. Fenley (location unknown) to Teofilo Otero.
Lots 1 and 2, the Southeast quarter of the Northwest (SE¼NW¼) quarter and the Southwest quarter of the Northeast (SW¼NE¼) quarter of Section 6; Township 21 South, Range 13 East.

April 19, 1933. Quit Claim Deed.[74]
F.W. Hannah and Ethyl Hanna of Nogales, AZ to Teofilo Otero.
South one-half of Southeast (S½SE¼) quarter of Section 19; Township 20, Range 13; less 4.56 acres R.R. right of way; and North one-half of Northeast (N½NE¼) quarter of Section 30; Township 20, Range 13, less 4/60 acres R.R. right of way containing 150.81 acres.

Teofilo Otero's heavy interest in real estate transactions also included a deed to the West Coast Cattle Company for part of Sections 7-18, Township 15 South, Range 7 East; part of Section 27, Township 16 South, Range 7 East for $10.00 in consideration,[75] and he obtained a mortgage from John T. Clark for parts of Lots 10-11, Block 56 at Tucson, AZ for $2,500.00[76] in December of 1917. The next year in 1918, Teofilo took out a mortgage from Pedro Antillon and wife for parts Lots 10-11, Block 53, Tucson for $2,500.00,[77] and obtained a mortgage for $7,500.00 from Arturo Carrillo and wife.[78]

In December of 1919, Teofilo issued a release to T.J. Hughes *et al.* for Lots 8 and 9, Block 196 at Tucson.[79] He acquired Lot 4, Block 117 at Tucson, AZ from B. Bachmann for $10.00 consideration in March of 1921.[80] Teofilo also took out a mortgage for $8,000.00 from M.M. Montipo for Lot 10, Block 258 at Tucson in September, 1921.[81] In a second land transaction with Arturo Carrillo, Teofilo issued a mortgage to Carrillo recorded on the Pima County Mortgage Book 44, page 135.[82]

To protect his real estate interests, Teofilo defended his *terrenos* when necessary. In one 1919 civil suit, Teofilo filed an action against Abraham Joseph and his wife Rosa for the payment of a $7,500 promissory note secured by a mortgage on Tucson lots.[83] The suit resulted in Teofilo's favor and he received a certificate of sale after purchasing the Joseph land for $8,583.80 at a Sheriff sale.[84]

After Teofilo's death in 1941, the ink was hardly dry on Teofilo Otero's Last Will and Testament and the Teofilo Otero estate litigation had just been settled when Otero land holdings were rapidly sold to outside interests. The home at 39 Driscoll Street between East Pennington and Alameda Streets at Tucson was sold from the Teofilo Otero Estate to Alice J. Aridner and Mabel Elizabeth Whited in August of 1942.[85] It was previously occupied by Teofilo's niece Brijida Castro Coenen, former Otero land grant owner, and her father Mauricio Castro. A business property at West Broadway and South Convent Street was sold from the Teofilo Otero Estate to Mr. and Mrs. Harry O. Juliani, the former chief deputy state attorney general of Arizona for an approximate consideration of $27,500.00.[86]

Of the numerous properties once owned by the Otero family of Tubac, there are a few notable Otero properties that deserve a special recognition in Arizona history: Otero Hall, the Rojas (Otero) House at Tubac, and El Tiradito and the House on Main Street at Tucson.

OTERO HALL (SOLAR)

The Tubac Presidio State Historic Park is the State of Arizona's second state park[87] and focal point of the Tubac Townsite Historic District listed in the National Register of Historic Places.[88] Initial historic buildings and land were gifted by Olga K. Griffin, wife of Frank J.C. Griffin on November 21, 1957 to the "State of Arizona by and through the Arizona State Parks Board" as her sole and separate property. Home to two major archaeological locations, the gifted land was intended "to restore the Presidio of Tubac utilizing said property as the nucleus of said Historical Monument." [89] It consisted of "Lots 8, 9 and 18, Block 7, Tubac Townsite, according to the map thereof dated June, 1916, and recorded in the office of the County Recorder of Santa Cruz County, Arizona, on October 25, 1916, in Book 1 of Maps, at page 7." [90]

Figure 5.20. (above) View of the 1885 Tubac School House to the left and newly built Otero Hall in 1917. (Courtesy Shaw Kinsley. Director Tubac Presidio State Historic Park).

The Tubac Presidio State Historic Park was opened and dedicated on September 28, 1958. Because few *presidio* sites are open nationally to the public for interpretation, the State Park system agreed with Mrs. Griffin that the

Park's "primary purpose [would be] to preserve the ruins of the oldest Spanish Presidio site in Arizona, San Ignacio de Tubac."[91] On March 13, 1993, Otero Hall and the Rojas House were nominated by the Arizona State Park for inclusion in the *Tubac Townsite Historic District* having been reviewed by Jim Woodward, Architectural Historian of Tempe, Arizona on September 1992. Both structures were listed among the twenty-two buildings for recognition in the National Register of Historic Places in 1994.

Figure 5.21. (opposite page at top) 1915 view of the old Spanish Highway/Anza Trail that ran down the center of 1880s Tubac's commercial area. The road passed newly built Otero hall located in the center background. (Courtesy Shaw Kinsley. Director Tubac Presidio State Historic Park).

According to the National Register of Historic Places:

> The Otero Social Hall is a plain, Neo-Classical Revival Style building. It is built with the characteristic hipped gable roof over a rectangular plan, and has a central wood panel door with sidelights. The cave rafters are exposed, illustrating the Bungalow Style influence on its design."[92]

Teofilo Otero deeded Otero Hall and adjacent land to the Tubac School District Number 5 of Santa Cruz County on July 4, 1938. The property was ordered condemned on

April 6, 1973 so that title could vest in favor of the People of the State of Arizona for use as a state park. [93] Though not mentioned in the National Register of Historic Places, Otero Hall is located at the site where the Otero *Solar*, Arizona's first European privately-owned residence, was located having also been used as a store for the people of Tubac.

Figure 5.22. Teofilo Otero (standing) and Sabino Otero (seated) were each known in their own right as Cattle Kings of Tubac. New research reveals these men were also active investors in real estate. These newly-acquired *terrenos* helped the Otero family prosper when drought and the fencing in of open ranges affected the stock raising industry. (Arizona Historical Society Image 9313).

Figure 5.23. Modern view of Otero Hall at the Tubac Presidio State Historic Park. (Photograph by the author).

Figure 5.24. Building on far left predates Otero Hall. This is a view of the Tubac School, hall, church, and presidio grounds from the Rojas House. Luisa Rojas Yoas identified the building on the far left as the hope built by Don Torivio Otero as the *Solar* and was the home where Fernando Otero, Luisa's contemporary, was born. (Courtesy Shaw Kinsley. Tubac Presidio State Historic Park).

OTERO/ROJAS HOUSE

Figure 5.25. 1880s Rojas House was identified on the 1882 Tubac Townsite Map as a building owned by Sabino Otero. The US Register of Historic Places states the Rojas house was built circa late 1880s. This is an apparent error as the building's true ownership was unknown at the time the Rojas House was placed on the Register. Reymundo Rojas likely remodeled the then-existing Otero building or moved into the then-standing structure. (Photograph by the author).

The adobe Rojas House is also listed on the U.S. Department of Interior's National Park Services National Register of Historic Places. It is located across from Otero Hall on the east side of the historic Spanish Highway on Tubac's Presidio State Park and Museum grounds. The Inventory of Historic Buildings in the Tubac Historic District reports that the Rojas House is an "Adobe Row House archtype, with its linear, single story massing punctuated by discrete windows and doors," built circa 1882-1893.[94] In 2006, museum curator for Arizona State Parks Michael Freisinger reported that the Rojas House was built by Reymundo and his wife Inez during the mid-1890s.[95] The house was likely built before the mid-1890s since Francisco Rojas was born at Tubac on November 27, 1889.[96]

According to the 1882 T. Lillie Mercer Tubac Townsite Plat discovered at the Arizona State Archives, Sabino Otero was the owner of an existing building located in the exact location of the Rojas House.[97] Reymundo Rojas immigrated to the United States from Mexico during the same year. According to the 1910 United States Federal Census of Tubac, Reymundo and his son Francisco were employed as general farm laborers.[98] Local Tubac oral history reports that the Rojas men worked at the Rancho de Otero. As Francisco Rojas, son of Reymundo and Inez Rojas, was the only individual with that name on the 1920 U.S. Federal Census of Tubac,[99] it is highly likely that he is the same Francisco Rojas who was employed by Teofilo Otero and was involved in the truck-motorcycle accident whose case reached the Arizona State Supreme Court in 1926.

The Rojas family consisted of Reymundo and Inez, and their children Francisco, Louisa, Jose Maria, and Juanita.[100] Louisa Rojas, wife of William Yoas, was born in the Otero/Rojas house in 1894.[101] She reportedly identified an image of an adobe house at the location of Otero Hall as the original site of the Otero *Solar* and place where Fernando Otero was born. Based on the 1882 T. Lillie Mercer Tubac Townsite Plat, it is unknown whether the building later known as the Rojas House was built on top of the then-standing 1882 Sabino Otero building or if the existing Otero structure was refurbished as a residence by Reymundo Rojas. Like Otero Hall, the Rojas House is adjacent to a historic road at the Tubac Presidio State Park and Museum called Otero Street that once intersected the Old Spanish Royal Highway. The close proximity of these two Otero buildings to the *presidio* at Tubac and the Spanish Highway strongly suggests the Otero family held high social status within Tubac's Spanish community.

Figure 5.26. View of Otero Street. Today Otero Street is a little alley immediately south of Otero Hall at the Tubac Presidio State Historic Park. On the 1882 Tubac Townsite, Otero Street was located just north of Mercer Street. The street passed directly south of Otero Hall and went directly to the second Sabino Otero House known today as the Rojas House. (Photograph by the author).

EL TIRADITO

Otero Social Hall at Tubac was not the only real estate donated by Teofilo Otero for community use. In 1927, Teofilo deeded a lot to the City of Tucson in an historic section of town within the Barrio Libre National Historic District and the Barrio Historico City Historic Preservation Zone. Located at 418 South Main Avenue, Tucson, Pima County, Arizona, this tiny parcel is situated south of the southwest corner of Main Avenue and Cushing Street.[102] Known as The Wishing Shrine or El Tiradito, the lot is the only known shrine in the contiguous United States dedicated to the soul of a sinner. Mexican folk customs are preserved at the site by the faithful as they visit the shrine in search of answers to their prayers.

The legend of the shrine involves a young man Juan Oliveras who was having an affair with his mother-in-law. One unfortunate day, Juan's father-in-law caught the pair together. An altercation ensued, and the father-in-law picked up an axe and bludgeoned the young man to death. Since he was a sinner, Juan could not be buried on consecrated ground. The locals buried Juan on the spot where he fell, hence the term Tiradito loosely translated as "Castaway" but more appropriately "he who was thrown away."

Figure 5.27. View of El Tiradito at Tucson. Land was donated by Teofilo Otero. This is a historical site where faithful visit to have their prayers answered. (Photograph by the author).

Locals continued to visit El Tiradito to pray for Juan's poor soul bringing candles reinforced with tin cans. In the process, locals discovered that their own prayers could be answered if their petitions were sincere.[103] The original El Tiradito shrine was located west of Meyer Street in the center of present-day Simpson Street near the historic Carrillo Gardens. A new shrine location became necessary due to road realignment.

The La Placita Committee members joined forces with the Tucson-Pima County Historical Commission to save the important cultural site.[104] Teofilo Otero deeded a lot to the City of Tucson to use as a permanent site for the shrine. A U-shaped wall was built in 1940s by the National Youth Administration in which devotees place their handwritten prayers into the crevices of the wall.[105]

Figure 5.28. Teofilo Otero donated lands for public use, Otero Hall at Tubac and El Tiradito at Tucson. (Courtesy Martha Desoto Green).

Was it pure generosity or some other motivation that persuaded Teofilo Otero to donate land for the El Tiradito shrine? We may never know but his sibling Sister Clara Otero may have likely interpreted Teofilo's donation as a silent prayer of intercession for his own indiscretions. Sister Clara was concerned that her brother Teofilo was indifferent about religion and that after God, only a faithful sister and a good wife would benefit his mortal well-being.[106] Sister Clara Otero was a teacher who lived a benevolent life caring for the welfare of others. She was posthumously inducted into the Arizona Women's Hall of Fame in 1988 for being among the first pioneers to enter a religious order.

Figure 5.29. Illustration of Sister Clara Otero by Dorotea Cvijanovic commissioned exclusively for *Terrenos* © 2018 Diana DeLugan. All rights reserved.

HOUSE ON MAIN STREET-TUCSON

Like the Rancho de Otero in Tubac, the house at Tucson on South Main Street remains an iconic symbol of Arizona's pre-statehood period. Manuel Otero, grandson of Torivio de Otero Spanish land grantee, built the adobe home at 219 South Main Street around 1861. It was erected on a small hill overlooking the old Tucson courthouse using sunbaked adobe bricks from the very foundation of Old Tucson.[107] Manuel moved his family from Tubac to Tucson in 1863 to avoid Apache depredations.[108] Rebuilt by Sabino Otero in 1874,[109] the house sat on an elevated lot buttressed by an adobe wall with ten narrow stairs that led to the front porch supported by ornate green posts.[110] Multiple fireplace stacks protruded from its roof. The home was surrounded by a manicured lawn with fig and pomegranate trees and Teofilo Otero's beloved cactus garden.[111]

The Otero house on Main Street was "one of the first Tucson homes to be completely furnished with items supplied locally" from Leo Goldschmidt Furniture Co. at Main St. and Congress. Like the Hacienda de Otero building at Tubac, its massive wood beams were cut by hand and transported from the Santa Rita Mountains by mule teams.[112] Many fine adornments decorated the home. During the 1880's, Teofilo Otero returned from a trip to France with a portrait of a mother holding her unclothed baby. The nudity shocked his sister's sense of morality who was an artist in her own right. Sister Clara Otero of the Sisters of St. Joseph of Carondolet reportedly absconded with the naked baby's portrait to St. Joseph's Academy and returned it safely with the baby newly clothed.[113]

The House on Main Street was a safe haven for the Otero family during the first few years after the house was built in 1861. The Otero family lived primarily at Tubac but traveled the perilous journey back to the house on Main Street to escape Apache depredations. After Sabino's death in 1914, his niece Ana Maria Comadurán Coenen inherited the property. Anna's daughter Anita C. Maldonado subsequently inherited the property after Ana Maria died, then the house was "held in trust at the Southern Arizona Bank & Trust Co.[114] During the mid-1960s, the City of Tucson redistricted the area that included the historic Otero family home to make room for "an exhibition hall in the new Urban Renewal Complex."[115] Urban sprawl soon claimed the Otero home despite citizen outcry to preserve the Fremont and Otero homes, and La Placita, the last three historic buildings set for demolition.[116] All that remains of the Otero town home at Tucson is the patio. It escaped demolition and is now a permanent exhibit at the Arizona Historical Society (AHS) Museum at Tucson. Donations to the AHS Museum are accepted by the museum to fund the continued preservation of the Otero Exhibit.

Figure 5.30. Illustration of Maria Clara Martinez Otero by Dorotea Cvijanovic commissioned exclusively for *Terrenos* Maria Clara's husband Manuel Otero built the house at 219 South Main Street circa 1861. Their youngest child Teofilo was born at the house.

Figure 5.31. The house at 219 Main Street in Tucson gave generations of Otero descendants' fond memories. (left-to-right) Mary Sentell Coenen holding her daughter Mary Ann Coenen, Ana Maria Comadurán (center), then Anita Carmen Coenen holding her granddaughter Nancy Ann Coenen. After Maria Clara Martinez de Otero passed away, Ana Maria became the matriarch of the house on Main Street. In this image there are four generations of Otero descendants. (Courtesy Teresa Anita Coenen Seaman).

Figure 5.32. House at 219 Main Street, Tucson before it was destroyed due to urban renewal. Only the façade of the porch was preserved and remains on permanent exhibit at the Arizona Historical Society Museum at Tucson, AZ. (University of Arizona Libraries, Special Collections: images from Arizona & Southwest Photograph files, "Tucson Ariz. – Urban Renewal album, Otero House).

Figure 5.33. Otero Porch Façade Exhibit at the Arizona Historical Society Museum. This is a permanent exhibit that celebrates the history of the Otero family of Tubac/Tucson.

CONCLUSION

The Otero family's Spanish land grant story provides important insight into Arizona's Hispanic history. Challenges for U.S. recognition of ancestral lands were experiences shared with other Spanish and Mexican land grant owners. Justice was not always swift or fair. To preserve a right to land, there were sometimes insurmountable legal challenges that did not favor foreign land grant owners. Despite and perhaps because of multiple adversities faced and won, the Otero story is celebrated by our federal and state governments. The Pacific Region of the United States National Archives and Records Administration celebrated both the January 10, 1789 land grant document and the Otero family of Tubac during the 2011 Hispanic Heritage Month saying:

> The grant is a beautiful document covered in ornate official seals and written in a hand easy to admire... by 1880 Otero descendants faced many significant challenges in both working and keeping the land. They survived drought, Indian raids, squatters, and justified their claims to both the Mexican and then the American governments.[1]

Although the Otero land grant was not among the largest Spanish or Mexican grants of land in Arizona, it remains significant as the first European private title to land. As you visit Elkhorn Ranch at the Baboquivari Mountains, Agua Linda Farms at Amado, the Arizona Historical Society Museum's Otero porch exhibit from the House on Main Street or El Tiradito at Tucson, Otero Hall, the Rojas House, or the Hacienda de Otero at the Tubac Golf Resort & Spa at Tubac; remember that these remaining structures were once on *terrenos* owned by the Otero family. They remain tangible symbols of Arizona's

Hispanic heritage and confirm the resilience of one Arizona pioneer family.

Family, home, and humble industry gave purpose to life. Perhaps Don Torivio de Otero's desire to give his family a permanent home can inspire others to give the same for their future generations. We celebrate Don Torivio de Otero as Arizona's first documented lay teacher at Tubac since 1787. Education has always been important to Arizona's pioneers.

Don Torivio's great-granddaughter Sister Clara Otero was inducted posthumously into Arizona Women's Hall of Fame in 1988. She was honored, in part, or her contributions as a young Hispanic teacher when Arizona was a young territory of the United States. Education uplifts families and communities, one student at a time.

On October 2, 2015, Arizona's governor Doug Ducey issued a proclamation to celebrate several of Don Torivio de Otero's personal achievements as part of Arizona's Hispanic Heritage Month. These Arizona firsts included Arizona's first privately-owned irrigation system, Arizona's first lay teacher, Arizona's first private European residence, and Arizona's first European private title to land. These historic milestones all occurred at the small town called Tubac. As the first northernmost frontier settlement in *Pimería Alta,* land of the upper Piman Indians, Tubac once belonged to Spain. Although the Otero land grant story is but a fraction of Arizona's rich Hispanic history yearning to be explored, always remember that Arizona's pioneer story began at Tubac.

Douglas A. Ducey
Governor

Office of the Governor

WITH SPECIAL RECOGNITION

WHEREAS, the legacy of Don Torivio de Otero has been established throughout southern Arizona for nearly 230 years; and

WHEREAS, Don Torivio de Otero received the first recorded title to land at the Tubac Presidio authorized by the King of Spain on January 10, 1789; and

WHEREAS, the land granted to Don Torivio de Otero is part of the Tubac Golf Resort and Spa today; and

WHEREAS, as the first documented European title holder to land, Don Torivio de Otero understood that ownership came with responsibilities and cultivated the desert land and built the first private irrigation system in Arizona; and

WHEREAS, his descendants used Otero ranch water to sustain local municipalities from Tumacacori to Tucson; and

WHEREAS, as the first lay teacher in Hispanic Arizona, Don Torivio de Otero believed in the value of education that was instilled in his descendants; and

WHEREAS, these accomplishments by Don Torivio de Otero strengthened our state and uplifted the Hispanic community.

NOW, THEREFORE, I, Douglas A. Ducey, Governor of the State of Arizona, do hereby honor Don Torivio de Otero's legacy and encourage residents and visitors throughout to discover the rich history in Tubac, Arizona.

IN WITNESS WHEREOF, I have hereunto set my hand and caused to be affixed the Great Seal of the State of Arizona

GOVERNOR

DONE at the Capitol in Phoenix on this second day of October in the year Two Thousand and Fifteen, and of the Independence of the United States of America the Two Hundred and Fortieth.

ATTEST:

Secretary of State

Figure 5.34. Proclamation honoring Don Torivio de Otero by Arizona Governor Douglas A. Ducey on 10/2/2015. The original signed proclamation is on permanent display at the Tubac Presidio State Historic Park. (Public domain).

APPENDIX A

Tubac/Otero Family Timeline of Important Events

Famous Dates in Tubac/Otero History
Spanish Tubac

- 1691: Tubac, a Pima Indian Rancheria, was visited by Jesuit Father Eusebio Francisco Kino; Kino's visits continue to 1711
- 1695: First Pima Revolt
- 1700: Tubac became a visita under Guevavi Mission during the early 18th century
- 1720: Missionaries report Tubac wiped out by this date
- 1730: Tubac became a mission ranch occupied by both Spaniards and indigenous people by the end of the 1730s
- 1736: Discovery of Planchas de Plata between Ranch of Arizona and Guevavi reported by Captain Juan Bautista de Anza in October
- 1751: Mission of Santa Gertrudis established; Second Pima Uprising against Spanish missions and settlements led by Piman Chief Luis of Saric results in Tubac deserted; Lt. Col. Diego Ortiz Parrilla, interim Governor of Sonora recommends establishment of fort with 30 troops at Tubac
- 1752: Presidio San Ignacio de Tubac established by formal decree on January 31st with Capt. Juan Tomas de Belderrain as its first commander and the fort becomes Spain's northernmost outpost
- 1759: Capt. Juan Tomas de Belderrain dies at Guevavi on September 7th
- 1760: Juan Bautista de Anza assumes command of Tubac on February 19th
- 1761: Soldiers moved 3 miles south to Tumacácori due to evil spirits
- 1764: Juan Bautista de Anza revives Tubac presidio
- 1765: Urrutia Map reveals early community of Tubac with the Spanish presidio at the center of the community, 49 dwellings south of the presidio, 11 dwellings north of the presidio, 64 milpas (farming

lots) east of the presidio on the banks of the Santa Cruz River, and a cemetery adjacent to the village; building located immediately south of east wing of presidio is later site of the Otero Solar, Arizona's first privately owned residence

- 1774: Jesuits expelled by King Carlos III of Spain
- 1774: Juan Bautista de Anza accompanied by Franciscans Juan Díaz & Francisco Tomás Hemenegildo Garcés embark on their first interior exploration to California departing from Tubac with 34 solders on January 8th
- 1775: Juan Bautista de Anza and colonists leave Tubac on October 23rd on orders from Charles III of Spain to settle at San Francisco to stop further colonization by Russians who were moving down the coast from Alaska, 63 persons joined at Tubac to the 177 persons from Horcasitas
- 1776: Tubac Presidio moved to Tucson leaving Tubac citizens exposed to Apache raids
- 1777: Juan Bautista de Anza returns to Tubac, Spain then departs south deeper into Pimería Alta, Nueva España
- 1779: Don Torivio de Otero marries Maria Ygnacia Salazar at Santa Ana, Sonora; Francisco Nunez receives grant for rental land at Tucson Presidio
- 1784: Mission of Santa Gertrudis replaced by church of Santa Anna (St. Anne's)
- 1787: San Rafael Royal Fort with Pima troop located at Tubac to defend residents and guard band of pacified Apaches on nearby reservation; Torivio de Otero moves his family to Tubac and begins teaching at the Tubac presidio
- 1789: Torivio de Otero receives first private land grant in Arizona on January 10th
- 1796: Santa Anna Iglesia (St. Anne's Church) completed

- 1804/7: Torivio de Otero wins squatter land challenge and reports he has been a teacher at the Tubac Presidio for 20 years; 88 Spanish military and their families, other non-military settlers, and 20 indigenous people reside on Tubac presidial land
- 1806: End of Pima garrison; citizens remain at Tubac despite lack of military defense
- 1807: Don Torivio de Otero petitions for land to be returned from squatters

Mexican Tubac

- 1821: Mexico gains independence from Spain, making Tubac part of Mexico; Otero family become Mexican citizens due to residency
- 1830: Tubac raided by Apaches during the 1830s; Tubac and Tucson remaining major settlements in Arizona
- 1834: All Arizona establishments organized as a Partido with San Ignacio de Tubac
- 1838: Tubac receives Pueblo status under Mexican law and is enlarged to 62 ½ miles; Jose Maria Martinez receives land grant at Tubac
- 1839: Atanacio Otero issues a promissory note to be paid by proceeds from mescal brandy
- 1840: Tubac raided by Apaches during the 1840s; population estimate 400
- 1842-3: Rancheria of friendly Apaches at Tubac
- 1846: Tubac soldiers Mexican garrison called in defense of Lt. Colonel Philip St. George Cooke's Mormon Battalion in December at Tucson; estimated population of 400 at Tubac
- 1848: No military citizen population at Tubac; 249 civilian inhabitants
- 1849: Depopulation of Tubac by hostile Apaches in summer; casualties buried by Ozark travelers to California
- 1851: Mexican repopulation of Tubac

- 1852: Captain Gomez formerly at Fronteras placed in charge of Tubac; population 100
- 1853: Gadsden Purchase of land from Mexico puts Tubac in Territory of New Mexico, United States, signed by US and Mexico on December 30th; 112 friendly Apaches reported at Tubac in July

Tubac in the United States of America

- 1854: Gadsden Treaty proclaimed law by President Pierce on June 30th and added to New Mexico by Act of Congress on August 4th; Poston and Ehrenberg explore Santa Cruz Valley resources including Tubac; Tubac abandoned by military local families remained; Otero family become U.S. citizens by residency
- 1855: New Mexico Legislation attached Gadsden Purchase to Doña Ana County on January 18th
- 1856: Charles D. Poston arrives at Tubac to establish headquarters of Sonora Exploring & Mining Co.; Tubac occupied by non-military Mexican families
- 1859: Jose Maria Martinez conveys land south of the Otero land grant to Manuel Otero; Arizona's first newspaper, the weekly *Arizonian*, first issue published on March 3rd
- 1860: New Mexico Legislature creates Arizona County with Tubac as its county seat from western Doña County on February 1st but law not enforced
- 1861: South part of New Mexico was declared as Territory of Arizona for the Confederacy by Lt. Col. John R. Baylor at Mesilla, New Mexico on August 1st; Civil War causes withdrawal of US troops from Tubac opening area to Apache raids; Charles D. Poston departs to California
- 1862: Confederate Congress declares a Territory of Arizona, Tubac included as part of the Confederacy; New Mexico Legislature abolishes Arizona County and re-annexes territory to Doña Ana County on January 18th; westernmost Civil War skirmish occurs

at Picacho Peak on April 15th; Union recovers Tucson on May 20th

- 1863: President Lincoln declares Arizona a Territory of the United States on February 24th after Bill passed Congress on February 20th; AZ Territorial Governor John N. Goodwin formally organized government of Arizona at Navajo Springs on December 29th
- 1864: Tubac becomes a military camp for a brief period; Tubac revisited by Charles D. Poston and J. Ross Browne; Manuel Otero appointed Alcalde of Tubac
- 1870: Manuel Otero dies of pneumonia; Sabino Otero takes over as head of household
- 1876: Ten Tubac citizens petition the Pima County School District No. 4 for the establishment of a school at Tubac on December 1st
- 1878: Charles D. Poston and associates petition for formation of Tubac Townsite, no further action taken
- 1879: Otero siblings petition for the confirmation of ancestral land through the U.S. Surveyor General's Office
- 1880: Dario Martinez issues a Quit Claim Deed to Sabino Otero for his father Jose Maria Martinez's land south of the Otero land grant on June 20
- 1882: Tubac Townsite is established by T. Lillie Mercer, Sabino Otero, and others
- 1884: President Chester A. Arthur authorizes Tubac Grant
- 1885: Tubac's first schoolhouse built during U.S. era built by T. Lillie Mercer
- 1893: Otero family removes its petition for confirmation of ancestral lands from the Court of Private Land Claims and petitions for a Homestead for the Otero land grant property
- 1899: Tubac becomes part of Santa Cruz County

- 1910: Dances held at Tubac Schoolhouse to raise money to build a church
- 1912: President William Taft confirms the Otero Homestead Patent to protect the Otero land grant property; St. Anne's Church construction started; Arizona becomes a state on February 14th
- 1914: Sabino Otero dies; Teofilo Otero builds Otero Hall serves as community center
- 1916: Baca Float #3 depletes Tubac population
- 1920: St. Anne's Church walls cave in, partial frame erected and narrower foundation laid
- 1929: St. Ann's Church constructed on the site of the Iglesia de Santa Gertrudis de Tubac (St. Gertrude's Church)
- 1934: Otero Hall serves as school for fourth graders
- 1937: Teofilo sells the Rancho de Otero to Addison Pelletier
- 1939: Tubac population: 365
- 1941: Teofilo Otero dies
- 1948: Tubac established as an artists' community
- 1957: Olga K. Griffen conveys Tubac Presidio land on December 21st to the State of Arizona by the Arizona State Parks Board for use as a historical State Park
- 1958: Arizona State Parks Board formally accepts Tubac Presidio land and establishes Arizona's second State Park; Tubac State Park, an Arizona State Monument, dedicated on September 28th with an invocation by Reverend Patrick J. Callahan of St. Ann's Church at Tubac, speeches by AZ Governor Ernest W. McFarland and Mexican Governor of the State of Sonora Alvarado Obregon, with AZ Senator Neilson Brown as Master of Ceremonies
- 1960: Tubac Festival of the Arts established
- 1967: Tubac Presidio Museum opened; Wallace Vegors director of the Tubac Presidio State Museum and then-president of the Tubac Historical Society

join Tubac citizens to prevent the sale of the 1885 Tubac Schoolhouse at public auction

- 1974: Arizona State Parks contracts University of Arizona to excavate part of the Tubac Presidio; President Gerald Ford and Mexican President Luis Echeverria visit Tubac on October 21st dining at the Hacienda de Otero, the then executive meeting room at the Tubac Valley Country Club
- 1976: Portion of Tubac Presidio archeological site enclosed as permanent Arizona State Park display
- 1989: Bicentennial Otero Family Reunion held at Tubac and Tucson
- 2011: U.S. National Archives and Records Division honors the Otero Family for the Otero Land Grant of 1789
- 2015: AZ Governor Douglas Ducey Proclaims Don Torivio de Otero Day

APPENDIX B

Otero Family Tree

1. Jose de Otero + Francisca Granillo

2. DON TORIVIO DE OTERO + MARIA YGNACIA SALAZAR

3. Atanacio Otero + Carment Quijada

4. Manuel Otero + Maria Clara Martinez

5. Teofilo Otero + Leonor Kaphan

6. Ricardo Otero + Francisca Quijada

7. Rosa Otero + Leopoldo Sinohui

8. Celia Sinohui + Fidencio Hinojosa

9. DIANA HINOJOSA + *James DeLugan*

10. Alma

11. Jesse

11. Cesar (Nicole)

12. ♂

11. Jorge (Maria)

12. ♀ ♀

11. Juan

10. Christopher

11. ♀

11. ♀

11. ♀

11. ♂

10. Reynaldo

OTERO FAMILY OF ARIZONA

APPENDIX C

Otero Family of Tubac Biofile

The following Biofile contains a non-exclusive synopsis of important figures in the Otero family of Tubac that currently spans more than ten generation of Arizonans. Although this Biofile does not reference every individual in the family tree, efforts have been made to include persons who were prominently involved in the Otero land grant story.

Avila, Rita Otero

See Otero, Rita

Brown, Anna

Anna Brown Otero was also known as Anita Brown, Anna B. de Sainz (alternate spelling Saenz), and Chonita Sainz.[1] She was born on 5/25/1879 to Ambrosio Brown of Texas and Crisanta Lopez of Arizona at Tucson, Arizona.[2] Anna filed a lawsuit on 11/19/1910 for recognition as common law wife of Teofilo Otero, for the distribution of half of Teofilo Otero's personal and real property, child support and alimony. She lost her claim due to defendant's successful anti-miscegenation defense. In Case 4820 titled *Anna B. Otero vs. Teofilo Otero*, Anna reported that she cohabitated with Teofilo from 9/24/1898 until 8/1910 becoming husband and wife by virtue of the Statutes of Arizona of 1901.[3] Four children were reported to have resulted from the union: Edward aka Eduardo born in 1902, Anita aka Ana born in 1905, and Alberto and Henry born in 1904 who died in infancy.[4] Anna was the owner of a home located on Stone Avenue in Tucson, Territory of Arizona with a mortgage value of $1,700 in 1898.[5]

Anna also lost her claim as co-petitioner against Leonardo Moreno, Executor of the Teofilo Otero Estate case #21553 in 1942. On 4/6/1942, petitioners' attorney E. Cusick of the law firm Cusick & Lyons of Tucson, AZ, wrote to Anna's daughter Mrs. Ana Provencio saying:

> "The truth is that Ysidro Otero is receiving the same amount as you and your brother, but his Mother is receiving twice as much as the children for the reason that she has a claim as a common law wife. Your Mother, by virtue of having sued for a divorce and a division of the community property, and having lost, was thereafter forever precluded from again raising this question. I explained this to you and your brother before."[6]

Anna B. Otero died on 3/4/1949 of apoplexy due to arterial hypertension. She was buried on 3/7/1949 at Holy Hope Cemetery at Tucson, AZ.[7]

Capan Otero, Leonor

See Kaphan, Leonor

Castro, Brijida aka Brigida

Brijida was born on 2/17/1866 at Tubac, Territory of Arizona, only surviving child of Maria Elena de Jesus Otero and José Mauricio Maximiano Castro.[8] After her mother Elena died in February 1868, Brijida was raised by her grandparents Manuel Otero and Maria Clara Martinez de Otero at Tubac and Tucson. Her father Mauricio remarried in August of 1868 at Tucson. He had three children, Brijida's step-siblings, with new wife Ana María Luques.[9] Despite their separation after Elena Otero's death, father and daughter remained close. Before his death, Mauricio lived with Brijida.

In 1883, Brijida married Anthony Coenen of Belgium who passed away on 5/27/1926. After Anthony's death, she ran a boarding home with her daughters Mary and Imelda.[10] Age 80, she died a widow at 4:00 am on 1/20/1947 of natural causes and is buried at Holy Hope Cemetery.[11] Her obituary states she was survived by Joseph and Carl A. Coenen and daughters Miss Imelda Coenen, Mrs. Clara C. (Rudolph) Soto, Mrs. Helen G (Joseph) Penunuri, Mrs. Melanie (Alberto) Sanchez, and Mrs. Bridget (Frank) Molina. Other children preceded her in death include Henry J.,[12] Luis J.,[13] and Mary[14]. According to Brijida's death record, her last residence was 195 South Main Street, Tucson, AZ.

Brijida's official Arizona death record incorrectly report her aunt and uncle Ramon Comadurán and Francisca Otero as her parents.[15] Brijida was a 5th generation heir of the Otero land grant and was one of the last owners of the historic land grant at Tubac. She possessed a one-third ownership interest in the Otero ranch lands which she sold to her uncle Teofilo Otero.

Castro, María Elena de Jesus Otero de

See Otero, María Elena de Jesus

Castro, Mauricio

José Mauricio Maximiano Castro was born in 1847 in Tucson, Sonora, Mexico, son of Ramon Castro and Brigida Higuera, and grandson of Saturnino Castro (Tucson *presidio* soldier in 1818) and Eulalia Pacheco.[16] He was baptized on January 2, 1848.[17]

According to the Presidio Families report by J. Homer Thiel, Mauricio married Maria Elena de Jesus Otero on March 29, 1864 witnessed by Jesús María Ortiz and Encarnación Comadurán. The 1864 Territorial Census of Arizona First, Second and Third Judicial Districts report Mauricio and Elena lived at Tucson in the same household with Mauricio's parents. At the time of their marriage, Mauricio was 17 and Elena Otero was 18 years old. The Tucson National Cemetery reports a second child Eloisa Castro died on 9/2/1866 as an infant.[18] After Elena died in February 1868, their daughter Brijida was raised by her maternal Otero grandparents at Tubac and Tucson. Mauricio died at Tucson on 6/17/1922 of natural causes and was buried at Holy Hope Cemetery at Tucson, AZ, Occupation: Farmer/Stock raiser.[19] He owned an Arizona livestock brand.[20] His last residence was 39 North Driscoll, Tucson, AZ.[21]

Coenen, Ana (Anna) Maria Comadurán de

See Comadurán, Ana Maria

Coenen, Anthony

Born Antonius Ghislenus Theodorius on 7/25/1847 at Zoutleeuw (Léau), Belgium. Among his several accomplishments, Anthony served as a Papal Zouave, reached the rank of Colonel of the French Zouaves, and was decorated by Pope Leo XIII for his service. He immigrated to the United States in 1872 via Kentucky then arrived at Tucson, Territory of AZ in 1873. He married Brigida Castro in 1883, daughter of Maria Elena de Jesus Otero and José Mauricio Maximiano Castro; and the granddaughter of Manuel Otero and Maria Clara Martinez. Together, Anthony and Brigida had numerous children including Anthony Coenen, Jr.[22]

Anthony was a close confidant of uncle-by-marriage rancher/stock raiser Sabino Otero and likely used his financial business acumen to help himself and the Otero family as a whole.

Occupation: Tax Collector and Assessor, Notary Public, and stock raiser. Anthony worked his way up from Money Order Clerk then eventually held the prestigious positions of Tax Collector and Assessor, a gubernatorial appointment as notary public for Tucson, and he helped administer Civil Service examinations for government posts. During his campaign for election, it was common to see ads from others vouching for Anthony's high moral character and financial savvy.

Like the Oteros, Anthony was a successful rancher. Perhaps to avoid the appearance of impropriety given his tenure as a tax collector/assessor, Anthony Coenen had Sabino Otero act as the statutory agent for Coenen & Co Cattle, Company. In 1893, Anthony's cattle company had 520 head of cattle valued at $2,940 (a 2016 value of $74,325.81). This was a nice complement to his personal property wealth of $6,890.00 reported almost ten years prior in 1884 ($161,282.71 using a 2016 conversion rate).[23] Anthony also provided surety for Manuela Otero de Quesse in her claim to facilitate her appointment as Administrator in the *Matter of the Estate of Louis Quesse.*[24] He died at 11 pm on 5/27/1926 of natural causes at 79 years of age.[25]

Coenen, Brigida Castro de

See Castro, Brijida

Coenen, Eugenio

Born Franciscus Josephus Eugenius (twin) on 5/30/1852 in Belgium. Eugenio immigrated to Kentucky with his younger brother Anthony Coenen, then they traveled Arizona to make Tucson their home. Occupation: Eugenio was a farmer,[26] stock raiser, and teacher at the Marist Brothers' school.[27] He spoke 13 languages. Teofilo Otero, youngest child of Manuel and Maria Clara Otero, was his former student. Teofilo regularly escorted his niece Ana Maria Comadurán to school. Ana Maria caught Eugenio's gaze and they eventually married. He was five years her senior. The 1880 US Federal Census reports Eugenio and Ana Maria lived at the township of Hacienda de Santa Rita in Sonoita Valley. Eugene died in an equestrian accident on 1/10/1884, just a few years after he married Ana Maria.[28]

Comadurán, Ana (aka Anna) Maria

Ana Maria was born at Tubac, Territory of New Mexico in 1859, daughter of Ramon Comadurán and Francisca Otero of Tubac, Territory of New Mexico.[29] Francisca was the eldest child of Manuel Otero and Maria Clara Martinez. Francisca's husband died in 1884 from wounds inflicted during an Apache attack.[30] By 1870, Ana Maria and her widowed mother Francisca resided with her grandmother Maria Clara Martinez de Otero after her father Ramon Comadurán's death.[31] Francisca died on 1/28/1871 and is buried at Tumacácori Mission, Santa Cruz County, AZ.[32] After her mother's death, she was raised by her maternal grandmother Maria Clara at Tubac and at El Reventon Ranch.

Ana Maria married Eugenio Coenen,[33] elder brother of Anthony Coenen. They had four children: Ramond, Antonio, Alfonso, and Anita.[34] Ana Maria was one of the co-petitioners to the Court of Private Land Claims No. 13 who requested that the Otero Spanish land grant of 1789 be perfected under U.S. law. Her right to claim the land grant was as her mother Francisca Otero's sole heir-at-law.

Uncle Sabino Otero bequeathed a one-third ownership interest of the Otero land grant to Ana Maria upon his death in 1914. She subsequently moved to the Hacienda de Otero at Tubac with Uncle Teofilo Otero, who also owned a one-third interest in the Otero land grant. Ana Maria eventually sold her ownership interest to Teofilo. She was instrumental in raising funds to establish St. Ann's Church in collaboration with Monsignor Louis Duval. She returned to Tucson in her final years.

In 1930, Ana Maria was the head of household at Tucson with her daughter Anita Coenen, and Sophia Polanco and Mercedes Madrid.[35] Age 86, she died a widow at 11:30 am on 1/23/1946 of natural causes (gangrene of both feet) and is buried at Holy Hope Cemetery. Her usual occupation was housewife but family considers her the matron of the Hacienda de Otero. Ana Maria was a 5th generation heir to the Otero land grant. Historical documents use Anna and Ana interchangeably. Her personal signature in court records reflect she went by the first name "Ana."

Comadurán, Francisca Otero de

See Otero, Francisca

Comadurán, Ramón

Ramón Comadurán was born in 1826, son of Tucson presidio *Comandante* Jose António Comadurán and Ana Maria Ramirez and grandson of Miguel Antonio Comadurán and Ramona Díaz del Carpio.[36] He served as a Corporal then Sergeant in the Spanish Calvary[37] and had more than one encounter fighting hostile Indian attack. Ramón married Francisca Otero, eldest child of Manuel Otero and Maria Clara Martinez Otero. The 1860 Census for the Territory of New Mexico reports he lived in Tubac with his wife Francisca and their one-year-old daughter Ana Maria. He was 13 years older than his wife. He was "ambushed and slain in 1861, shortly after the Chiricahuas resumed their attacks."[38]

Hinojosa, Celia Sinohui

Celia was born in Ruby, Arizona on May 28, 1936, eldest child of Leopoldo Sinohui and Rosa Otero. Arizona birth records erroneously listed her as a male at birth. Her maternal grandparents were Ricardo Otero (son of Teofilo Otero and Leonor Kaphan) and Francisca Quijada. Celia's lifelong desire to know the truth about her family history inspired the research that resulted in this book, *Terrenos Illustrated History of the Otero Land Grant*. She died on May 28, 2013, beloved matriarch of five generations. Mass was held at St. Mary's Basilica, Phoenix, AZ on June 1, 2013, followed by burial at St. Francis Cemetery.

Celia was a 7th generation descendant of the Otero land grant family of Tubac. She was preceded in death by her husband Fidencio Garcia Hinojosa and daughter Alma Diana. She was survived by her sister Maria Velia (Manuel) Lopez, daughters Cricelia Francisca Hinojosa, Maria Cristina (Joe) Gerardo, and Criselda Diana (James) DeLugan, son Joel (Karen) Hinojosa, and many grandchildren, great-grandchildren, and great-great grandchildren.

Kaphan, Leonor

Leonor was the daughter of Joseph Kaphan and Juana Mendez. She was born 1/1/1873. Leonor moved from Tubac to Calabasas where she held an Arizona Livestock brand in her name,[39] then moved to San Bernardino, CA where she died at on 2/14/1943 within two years of Teofilo Otero's death.[40]

She had two children with Teofilo Otero, last heir of the Otero land grant: Ysidro and Ricardo Otero.[41] Leonor claimed legal status as common law wife of Teofilo Otero as co-petitioner of one of two cases against the Executor of the Teofilo Otero Estate. She received $5,000.00 as a settlement for her claim which was reduced to $10.00 through actions of her son Ysidro Otero. Her father was Joseph Kaphan who immigrated from Berlin, Germany in 1871,[42] and her mother was Juana Mendes. Joseph successfully petitioned for a homestead and received land patent number 7783.[43]

The Kaphan homestead is the historic site of the current Chavez Siding Road exit property at Tubac. At the time Kaphan owned the homestead, the property shared boundary lines with Teofilo Otero's Reventon Ranch to the north and the present-day Tubac Golf Resort & Spa, historic site of the Rancho de Otero Spanish land grant property.

Kaphan, Susana

Susana Kaphan was born at Tubac, Territory of Arizona to Joseph Kaphan of Berlin, Germany and Juana Mendez of Mexico. She had a daughter Rita Otero with Fernando Otero, 4th generation heir-at-law of the Otero land grant. Susana married Raphael Aldecova and died on 4/25/1964 in Los Angeles, CA.[44] She was the sister of Leonor Kaphan who had two children with Fernando's brother Teofilo: Ysidro and Ricardo Otero. Daughter Rita Otero married Albert Avila and moved to Yuma, AZ where they had four known children: Paulina Eva, Mary Louise, Albert Jr., and Ruben Arthur.

Litel, Olga Maria Otero

See Otero, Olga Maria

Martinez, Maria Clara

Spouse of Manuel Otero, grandson of Spanish land grantee Don Torivio de Otero, Maria Clara was a child bride. She was thirteen years younger than her husband Manuel. Born circa 1823, Maria was about fourteen years old when she gave birth to her eldest child Francisca. She was also illiterate, unable to read or write.[45] Due to Apache depredations, the family lived in Tucson periodically.

After her husband Manuel died in 1870 of pneumonia, Maria Clara kept house and cared for her two young sons Fernando and Teofilo. In the same home, daughter Francisca cared for her own daughter Ana Maria Comadurán while daughter Gabriela helped care for granddaughter Brijida Castro. After Francisca died in 1871, Maria Clara became the primary caregiver for granddaughters Ana Maria and Brijida.

Maria Clara also homesteaded 160 acres at Amado under her own name according to Tucson land office records. The land was locally known as El Reventon Ranch. Homestead depositions report she first arrived at the property on May 16, 1890 and only left the Amado homestead a few days when she was sick or for trips to Tucson for supplies. She reported that four children lived with her, no other adults. Caring for children at an estimated 67-years-of-age must have been challenging for anyone. Unable to write, her son Teofilo, a Frank Smith, and grandson-in-law Anthony Coenen witnessed her "x" mark on her Amado homestead papers.

James Officer, author of the book Hispanic Arizona 1536-1856, stated in a footnote that he suspected that Maria Clara may have belonged to the family of Jose Maria Martinez, the Mexican land grant owner who sold his property to Maria Clara's spouse Manuel Otero.[46] ArchaeologySouthwest.org reported in its Presidio Families report that Maria Clara was "probably Jose Maria's sister." A close look at documents and dates is inconclusive. No birth, baptismal, or other primary source records have been located to date to confirm that Maria Clara Martinez was Jose Maria Martinez's sister or relative. But the family theory persists. A thesis published in 2011 by the College of Sonora at Hermosillo about Jose Urrea's armed conflict with Manuel Maria Gándara from 1837-1845 reports that Maria Clara was likely a relative of Jose Maria Martinez. No specific relation was listed.[47]

According to the Presidio Families list by J. Homer Thiel, Tubac land grantee Jose Maria Martinez married Felipa Yrigoyen [ear-ee-go-yen] in 1833, he received a land grant at Tubac in 1838, and the couple had approximately 10 children from 1836 to 1856; then Jose Maria married Jesusa Quintero and had five children from 1858 to 1865.

It is about here where family connections get confusing. It has been suggested Jose Maria Martinez land grantee at Tubac was allegedly the same person who was later granted the Rancho de Martinez land at San Xavier on February 23, 1851 and died in 1874. Jose Maria Martinez conveyed his Tubac land grant to Manuel Otero in 1858 by informal deed. According to US Surveyor General John Wasson, the land from Martinez to Otero was subsequently formally conveyed by Jose Maria Martinez's sole surviving heir Dario Martinez on June 24, 1880. But just 2 years later, the petition for the Jose Maria Martinez ranch at San Xavier was submitted on January 10, 1882 by Nicolas Martinez and co-heirs claiming to be Jose Maria Martinez's true heirs-at-law. Dario Martinez was not mentioned. The search for Maria Clara Martinez de Otero's ancestral tree continues.

Otero, Ana Brown

Ana Brown Otero was also known as Anita Provencio and Ana Brown Provencio. She was born on 10/20/1905 at Tucson, Territory of AZ. Her parents were Teofilo Otero and Anna Brown Otero.

Her birth record was recorded before Justice of the Peace Lewis W. Howard at Calexico, CA on 10/23/1933, 28 years after her birth. Her 1933 birth certificate reports she was one of four siblings then alive with two siblings that died before her birth.[48] She had one child with Ramon M. Provencio named Ramon Armando Provencio who was born at Tucson, AZ.[49] Ana was a co-petitioner against Leonardo Moreno, Executor of the Teofilo Otero Estate in 1942 and received a $2,500.00 settlement in the matter. Ana was a 5th generation Otero of the land grant family of Tubac.

The Estate of Anna Otero Provencio was filed on 1/12/1999 as Case Number P29773 before presiding judge Kyle Bryson. Her son Armando Provencio was her duly appointed Fiduciary.[50]

Otero, (Don) Joséf Atanacio (aka Atanasio)

Josef Atanacio was born in 1772 at Tubac. Don Torivio and his wife Maria Ygnacia Salazar de Otero baptized their son Josef Atanacio Otero Salazar on March 5, 1772 at the church of Santa Maria in Magdalena, Sonora, New Spain.[51] US National Park Service Mission 2000 database reflects Atanacio was deeply involved in community affairs: Atanacio witnessed the marriages of Juan Samatiz and Maria Ignacia Peña at Tubac on 8/5/1816, marriage of Tomás Rios and Juana Pineda at Tumacácori on

4/15/1816, Maximo Otero and Carmen Quijada at Tumacácori on 4/22/1820; all officiated by Fray Narciso Gutiérrez, priest in charge of Tubac. On 4/141816, Atanacio and wife Carmen Quijada were also godparents to Tomás, surname unknown, at Tumacácori. Daughter Magdalena was buried at Tumacácori Mission on 2/22/1821.

Atanacio was the constitutional Alcalde (mayor) of Tubac in 1833 and first legal heir-at-law of the Otero Spanish land grant at Tubac. An industrious man, he supplemented his agricultural pursuits with the sale of mescal to the Tubac and Tucson Presidios:

> I, Atanasio Otero, say that I am obliged to pay a certain debt in the amount of ---pesos to Mr. Jesús María Corella on the 24th day of June of the upcoming year that we will compute as 1844. The sum to be payed with proceeds from the business of selling the distillation of mescal at the presidios of Tubac and Tucson, payment for which is in current ---money. I will offer the same for payment of the debt when it is due, in conjunction with various present and future goods, the receipt of which will be verified upon demand. For these truths I document and will execute the most secure payment to him in whom I have obligated my person, without which no defense could protect me. I certify and give surety to this writing in which I am justly obligated, at Arizpe on June 29, 1839.
>
> Atanacio Otero (rubric)

(Sealed with the two-real arbitrator's stamp for the years 1838 and 1839.)[52] *See* Figure 2.5.

The 1831 Census of Tubac reflects Atanacio was listed with the title "Don," a person of high social status.[53]

Otero, Eduardo Brown

Eduardo was born on 10/13/1902 at Tucson, AZ Territory as son of Teofilo Otero and Anna Brown. His birth certificate was issued 33 years after his birth at Calexico, CA on 7/11/1934 before Justice of the Peace Lewis H. Howard that stated he had two siblings.[54] He died on 3/17/1975 at Tucson, AZ and is buried at Holy Hope Cemetery.[55]

He ran an unsuccessful bid for Sheriff of Tucson.

Along with his mother and sister, they were co-petitioners against the Executor of Teofilo Otero Estate asking for Teofilo's last will and testament be invalidated. He received $2,500.00 as a settlement in the matter. Eduardo was a 5th generation Otero of the land grant family of Tubac.

Otero, Fernando

Fernando Otero was the middle son of Manuel Otero and Maria Clara Martinez. He was born in 1860 at Tubac, AZ.[56] Occupation: Stock raiser[57] and miner. After his father's death in 1870, Fernando was raised by his mother Clara, sisters and 26-year-old brother Sabino. Although Fernando became intimately involved in certain business transactions with his siblings,[58] he had other business ambitions. Arizona Historical Society records report Fernando issued notice to homestead 160 acres known as Rio Venton, likely corruption of the ranch historically known as Reventon north of Tubac.

The Florence, AZ Land Office also reports he claimed a homestead but lost it over a land dispute. As the cattle industry began to wane due to severe drought and over-grazing, Fernando shifted his focus to the mining industry. On March 13, 1881, Fernando filed a mining claim at the Pima County Recorder's Office for a mining site at the Santa Rita Mountains near Tubac.[59] He was also one of the co-petitioners to the Court of Private Land Claims No. 13 to have the Otero Spanish land grant of 1789 ratified under U.S. law.

He had one daughter, Maria Rita Otero[60] with Susana Kaphan. Susana was the sister of Leonor Kaphan who had two sons Ysidro and Ricardo with Fernando's younger brother Teofilo Otero. Maria Rita married Alberto Avila and moved to Yuma, Arizona to raise a family.

Family oral history reports that Fernando lived with his siblings until the turn of the 20th century. Then, the unspeakable happened. On September 25, 1901, Sherriff A.V. Lewis issued a summons for nine jurors to gather under the authority of The District Court for the First Judicial District for the County of Cochise and determine the cause of death for the body of a Mexican found dead. This Inquest led by Coroner Chas S. Clark was to determine the cause of death for the body identified as Fernando Otero.

Inquest Jurors included Peter Connor, Andy Griffin, Robert Todd, John Wilson, and S. P. Gallen. The primary witness at the inquest was N. E. Holmes, manager of the Exposed Reef Mining Company who testified that Fernando had been working for the mining company as a laborer. During the early morning of February 24, 1901, Fernando was dispatched to retrieve a wagon wheel at the mining company storehouse located at the foot of the Hill Carro Canon Huachuca Mountain in Cochise County Arizona. Unfortunately, Fernando never returned. Mr. Holmes discovered Fernando's lifeless body sprawled across the Exposed Reef Mining Company's own road on the following afternoon around 2:45 pm.

Unaware of his assailant, Fernando, was shot from the back. The fatal bullet entered Fernando to the right of the back bone about one and one half to two inches moving in an upward trajectory until it passed through his body out of the right side of the sternum bone exiting about four inches below the arch of the areola on the right portion of his breast bone.

On November 6, 1901, Inquest jurors unanimously held that Fernando Otero had been murdered. The Exposed Reef Mining Company was incorporated on September 11 of 1899. One year after Fernando's murder in 1901, a second man John Powell was murdered at the Exposed Reef mine. Two murders – two years. At Fernando's crime scene, there was no evidence of a struggle. It appeared that his body had been rolled over after his murder – suggesting the killer needed to verify his identity. This was not simply a robbery gone wrong. Fernando carried from $30 to $80 dollars on his person and was still wearing a new gold watch from a Montgomery Ward & Company ad.

Otero, Fernando Kilbray

Fernando Otero was born on 2/1/1909 at Tubac, Territory of AZ as the son of Manuel Otero and Angelita Kilbray. Occupation: Building contractor. He married Otila "Tila" Moreno.[61] Fernando gave an interview to the *Mexican Heritage Project* about the Otero Family. The *Mexican Heritage Project* resulted in the book *Los Tucsonenses.* None of Fernando's interview was used in the book. Fernando died in 1989 and is buried in Holy Hope Cemetery in Tucson, AZ. His estate was filed as Case Number RP835 with the Clerk of Superior Court at Tucson, AZ on 6/22/1990. His wife's estate was filed on 3/9/1992 as Case Number P21377 with the same court.

Otero, Francisca

Francisca was born approximately 1841, the eldest daughter of Manuel Otero and María Clara Martinez. She was a 4th generation heir of the Otero land grant. She married Ramón Comadurán of New Spain (Mexico).[62] She died a widow at 30 years of age on 1/28/1871.[63] Her daughter Ana Maria Comadurán represented her mother Francisca's interest as a co-petitioner to the Court of Private Land Claims No. 13.

Otero, Gabriela

See Otero, Sister Clara

Otero, Joséf de

Joséf aka Joseph married Francisca Granillo. They were the parents of Torivio de Otero, Otero land grant recipient. During the late 1770's, parents and son lived in northern New Spain in Cucurpe, present-day Sonora. Joséf and Francisca witnessed Torivio and Maria Ygnacia Salazar's marriage at Santa Ana, New Spain (Mexico) on 2/16/1779.[64] Although no known documents have been located to confirm the assertion, it has been suggested that Joséf's father may have been Dos Santos de Otero,[65] the eyewitness to the 1754 Piman uprising at Arivaca and surrounding areas.

Otero, Josephus Emmanuel Teofilus "Teofilo"

Teofilo was born on 10/22/1863 at the Otero home at 219 South Main Street, Tucson, Territory of AZ, youngest child of Manuel Otero and Maria Clara Martinez. He was one of the co-petitioners to the Court of Private Land Claims No. 13 to have the Otero Spanish land grant of 1789 ratified under U.S. law. Occupation: Stock raiser and Agriculturalist. He also owned an Arizona livestock brand.[66] In 1910, he and brother Sabino lived in the same household as Ana Maria Coenen, her children and grandchildren at 219 South Main Street, Tucson, Territory of AZ.[67]

Like his philanthropist brother Sabino, Teofilo did not hesitate to help those in need. Teofilo was a founding member of La Alianza Hispano Americano. La Alianza was founded on January 14, 1894 at Tucson. A fraternal mutual-aid society, La Alianza provided aid to Mexican-American communities throughout the southwest and eventually joined forces with the NAACP in 1954 to fight discrimination.[68] The names of some of its principal founders is memorialized in an engraved block at the former office of C.Y. Velasco at Tucson with dates and names: C.Y. Velasco, J.C. Merino. C.C. Jacome, M. Aguirre. D. Gil, J.O. Sainz, C.C. Goodwin, D.S. Valencia and T. (Teofilo) Otero.[69]

Teofilo was elected and served as President of La Alianza. He was installed on January 14, 1900 at the La Alianza Supreme Lodge.[70] In May of 1914, he loaned La Alianza Hispano-Americana $20,000.00 to erect its new building on West Congress Street.[71] Teofilo was also active at Tucson in support of World War I Bonds. He purchased $5,000.00 of Liberty Bonds in the *Make It a Million* sale.[72] Teofilo was also responsive to the needs of community. In 1927, he donated land to the City of Tucson for *El Tiradito: Shrine to the Sinner*,[73] and provided Otero Hall to the Town of Tubac for educational and community needs which has since been added to the Tubac Presidio State Park and Museum.

Teofilo died at 7:22 am on 5/15/1941 of penile cancer at Tucson, AZ and is buried at Holy Hope Cemetery.[74] Upon his death at 77 years old, he was survived by two nieces, Ana Maria Coenen and Brijida Coenen, and a number of grandnieces and grandnephews. He had two children with Anna Brown: Ana Brown Provencio and Eduardo Otero; and two children with Leonor Kaphan. Teofilo's obituary said "[d]uring the last days of the open range, Teofilo Otero's cattle, one of the largest herds in Southern Arizona, ranged from Casa Grande to the Mexican border."[75]

Otero, Leonor Kaphan (Capan)

See Kaphan (Capan), Leonor

Otero, Magdalena

Magdalena was born approximately 1817 and died on 2/22/1821. Her parents were Atanacio Otero and Carmen Quijada. She was buried at the Tubac Presidio Cemetery and was a 3rd generation heir to the Otero land grant.[76]

Otero, Manuel Ochoa

Manuel Otero was born on 7/14/1867 in Tubac.[77] He was the son of Sabino Otero and Manuela Ochoa,[78] however his mother is also reported to have been named Concepcion.[79] Occupation: Freighter.[80] Manuel married Angela, affectionately known as "Angelita" Kilbray aka Gilbray of Pinal County, AZ. He filed a lawsuit against his uncle Teofilo Otero as the Executor of the Sabino Otero Estate that claimed he had a superior right to the Sabino Otero estate as Sabino's natural son. The case was dismissed. Manuel was a 5th generation Otero of the land grant family of Tubac.

Manuel's son Fernando reported that his father was raised by Sister Clara Otero. He also said his grandfather Sabino paid Santiago Gastelum to care for his son.[81] Census records from 1860-1910 for the households of Sister Clara Otero aka Gabriela Otero or Santiago Gastelum fail to support Fernando's claim.

Manuel died on 9/3/1958[82] and his last known residence was 934 South 11th, Tucson, AZ. His obituary published on 9/5/1958 stated:

> Manuel O. Otero, 91, of 142 W. 31st St., died Wednesday at Pima County Hospital. Native of Tubac. Husband of Angelita. Father of Fernando K., Mrs. Louis Verdugo, Mrs. Frank Vega, Mrs. Agustine Estrada, Mrs. Carlos Morales and Mrs. William Flores Jr. Twenty-one grandchildren and eight great-grandchildren. Rosary at 8 p.m. tomorrow at Tucson Mortuary Chapel. Mass at 10:30 a.m. tomorrow at San Agustin Cathedral. Burial Sunday in Holy Hope Cemetery.[83]

Otero, Manuel Quijada

Census records taken during Manuel Otero's life state he was born at Tubac, Sonora, Mexico about 1810.[84] US National Park Service Database Mission 2000 disagrees and reports he was born in Alamos, Sonora, Mexico about 1809.

Confusion regarding Manuel's birth location exists because another man named Manuel Otero married to Maria de las Nieves Esquer was born in Alamos, Sonora, Mexico and was a contemporary of Manuel Otero of Tubac. Historical records and Otero oral family history suggest they are cousins.

Manuel Otero of Tubac was listed as an adult living with his parents Joséf Atanacio Otero and Carmen Quijada, and grandfather Spanish land grantee Don Torivio de Otero in 1831.[85] J. Homer Thiel's *Presidio Families of Tucson* reports Manuel was the eldest of six siblings including: Magdalena, Maria, Fernando, Piedad, and Jesus.

In 1845, Manuel was one of seven residents who signed a report in support of recent Mexican government changes placing General José Cosme de Urrea in power over all of Sonora, Mexico.[86] Manuel married Maria Clara Martinez and they had seven children: Francisca, Sabino, Maria Elena de Jesus, Maria Manuela, Gabriela, Fernando, and Teofilo. Manuel purchased a Mexican deed of land adjacent to the Otero land grant from José Maria Martinez, effectively expanding the boundaries of El Rancho de Otero. AZ territorial Governor Goodwin appointed Manuel as Alcalde (mayor) of Tubac on 1864. Manuel died in 1870 of pneumonia.

Otero, María Elena de Jesus

Daughter of Manuel and Maria Clara Martinez Otero, she was born in Tubac on 8/17/1846[87] and was baptized on 9/8/1846 at Tumacácori Mission.[88] She married José Mauricio Maximiano Castro on 3/29/1864 at Tucson officiated by Father Bosco.[89] They had two children, Brijida and Eloisa, the latter died in August of 1868.[90] Maria Elena died February 1868 at Tubac and was buried in Tucson according to the Diocese of Tucson Burial Registry 1863-1887.[91]

Otero, Maria Manuela

Manuela Otero, she was born at Tubac, Mexico (AZ). She was also baptized at Tubac witnesses by godparents Jesus Maria Orozco and Nicolas Herrera.[92] Manuela married Louis Quesse who was 19 years her senior.[93] Louisa born approximately 2/1870,[94] Occupation: Housewife.[95] After her husband's death, Manuela assumed his role managing the family's herd of cattle and real estate[96] and owned an Arizona livestock brand.[97] She was one of the co-petitioners to the Court of Private Land Claims No. 13 to have the Otero Spanish land grant of 1789 ratified under U.S. law, and 4th generation heir-at-law of the Otero land grant.

Her brother Sabino was appointed as the Administrator of her estate[98] with Richard Starr, Severin Rambaud, and Manuel Amado as appraisers. At the time of her death, she owned about 450 head of cattle ranging in Pima and Santa Cruz counties, Territory of Arizona. She also owned real property in Tucson known as Lot 5, Block 209; Lot 6, Block 214; and parts of Lots 7 and 11 in Block 221, reported on official survey as Subdivisions 11 and 29 of Block 221 totaling and estate value of $9,100.00.[99] The cattle brand owned by Maria Manuela is considered the oldest Otero brand, possibly inherited from her father Manuel Otero.[100]

She died a widow on 7/20/1898 intestate in Pima County, AZ.[101] Upon her death, she was survived by brothers Sabino and Teofilo Otero, and Gabriela Otero aka Sister Clara Otero. Teofilo and Sister Clara each surrendered their lawful portion of Manuela's estate via Deed to Sabino Otero in exchange for "one dollar and love and affection."[102]

Otero, Maria Ygnacia

Maria was a sister of Torivio de Otero, Otero land grant recipient. She was married to Pedro Sebastian Villaescusa and they had several children: Juan José[103] Maria Ygnacia baptized Andrés Durán before Fray Balthasar Carrillo on 12/1/1787.[104]

Otero, María Ygnacia Salazar de

See Salazar, María Ygnacia

Otero, Olga Maria

Olga was born on 6/4/1935 daughter of Fernando Otero and Otila Moreno at Tucson, AZ. At the time of her birth, her family resided at 814 South 10th Avenue.[105]

Olga is remembered for her efforts to save the Otero family home at 219 South Main Street. The Otero family home façade is preserved at the Arizona Historical Society Museum at Tucson, AZ. Olga is a 6th generation Otero of the land grant family of Tubac.

Otero, Ricardo Kaphan

Ricardo was the second son of Teofilo Otero and Leonor Kaphan. He was born on 4/26/1891[106] at Tubac, AZ Territory. He died on 3/20/1946 at Nogales, AZ of Silicosis, a form of lung disease.[107]

Occupation: Vaquero and Miner. During his youth, he was a vaquero at local Santa Cruz Valley ranches including Baca Float and La Canoa. Ricardo left Tubac to become a miner working the mines at Twin Buttes, Harshaw, Lochiel, Ruby, Silverbell and Tiger. He married Francisca Quijada of Saric, Sonora Mexico at Amado, AZ. They had numerous children including: Rosa,[108] Ricardo, Maria Reina, Ramon,[109] Manuel,[110] Ruben,[111], and Rita, and they raised nephew Jose Garcia as their own. His last residence was 153A Beck Street, Nogales, AZ. He is buried at the old Nogales Cemetery.[112] Ricardo was a 5th generation descendant of the Otero land grant family of Tubac. Stories Ricardo told his granddaughter Celia Sinohui Hinojosa about the Otero land grant family ignited her lifelong curiosity to discover more about the family's history. Although he was not a petitioner against his father Teofilo Otero's estate, he was awarded $2,500.00 in settlement as the son of Teofilo Otero which was reduced to $10.00 through actions taken by his brother Ysidro.

Otero, Rita

Rita was born est. 1885 at Tubac, Territory of AZ, daughter of Fernando Otero and Susana Kaphan. She was a 5th generation Otero of the land grant family of Tubac. Rita married Albert Avila of Yuma, AZ. They had 4 children: Eva, Mary E., Albert, and Ruben.[113]

Otero, Sabino

Sabino was born on 12/30/1842 at Tubac, Sonora, Mexico, eldest son of Manuel Otero and Maria Clara Martinez. He was one of the co-petitioners to the Court of Private Land Claims No. 13 to have the Otero Spanish land grant of 1789 ratified under U.S. law and 4th generation heir-at-law to the Otero land grant.

Occupation: Stock raiser[114] and owner of multiple Arizona livestock brands.[115] Sabino was civic-minded. He regularly served as a jurist,[116] was nominated for positions within the Pima County Democratic Party[117] and state legislature;[118] served as Militia Captain for the Upper Santa Cruz district,[119] and as an Election Official at Tubac and Bosque.[120] Diverse in his endeavors, he also served as a coroner.[121]

In furtherance of his pursuits as a stock raiser, Sabino was active in the Arizona Live Stock Ranchmen's Association,[122] the Pima County Cattle Ranchers Association,[123] and the Santa Cruz Stock Growers Association.[124] He was a "shrewd and influential citizen" of Tubac who travelled across Europe and attended the Paris Exposition of 1878.[125] He was the Attorney for the Estate and Administrator of his sister Manuela O. de Quesse's estate,[126] Attorney for and administrator of the Estate of Louis Quesse,[127] and Petitioner of the Otero Land Grant Claim for the Heirs of Clara Martinez Otero. He was also an incorporating officer of the Santa Cruz Land and Water Co. along with Frank L. Proctor, George J. Roskruge, John Anderson, and Manley S. Snyder.[128]

Lauded for his charitable endeavors, Sabino was a patron to local Catholic diocese at Tucson and the Sisters of St. Joseph at Tucson, Phoenix, Prescott and Los Angeles. Although he was once reported to have been close to marriage,[129] Sabino remained single throughout his life.

Sabino's last residence was 84 Main Street, Tucson, AZ.[130] In 1886, Sabino remodeled the home at 219 South Main Street built by his father Manuel Otero. Mr. H.C. Sigfried had the remodeling contract.[131] The façade of the old Otero home at Tucson is preserved as an historical exhibit at the Arizona Historical Society Museum at Tucson.

He died at 1:00 am on January 22, 1914 at Tucson, AZ of cirrhosis of the liver. He was survived by younger brother Teofilo Otero, two nieces, Ana Maria Coenen and Brigida Coenen, grandnephews Alfonso and Eugene E. Coenen, and a number of grandnieces and grandnephews. He had one known child, Manuel Ochoa Otero.

Otero, Sister Clara

Sister Clara Otero was born Gabriela Otero in 1849 in Tubac, youngest daughter of Manuel Otero and Maria Clara Martinez.[132]

Sister Clara (Gabriela) was only three-years-old when Tubac was sold by Mexico to the United States government pursuant to the Gadsden Purchase. As a devoted daughter, she helped her mother Maria Clara Martinez de Otero with household chores and helped care for her younger siblings Fernando and Teofilo Otero and nieces Ana Maria Comadurán and Brijida Castro. When she turned 13, Gabriela witnessed the Civil War operations at Tubac and experienced the creation of the Arizona Territory in 1863. Occupation: Gabriela's quiet domestic life drastically changed when she met the Sisters of St. Joseph's Academy. She attended the Academy as an award-winning student[133] and was active in school events.[134]

Gabriela formally entered the St. Joseph's Convent and Academy for Females at Tucson on February 2, 1878.[135] The convent and academy was originally established in 1870 adjacent to the old San Augustine Cathedral when the entire Arizona Territory had less than 10k inhabitants. It was also known as the "French School" because the founding nuns spoke French.[136] Her name was officially changed from Gabriela Otero to Sister Clara of the Blessed Sacrament when she took her final and perpetual vows on March 12, 1880 before Bishop Salpointe. As an educator, she was diverse. She taught Spanish, drawing, painting, piano, harp, guitar, and violin. Sister Clara helped establish numerous institutions in Arizona including St. Mary's Hospital, St. Joseph's Academy, and San Xavier School for Children at Tucson; the school at Komatke near Laveen; and schools in Yuma, Florence, and Prescott.[137]

Sister Clara was posthumously inducted into the Arizona Women's' Hall of Fame on 10/29/1988 for being "one of the first young Hispanics in Tucson to join the Sisters of St. Joseph. Her online biography at the Arizona Women's Hall of Fame website misstates certain facts.[138] It reports that Sister Clara was born at Tucson. Census records taken during the 1860s report that she was in fact born at Tubac. Second, the bio reports her family moved to Tucson prior to her birth. Census records reveal that the Otero family did not move to Tucson until just prior to 1863 when her younger brother Teofilo was born.

Sister Clara died of consumption at St. Joseph's Academy on 9/4/1905 at the age of 56. In her honor, a quilt with her image was made by the Arizona Quilters Guild and placed on permanent display at the Carnegie Center, 1101 W. Washington St, in downtown Phoenix. Her image is also available online at the Arizona Memory Project. She was one of the co-petitioners to the Court of Private Land Claims No. 13 to have the Otero Spanish land grant of 1789 ratified under U.S. law, and 4th generation heir-at-law of the Otero land grant.

Otero, (Don) Torivio (Toribio) de

Torivio's birth and death dates are unknown. He was the recipient of the Otero Spanish land grant of 1/29/1789. He married Maria Ygnacia Salazar at Santa Ana, New Spain (Mexico) on 2/16/1779. Present at the nuptials were Maria Josefa de Urrea, Juan Tomás de Belderrain, Francisco Xavier Ignacio Salazar, José de Otero, Francisca Granillo officiated by Fray Francisco Sánchez Zúñiga. The marriage record stated:

> On February 16, 1779, the requirements mandated by the Holy Council of Trent having been complied with and the sacred doctrinal laws having been met with no impediment resulting to prevent the marriage, the following were married and veiled before me, minister for His Majesty in this mission of San Ignacio, in *faciœ et justa ritual ecclesiœ*, Don Toribio de
> Otero, a single man, son of Don Josef de Otero and Doña Francisca Granillo, residents of the place called Cucurpe, and María Ignacia Salazar, a young maiden, daughter of the late Don Vicente Salazar and his legitimate wife Doña Josefa de Urrea, residents of this place called Santa Ana. Witnesses were Don Francisco Salazar and Don Juan Tomás Belderrain, for which truth I signed on the said day, month, and year as above. Fr. Francisco Zuñiga (rubric) Minister of Doctrine for His Majesty.[139]

Torivio received the first private title to Spanish (Arizona) land at Tubac on 1/10/1789. A highly respected citizen, Torivio was called upon by Tubac *presidio* commanders to act as a witness of several important land transactions. He witnessed the signatures of Manuel de Leon and Jose Manuel Soto Mayor for the original Tumacácori land grant claim[140] and the second Francisco Nuñez land transaction at Tubac.[141]

It has been suggested that Dos Santos Antonio Otero y Peon may have been Torivio's grandfather, from the family of Pedro Luciano de Otero, part owner of the La Valencia silver mine at Guanajuato, Mexico.[142] No documents have surfaced to date to support these claims.

Otero, Ysidro (aka Isidro) Kaphan (Capan)

Ysidro was born on 12/18/1890[143] as the eldest son of Teofilo Otero and Leonor Kaphan. He married Porfiria "Cachita" Olivas in 1912 at Tubac, Territory of AZ[144] and they had 10 children: Francisco,[145] Ysidro,[146] Jose,[147] Joe,[148] Elvira,[149]Rosa,[150] Elena,[151] Ysidro,[152] Juan Ysidro,[153] and Leonardo (Feliciano)[154].

Occupation: Farmer, both ranching and agriculture.[155] Ysidro worked at the Rancho de Otero and his own farm. He was respected locally for his knowledge of agriculture and correspondence indicates he had an amicable relationship with his father. Ysidro owned twenty-four lots in Tubac Townsite. He died on 1/21/1978 at Roseville, Placer, CA[156] and is buried at the Tubac, AZ cemetery. Ysidro was a 5th generation Otero of the land grant family of Tubac.

Provencio, Ana Brown Otero

See Otero, Ana Brown

Quesse, Louis

Born in Minder, Prussia, Louis married María Manuela Otero. At age 22, Louis enlisted with the U.S. Army 3rd Infantry on July 14, 1845 at New Orleans, LA employed as a blacksmith.[157] In 1870, Louis owned an estimated $500.00 in real estate and $3,500.0 in personal estate.[158] Occupation: Farmer.[159]

Quesse, Maria Manuela Otero de

See, Otero, Maria Manuela

Quijada, Carmen

According to numerous historical documents at the US National Park Service Database Mission 2000, Carmen Quijada is the spouse of Josef Atanacio Otero, son of Spanish land grantee Don Torivio de Otero. The same database also lists Carmen as the wife of Maximo Otero married on 4/22/1820 at Tumacácori witnessed by Tubac presidio soldier Francisco Xavier Marqués and Ensign of the Buena Vista Presidio Ignacio Elias Gonzales.

Salazar, María Ygnacia

María Ygnacia was the wife of Torivio de Otero, Otero land grantee. Her parents were Vicente Prudencio Salazar and María Josefa de Urrea of Santa Ana, New Spain (Mexico).[160]

Urrea, Bernardo de

Bernardo was a Basque criollo born at Culiacan, Sonora Nueva España in 1710 and died on April of 1777. Grandfather-in-law to Don Torivio de Otero, Spanish land grantee, Bernardo holds the distinction of being the person to own a ranch in northern Sonora, Mexico from which Arizona takes its name.[161]

APPENDIX D

Francisco Nunez 1773 Land Grant

National Archives and Records Administration. The National Archives at Riverside. 49, Records of the Bureau of Land Management. Arizona Court of Private Land Claims. Miscellaneous Files 1789-1907. Spanish Documents from Miscellaneous Files. Box No. 27.

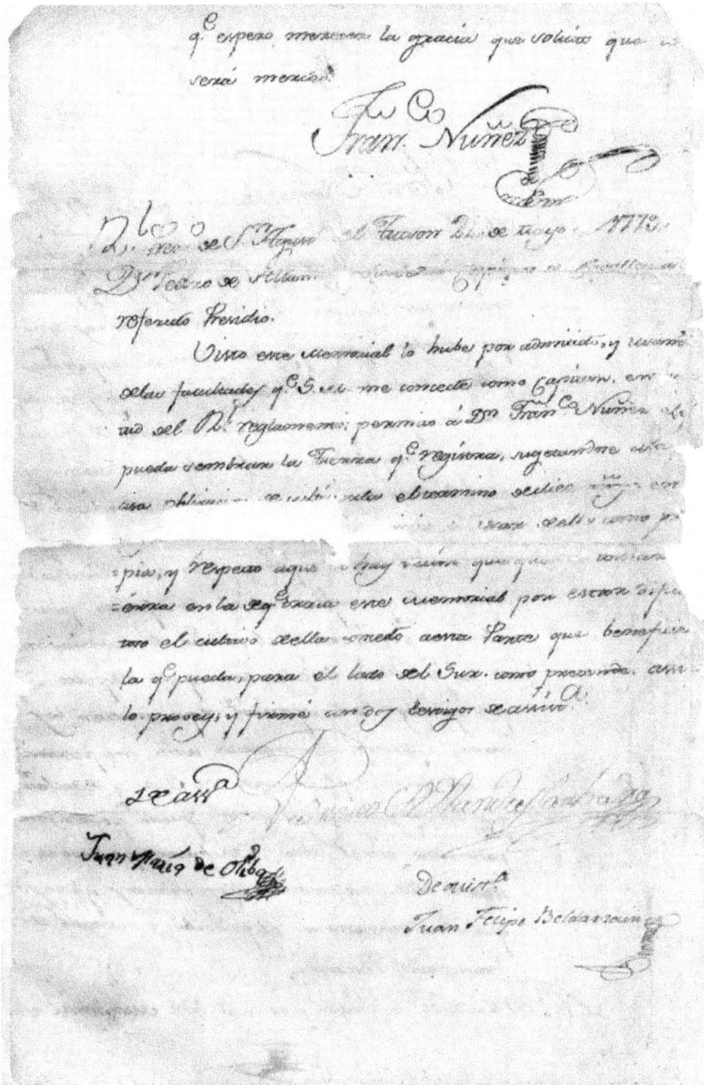
q.e espero merecer la gracia que solicito que [illegible] será merced.

Fran.co Nuñez

R.l Pres.o de S.n Agustin del Tucson 2[illegible] de mayo 1777.

D.n Pedro de Allande [illegible] Capitan [illegible] de Cavalleria de referido Presidio.

Visto este Memorial lo hube por admitido, y usando de las facultades q.e S. M. me concede como Capitan en [illegible] del R.l reglamento; permito a D.n Fran.co Nuñez [illegible] pueda sembrar la tierra q.e registra, [illegible] el camino [illegible] como [illegible] pies, y respecto aque [illegible] hay razon que [illegible] en la [illegible] este memorial por estar [illegible] el cultivo de ella [illegible] parte que beneficia la q.e pueda, para el lado del Sur como [illegible]. Assi lo provey, y firmé con dos testigos de asistencia.

Pedro de Allande y Saabedra

De asist.a

Juan Maria de Olibas

De asist.a

Juan Felipe Beldarrain

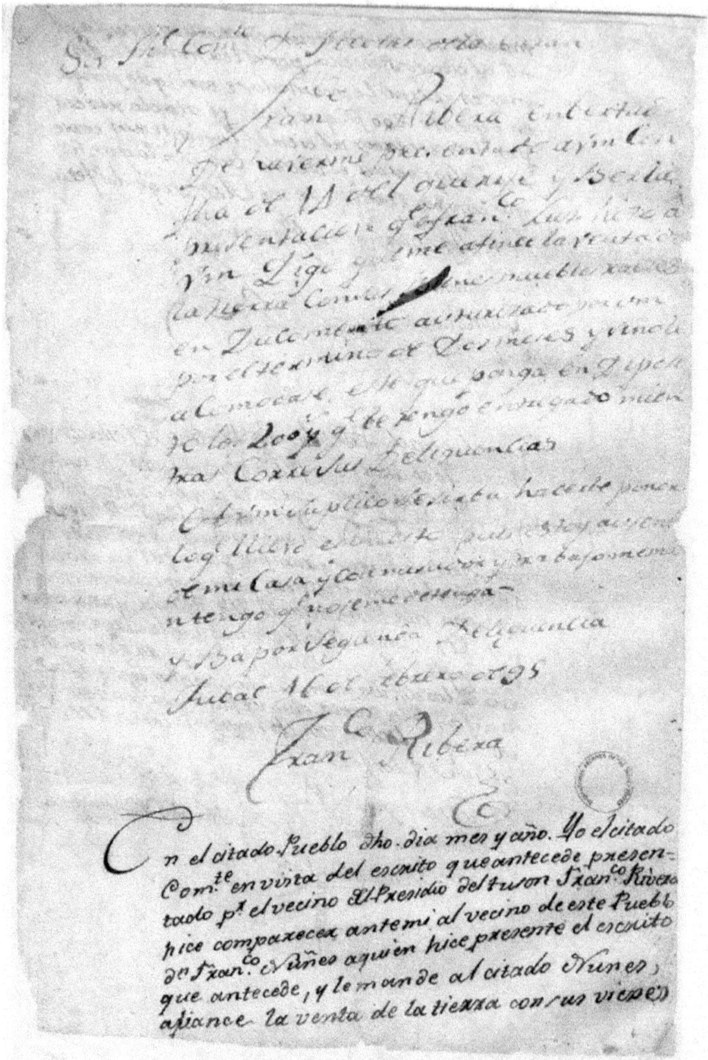

Fran.co Ribera

En el citado Pueblo dho. dia mes y año. Yo el citado Comte en vista del escrito que antecede presentado pr el vecino del Presidio del Tuson Fran.co Rivera hice comparecer ante mi al vecino de este Pueblo Dn Fran.co Nuñes a quien hice presente el escrito que antecede, y le mande al citado Nunes, afiance la venta de la tierra con sus vienes

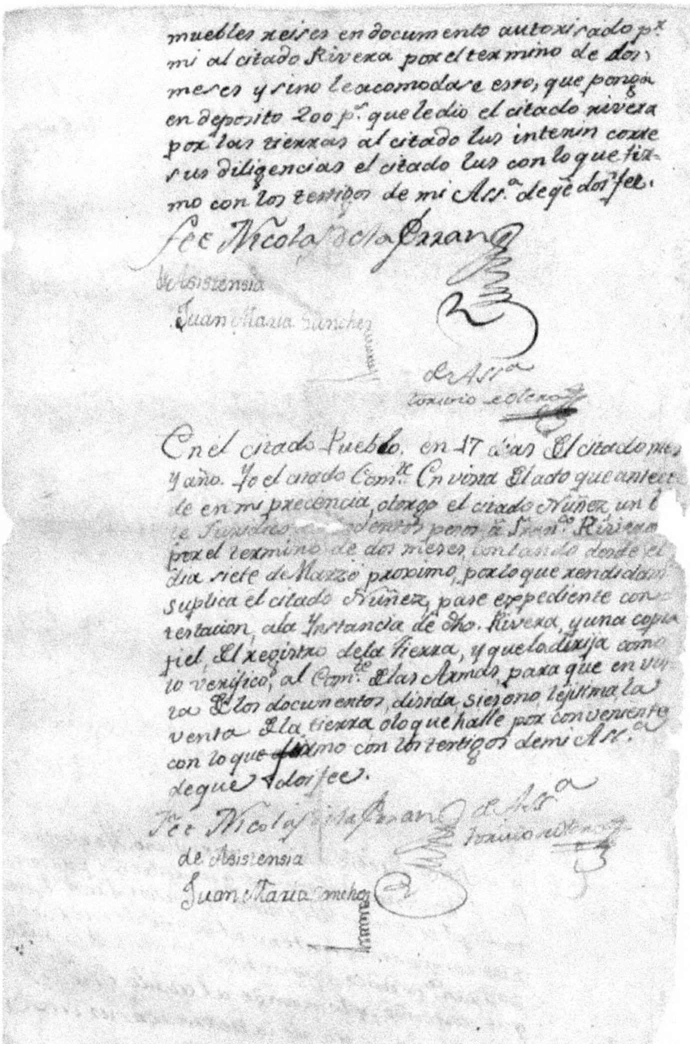

muebles reises en documento autorizado pr.
mi al citado Rivera por el termino de dos
meses y sino le acomodare esto, que ponga
en deposito 200 ps. que le dio el citado rivera
por las tierras al citado Luis interin corre
sus diligencias el citado Luis con lo que firmo con los testigos de mi Asa. de qe. doy fee.

Fee Nicolas de la [illegible]
de Asistensia
Juan Maria Sanchez
de Asa.
Antonio [illegible]

En el citado Pueblo en 17 dias el citado mes
y año. Yo el citado Comte. en vista de lo que antecede en mi presencia, otorgo el citado Nuñez un [illegible]
[illegible] pero a [illegible] Rivera
por el termino de dos meses contando desde el
dia siete de Marzo proximo, por lo que rendidam[ente]
suplica el citado Nuñez, pase expediente con-
testacion, a la Instancia de dho. Rivera, y una copia
fiel del registro de la tierra, y que la dirija como
lo verifico, al Comte. de las Armas, para que en vista de los documentos, decida si es o no legitima la
venta de la tierra o lo que halle por conveniente
con lo que firmo con los testigos de mi Asa.
de que doy fee.

Fee Nicolas de la [illegible]
de Asa.
Antonio [illegible]
de Asistensia
Juan Maria Sanchez

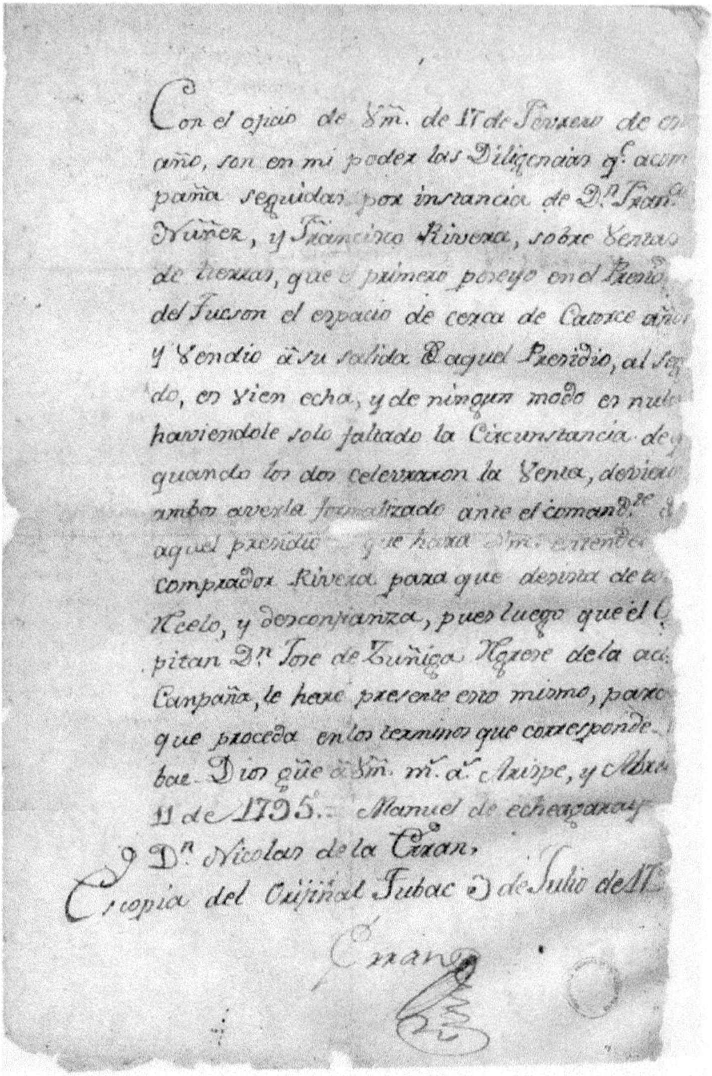
Con el oficio de Vm. de 17 de Febrero de este
año, son en mi poder las Diligencias q.e acom-
paña seguidas por instancia de D.n Fran.co
Nuñez, y Francisco Rivera, sobre venta
de tierras, que el primero poseyo en el Presidio
del Tucson el espacio de cerca de Catorce años
y vendio à su salida de aquel Presidio, al seg[un]
do, es vien echa, y de ningun modo es nula
haviendole solo faltado la Circunstancia de q.
quando los dos celebraron la Venta, devieron
ambos averla formalizado ante el comand.te de
aquel presidio que hara Vm. entender al
comprador Rivera para que desista de su
rezelo, y desconfianza, pues luego que el Capitan D.n Jose de Zuñiga regrese de la ac-
Campaña, le hare presente esto mismo, para
que proceda en los terminos que corresponde.
Dios güe à Vm. m.s a.s Arizpe, y Abril
11 de 1795.= Manuel de echegaray
S. D.n Nicolas de la Erran.
Es copia del Original Tubac [illegible] de Julio de 17[illegible]
Erran

por escrito con lo que firmo con los testigos de mi Asistencia de que doy fee.

Tte Nicolas de la Garza

de Asistencia Juan Maria Sanchez

de Asistencia Tomas de Otero

APPENDIX E

UNITED STATES DEPUTY SURVEYOR GEORGE J. ROSKRUGE 1881 FIELD NOTES - OTERO LAND GRANT

Arizona State Library, Archives & Public Records. *Field Notes of the Preliminary Survey of House lot in Tubac, Pima Co. Arizona Territory. Sabino Otero et al claim.* Microfiche. From NARA U.S. Bureau of Land Management records.

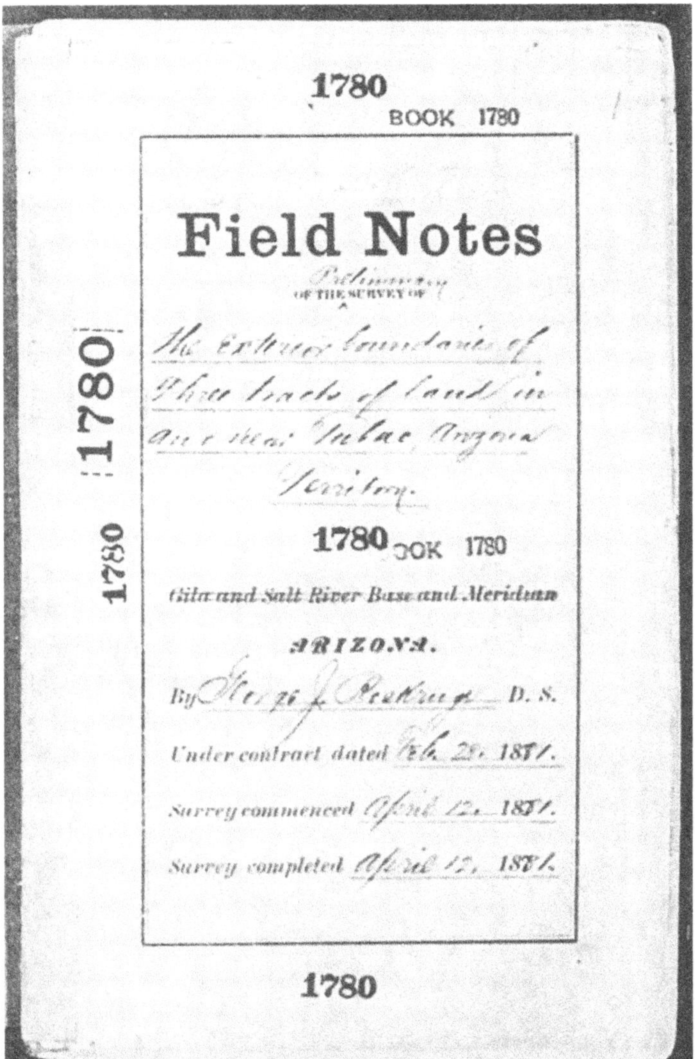
1780

BOOK 1780

1780

1780

Field Notes

Preliminary
OF THE SURVEY OF

the exterior boundaries of three tracts of land in and near Tubac, Arizona Territory.

1780 BOOK 1780

Gila and Salt River Base and Meridian

ARIZONA.

By George J. Roskruge D. S.

Under contract dated Feb. 28. 1881.

Survey commenced April 12. 1881.

Survey completed April 12, 1881.

1780

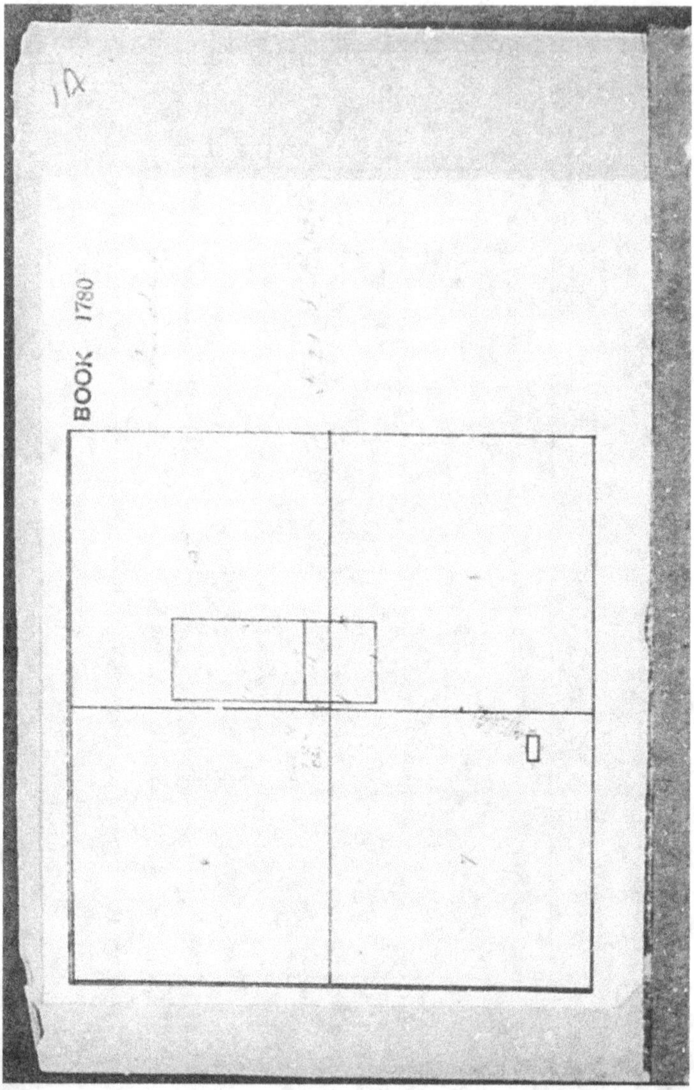
BOOK 1780

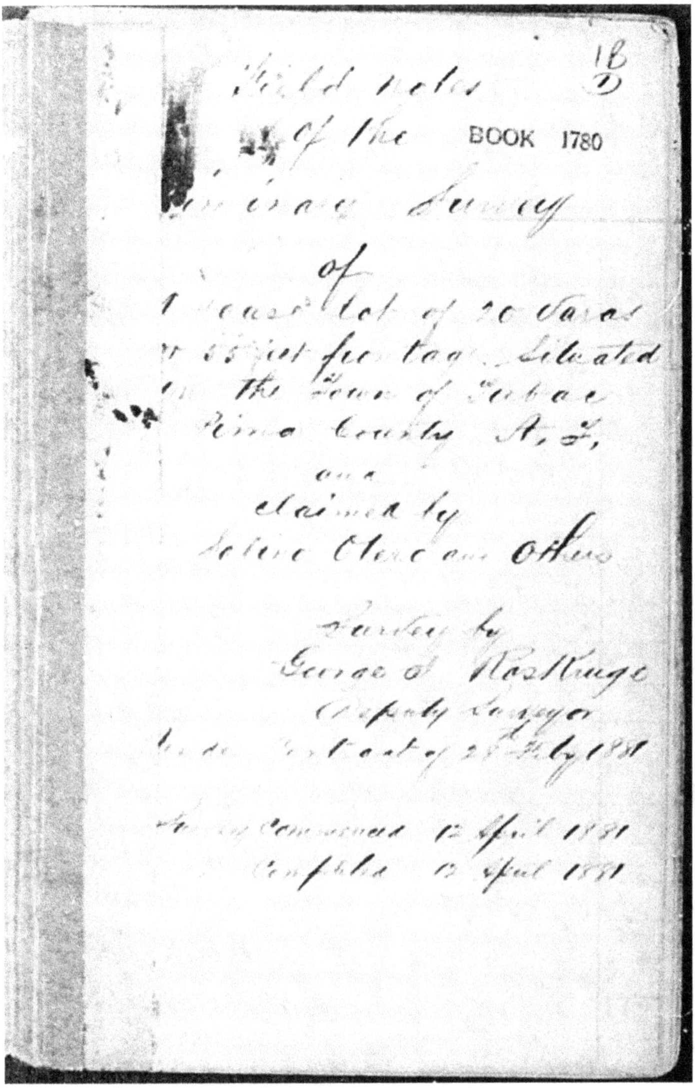

1B
D

Field notes
of the
BOOK 1780
Preliminary Survey
of
1 House Lot of 20 Varas
or 55 feet frontage situated
in the Town of Tubac
Pima County A. T.
and
claimed by
Sabino Otero and Others

Surveyed by
George J. Roskruge
Deputy Surveyor
under Contract of 28th Feby 1881

Survey Commenced 12 April 1881
Completed 12 April 1881

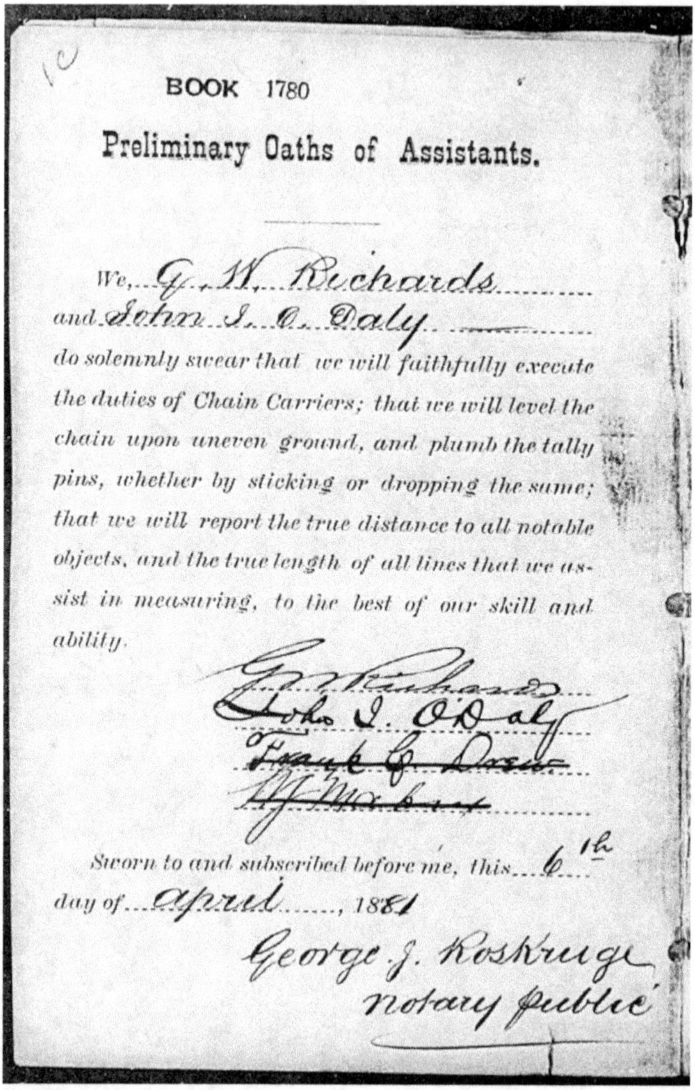

1c

BOOK 1780

Preliminary Oaths of Assistants.

We, G. W. Richards
and John I. O. Daly
do solemnly swear that we will faithfully execute the duties of Chain Carriers; that we will level the chain upon uneven ground, and plumb the tally pins, whether by sticking or dropping the same; that we will report the true distance to all notable objects, and the true length of all lines that we assist in measuring, to the best of our skill and ability.

G. W. Richards
John I. O'Daly
~~[illegible]~~
~~[illegible]~~

Sworn to and subscribed before me, this 6th
day of April, 1881

George J. Roskruge
Notary Public

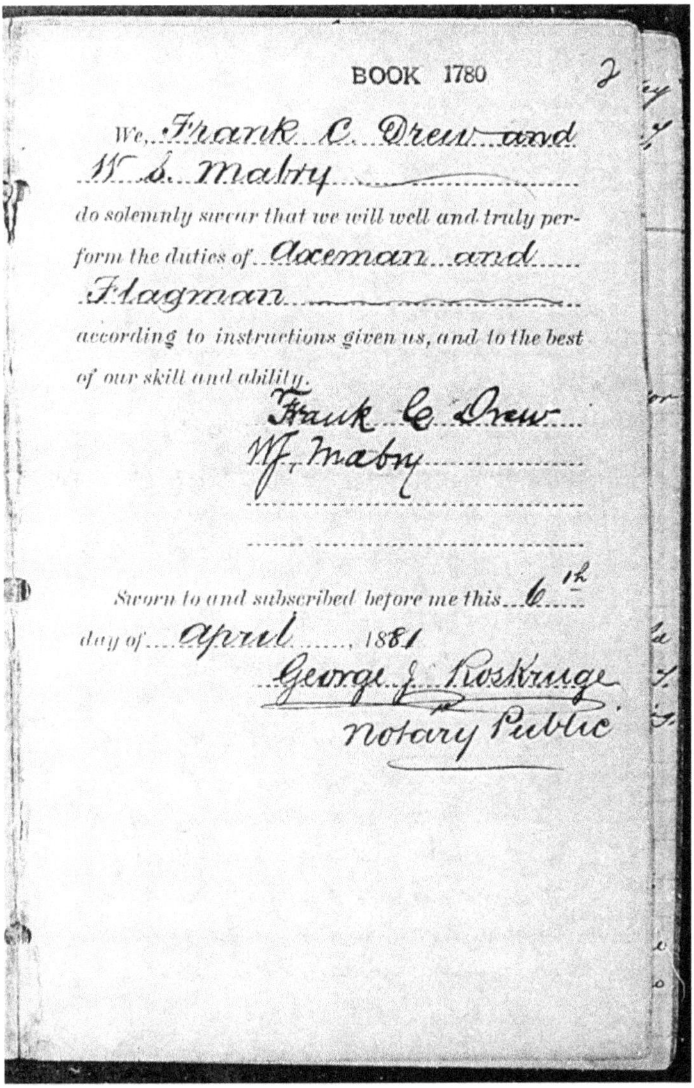

BOOK 1780 2

We, Frank C. Drew and W. S. Mabry

do solemnly swear that we will well and truly perform the duties of Axeman and Flagman

according to instructions given us, and to the best of our skill and ability.

Frank C. Drew

W. S. Mabry

Sworn to and subscribed before me this 6th day of April, 1881

George J. Roskruge

Notary Public

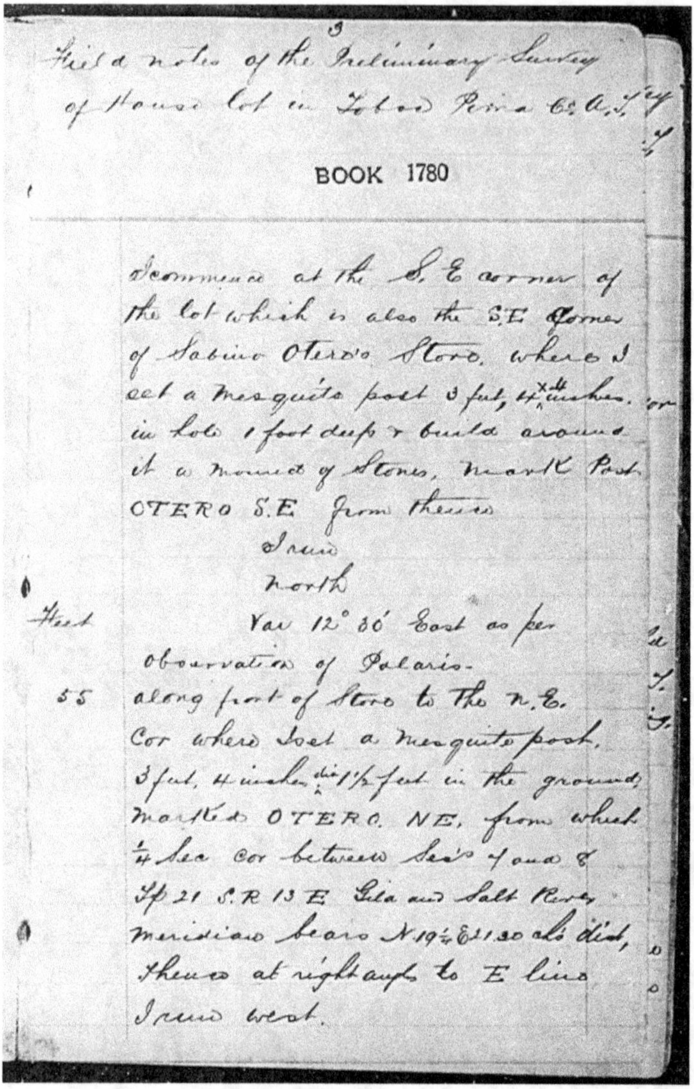

3

Field notes of the Preliminary Survey
of House lot in Tubac Pima Co. A.T.

BOOK 1780

I commence at the S.E corner of
the lot which is also the S.E Corner
of Sabino Otero's Store, where I
set a mesquite post 3 feet, 4x4 inches. or
in hole 1 foot deep & build around
it a mound of Stones, mark Post
OTERO S.E from thence
I run
North
West Var 12° 30' East as per
observation of Polaris-
55 along front of Store to the N.E.
Cor where I set a mesquite post,
3 feet, 4 inches dia 1½ feet in the ground,
marked OTERO NE, from which
¼ Sec Cor between Sec's 7 and 8
Tp 21 S.R 13 E Gila and Salt River
meridian bears N 19¼ E 21.30 chs dist,
thence at right angles to E line
I run west.

4

Field notes of the Preliminary Survey
of House lot in Tubac Pima Co. A.T.

BOOK 1780

Feet — Var 12° 30' East

110 to the N.W. Cor of lot where I set
a mesquite post 3 feet. 3"x3" in
1 foot in ground and build
around it a mound of stones.
Mark post OTERO, N.W.
Thence at right angles to north
line,

True South

Var 12° 30' East

55 to the S.W. cor where I set a
mesquite post 3 feet. 4"x4" in in.
pit 1 foot deep and build
around it a mound of stones,
mark post OTERO, S.W.
Thence at right angles
to west line,

True East

Var 12° 30' E.

110 to place of begining

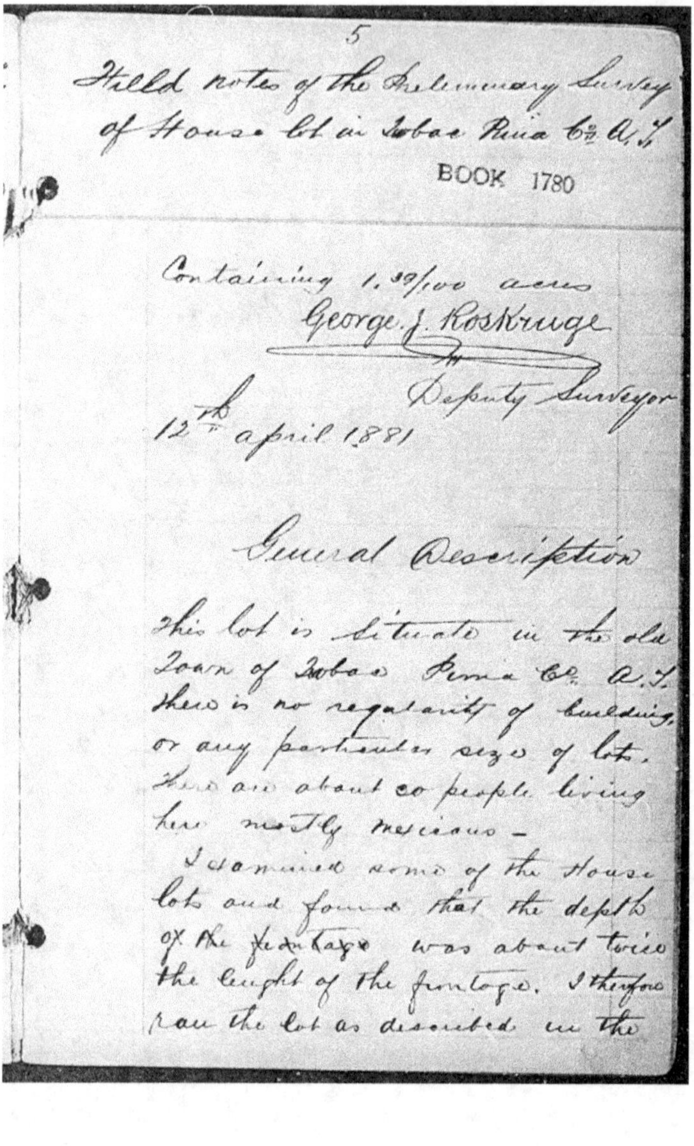
5

Field notes of the Preliminary Survey of House lot in Tubac Pima Co. A.T.

BOOK 1780

Containing 1.39/100 acres

George J. Roskruge

Deputy Surveyor

12th april 1881

General Description

This lot is situated in the old Town of Tubac Pima Co. A.T. there is no regularity of building or any particular size of lots. There are about 60 people living here mostly mexicans -

I examined some of the House lots and found that the depth of the frontage was about twice the length of the frontage. I therefore ran the lot as described in the

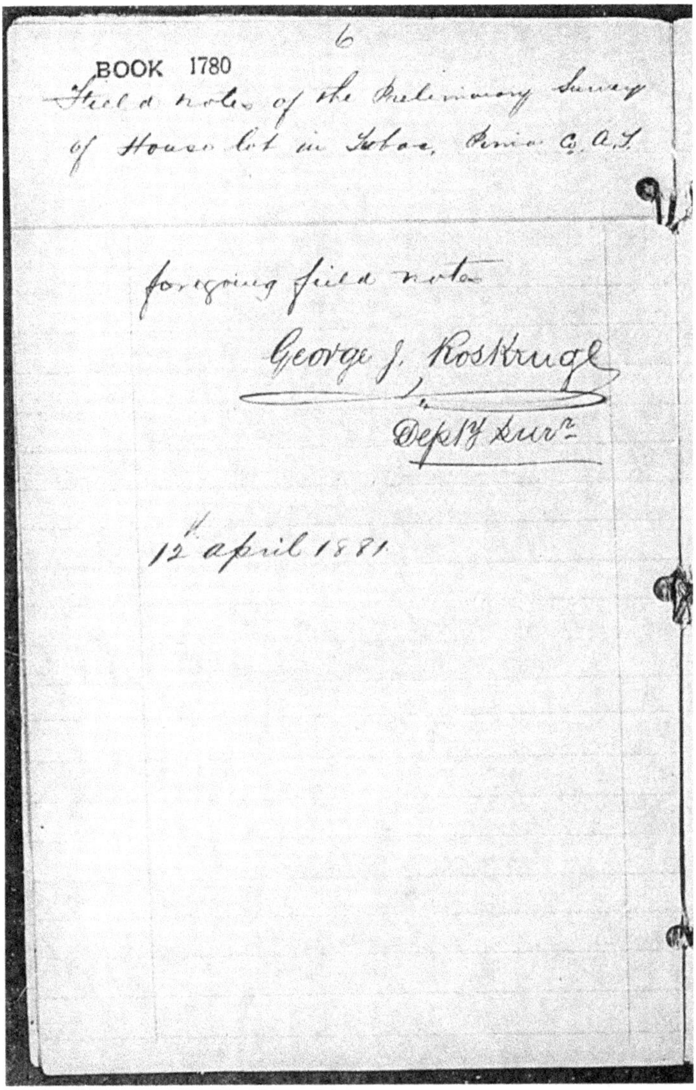

6

BOOK 1780

Field notes of the Preliminary Survey of House lot in Tubac, Pima Co. A.T.

foregoing field notes

George J. Roskruge

Dep'ty Surv'r

12th April 1881

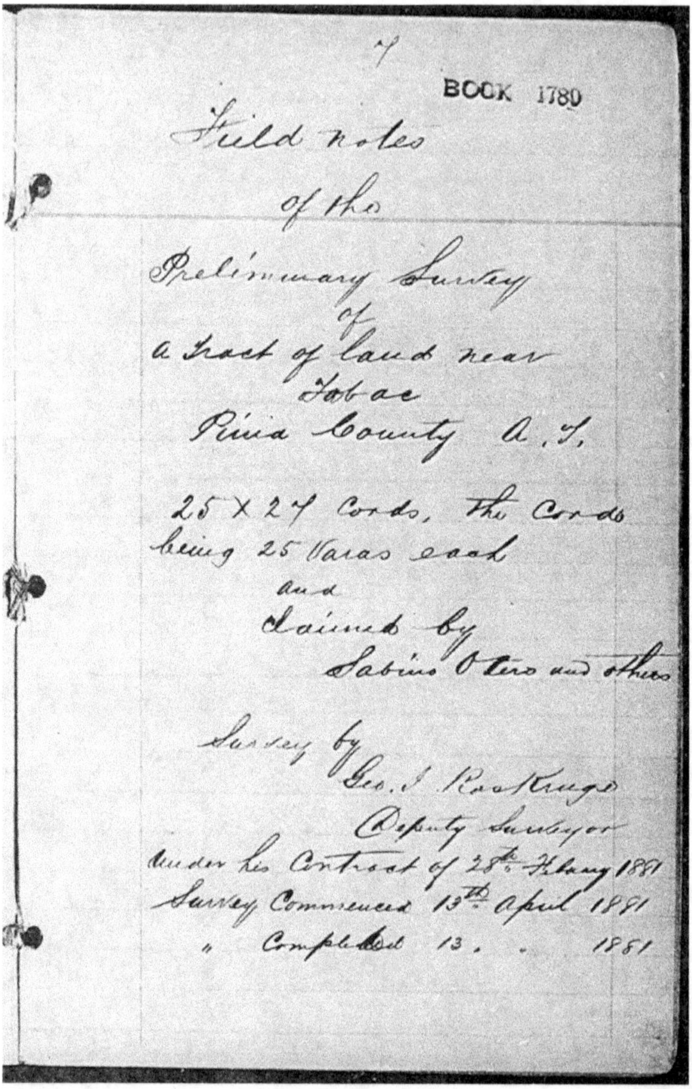

7

BOOK 1780

Field notes
of the
Preliminary Survey
of
a Tract of land near
Tubac
Pima County A.T.

25 X 27 Cords, the Cords
being 25 Varas each
and
claimed by
Sabino Otero and others

Survey by
Geo. J. Roskruge
Deputy Surveyor
under his Contract of 28th February 1881
Survey Commenced 13th April 1881
" Completed 13 " 1881

8

Field notes of the Preliminary Survey
of a Tract of land near Tubac 20 x 27 cords
the cords being 25 varas each,

BOOK 1780

I am now at the old ruins
of the House where Sabino Otero's
Grandfather lived, when he
Cultivated the following described
tract of land, and which is
now Cultivated by Sabino Otero,

I set a willow post 4 feet, 4" 4 in
2 feet in the ground and mark it
on the south side OTERO, N.W
from which old ruins of House bears west
60 lks dist.
Stake in mound of earth with
pits and 3 Trees for Cor to secs
5.6.7&8 of Tp 21, S. R 13 E Gila and
Salt River meridian bears
S 12½° W 4.72 chains distant
from willow post.
Thence
Var 12°.30' E as per

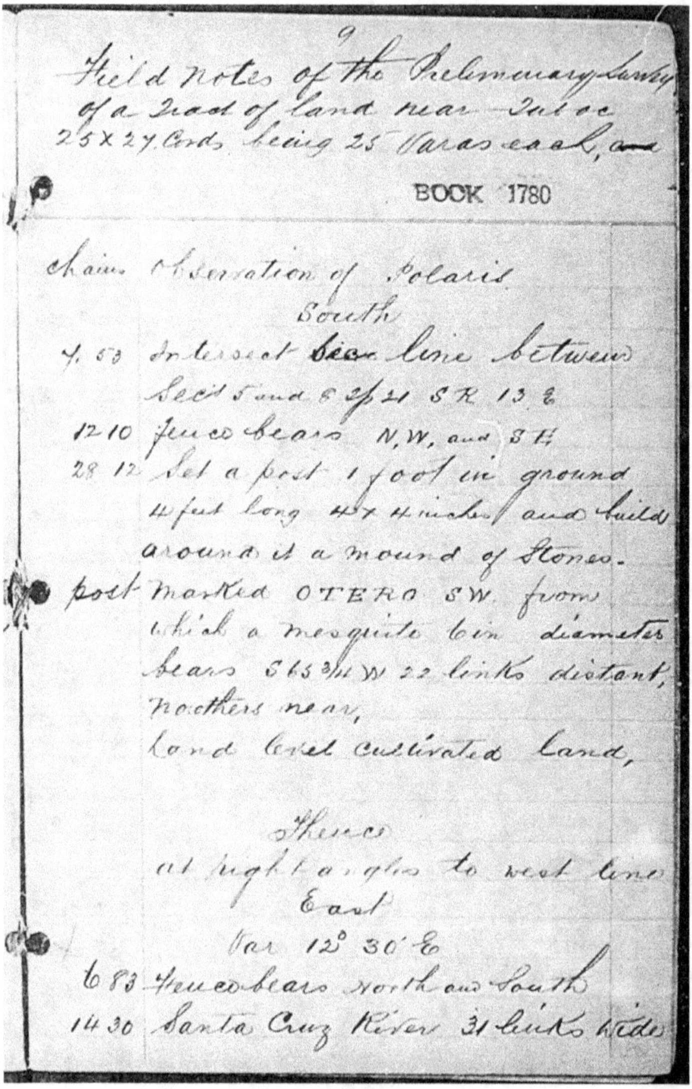

9

Field Notes of the Preliminary Survey
of a Tract of land near Tubac
25 X 27 Cords being 25 Varas each, and

BOOK 1780

Chains Observation of Polaris
South
7.50 Intersect Sec. line between
Secs 5 and 8 Tp 21 S R 13 E
12 10 fence bears N, W, and S E
28 12 Set a post 1 foot in ground
4 feet long 4 x 4 inches and build
around it a mound of Stones.
post marked OTERO SW. from
which a mesquite 6 in diameter
bears S 63 3/4 W 22 links distant,
Northers near,
Land level cultivated land,

Thence
at right angles to west line
East
Var 12° 30' E
6 83 Fence bears North and South
14 30 Santa Cruz River 31 links wide

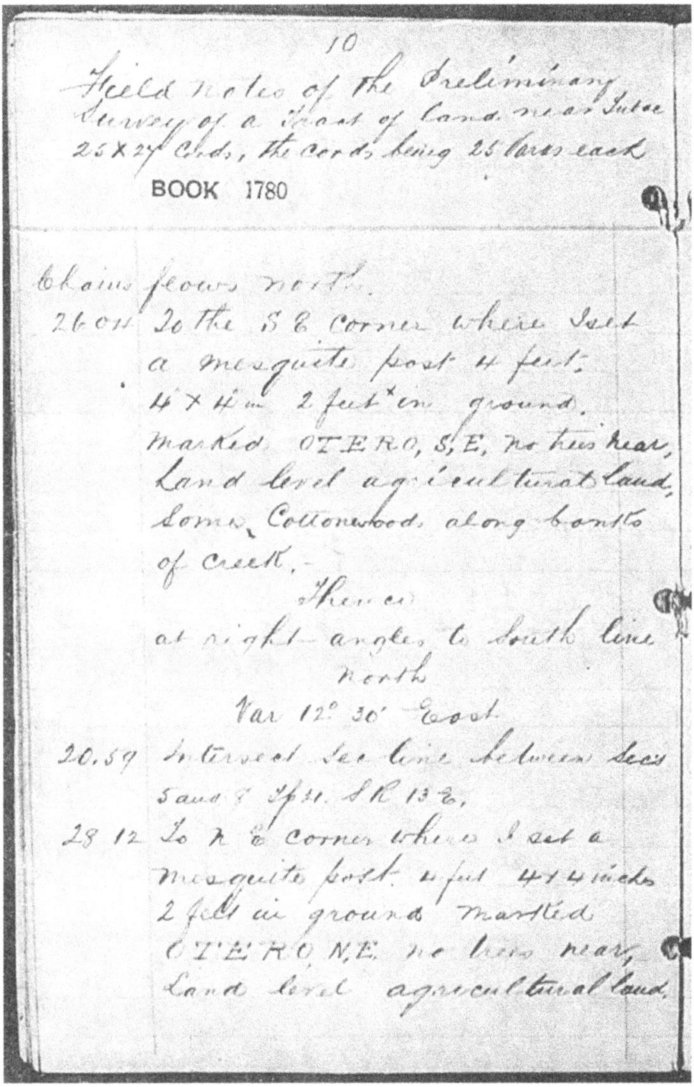

10

Field notes of the Preliminary Survey of a Tract of Land near Tubac 25 x 27 Cords, the cords being 25 varas each

BOOK 1780

Chains flows north.

26.04 To the S E Corner where I set a mesquite post 4 feet. 4 x 4 in 2 feet in ground. marked OTERO, S,E, no trees near, Land level agricultural land, Some Cottonwoods along banks of creek.-

Thence at right angles to South line north

Var 12° 30' East

20.59 Intersect Sec line between Secs 5 and 8 Tp 21. S R 13 E,

28.12 To N E Corner where I set a mesquite post 4 feet 4 x 4 inches 2 feet in ground marked OTERO N,E, no trees near, Land level agricultural land,

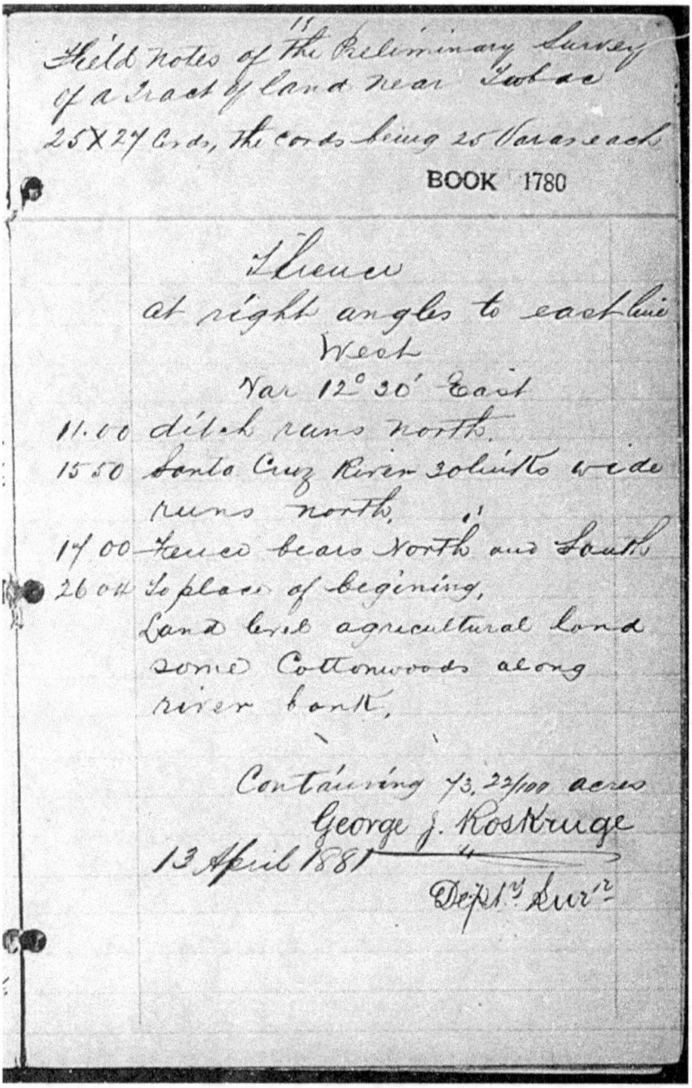

11

Field notes of the Preliminary Survey
of a Tract of land near Tubac
25 X 27 Cords, the cords being 25 Varas each

BOOK 1780

Thence
at right angles to east line
West
Var 12° 30' East
11.00 ditch runs north.
15 50 Santa Cruz River 30 links wide
runs north.
17 00 Fence bears North and South
26 00 To place of begining,
Land best agricultural land
some Cottonwoods along
river bank,

Containing 73.22/100 acres
George J. Roskruge
13 April 1881
Dep't Sur'r

BOOK 1780 12

General description

This tract of land is about ¼ of a mile North of the town of Tubac in the valley of the Santa Cruz. it is situated in Sec 5 and 8 Tp 21. S.R 13 East Gila and Salt River Meridians, the Santa Cruz River runs through it from South to north ditches being run over the land bringing under a high state of Cultivation, the soil is a rich valley loam,

There are some Cottonwoods trees along the river banks and some very old pear trees growing on the land near the old buildings

George J. Roskruge

13th April 1881 Depy Survr

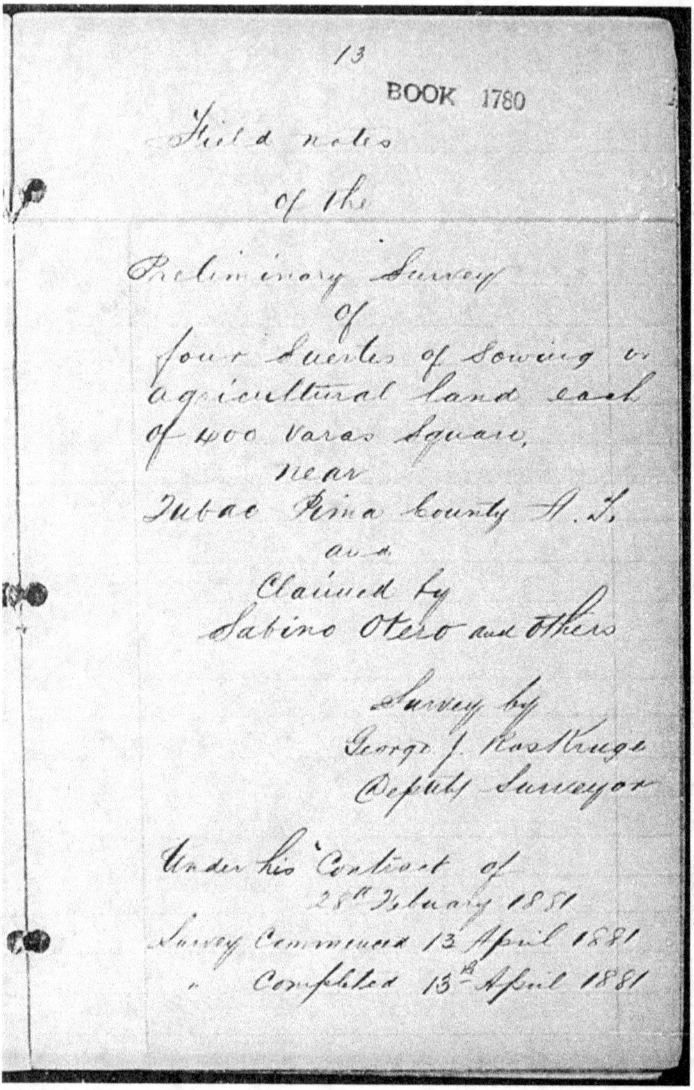

13

BOOK 1780

Field notes
of the
Preliminary Survey
of
four Suertes of Sowing or
agricultural land each
of 400 Varas Square,
near
Tubac Pima County A. T.
and
Claimed by
Sabino Otero and others

Survey by
George J. Roskruge
Deputy Surveyor

Under his Contract of
28th February 1881
Survey Commenced 13 April 1881
" Completed 13th April 1881

14

Field notes of the preliminary Survey of 4 Suertes of land of 400 Varas each near Tubac Pima Co. A. T.

BOOK 1780

I am now at the willow post marked on South Side. OTERO, N.W, near the old Otero's House, from which corner to secs 5.6.7.&8 Tp 21. S.R. 13. E bears S 12½ W. 7.72 chs distant, and from observation find that to include 4 Suertes of Cultivated land, I shall have to run my North and South lines of equal length to the tract just run namely 26.04 chains and the east and west lines 42.66 chains.

I therefore mark the willow post on the north side OTERO S.W.

and run thence

North

Var 12° 30' E

as per observation of Polaris

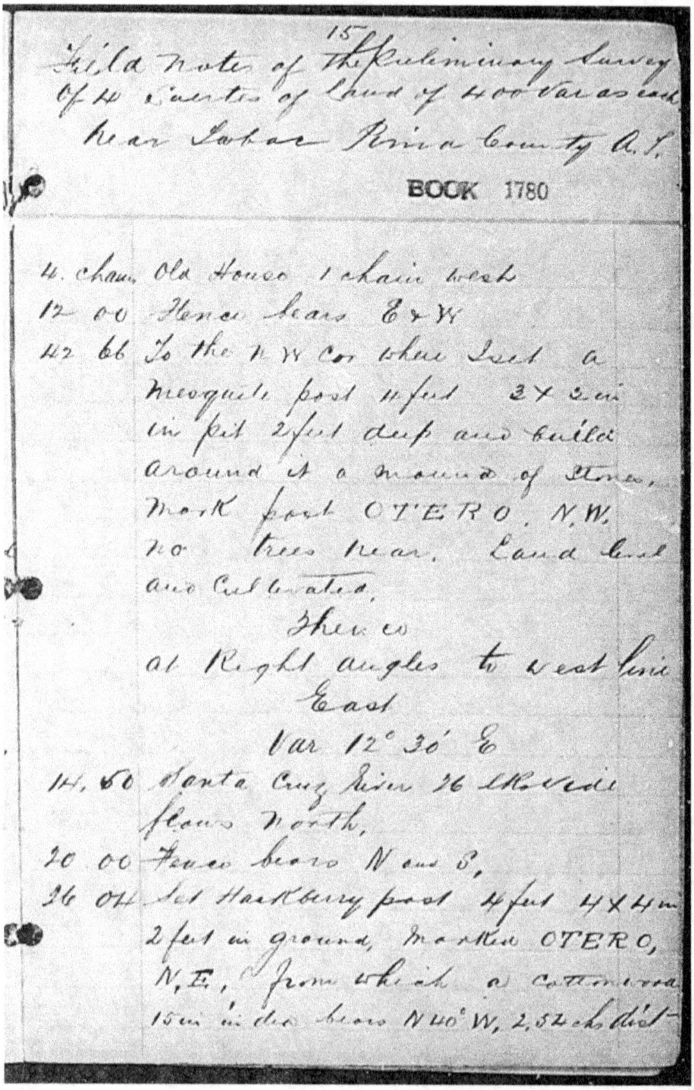

15

Field Notes of the Preliminary Survey
Of 4 Quarters of Land of 400 Varas each
near Tubac Pima County A.T.

BOOK 1780

4. chain Old House 1 chain west
12 00 Fence bears E & W
42 66 To the N W Cor where I set a
mesquite post 4 feet 3 x 3 in
in pit 2 feet deep and build
around it a mound of stones.
Mark post OTERO. N.W.
No trees near. Land level
and Cultivated.

Thence
at Right angles to west line
East
Var 12° 30' E

14.50 Santa Cruz River 26 lks wide
flows North.
20.00 Fence bears N and S.
26 04 Set Hackberry post 4 feet 4 x 4 in
2 feet in ground, marked OTERO,
N.E., from which a Cottonwood
15 in in dia bears N 40° W, 2.52 chs dist

Field notes of the 16 preliminary
Survey of 4 Suertes of land, of 400 Va.
each, near Tubac Pima Co, A.T.

BOOK 1780

Cor

A Cottonwood 12 in in dia bears
N 84° W 3.64 chs distant,
Land level and Cultivated,
Some Cottonwoods along River bank,

Thence

at right angles to north line

South

Var 12° 30' East

6.70 Fence bears E & W and leaves
Cultivated field and line, runs
across point of uncultivated
land,

11 00 ditch runs N. & S.,

30 00 Enter Cultivated land,

42 66 To the mesquite post marking
the NE cor of tract last surveyed
I now mark on north side of
post OTERO, S, E,
Land mostly level agricultural
Land,

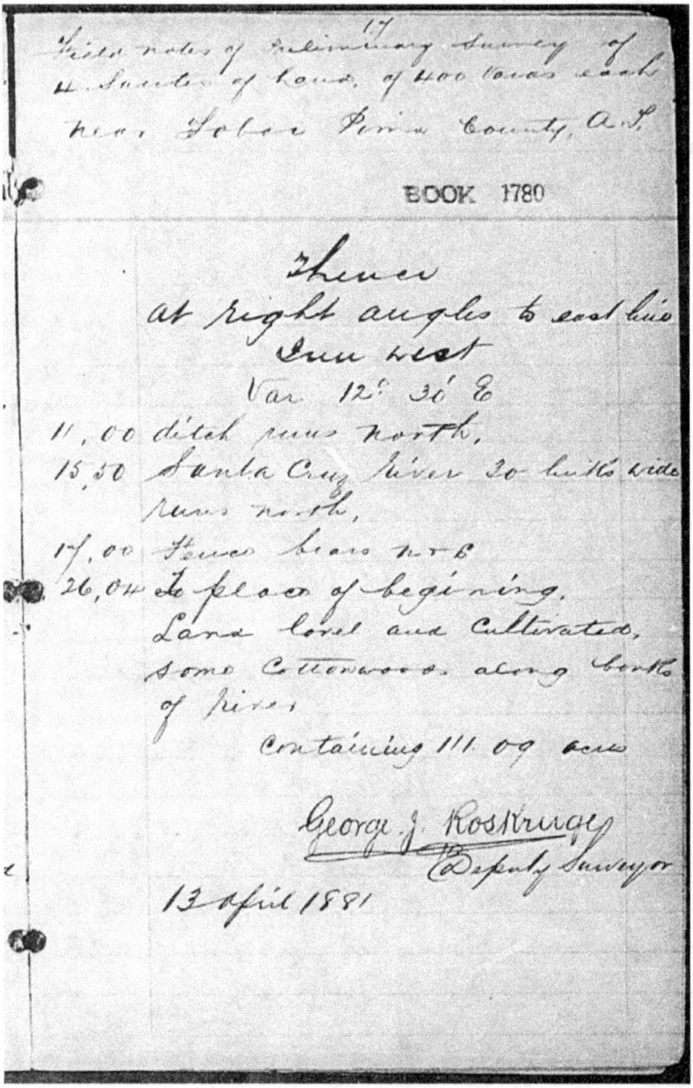

17

Field notes of Preliminary Survey of
4 Suertes of Land, of 400 Varas each
near Tubac Pima County, A.T.

BOOK 1780

Thence
at right angles to east line
Due West
Var 12° 30' E

11,00 ditch runs north,
15,50 Santa Cruz River 30 links wide
runs north,
17,00 Fence bears N & S
26,04 to place of begining.
Land level and Cultivated,
some Cottonwoods along banks
of river

Containing 111.09 acres

George J. Roskruge
Deputy Surveyor

13 April 1881

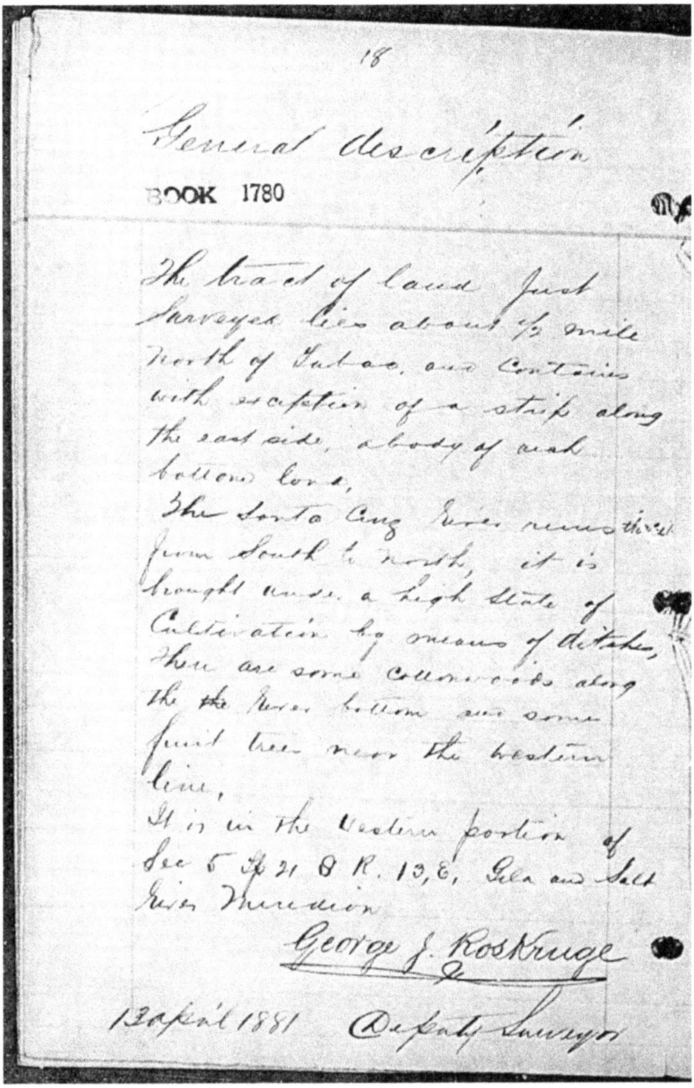

18

General description

BOOK 1780

The tract of land just surveyed lies about 1/2 mile North of Tubac, and contains with exception of a strip along the east side, a body of rich bottom land.

The Santa Cruz River runs through from South to north, it is brought under a high state of Cultivation by means of ditches, there are some cottonwoods along the the river bottom and some fruit trees near the western line.

It is in the western portion of Sec 5 Tp 21 S R. 13, E, Gila and Salt River Meridian

George J. Roskruge

13 April 1881 Deputy Surveyor

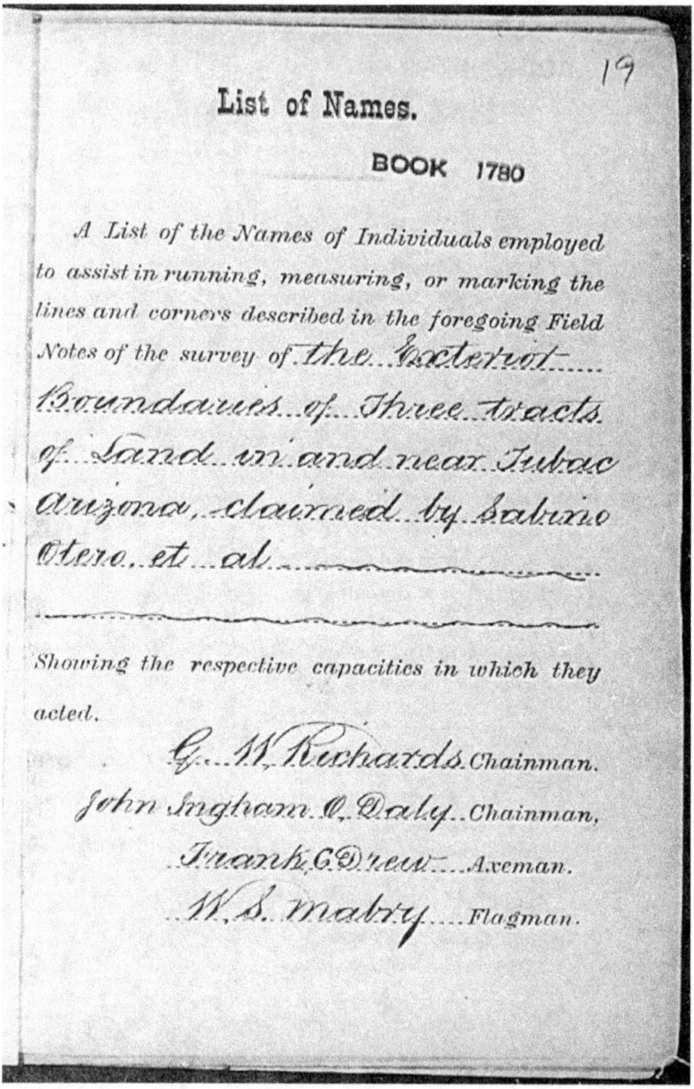

19

List of Names.

BOOK 1780

A List of the Names of Individuals employed to assist in running, measuring, or marking the lines and corners described in the foregoing Field Notes of the survey of the Exterior Boundaries of Three tracts of Land in and near Tubac Arizona, claimed by Sabino Otero et al

Showing the respective capacities in which they acted.

G. W. Richards *Chainman.*

John Ingham O. Daly *Chainman,*

Frank C. Drew *Axeman.*

W. S. Mabry *Flagman.*

70 BOOK 1780

Final Oath of Assistants.

We hereby certify that we assisted George James Roskruge *U. S. Deputy Surveyor, in surveying* the Exterior Boundaries of Three tracts of land in and near Tubac, Arizona claimed by Sabino Otero et al.

and that said Survey has been in all respects, to the best of our knowledge and belief, well and faithfully executed, and the boundary monuments planted according to the instructions furnished by the Surveyor-General.

J. B. Richards *Chainman.*
John Inglis *Chainman.*
Frank Drew *Axeman.*
W. J. Mabry *Flagman.*

Sworn to and subscribed before me, this 14th *day of* April, 1881

George J. Roskruge
Notary Public

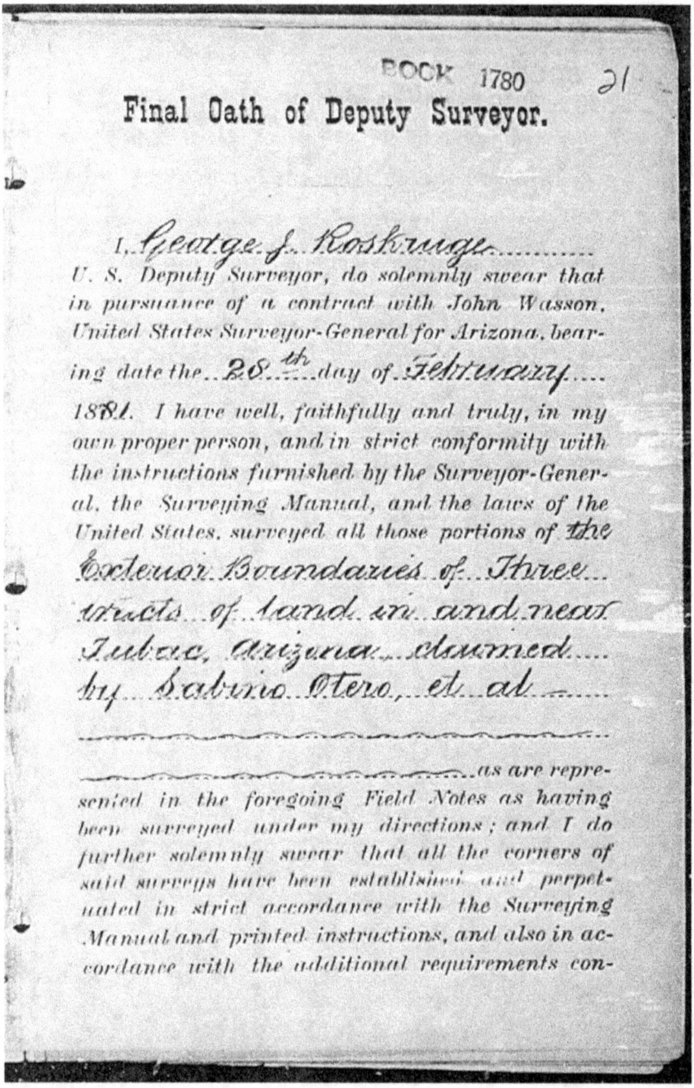

BOOK 1780 21

Final Oath of Deputy Surveyor.

I, George J. Roskruge U. S. Deputy Surveyor, do solemnly swear that in pursuance of a contract with John Wasson, United States Surveyor-General for Arizona, bearing date the 28th day of February 1881. I have well, faithfully and truly, in my own proper person, and in strict conformity with the instructions furnished by the Surveyor-General, the Surveying Manual, and the laws of the United States, surveyed all those portions of the Exterior Boundaries of Three tracts of land in and near Tubac, Arizona claimed by Sabino Otero, et al as are represented in the foregoing Field Notes as having been surveyed under my directions; and I do further solemnly swear that all the corners of said surveys have been established and perpetuated in strict accordance with the Surveying Manual and printed instructions, and also in accordance with the additional requirements con-

27 BOOK 1780

tained in circular instructions from the U. S. Surveyor-General for Arizona, dated September 1, 1873, regarding the establishment of corner boundaries of public surveys, and that the foregoing are the true and original Field Notes of such surveys.

George J. Roskruge
Deputy Surveyor.

Sworn to and subscribed before me, this 26th
day of May 1881

William J. Oldham

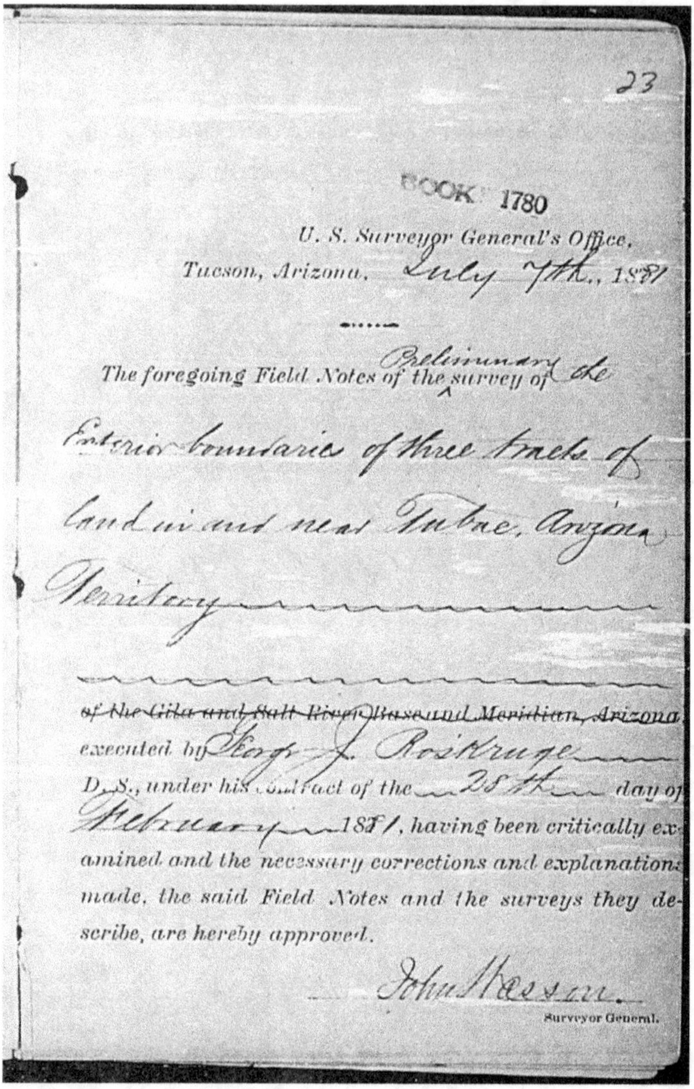

23

BOOK 1780

U. S. Surveyor General's Office,
Tucson, Arizona, July 7th., 1881

The foregoing Field Notes of the Preliminary *survey of* the Exterior boundaries of three tracts of land in and near Tubac, Arizona Territory

~~of the Gila and Salt River Base and Meridian, Arizona,~~ *executed by* George J. Roskruge *D. S., under his contract of the* 28th *day of* February *18*81, *having been critically examined and the necessary corrections and explanations made, the said Field Notes and the surveys they describe, are hereby approved.*

John Wasson.
Surveyor General.

NOTES

NOTES

Chapter One: The Otero Land Grant

[1] U.S. Library of Congress. *Father Eusebio Kino* reports that Kino is also accredited for the introduction of horses and cattle to *Pimería Alta*. Accessed at http://international.loc.gov/intldl/eshtml/es-1/es-1-3-3.html on 8/13/2016.

[2] San Xavier Mission. *A Brief History of Mission San Xavier del Bac*. Accessed at http://www.sanxaviermission.org/History.html on 8/13/2016.

[3] Officer, James. *Hispanic Arizona, 1536-1856.*The University of Arizona Press. Tucson: 1987:35.

[4] Arizona State Parks. *Tubac Presidio State Historic Park: Cultural History*. http://azstateparks.com/Parks/TUPR/science.html (Accessed on 12/3/2016).

[5] GVHC.org. *St. Ann's Church – Tubac*. Accessed at http://www.gvrhc.org/Library/StAnnsChurch-Tubac.pdf on 7/31/2016.

[6] *Ibid.*

[7] U.S. Bureau of Land Management. *The Archaeology of Southeast Arizona*. Accessed at http://www.blm.gov/style/medialib/blm/wo/Planning_and_Renewable_Resources/coop_agencies/new_documents/az.Par.62735.File.dat/arizona_2.pdf on 8/13/2016.

[8] The 1762 Map at the Biblioteca Digital Hispánica *Mapa de una Porcion de la provincial de Zonora que manifesta la Posicion de los enemigos* by Cartographer Francisco Ferten at the Biblioteca Digital Nacional de España depicts a second Tubac located approximately 200 miles south from Tubac, Santa Cruz County, Arizona. http://bdh.bne.es/ (Accessed 10/10/2016). The second Tubac is located in present-day Sonora, Mexico in the area once known as Pimería Bajo, land of the lower Piman Indians just slightly northwest of the Spanish colonial fort named Buena Vista.

[9] DeLugan, Diana. *Otero Research Collection*. Historian and Retired Hydrologist Philip Halpenny. *Barrio de Tubac Archaeological Preserve Lecture*. Audio file taken at Tubac Presidio State Park and Museum. 10/22/2016.

[10] The Archaeological Conservatory. *Barrio de Tubac Archaeological Preserve* brochure. Undated.
[11] Dobyns, Henry F. *Tubac Through Four Centuries; An Historical Resume and Analysis.* Published by the Arizona State Parks Board and Reformatted by the Tubac Presidio State Historical Park. Accessed at http://parentseyes.arizona.edu/tubac/ on 7/15/2016.
[12] Bancroft, Hubert Howe. *The Works of Hubert Howe Bancroft. History of Arizona and New Mexico. 1580-1888.* [Image]. Map of the Northwest in 1539. The History Company, Publishers. San Francisco: 1889.
[13] U.S. Bureau of Land Management. *The Archaeology of Southeast Arizona.* Accessed at http://www.blm.gov/style/medialib/blm/wo/Planning_and_Renewable_Resources/coop_agencies/new_documents/az.Par.62735.File.dat/arizona_2.pdf on 8/13/2016**.** The Presidio of San Ignacio de Tubac consisted of fifty troops under the command of Captain Belderrain.
[14] Donaldson, Thomas. *The Public Domain Its History, With Statistics.* Washington: 1884:p.1126.
[15] *Ibid. Real audencia* translated is the Royal audience. Since the Spanish Monarchy was unable to receive land petitioners in person, his royal interests were reviewed by a tribunal that held authority in his absence.
[16] Land of the upper Piman Indians.
[17] Virrey of Spain. *Reglamento e instrucciones para los presidios que han de forman la linea de la frontera de la Nueva España.* La Aguila Printers. Mexico: 1834, Royal Ordinance 10, Title 14§3 (*Cordon de Presidios-Tubac.*). "At least forty leagues from the former presidio [of Altar] Tubac is found, with a competent neighborhood which has gathered in the shade of its garrison, and the neighbors can subsist in that place; the garrison will be moving to another location within its vicinity, where the ground must be of the requisite proportions, and at precisely the same distance of forty leagues from Altar, as far as possible to the west, in order to secure their reciprocal communication, promiscuously cut trails in the intermediate terrain, and impregnate the entrances of the enemies of the inner country." Translation by the author.
[18] Garcés, Francisco. *On the Trail of a Spanish Pioneer: The Diary and Itinerary of Francisco Garcés* (missionary Priest) in

His Travels Through[ou]t Sonora, Arizona, and California, 1775-1776, Vol.1. F. P. Harper. New York: 1900, p.79.

[19] *Ibid.* Reports estimated 1,000 persons. *See* Bancroft, Hubert. *History of the Pacific States of North America: Arizona and New Mexico.* A.L. Bancroft & Company. British Columbia: 1888, p.382. Bancroft reports a high population at Tucson of 2,000, including families of soldiers.

[20] Bolton, Herbert. *Texas in the Middle Eighteenth Century: Studies in Spanish Colonial History and Administration.* University of California Press. Texas: 1915, p.385.

[21] Dobyns, Henry. *Tubac Through Four Centuries An Historical Resume and Analysis.* The Arizona State Parks Board. 1959. http://parentseyes.arizona.edu/tubac/cpt6-L.htm

[22] Tucson presidio solders were badly outnumbered, 350 Apaches to 15 soldiers, during an attack on the fort on November 6, 1779. Another significant attack brought 600 Apaches against 20 soldiers who defended the presidio on May 1, 1782. Thiel, Homer. Archaeology Southwest. *Pioneer Families of the Presidio San Agustín del Tucson.* www.archaeologysouthwest.org/pdf/presidiofamilies.pdf. Accessed 7/4/2014..

[23] National Archives and Records Administration. Record Group 49, BLM Records; Arizona Court of Private land Claims; Series Miscellaneous Files 1789-1907: Folder title – Spanish Documents form Miscellaneous Files; Box 27.

[24] *Ibid.*

[25] Dobyns, Henry. *Tubac Through Four Centuries An Historical Resume and Analysis.* The Arizona State Parks Board. 1959. http://parentseyes.arizona.edu/tubac/cpt7.htm. Dobyns reports that approximately forty families remained at Tubac after the troops departed to Tucson.

[26] *Ibid.*

[27] Bancroft, Hubert. *History of the Pacific States of North America: Arizona and New Mexico.* A.L. Bancroft & Company. British Columbia: 1888, p.383.

[28] Dobyns, Henry. *Tubac Through Four Centuries An Historical Resume and Analysis.* The Arizona State Parks Board. 1959. http://parentseyes.arizona.edu/tubac/cpt7.htm.

[29] Virrey of Spain. *Reglamento e instrucciones para los presidios que han de forman la linea de la frontera de la Nueva España.*

La Aguila Printers. Mexico: 1834, Royal Ordinance 10, Title 11 §1-2 of Spain (*Gobierno politico*). Translation by the author.

[30] Arizona Historical Society. *1807 Petition by Don Torivio de Otero.* MS 638 Otero Family Papers, 1807-1957. Tucson.

[31] U.S. Department of Interior National Park Service. *Mission 2000 Database.* Event ID:4295. https://home.nps.gov/applications/tuma/detail2.cfm?Event_ID=4295

[32] Officer, James. *Hispanic Arizona, 1536-1856.* The University of Arizona Press. Tucson: 1987, p. 346, fn 8 citing Atienza, *Nobiliario Español,* 1045, that reports the Otero family's surname is linked to Spanish Castillian nobility.

[33] U.S. Department of Interior National Park Service. *Mission 2000 Database.* Event ID:4295. https://home.nps.gov/applications/tuma/detail2.cfm?Event_ID=4295

[34] *Ibid.* Personal ID: 6714. https://home.nps.gov

[35] *Ibid.* Event ID: 4307, Book: Santa Ana-B, p.3. Juan Francisco Salazar and Maria Dolores Otero baptized José Dolores Martinez. Also present were José Martinez and Maria de la Luz parents and Father Matías Gallo who was the officiant.

[36] "México bautismos, 1560-1950," database, *FamilySearch* (https://familysearch.org/ark:/61903/1:1:NLBT-L7H : 12 December 2014), Joseph Francisco Salazar Otero, 21 Jul 1774; citing Santa Maria Magdalena, Magdalena, Sonora, Mexico, reference ; FHL microfilm 682,356. The National Park Services Mission 2000 database translated a portion of the document saying, "I found the following three entries (2450, 2451, and 2452) on three loose sheets of paper and, so that they would not be lost, I copied them as follows:---and in verification of the truth of these three entries, I signed on November 18, 1776. F. Pedro Font." The original document is located at the Bancroft Library, Berkeley, CA.

[37] "*Ibid.* (https://familysearch.org/ark:/61903/1:1:NLB5-G98 : 12 December 2014), Maria Guadalupe Salazar Otero, May 1777; citing Santa Maria Magdalena, Magdalena, Sonora, Mexico, reference ; FHL microfilm 683,037.

[38] *Ibid.* (https://familysearch.org/ark:/61903/1:1:JS82-G4Y : 12 December 2014), Jose Ygnacio Loreto Salazar Otero, 18 Sep 1787; citing Santa Maria Magdalena, Magdalena, Sonora, Mexico, reference ; FHL microfilm 683,037.

[39] Father Pedro de Arriquibar officiated baptismals at the pueblo of San Ignacio de Tubac after the presidio was moved to Tucson in 1775. Atanacio Otero, son of Don Torivio and Maria Ygnacia was born in the pueblo of San Ignacio de Tubac. Josef Atanacio's baptismal register reported he was baptized in "the year of our Lord one thousand seven hundred eighty-two, in the 5th of March." He was the legitimate son of Don Torivio Otero and Doña Maria Ygnacia Salazar, neighbors of Santa Ana, and his godparents were Don Francisco Salazar and Doña Dolores Otero. "México, Sonora, registros parroquiales, 1657-1994," database with images, FamilySearch (https://familysearch.org/ark:/61903/3:1:9Q97-YSPWFZM?cc=1473203&wc=MKRQ-W3J%3A45353801%2C45353802%2C45353803 : 21 May 2014), Magdalena > San Ignacio > Bautismos 1777-1828 > image 13 of 68; Parroquias de la Iglesia Católica, Sonora (Catholic Church parishes, Sonora).

[40] Arizona Historical Society. *1807 Petition by Don Torivio de Otero.* MS 638 Otero Family Papers, 1807-1957. Tucson.

[41] U.S. Department of the Interior, National Park Service. Mission Tumacácori Mission 2000 Searchable Database. Event ID: 2089. https://www.nps.gov/applications/tuma/detail2.cfm?Event_ID=2089. Pedro Sebastian Villaescusa was born on 6/29/1744 and baptized on 6/30/1744 in the village of Alpera, Spain. His parents were Juan de Villaescusa Harnedo [likely Arnedo not Harnedo and a scrivenor's error] and Josepha Arnedo Vicente. His paternal grandparents were Sebastian de Villaescusa Lopez and Antonia Arnedo. Maternal grandparents were Pedro Arnedo Zortosa and Josepha Vicente.

[42] *Ibid.* Personal ID: 5616. https://home.nps.gov/applications/tuma/Detail.cfm?Personal_ID=5616. Don Torivio de Otero's sister was Maria Ignacia Otero de Villaescusa. Mission 2000 database reports she baptized Andres Durán on December 1, 1887 at Tubac. Fray Balthasar Carrillo officiated the ceremony. See Mission 2000 Event ID: 3031.

[43] Thiel, Homer. Archaeology Southwest. *Pioneer Families of the Presidio San Agustín del Tucson.* On February 15, 1787, Don Torivio witnessed the marriage of Juan Felipe Zurubua and Juana Olguin at Tubac.

www.archaeologysouthwest.org/pdf/presidio_families.pdf Accessed 7/4/2014, p. 207, citing US National Park Service Mission 2000 Database Event ID: 4302 that reports Don Torivio was the witness to the marriage of Juan Felipe Zurubua and Juana Olguin at San Ignacio on 2/15/1787. The *presidio* of San Ignacio was newly located at Tubac in the same year.

[44] U.S. National Park Service. Mission Tumacácori Mission 2000 Searchable Database. Personal ID: 10040. https://home.nps.gov/applications/tuma/Detail.cfm?Personal_ID=10040 Nicolás de la Errán achieved title of Teniente Comandante del Presidio de Tubac and Capitán de Tubac. He was married to Doña Loreta Marques. *See* Dobyns, Henry. *Tubac Through Four Centuries An Historical Resume and Analysis.* The Arizona State Parks Board. 1959. http://parentseyes.arizona.edu/tubac/cpt8-C.htm.

[45] U.S. National Archives and Records Administration. The National Archives at Riverside. RG 49, Records of the Bureau of Land Management. Arizona Court of Private Land Claims. Series: Surveyor General of Arizona Case Files 1860-1891. Folder Title: Sabino Otero Grant, Box 2. *Otero Land Grant Translation.*

[46] *Ibid.* The land grant copy is recorded in the US Surveyor General's Journal 3rd Vol, pp. 32-6. The 1789 Otero land grant is the most ancient document held at NARA's pacific repository.

[47] For more than two centuries, writings reflect several variations of Otero's first name: *e.g.* U.S. Surveyor-General Opinion of 3/1/1881 "Torevio;"Otero, Lydia. *La Calle.* The University of Arizona Press: Tucson, 2010, 159 "Toribido"; Officer, James. *Hispanic Arizona.* The University of Arizona Press: Tucson, 1987:66, 79,121, 346 n. 38 "Toribio."; Sheridan, Thomas. *Arizona A History.* The University of Arizona Press: Tucson, 1995, 48 "Toribio;" Brownell, Elizabeth. *They Lived in Tubac.* Westernlore Press: Tucson, 1986: 4, 23, 77, 79 "Toribio;" Kessel, John. *Spain in the Southwest.* University of Oklahoma: 2002, 312 "Toribio." This confusion likely stems from a scrivener's error in the text of the land grant. The land grantee's name is Torivio. Correct spelling of his name was verified against his signature as a witness on several 18th century *presidio* documents located at the United States National Archives.

[48] Numerous published writings report Torivio de Otero was required to build a school on his land. This assertion is memorialized in the plaque located outside the historic schoolhouse at Tubac. This is incorrect. The 1789 Otero Spanish land grant makes no such requirement.
[49] Translation is by the United States National Parks Service. Mission 2000 Spanish Records Database. The translation was by the late Don Garate, chief translator at the Tumacácori Mission. Retrieved on August 31, 2014 from home.nps.gov/applications/tuma/Detail.cfm?Personal_ID=11050
[50] Other translation of the Otero Spanish land grant are available, including one at the United States National Park Service Website *Mission 2000 Database.* https://www.nps.gov/tuma/learn/historyculture/mission-2000.htm, and in an article published by the Arizona Weekly Citizen newspaper of Tucson, AZ on 3/6/1881.
[51] National Archives and Records Administration. The National Archives at Riverside. Record Group 49, Records of the Bureau of Land Management. Arizona Court of Private Land Claims. Surveyor General of Arizona Case Files 1860-1891. [Image Otero Land Grant] Sabino Otero Grant, Box #2.
[52] Taylor Jr., Dr. Quintard. *United States History: Timeline: 1800-1900.* University of Washington. http://faculty.washington.edu/qtaylor/a_us_history/1800_1900_timeline.htm.
[53] Arizona Historical Society. *Don Torivio de Otero Land Squatter Challenge Papers.* MS 638 Otero Family Papers, 1807-1957. Tucson.
[54] *Ibid.* Manuel de León was the political commander and judge at Tubac. His refusal to settle the land challenge as the presiding judge at Tubac suggests he may have been uncertain of the appropriateness of his decision to lend Don Torivio's land in Torivio's absence. This is particularly suggestive given that de León knew Don Torivio had legal ownership of the land.
[55] *Ibid.* According to the plain language of the 1789 Spanish land grant, Don Torivio acquired sole dominion over the land grant property after the mandatory four year waiting period and was able to sell it unencumbered to anyone of his choosing.
[56] *Ibid.*
[57] Arizona Historical Society. *Don Torivio de Otero Land Squatter Challenge Papers.* MS 638 Otero Family Papers, 1807-

1957. Tucson. Governor Conde's order instructed that military commander and judge de León expedite his order which only seems fair given the length of time that Don Torivio had to wait for justice.
[58] According to both the 1789 Otero land grant and the 1804/1807 land squatter challenge documents, Don Torivio de Otero dug new canals and a erected dam on his private land at Tubac.
[59] Humboldt, Alexandre Von. Graphic adaptation of *A map of New Spain, from the 16° to 38° North Latitude reduced from large map.* [London, Longman, Hurst, Rese, Orme and Browne, Paternoster Row, 1804]. Map. Retrieved from the Library of Congress www.loc.gov/item/2006626018/
[60] Garcia Cubas, Antonio. Image excerpt from Atlas pintoresco é historico de los Estados Unidos Mexicanos, Mexico. Debray Sucesores. 1885. From ethnographic map surrounded by illustrations. Retrieved from Library of Congress, Geography and Map Division at www.loc.gov/item/2008621671/
[61] Bowden, J.J. Office of the State Historian, Division of the Commission of Public Records, State Records Center and Archives. http://newmexicohistory.org/people/rancho-de-otero-grant.
[62] *See* U.S. BLM. *Plat Township 21 South, Range 13 East. G&SRM, Arizona.* 2/4/1877. Filed at the Surveyor General's Office. Tucson.
[63] Bashford, Coles, Compiler. *The Compiled Laws of the Territory of Arizona including the Howell Code and the Session Laws from 1864 to 1871, inclusive, to which is prefixed the constitution of the United States, the Mining Law of the United States, and the Organic Acts of the Territory of Arizona and New Mexico.* Weed, Parsons and Company, Printers. Albany: 1871. Under the ACT that amended Chapter 29 of the Arizona Howell Code "Of Probate Courts," approved on 10/3/1867, a widow had superior right to her children to be the administrator of her husband's estate if he died intestate.; Amendment to Section 1 of Chapter 32 of the Arizona Howell Code "Of the Rights of Married Women" states, "All property acquired after marriage by either husband or wife, except such as may be acquired by gift, bequest, devise or descent, shall be common property;" and under Chapter 26 "Of Title to Real Property by Descent" Section 1.1, "When any person shall die

seized of any lands, tenements or hereditaments, or of any right thereto, or entitled to any interest therein, in fee simple, or for the life of another, not having lawfully devised the same, they shall descend, subject to his debts, in manner following: 1. In equal shares to his children, and to the issue of any deceased child by right of representation."

[64] U.S. *Report of the Commissioner of General Land Office to the Secretary of the Interior for the Year 1869.* Government Printing Office. Washington: 1870, p.18.

[65] *Ibid,* p.19.

[66] U.S. Department of the Interior Bureau of Land Management. *200 Years of a Land Office Business: A GLO Timeline.* https://www.blm.gov/es/st/en/prog/glo/glo_timeline.html accessed on 1/22/2017.

[67] *Ibid. Managing a Land Office Business.* https://www.blm.gov/es/st/en/prog/glo.html accessed on 1/22/2017.

[68] U.S. *Report of the Commissioner of General Land Office to the Secretary of the Interior for the Year 1869.* Government Printing Office. Washington: 1870.

[69] *Ibid,* p.46.

[70] There were two other claims for grants made at the Tubac *presidio* claimed by the heirs of Ignacio Cruz and by Carmen de O'Campos. The U.S. Surveyor General did not take any action on these claims as neither record of those grants could be located in the Mexican Archives. *See* Arizona State Library, Archives & Public Records. U.S. Bureau of Land Management Reels 10.1.21/22 containing NARA BLM records of the Journal of U.S. Surveyor General Records Miscellaneous Files; *see also.* Bowden, J.J. Office of the State Historian, Division of the Commission of Public Records, State Records Center and Archives. http://newmexicohistory.org/people/rancho-de-otero-grant, fn 2.

[71] United States. *Annual Report of the Commissioner of the General Land Office.* Government Printing Office. Washington: 1882, p.51.

[72] Arizona State Library, Archives & Public Records. U.S. Bureau of Land Management *Sabino Otero Grant et al and Misc.* Reels 10.1.21/22 containing NARA BLM records of the

Journal of U.S. Surveyor General John Wasson copy of the Otero Petition as recorded in Journal No. 3, pps 27-29.

[73] *See* Pima County Court, AZ. *Order of Appointing Administrator*. Manuela O. de Quesse died on July 20, 1898. Pima County Probate Court Journal 7.

[74] Arizona State Library, Archives & Public Records. U.S. Bureau of Land Management *Sabino Otero Grant et al and Misc.* Reels 10.1.21/22 containing NARA BLM records of the Journal of U.S. Surveyor General John Wasson copy of the Otero Petition as recorded in Journal No. 3, pps 27-29. Ana Maria Coenen's surname was misspelled in the petition and throughout the entire case proceedings as "Cunnen."

[75] Arizona State Library, Archives & Public Records. U.S. Bureau of Land Management *Sabino Otero Grant et al and Misc.* Reels 10.1.21/22 containing NARA BLM records of the Journal of U.S. Surveyor General John Wasson copy of the Otero Petition as recorded in Journal No. 3, pps 27-29.

[76] Arizona State Library, Archives & Public Records. U.S. Bureau of Land Management *Sabino Otero Grant et al.* Microfilm containing NARA BLM records of the U.S. Deputy U.S. Surveyor General George J. Roskruge. 4/18/1881.

[77] United States. Report of the Secretary of the Interior for the Fiscal Year Ending June 30, 1881. Government Printing Office. Washington: 1881, containing the report on *Spanish and Mexican Private Land Claims*. p.477.

[78] Arizona Weekly Citizen. *Rancho de Otero and House Lot. United States Surveyor-General's Opinion and Recommendation in the Case.* 3/6/1881.

[79] Bowden, J.J. Office of the State Historian, Division of the Commission of Public Records, State Records Center and Archives. http://newmexicohistory.org/people/rancho-de-otero-grant.

[80] Arizona State Library, Archives & Public Records. U.S. Bureau of Land Management *Rancho de Martinez*. Reels 10.1.21/22 containing NARA BLM records of the U.S. Deputy U.S. Surveyor General John Wasson.

[81] *Et al* is the short form of the legal phrase *et alia* meaning "and all others" in Latin. Since the late 1800s, historians have dropped the *et al* in reference to the "Sabino Otero *et al*" land grant petition erroneously suggesting that Sabino Otero was the only person with rights to the Otero land grant claim.

[82] United States. *Journal of the Senate of the United States of America.* Government Printing Office. Washington: 1881 at pp.233-34.
[83] Bowden, J.J. Office of the State Historian, Division of the Commission of Public Records, State Records Center and Archives. http://newmexicohistory.org/people/rancho-de-otero-grant.
[84] Governor of Arizona. *Report of the Governor of Arizona made to the Secretary of the Interior for the Year 1879.* Government Printing Office. Washington: 1879, p.24.
[85] 26 Stat. 854 (3 Mar 1891) [U.S. Comp. St. 1901, p.705]. An Act to Establish a Court of Private Land Claims.
[86] Arizona Weekly Citizen. *Untitled.* 1/26/1884.
[87] United States. *Annual Report of the Commissioner of the General Land Office.* Government Printing Office. Washington: 1882, p.51.
[88] Santa Fe Daily New Mexican. *The Land Court. In Full Blast at Tucson – List of Cases Filed for Arizona.* 2/22/1893.
[89] Bowden, J.J. Office of the State Historian, Division of the Commission of Public Records, State Records Center and Archives. *Rancho de Otero Grant.* http://newmexicohistory.org/people/rancho-de-otero-grant fn.2.
[90] *Ibid.* http://newmexicohistory.org/people/rancho-de-otero-grant.
[91] 3 Stat. 566, Ch. 51. *The Cash Act.* Enacted April 24, 1920.
[92] U.S. Bureau of Land Management. *Department of the Interior Bureau of Land Management Field Notes. Serial No: AZPHX:0011924.* Phoenix Land Office. Obtained 11/2/2011.
[93] United States Department of the Interior BLM General Land Office Records Online. *Theophilus A. Bagwell and Sabino Otero, Assignee, Accession Nr: 251724 for Serial Patent Document Nr: 013005; BLM Serial Nr: AZPhx 0013005.* Total 86.17 acres obtained under the authority of the May 20, 1862 Homestead Act (12 Stat. 392). Issued on 3/4/1912.
[94] *Ibid. Robert F. Donaldson, Sabino Otero Assignee, Accession Nr: 434913 for Serial Patent Document Nr: 013004; BLM Serial Nr: AZPhx 0013004.* Total 122.80 acres obtained under the authority of the May 20, 1862 Homestead Act (12 Stat. 392). Issued on 10/10/1914.
[95] *Ibid. Clara M. Otero, Document Nr: 011924. https://glorecords.blm.gov/*

Chapter Two: Tubac and the Solar de Otero

[1] U.S. Bureau of Land Management. *The Archaeology of Southeast Arizona.* Accessed at http://www.blm.gov/style/medialib/blm/wo/Planning_and_Renewable_Resources/coop_agencies/new_documents/az.Par.62735.File.dat/arizona_2.pdf on 8/13/2016.
[2] Dobyns, Henry. *Tubac Through Four Centuries An Historical Resume and Analysis.* The Arizona State Parks Board. 1959. http://parentseyes.arizona.edu/tubac/cpt6-C.htm
[3] Wasson, John. *Letter from the Secretary of the Interior transmitting The report and opinion of the surveyor-general of Arizona Territory, together with a duly authenticated copy of the title papers and testimony in the matter of the private land claim, No. 7, &c* (Tumacácori and Calabasas Land Grant). 46th Congress, 2d Session. Ex. Doc. No. 207, p.39.
[4] *Ibid,* p.40.
[5] Wasson, John. *Letter from the Secretary of the Interior transmitting The report and opinion of the surveyor-general of Arizona Territory, together with a duly authenticated copy of the title papers and testimony in the matter of the private land claim, No. 7, &c* (Tumacácori and Calabasas Land Grant). 46th Congress, 2d Session. Ex. Doc. No. 207, p.40.
[6] U.S. Department of the Interior. National Park Service. *Juan Bautista de Anza.* Accessed at https://www.nps.gov/juba/index.htm on 8/12/2016.
[7] Wasson, John. *Letter from the Secretary of the Interior transmitting The report and opinion of the surveyor-general of Arizona Territory, together with a duly authenticated copy of the title papers and testimony in the matter of the private land claim, No. 7, &c* (Tumacácori and Calabasas Land Grant). 46th Congress, 2d Session. Ex. Doc. No. 207, p.39.
[8] *Ibid.*
[9] Bents, Doris W. *The History of Tubac, 1752-1948.* University of Arizona. Tucson: 1949, p.21 Courtesy of Arizona State Library, Archives & Public Records. Call No. 979.1 H21B.
[10] *Ibid*; *see* Illustration of 18th Century Tubac, Chapter One, p.5/
[11] Williams, Jack. The Center for Spanish Colonial Archaeology. *A Proposed Plan for El Presidio De Tubac Archaeological Park.* March 1989. The Jack Williams describes the community of the

south barrio near the Tubac Presidio and identifies many of the ruins preserved within the protected park grounds.

[12] GVHC.org. *St. Ann's Church – Tubac.* Accessed at http://www.gvrhc.org/Library/StAnnsChurch-Tubac.pdf on 7/31/2016.

[13] Heintzelman, Samuel. *Sonora and the Value of Its Silver Mines. Report of the Sonora Exploring and Mining Co. Made To The Stockholders.* Railroad Record Print. Cincinnati: 1856, p.41.

[14] National Park Service, Tumacácori Historic Resource Study, *Fictitious Capital and Fictitious Landscapes: Baca Float No. 3.* Accessed at https://www.nps.gov/parkhistory/online_books/tuma/hrs/chap7.htm on 1/31/2017.

[15] Heintzelman, Samuel. *Sonora and the Value of Its Silver Mines. Report of the Sonora Exploring and Mining Co. Made To The Stockholders.* Railroad Record Print. Cincinnati: 1856, p.41.

[16] *Ibid,* p.9.

[17] *Ibid,* p.4.

[18] *Ibid,* p.8.

[19] *Ibid,* p.41.

[20] Heintzelman, Samuel. *Report of the Sonora Exploring and Mining Co., Made To The Stockholders.* Railroad Record Print. Cincinnati: 1857, p.5. Italics in original.

[21] *Ibid.*

[22] *Ibid,* p.7

[23] Officer, James. *Hispanic Arizona, 1536-1856.* The University of Arizona Press. Tucson: 1987, p.121. Census records of 1831 refer to Atanacio and his wife Carmen Quijada de Otero with the titles *Don* and *Doña* which signify they held a high social status in the Tubac community.

[24] Bents, Doris W. *The History of Tubac, 1752-1948.* University of Arizona. Tucson: 1949, p. 74. Courtesy of Arizona State Library, Archives & Public Records. Call No. 979.1 H21B, p. 74.

[25] Poston, Charles. *Building a State in Apache Land.* The Overland Monthly Publishing Co. San Francisco: 1894.

[26] Heintzelman, Samuel. *Report of the Sonora Exploring and Mining Co., Made To The Stockholders.* [Image Aribaca]. Railroad Record Print. Cincinnati: 1857.

[27] A full translation of this document is available online at the National Park Service U.S. Department of the Interior Mission

2000 database at https://home.nps.gov/applications/tuba/search.cfm.
[28] *Arizona miner.* (Fort Whipple, Ariz.), 10 Aug. 1864. *Chronicling America: Historic American Newspapers.* Lib. of Congress. http://chroniclingamerica.loc.gov/lccn/sn82016242/1864-08-10/ed-1/seq-3/
[29] *Arizona, Territorial Census Records, 1860.*
[30] No birth record has been located for Fernando Otero, son of Manuel and Maria Clara Otero. However, the 1860 Territorial Census reported that he was four months old residing at Tubac with his parents. On the 1864 Arizona Territory Census, Manuel Otero reported he and all of Fernando's older siblings had lived all their lives at Tubac. Based on the census records, it is highly likely that Fernando was born in Tubac, not Tucson.
[31] "Mexico matrimonios, 1570-1950," database, *FamilySearch* (https://familysearch.org/ark:/61903/t.t.JZ4G-X2F: accessed 6 May 2016), Ramon Comadieran [sic] and Franca. (Francisca) Otero, 29 Aug 1857; citing Santa Maria Magdalena, Magdalena, Sonora, Mexico, reference; FHL microfilm 682,378.
[32] James H. McClintock Collection. Burton Barr Library, Phoenix AZ. News clipping folder titled "*Cities and Towns, AZ-Tubac.*" Clip reference titled "Depopulated." 12/2/1916.
[33] The Weekly Arizonan. *Advertisements/Notice.* Tubac. 6/16/1859. Hoppin & Appel of Tubac ran an ad for the return of their runaway peon Juan Jose Arenas. The latter was alleged to be in his employer's debt for $82,68 ¾; *see* Arizona Miner. *Legislature.* Fort Whipple. 10/5/1864. Article advised new legislature called for the end of peonage.
[34] Longan, M.M. *Arizona in the Confederacy.* P.145. The Confederate Veteran Magazine 1922. Broadfoot's Bookmark publisher. Wendell, N.C. A Confederate convention was held at Tucson in 1861 electing Granville H. Oury as delegate to the Confederate Congress. Captain Hunter raised the Confederate flag at Tucson on 2/28/1862. The only clash between Union and Confederate soldiers occurred at Picacho Pass on 4/5/1862, later the site of the Southern Pacific Railroad; *see* Confederate States of America. *Confederate War Journal*, Vol. 1. War Journal Publishing Company, 1893 at p. 143 reporting the list of Territory of Arizona officers appointed by Confederate President Jefferson Davis: Governor John R. Baylor, Arizona;

Secretary Robert Joselyn, Mississippi; Chief Justice Alexander M. Jackson, New Mexico; Associate Justice Columbus Upson, Texas; Attorney General Russell Howard, Arizona; and M.H. McWillie as Delegate to Congress; *see also* United States. *United States Congressional Serial Set, Volume 3115.* U.S. Government Printing Office. Washington: 1893, p.20 reprint of Confederate Lieutenant Colonel John B. Baylor's proclamation claiming the Territory of Arizona for the Confederate States of America.

[35] Dioceses of Tucson Archives. *Baptismal Register 4/18/1863.* Eldest sister Francisca Otero was Teofilo's godmother. The register lists Teofilo's father Manuel Otero's Christian name as "Emmanuel."

[36] Longan, M.M. *Arizona in the Confederacy.* P.145. The Confederate Veteran Magazine 1922. Broadfoot's Bookmark publisher. Wendell, N.C.: 1922.

[37] James H. McClintock Collection. Burton Barr Library, Phoenix AZ. News clipping folder titled *Cities and Towns, AZ-Tubac.* Clip reference titled "Depopulated." 12/2/1916.

[38] James H. McClintock Collection. Transcript. Burton Barr Library, Phoenix AZ. Folder titled *Arizona-History-1862-1912.* Transcript of Arizona State Historian James McClintock "presented on the 'Union Oil Company of Arizona's Forward Arizona Program' as broadcast April 30, 1930, over KTAR, The Arizona Republican's Electrical Equipment Company's Radio Station Atop the Heard Building."

[39] Arizona Department of Health Services. *Arizona Genealogy Birth and Death Certificates. Manuel Otero Death Record State File No. 6850.* The informant to Manuel's death was his son Fernando. Fernando reported that Manuel's mother was Manuela Ochoa. This information directly conflicts with Fernando's own Mexican civil registry of birth dated July 10, 1910 at Tubatama, Sonora, Mexico on file at the Tubac Historical Society. Mexican civil registry of birth records in 1910 stated the maternal and paternal lineage of children and advised that Fernando Otero was the grandson of Sabino Otero, cattleman of Tubac, and deceased Concepcion Ochoa.

[40] A Sabino Otero bio note in the Carl Hayden file at the Arizona Historical Society research library at Tucson reports Sabino was nineteen-years-old when he took over responsibility to care for the Otero family that included a dozen children.

Census records confirm both facts are incorrect. His mother and sisters were caring for their own children for a total of eight persons in the family of four adults and four children. Sabino was 26-years-old when his father Manuel died. Nonetheless, these misstatements have been regularly reported by historians and journals proffered as fact since the early 20th century until present time.

41 Archaeologysouthwest.org. *Pioneer Families of the Presidio San Agustin del Tucson citing* St. Augustine Catholic Church Baptisms, 1:14 no. 115 reporting Francisca Otero also had one son José Ramon Comadurán. José Ramon was baptized on October 17, 1861; Officer, James. *Hispanic Arizona, 1536-1856.* The University of Arizona Press. Tucson: 1987, p.399 fn 44 reporting that Ramon Comadurán Sr., spouse of Francisca Otero was killed in 1861 by Apaches.

42 James H. McClintock Collection. Burton Barr Library, Phoenix AZ. News clipping folder titled *"Arizona Land Grants."* Clip reference titled "Surveyor Generals" states that John Wasson was originally a newspaper man who came to California by way of Panama. After he arrived in Arizona, he established the "Arizona Citizen" newspaper whose first issue appeared on Saturday, 10/15/1870. He died on 1/16/1909 at Pomona, CA.

43 Philip Halpenny was trained as an archeologist but spent his career as a land/water expert. Former officer of the Tumacácori Water Company, Inc. Halpenny is also a historian who regularly gives tours of the Tubac Spanish archeological ruins of the south barrio at the Tubac Presidio State Historic Park and Museum.

44 DeLugan, Diana. *Otero Research Collection. Philip Halpenny Email.* 7/24/2016.

45 Author Tom Sheridan reports in his book *Landscapes of Fraud Mission Tumacácori, The Baca Float, and the Betrayal of the O'odham* that Baca Float #3 was a government sanctioned land fraud that dispossessed early settlers, many at Tubac.

46 Brownell, Elizabeth. *They Lived in Tubac.* Tucson: Westernlore Press, 1986, p.66.

47 Tubac Arizonian. *Charles Poston, et al Application for Tubac Townsite.* Vol. II, No.II. Summer 1959. Courtesy of Arizona State Library, Archives & Public Records. Tubac Town News Clippings File.

[48] Brownell, Elizabeth. *They Lived in Tubac.* Tucson: Westernlore Press, 1986, p.14.
[49] Territory of Arizona. *Journals of the First Legislative Assembly of the Territory of Arizona.* Vol. 1. Prescott: 1865.
[50] Bents, Doris W. *The History of Tubac, 1752-1948.* University of Arizona. Tucson: 1949, p.188, fn. 13 *citing R.J. Hinton.* Courtesy of Arizona State Library, Archives & Public Records. Call No. 979.1 H21B; *see* Brownell, Elizabeth. *They Lived in Tubac.* Tucson: Westernlore Press, 1986, p. 61 *citing* The Arizona Citizen. *Untitled.* Tucson, AZ. 5/13/1876 reported that I. Goldberg intended to start a store at Tubac.
[51] Brownell, Elizabeth. *They Lived in Tubac.* Tucson: Westernlore Press, 1986, p.66 *citing* Pima County Recorder's Office, Land Claims Book. 1; p. 409.
[52] *Ibid,* p.77.
[53] *Ibid,* p.77.
[54] *Ibid.* Back book cover of hardback book.
[55] *Ibid*, p.67.
[56] *Ibid*, p.67.
[57] Because the list of petitioners in the Otero land grant claim was long, the name for the petitioners in the case was shorted in a common legal construct as "*Sabino, et al;*" *et al* is a Latin phrase that means "and others." Over time, the *"et al"* was forgotten or inadvertently dropped. During the 20th century, institutional memory faded, and subsequent historians have referred to the Otero land grant petition in error simply as the "Sabino Land Grant."
[58] Vegors, Wallace. *The Otero Solar at Tubac: "Home" for 150 Years.* History 399g class with Dr. Harwood Hinton. Undated. Tubac State Presidio Park and Museum Collection.
[59] Arizona Republic. *Battle Lines Drawn in Fight to Save Old School.* Phoenix. 3/19/1967; A copy of the Vegors paper on the Otero Solar was given to the Author by Shaw Kinsley. Kinsley was the Director of the Tubac Presidio State Park and Museum from 2010 to April of 2017. He retired due to health concerns. The revitalization success of the Tubac Presidio State Park and Museum has been attributed to Kinsley's hard work and enigmatic personality.
[60] Vegors, Wallace. *The Otero Solar at Tubac: "Home" for 150 Years.* History 399g class with Dr. Harwood Hinton. Undated. Tubac State Presidio Park and Museum Collection. P.15.

[61] *Ibid,* p.13. Tubac State Presidio Park and Museum Collection; A copy of the Vegors paper was provided courtesy of Shaw Kinsley, Director of the Tubac Presidio State Park and Museum.
[62] *Ibid,* p.15. Tubac State Presidio Park and Museum Collection.
[63] *Ibid,* p.16. Tubac State Presidio Park and Museum Collection.
[64] United States. Department of the Interior National Park Service. *National Register of Historic Places Continuation Sheet.* Interagency Resources Division. 1994. Section 7, p.3.
[65] Arizona State Library, Archives & Public Records.. *Plan of Tubac Town-site Pima County.*
[66] United States. Department of the Interior National Park Service. *National Register of Historic Places Continuation Sheet.* Interagency Resources Division. 1994. Section 7, p.3.
[67] Arizona Weekly Citizen. *Commissioners' Notice.* 8/20/1882. Frank W. Girard, James Peters, and H.W. Low were appointed commissioners of newly established Townsite of Tubac. A notice was issued on July 27, 1882 that a hearing was held on August 28, 1882 to partition the land "to the persons entitled to the same according to their respective interests the lots, squares or grounds to which each of the occupants thereof shall be entitled."
[68] U.S. Department of the Interior National Park Service. *National Register of Historic Places Continuation Sheet.* Interagency Resources Division. 1994. Section 7, p.3.
[69] The 1877 plat further reveals that the historic Spanish Royal Highway known as "Camino Real" from Tumacácori to Tucson's Mission San Xavier ran adjacent to and east of the *Solar*. The *Solar's* close proximity to the presidio and Royal Highway again suggests that the Otero family held high local prominence.
[70] Bents, Doris W. *The History of Tubac, 1752-1948.* University of Arizona. Tucson: 1949, p. 74. Courtesy of Arizona State Library, Archives & Public Records. Call No. 979.1 H21B, p. 188. "It is improbable that Tubac had two stores. It appears that Sabino Otero bought the Goldberg store and that Mercer kept it (Reminiscences of Sara M. Black) per Doris Bents.
[71] Brownell, Elizabeth. *They Lived in Tubac.* Tucson: Westernlore Press, 1986, p.78
[72] Arizona State Library, Archives & Public Records. *Field Notes of the Preliminary Survey of House lot in Tubac, Pima Co.*

Arizona Territory. Sabino Otero et al claim. Microfiche. From NARA U.S. Bureau of Land Management records, p.3.
[73] Brownell, Elizabeth. *They Lived in Tubac.* Tucson: Westernlore Press, 1986, p. 67.
[74] United States. Bureau of Land Management {XE"Bureau of Land Management"} *Land Patent Accession Number AZAZAA 010528.* Issued 12/30/1884.
[75] Bents, Doris W. *The History of Tubac, 1752-1948.* University of Arizona. Tucson: 1949, p. 214. Courtesy of Arizona State Library, Archives & Public Records. Call No. 979.1 H21B.
[76] Santa Cruz County Recorder Book of Deeds. Bk 10, 514.
[77] Santa Cruz County Recorder's Office. *Plat of the Tubac Townsite.* 3/3/1914.
[78] Bents, Doris W. *The History of Tubac, 1752-1948.* University of Arizona. Tucson: 1949, p. 215-7. Courtesy of Arizona State Library, Archives & Public Records. Call No. 979.1 H21B.
[79] Santa Cruz County Recorder Book of Deeds. Bk 23, pp.303-04.
[80] *Ibid.* Bk 23, pp.303.
[81] DeLugan, Diana. *Otero Research Collection.* Email from Carol Cullen of the Santa Cruz Unified School District No. 35. 8/3/2016.
[82] Arizona Historical Society. *James Officer Collection. MS 1155. Interview with Ana Maldonado de Fimbres.* Undated. Officer's interview with Mrs. Fimbres reports that Olga Otero Litel, Sabino Otero's great-granddaughter wanted to build a house on one of the newly contested Otero lots.
[83] Santa Cruz County Superior Court. *State of AZ vs Tubac Elementary School District No. 5. Case No. 6725. Final Order of Condemnation.* Tucson, AZ. 8/27/1973.
[84] Sonora Silver Mining Co. *Report of the Sonora Exploring and Mining Co., Made to the Stockholders.* Railroad Record Print. Cincinnati: 1857, p.6. House just right of center next to a large tree is an 1857 image of the Otero *Solar* or house lot.

Chapter Three: Rancho de Otero

[1] Ancestry.com. Arizona, Compiled Census Index, 1831-1880 [database on-line]. Provo, UT, USA: Ancestry.com Operations Inc., 1999.
[2] Arizona State Library, Archives & Public Records. *Field Notes of the Preliminary Survey of House lot in Tubac, Pima Co.*

Arizona Territory. Sabino Otero et al claim. Microfiche. From NARA U.S. Bureau of Land Management records, p.3 of United States Deputy Surveyor General George J. Roskruge's Filed Notes. 4/13/1881 and Plat dated 7/7/1881.

[3] *Ibid. U.S. Bureau of Land Management Assorted Grants & Miscellaneous papers.* Filmfile #10.1.22. United States Deputy Surveyor General George J. Roskruge's Filed Notes. 4/13/1881 and Plat dated 7/7/1881.

[4] Wagoner, J.J. *History of the Cattle Industry in Southern Arizona, 1540-1940.* Social Science Bulletin No. 20. University of Arizona. Tucson: 1952.

[5] *Ibid.*, p.5 *citing* Charles W. Hackett, *Historical Documents Relating to New Mexico, Nueva Vizcaya and Approaches Thereto, to 1873.* I, p.41.

[6] *Ibid*, p.8.

[7] *Ibid. citing* the works of Herbert E. Bolton.

[8] Arizona Republic. *State Pioneer Taken By Death (Teofilo).* Phoenix, AZ. 5/16/1941, p.8; *see* www.arizonahistoricalsociety.org/wp-content/upLoads/library_Otero-Family.pdf ("Sabino was known as the cattle king"); *see also* Portillo Jr., Ernesto. *Neto's Tucson: Otero family leaving lasting mark in S. AZ.* Accessed at http://tucson.com/news/local/neto-s-tucson-otero-family-leaves-lasting-mark-in-s/article_1b54e4cc-5262-57ba-b7f8-2c3c5e5bd2b8.html on 10/25/2010 (Teofilo's older brother was Sabino Otero, and together they were known as "Arizona's Cattle Kings").

[9] Unfortunately, many modern Arizona pioneer ranch history compilations omit any mention of the Otero stock farm. *eg.* Arizona Pioneer Stockmen was organized in 1977 to preserve and record early Arizona Ranch Histories. The Otero surname does not appear on any of the published stockmen biographies. *See: http://www.anls.org/p.aspx?pID=Get-Involved/Pioneer-Stockmen-Association/233.*

[10] Officer, James. *Hispanic Arizona, 1536-1856.* Image. "Cattle brands of old Spanish-Mexican families of Southern Arizona." The University of Arizona Press. Tucson: 1987, p.16.

[11] Santa Cruz County. *Our History.* Accessed at http://www.co.santa-cruz.az.us/304/Our-History

[12] Arizona Daily Star. *Of Interest to Cattlemen.* 10/4/1884, p.4.

[13] *Ibid. Cattlemen's Attention.* 8/21/1890, p.4.

[14] Arizona Weekly Citizen. *Cattle Inspection.* 7/3/1886, p.1.
[15] Arizona Daily Star. *Untitled.* 12/14/1886, p.4.
[16] Arizona Weekly Citizen. *South of Tucson.* Tucson, AZ. 2/26/1876, p.1.
[17] For more information on the ranch at Reventon, *see* Chapter Five.
[18] Arizona Weekly Citizen. *The Country Southward.* Tucson, AZ. 4/21/1877, p.2.
[19] *Ibid. Official Records.* 915/1883, p.4.
[20] Arizona Republic. *Arizona Days with Roscoe G. Willson.* Tucson, AZ. 1/19/1969, p.164 citing the Arizona Star dated 10/10/1884.
[21] The St. Johns Herald. *Untitled.* St. Johns, AZ. 7/16/1885, p.1.
[22] *Ibid.*
[23] Arizona Weekly Citizen. *Untitled.* Tucson, AZ. 7/18/1885, p.3.
[24] The St. Johns Herald. *Untitled.* St. Johns, AZ. 7/16/1885.
[25] *Ibid*, p.1.
[26] Arizona Daily Star. *A Big Cattle Drive.* Tucson, AZ. 7/14/1885, p.4.
[27] Governor of Arizona. *Report of the Governor of Arizona to the Secretary of the Interior.* Government Printing Office. Washington: 1885:6.
[28] *Ibid* at p.7.
[29] Arizona Daily Star. *Untitled.* Tucson, AZ. 3/9/1887, p.4.
[30] Oro Valley Historical Society. *Heritage Guide: George Push and Arizona Statehood.* Accessed at http://ovhistory.org/heritage-guide-george-pusch-and-arizona-statehood/ on 6/30/2016.
[31] Arizona Weekly Citizen. *Untitled.* 1/29/1887, p.2.
[32] Daily Alta California. *Arizona Cattle Kings.* 11/18/1888.
[33] Arizona Daily Star. *Untitled.* Tucson, AZ. 6/16/1889, p.4.
[34] Arizona Weekly Citizen. *Untitled.* Tucson, AZ. 4/12/1890, p.3.
[35] *Ibid.* 4/5/1890, p.4.
[36] El Fronterizo. *Sueltos de la Cuidad.* Tucson, AZ. 3/15/1890, p.3.
[37] Arizona Weekly Citizen. *Untitled.* Tucson, AZ. 1/30/1892, p.2.
[38] Arizona Daily Star. *Untitled.* Tucson, AZ. 4/9/1891, p.4.
[39] The Border Vidette. *Untitled.* Nogales, AZ. 10/6/1900, pg. 2.
[40] Arizona Daily Star. *All on Account of a Steer.* Tucson, AZ. 1/30/1895, p.4.

[41] Arizona Department of Corrections. *Historical Prison Register*. Accessed at https://corrections.az.gov/historical-prison-register-m on 6/30/2016.
[42] Arizona Daily Star. *All on Account of a Steer*. Tucson, AZ. 1/30/1895, p.4.
[43] Ramon Sardina, ex-constable of Tubac, had his own personal run in with Sabino Otero. Sardina was arrested and charged with the unlawful killing of Sabino's cattle in 1887 (Arizona Daily Star. *Untitled*. 6/3/1887, p.4.) Perhaps the recent case was more about Sardina then Eugenio Moreno. Sardina was later held in default of bail for not appearing before the grand jury on the matter (Arizona Weekly Enterprise. *Arizona News*. Florence, AZ. 6/11/1887, p.3.)
[44] Arizona Weekly Citizen. *Notice*. Tucson, AZ. 7/29/1876, p.2.
[45] The Border Vidette. *Increased Assessments*. Nogales, AZ. 8/8/1903, p.2.
[46] *Ibid. Assessments*. Nogales, AZ. 8/13/1904.
[47] Arizona Daily Star. *Assessments*. Tucson, AZ. 8/10/1909, p.7.
[48] Arizona Daily Star. *Assessments*. Tucson, AZ. 8/10/1909, p.7.
[49] *See* Sayre, Nathan F. *Ranching, Endangered Species, and Urbanization in the Southwest: Species of Capital*. The University of Arizona Press. Tucson: 2002. Exposé of Cattle Ranching in Arizona
[50] Arizona Daily Star. *Developments On Old Otero Grant*. Tucson, AZ. 7/18/1915, p.7.
[51] *Ibid. Western Engines Deliver Wet Goods. Schweitzer Outfits on Development Project at Tubac Get Results*. Tucson, AZ. 8/15/1915, p.7.
[52] *Ibid. This Equipment Delivers the Goods. Teofilo Otero Buys More Western Engines and Layne-Bowler Pumps*. Tucson, AZ. 10/3/1915, p.8.
[53] *Ibid*. 10/18/1917, p.5.
[54] The Weekly Portage Sentinel. *The Gila Gold Mines - Humbug Exploded*, Ravenna, OH: 3/10/1859, Image 2.
[55] Legislature of the Territory of Arizona. *Memorial and Affidavits Showing Outrages Perpetrated by the Apache Indians in the Territory of Arizona During the years 1869 and 1870*. Francis & Valentine Printers. San Francisco. 1871:19.
[56] The Weekly Arizonan. *July 18, 1879 Letter to the Editor*. Tucson, AZ. 7/30/1870.

[57] Legislature of the Territory of Arizona. *Memorial and Affidavits Showing Outrages Perpetrated by the Apache Indians in the Territory of Arizona During the years 1869 and 1870.* Francis & Valentine Printers. San Francisco. 1871:19.
[58] The Arizona Sentinel. *Tubac.* Yuma: 3/22/1879.
[59] United States Library of Congress Chronicling America. The Arizona Sentinel (Yuma, Arizona. March 22, 1879, Image 1. Provided by the Arizona State Library, Archives and Public Records; Phoenix, AZ.
[60] Arizona Citizen. *Apache Attack in Tucson.* Tucson, AZ. 7/27/1872.
[61] United States. *Report of the Acting Governor of Arizona Made to the Secretary of the Interior for the year 1881.* Government Printing Office. Washington: 1881:15.
[62] United States. *Report of the Governor of Arizona Made to the Secretary of the Interior for the Year 1883.* Government Printing Office. Washington: 1883:9.
[63] The Arizona Sentinel. *Tubac.* Yuma: 3/22/1879.
[64] "United States Census, 1880," database with images, *FamilySearch*(https://familysearch.org/ark:/61903/1:1:MH2H-7PD : 7 July 2016), Fernandez Otero in household of Clara Otero, Tubac, Pima, Arizona, United States; citing enumeration district ED 3, sheet 212C, NARA microfilm publication T9 (Washington D.C.: National Archives and Records Administration, n.d.), roll 0036; FHL microfilm 1,254,036. Record Image 33S7-9YY1-9RZH & 33S7-9YY1-9R8Y. Charles Poston made a number of errors on the 1880 census. He was friends with the Otero family. However, in the census he listed Manuela Quesse as the mother of Brijida Castro. Brijida was the daughter of Manuela's sister Maria Elena de Jesus. He reported Fernando Otero's first name as Fernandez. Poston also appears to list Sabino Otero as the son of Juanes Espinoso as he has Sabino grouped with Espinoso's family. These errors made to a family he knew well raises a question of Poston's veracity when it comes to the entire town's census.
[65] Arizona Republican. *Against the Papagoes.* 8/29/1896.
[66] *Ibid. All Over Arizona.* Tucson, AZ. 4/1/1898.
[67] Coconino Weekly Sun. *The Cattlemen of Pima.* Flagstaff, AZ. 9/3/1896; The Border Vidette. *County Central Committee.* Nogales, AZ. 10/27/1898.

[68] United States Department of the Interior BLM General Land Office Records Online. *Sacramento Granillo, Ascession No: AZAZAA 010530. https://glorecords.blm.gov/*. Mr. Granillo received a Serial Patent on 1/11/1892 at Tubac.
[69] District Court, of the First Judicial District, of the Territory of Arizona, In and For the Court of Pima. *Case # 2087. Sabino Otero et al v. Sacramento Granillo: Complaint.* 4/10/1892.
[70] *Ibid. Demurrer and Answer.* 4/30/1892.
[71] *Ibid. Injunction.* 4/19/1892.
[72] *Ibid. Teofilo Otero Affidavit.* 2/8/1893.
[73] *Ibid. Polonio Valdez Notice to Appear for Attempt Hearing.* 2/9/1893.
[74] Arizona Daily Star. *Arrested On a Warrant Sworn Out By His Wife.* Tucson, AZ. 9/3/1910, p.5.
[75] Arizona Daily Star. *Federal Court Continues Its Regular Grind.* Tucson, AZ. 10/296/1910, p.5.
[76] Davis, Ray Jay. *Antipolygamy Legislation.* Brigham Young University at http://eom.byu.edu/index.php/Antipolygamy_Legislation.
[77] Arizona Daily Star. *Federal Court Rapidly Draws to Adjournment.* Tucson, AZ. 10/28/1910, p.5.
[78] Arizona Sentinel and Yuma Weekly Examiner. *Court Empanels U.S. Grand Jury.* Yuma, AZ. 10/26/1911, p.4.
[79] Arizona Daily Star. *Says Brother Has Charge of His Property. So Wife of Teofilo Otero Wants Court to Have Sabino Otero Surrender to Her a Proper Portion.* Tucson, AZ. 11/20/1910, p.5.
[80] Tucson City Directories for 1899, 1901, and 1913 reflect Teofilo resided with his brother Sabino Otero at 219 S. Main Street, Tucson, AZ. No City Directories were located that reflect Anna Brown Otero and Teofilo Otero resided together as of the publication of this book.
[81] District Court First Judicial District of the Territory of AZ, Pima County. *Otero vs. Otero Complaint. Case 4820.* Tucson, AZ. 11/16/1910. The Complaint reports Anna Brown Otero and Teofilo Otero had two other minor children, Alberto and Henry, who died as infants in 1904. She also asked that Teofilo be enjoined from further disposing his property.
[82] *Ibid. Teofilo Otero Amended Demurrer & Answer. Case 4820.* Tucson, AZ. 5/16/1911.
[83] Arizona Revised Statutes of the Territory of Arizona. Title 45, Chapter 1, Paragraph 3092, Section 6. 1901.

[84] District Court First Judicial District of the Territory of AZ, Pima County. *Otero vs. Otero, Ana Brown Otero Demurrer. Case 4820.* Tucson, AZ. 5/26/1911.

[85] Term "Negro" is from the *Otero vs Otero* case.

[86] District Court First Judicial District of the Territory of AZ, Pima County. *Otero vs. Otero, Defendant's Brief on Demurrer. Case 4820.* Tucson, AZ. 5/26/1911.

[87] El Paso Herald. *Wealthy Arizonan is Held as Smuggler.* El Paso, TX. 4/26/1915.

[88] Arizona Daily Star. *Otero Under Arrest.* Tucson, AZ. 4/25/1915, p.3; *see* Arizona Daily Star. *Pima Automobile Directory.* Tucson, AZ. 3/20/1915, p.10 reports Teofilo Otero was the owner of a Mitchell Touring car and among the first to own an automobile in the newly formed State of Arizona.

[89] *Ibid. Case Will Be Set for Trial Next Week; Otero Pleads Not Guilty.* Tucson, AZ. 5/9/1915, p.3.

[90] Arizona State Board of Health. Bureau of Vital Statistics. Original Certificate of Death. *Sabino Otero.* State Index No. 250, County Registered No. 31 for the Town of Tucson, County of Pima, AZ.

[91] *E.g.* The Friday, January 23, 1914 edition of Arizona Daily Star of Tucson erroneously reported that a 19-year-old Sabino assumed the role as functional head of household after his father Manuel Otero died. This misstatement continues to be reported as fact to date despite federal census records that confirm Manuel died in 1870 when Sabino was 29-years-old; *see* Arizona Daily Star. *Useful Life of Sabino Otero Comes to End. Last Direct Male Descendant but One of Grantee of Otero Land Grant; Devoted Life to Aiding Others.*

[92] Arizona Daily Star. *In the Superior Court of Pima County, State of Arizona. Notice of Hearing Petition.* 2/15/1914, p.12.

[93] The Border Vidette. *Re: Estate of Sabino Otero.* Nogales, AZ; 2/7/1914, p.3.

[94] Superior Court of Pima County, AZ. *Manuel Otero vs. Teofilo Otero. Complaint. Case No. 5835.* Filed 10/19/1916.

[95] Superior Court of Pima County, AZ. *In the Matter of the Estate of Sabino Otero. Docket No. 2107. Last Will and Testament.* Filed 3/31/1914.

[96] Published census records fail to support that Sabino and Manuel Otero ever lived together.

[97] Sabino Otero signed his Last Will and Testament on 1/15/1914 which was witnessed by Anita C .Coenen and Tom K. Richey, both residents of Tucson, AZ. Sabino died on 1/22/1914.
[98] Superior Court of Pima County, AZ. *Manuel Otero vs Teofilo Otero. Complaint. Case No. 5835.* Filed 10/19/16.
[99] Black's Law Dictionary Free 2nd Ed and The Law Dictionary. *Demurrer.* https://thelawdictionary.org/demurrer/
[100] Superior Court of Pima County, AZ. *Teofilo Otero Demurrer and Answer. Case No. 5835.* Undated.
[101] *Ibid. T. Otero vs J. Otero.* Case No. 5904. *Promissory Note between Teofilo Otero, Jose T. Otero, and Ana Maria Coenen.* 1/20/1916.
[102] *Ibid. T. Otero vs J. Otero.* Case No. 5904. *Complaint.* 8/12/1916.
[103] *Ibid. T. Otero vs J. Otero.* Case No. 5904. *Complaint.* 8/12/1916. The Complaint alleged default of numerous promissory notes payable by Jose T. Otero to Teofilo Otero in gold coin: $10,000 on 1/20/1916, $1,200 on 2/19/1916, $500 on 2/23/1916, $500 on 3/11/1916, $1,200 on 3/18/1916, $1,000 on 4/4/1916, $2,000 on 5/2/1916, $1,000 on 5/15/1916, $1,000 on 5/29/1916, $500 on 6/12/1916, and $249.41 on 7/12/1913.
[104] 2017 figured determined by using an inflation rate of 3.13% per year in accordance with figures reported by the U.S. Department of Labor Statistics.
[105] Superior Court of Pima County, AZ. *T. Otero vs J. Otero.* Case No. 5904. *Reply to Answer and Answer to Counter-Claim.* 10/10/1916.
[106] Arizona Republic. *In Supreme Court.* Tucson, AZ. 1/24/1918, p.6.
[107] Arizona Supreme Court Case No. 1630. *Mandate.* 5/20/1919.
[108] Garcia y Alva, Federico. *"Mexico y sus progresos": "Album-directorio del estado de Sonora."Obra hecha con apoyo del gobierno del estado.* Impresa oficial dirigida por A.B. Monteverde. Sonora. 1905; *see* section on "Hacienda de 'Jupateco." Not paginated.
[109] Venustiano Carranza Garza was the President of the Mexican United States from 5/1/1917-5/21/1920.
[110] Fold3. *Mexican FBI Files. M1085.* "Juan Ortiz-In Re: Mexican Activities." Wm. Neunhoffer. Tucson, AZ. 7/6/1916, p.3.
[111] *Ibid, p.5.* "Juan Ortiz-In Re: Mexican Activities." Wm. Neunhoffer. Tucson, AZ. 7/25/1916, p2.

[112] Fold3. *Mexican FBI Files. M1085.* "In Re-H. Yzurieta et al." Tucson, AZ. 7/17/1916, p.2.
[113] *Ibid,* p.3.
[114] *Ibid.* AZ. 6/28/1916.
[115] *Ibid.* "In Re: Mexican Activities." Interview of General Santiago Rivero by Wm. Neunhoffer. AZ. 7/28/1916.
[116] *Ibid.* "In Re: Mexican Activities." Interview of Colonel Francisco Cardenas by Wm. Neunhoffer. AZ. 8/10/1916.
[117] Tubac Historical Society. *Anna Maldonado Fimbres. "Voices of the Valley" Tubac Historical Society Oral History Project.* Tubac, 3/16/1990, pp.29-33.
[118] *Ibid,* p.29.
[119] Tubac Historical Society. *Anna Maldonado Fimbres. "Voices of the Valley" Tubac Historical Society Oral History Project.* Tubac, 3/16/1990, p.14.
[120] Arizona Republic. *Historic Tubac is Preparing to Hold Annual Festival.* 6/7/1925, p.6; *see* Tubac Historical Society. *"Voices of the Valley." Tubac Historical Society Oral History Project.* Interviewer Betty J. Lane. 2/27/1990 and 3/16/1990 at pp.5-6. Interview of Anna Maldonado Fimbres detailing how Ana Maria Comadurán Coenen raised money from Uncle Teofilo Otero and local citizens to fund the building of St. Ann's Church. Speculation exists that St. Ann's church and Ana Maria share the name of the same patron saint.
[121] Arizona Daily Star. *51-Pound Melon.* Tucson, AZ. 8/13/1918, p.8.
[122] Tubac Historical Society. *Anna Maldonado Fimbres. "Voices of the Valley" Tubac Historical Society Oral History Project.* Tubac, 3/16/1990, p.22.
[123] Arizona Supreme Court. Otero & Rojas v. Soto & Gonzalez. No. 2702. Appeal from Supreme Court of Arizona. 6/27/1928.
[124] Definition Guardian ad litem: "When a person involved in a suite cannot adequately represent his or her own interests, the court may appoint an guardian ad litem to protect the person's interests...Generally, courts appoint guardians ad litem to represent legal infants and adults who are actually or allegedly incapacitated." Cornell Law School. *WEX, Legal Information Institute.* Accessed at https://www.law.cornell.edu/wex/guardian_ad_litem
[125] Arizona Republic. *Two Cases Argued.* Phoenix, AZ. 4/22/1928, p.4.

[126] Arizona State Board of Health Bureau of Vital Statistics. *Standard Certificate of Death Teofilo Otero. State File No. 422; Registrar's No. 414.* Witnessed on 5/16/1941. Teofilo died of cancer of the penis which he contracted three years prior to his death.
[127] Superior Court of Pima County, AZ. *Complaint for Declaratory Judgment. Leonor and Ysidro Otero vs Leonardo Moreno et al. Docket No. 21094.* Tucson: 8/15/19941, pp.1-6.
[128] *Ibid. Separate Answer of Defendant Leonardo Moreno, as Executor. Docket No. 21094. Leonor and Ysidro Otero vs Leonardo Moreno et al. Docket No. 21094.* Tucson: 9/6/1941, pp.1-4.
[129] *Ibid. Motion to Dismiss Cause as to the Plaintiff Ysidro Otero. Docket No. 21094.* Tucson: 9/6/1941, p.1.
[130] *Ibid. Deposition of Anna Maria Coenen. Docket No. 21094.* Held 10/17/1941, p.3.
[131] *Ibid. Deposition of Anna Maria Coenen. Docket No. 21094.* Held 10/17/1941, pp.3-6.
[132] *Ibid. Deposition of Anna Maria Coenen. Docket No. 21094.* Held 10/17/1941, pp. 15-19.
[133] *Ibid. Anna Brown Otero, Ana O. Provencio and Edward Otero vs Leonardo Moreno et al. Docket No. 21553.*
[134] *Ibid. Transcript of Testimony. Docket Nos. 8334 (In the Matter of the Estate of Teofilo Otero) No. 21094 (Leonor Capan Otero and Ysidro Otero vs Leonardo Moreno et al) and 21553 (Ana O. Provencio and Edwardo Otero vs Leonardo Moreno et al).* Held 3/31/1942. pp. 3-12.
[135] *Ibid. Transcript of Testimony. Docket Nos. 8334 (In the Matter of the Estate of Teofilo Otero) No. 21094 (Leonor Capan Otero and Ysidro Otero vs Leonardo Moreno et al) and 21553 (Ana O. Provencio and Edwardo Otero vs Leonardo Moreno et al).* Held 3/31/1942.
[136] *Ibid. Transcript of Testimony. Docket Nos. 8334 (In the Matter of the Estate of Teofilo Otero) No. 21094 (Leonor Capan Otero and Ysidro Otero vs Leonardo Moreno et al) and 21553 (Ana O. Provencio and Edwardo Otero vs Leonardo Moreno et al).* Held 3/31/1942, pp.28-
[137] *Ibid. (In the Matter of the Estate of Teofilo Otero) No. 21094 (Leonor Capan Otero and Ysidro Otero vs Leonardo Moreno et*

al) and 21553 (Ana O. Provencio and Edwardo Otero vs Leonardo Moreno et al). Held 3/31/1942, pp. 31-32.
[138] *Ibid. Order Authorizing Executor to Compromise Suits. Docket Nos. 8334 (In the Matter of the Estate of Teofilo Otero).* Filed 3/31/1942.
[139] DeLugan, Diana. *Otero Research Collection. Maria Reina Otero Interview.* 4/7/2010. Maria Reina Otero is the daughter of Ricardo Otero who had first-hand knowledge of her father's understanding of the Teofilo Otero probate challenge.
[140] Arizona Daily Star. *Court Settles Otero Estate; Monthly Payments of $30 to $125 Provided for Relatives, Friends.* Tucson, AZ. 7/29/1942.

Chapter Four: Rancho de Otero Legacy

[1] Santa Cruz County Recorder Book of Deeds. Bk 8, 148.
[2] *Ibid.* Bk 10, 285.
[3] Tubac Golf Resort and Spa. *About Us.* Accessed at http://www.tubacgolfresort.com/about/ 9/15/2016.
[4] Santa Cruz County Recorder Book of Deeds. Bk 20, pp.513-15.
[5] *Ibid.*
[6] *Ibid,* pp.566-68.
[7] State of Arizona. Department of Revenue. *Parceling Standards.* Revised 2/25/2011. Accessible online at https://azdor.gov/Portals/0/Property/2011Part6Chapter1.pdf. Standards explain that a Section of land equal 160 acres. Each Section is divided into 4 equal quarters of 160 acres each, and each quarter of a quarter section equals 40 acres.
[8] Arizona Republic. *Weekly Is Thriving Enterprise.* Phoenix, AZ. 3/18/1953, p.53.
[9] DeLugan, Diana. *Otero Research Collection. Email from Georgia Bowman Allen.* 3/4/2017.
[10] Panchos. *About.* Accessed at http://panchosdesign.com/about/
[11] Tucson Daily Citizen. *Bowman Sells Famous Old Ranch Near Tubac.* Tucson, AZ. 2/16/1946, p.2.
[12] Tucson Daily Citizen. *Hacienda Otero Ranch.* Tucson, AZ. 1/3/1948, p.10.
[13] Arizona Republic Sun. *Grace & Grace Realtors.* Phoenix, AZ. 2/8/1948, p.41.
[14] *Ibid.*
[15] Santa Cruz County Recorder Book of Deeds, Bk 28, pp.238-40.

[16] Tucson Daily Citizen. *Bowman Sells Famous Old Ranch Near Tubac.* Tucson, AZ. 2/16/1946.
[17] *Ibid.*
[18] Tucson Daily Citizen. *Manufacturer Is New Owner of Otero Ranch.* Tucson, AZ. 2/18/1946, p.46.
[19] Joanna Fay Shankle had two sons with former husband Clarence E. "Dutch" Shankle, Joseph Fay Shankle and John Dyer Shankle. She also had two children with second husband Walter C. Davis. Davis-Monthan Aviation Field Register/Joan Fay Shankle website. http://dmairfield.com/people/shankle_jf/. Accessed on 10/26/2010.
[20] The P.M. Ranch site was originally the Joseph Kaphan Federal land patent. Subsequently, it was sold and became the Chavez Ranch at Tubac, Az's Chavez Siding Road Exit. It was eventually sold to Thomas Casanega who in turn sold the property to Army Aviator E.C. Shankle for $50,000. *See* Rosenfield, Marie. *Desert Aristocrats.* Green Valley News. Green Valley: 6/27/1968.
[21] Arizona Republic. *Famous Ranch in Tubac Sold.* Phoenix, AZ. 6/26/1948, p.11.
[22] Davis-Monthan Aviation Field Register/Joan Fay Shankle website. http://dmairfield.com/people/shankle_jf/. Accessed on 10/26/2010.
[23] See Davis-Monthan Aviation Field Register at http://dmairfield.com/people/shankle_jf/.
[24] DeLugan, Diana. *Otero Research Collection.* According to John Shankle, son of Joanna Fay Davis (formerly Shankle), PM stood for *pajaritos migratorios*, translated migratory birds. Email from John Shankle to Diana DeLugan, 10/0/2010.
[25] Davis-Monthan Aviation Field Register/Joan Fay Shankle website. http://dmairfield.com/people/shankle_jf/. Accessed on 10/26/2010.
[26] DeLugan, Diana. *Otero Research Collection. John Shankle email.* 10/30/2010.
[27] Tucson Daily Citizen. *Sanity Hearing Under Way for Mrs. W.C. Davis.* Tucson, AZ. 9/28/1948, p.2; Arizona Republic. *Wealthy Rancher Ruled Incompetent.* Phoenix, AZ. 3/3/1950, p.23.
[28] Davis-Monthan Aviation Field Register/Joan Fay Shankle website. http://dmairfield.com/people/shankle_jf/. Accessed on 10/26/2010.

[29] To learn more about Joanna Fay Shankle's history as an aviator visit http://dmairfield.com/people/shankle_jf/.
[30] Tucson Daily Citizen. *1,000 Homes Planned on Tubac Ranch.* Tucson, AZ. 3/28/1958, p.13.
[31] *Ibid.*
[32] *Ibid. The Town that Won't Stay Dead.* Tucson, AZ. 2/3/1960, p.25.
[33] *Ibid. Joins Country Club Bing Crosby Buys Land Near Tubac.* Tucson, AZ. 5/11/1959, p.1.
[34] *Ibid.*
[35] Arizona Republic. *Untitled.* Phoenix, AZ. 10/27/1963, p.107.
[36] *Ibid. Arizonans Plan to Attend Meet.* Phoenix, AZ. 3/8/1959, p.86.
[37] Tucson Daily Citizen. *Bing Crosby Buys Land Near Tubac.* Tucson, AZ. 5/12/1959, p.1.
[38] *Ibid. Bing Crosby Heads Tubac Club Board.* Tucson, AZ. 6/8/1959, p.35; According to the Arizona Daily Sun article *Star Elected Board Chairman"* on 1/21/1960, Crosby was also elected Chairman of the Board of Directors of the First National Bank of Holbrook.
[39] *Ibid. Bing Gets Option On Tubac Land.* Tucson, AZ. 10/23/1959, p.2; Arizona Republic. *Bing Leases Tubac Land.* Phoenix, AZ. 10/26/1959, p.34.
[40] *Ibid. Joins Country Club Bing Crosby Buys Land Near Tubac.* Tucson, AZ. 5/11/1959, p.1.
[41] *Ibid. The Town that Won't Stay Dead.* Tucson, AZ. 2/3/1960, p.25.
[42] *Ibid. On Site of Old Presidio.* Tucson, AZ. 11/21/1960, p.58; Golf course designer Red Lawrence designed the Litchfield Park Course in Phoenix, AZ. *Id*; Bob Stacey was the contractor for the course designed by Mr. Lawrence. Tubac Daily Citizen. *Tubac Sets Deadline Date.* 8/10/1959, p.26.
[43] *Ibid. 'Thinking Man's Course' Tubac Golf Course Rises on Site of Old Presidio.* Tucson, AZ. 11/21/1960, p.60.
[44] *Ibid. On Site of Old Presidio.* Tucson, AZ. 11/21/1960, p.58.
[45] *Ibid.*
[46] *Ibid. Pro Campaigner Souchak Puts Golf Earnings Back Into Tubac's Course.* Tucson, AZ. 5/1/62, p.20. Souchak was induced to invest in the Tubac course by O. H. Gahlberg and William "Bill" Gahlberg. William ran the course and was formally a golf captain at the University of Arizona.

---

[47] *Ibid. Tubac Stockholder Stalks 'Trespasser.'* Tucson, AZ. 2/9/1963, p.11.
[48] Arizona Republic. *Untitled.* 11/23/1963, p.82.
[49] *Ibid.*
[50] *Ibid.*
[51] Tucson Daily Citizen. *Tubac Golf Course Sold to Pollock.* Tucson, AZ. 6/10/1969, p.22; "Pollock said that his former partners will receive part cash for their interest and retain their interest in the acreage which surrounds the golf course." *Id.*
[52] *Ibid. Magdalena Really Spruces Up.* Tucson, AZ. 10/16/1974, p.1.
[53] *Ibid. Tubac Golf Course Sold to Pollock.* Tucson, AZ. 6/10/1969, p.22.
[54] *Ibid.*
[55] Tucson Daily Citizen. *Magdalena Really Spruces Up.* Tucson, AZ. 10/16/1974, p.1
[56] *Ibid. Mexico Prepares for Visit.* Tucson, AZ. 10/16/1974, p.6.
[57] *Ibid. But Tubac Stop Offers Relief.* Tucson, AZ. 10/22/1974; Gerald R. Ford Presidential Library. *Pool Report – Tubac/Davis-Monthan/Oklahoma City.* 10/21/1974.
[58] Gerald R. Ford Presidential Library. *Pool Report – Tubac/Davis-Monthan/Oklahoma City.* 10/21/1974.
[59] Juarez Jr., Macario. The Arizona Daily Star. *Ronald D. Allred Acquired the Tubac Golf Resort for $7.28 million; Visions the 400-acres as Potential World-class Resort.* Obtained at http://www.hotel-online.com/News/PR2002_4th/Oct02_Tubac.html. Accessed on 11/26/17.
[60] Arizona Corporation Commission. *Entity Search. File No. L10412751.* Obtained on 11/26/17.
[61] *See* Arizona Corporation Commission *Tubac Allred, L.C.C. File Number L10412693.*
[62] *See* Arizona Corporation Commission *Dann Holdings, Inc. File Number 10585487.*
[63] Juarez Jr., Macario. The Arizona Daily Star. *Ronald D. Allred Acquired the Tubac Golf Resort for $7.28 million; Visions the 400-acres as Potential World-class Resort.* Obtained at http://www.hotel-

online.com/News/PR2002_4th/Oct02_Tubac.html. Accessed on 11/26/17.

[64] PRWeb. *Tubac Golf Resort & Spa Owner, Ron Allred, To Be Inducted Into Colorado Ski & Snowboard Hall Of Fame.* Obtained at http://www.prweb.com/releases/2011tubacgolfresort/06tucsonresort/prweb8608099.htm. Accessed on 11/26/17

[65] Historic Hotels of America. *About.* Obtained at http://m.historichotels.org/smartphone/index.php/about. Accessed on 11/26/17.

[66] Arizona Republic. *Film Glamorizes Historic Hacienda.* Phoenix, AZ. 5/22/1955, p.51.

[67] Wikipedia. *Strange Lady in Town.* Obtained at https://en.wikipedia.org/wiki/Strange_Lady_in_Town. Accessed 6/29/2016.

[68] *Ibid. Tin Cup.* Obtained at https://en.wikipedia.org/wiki/Tin_Cup. Accessed 6/29/2016.

[69] Arizona Republic Sun. *1 Long Drive Gets You To 'Tin Cup.'* Phoenix, AZ. 9/8/1996.

[70] *Ibid. Get Out Your (family) and Hit the 'Tin Cup.'* Phoenix, AZ. 9/8/1996, p.176.

[71] *Ibid.*

[72] *Ibid.*

Chapter Five: Baboquivari and Other Terrenos

[1] Ring, Bob. *Time Travel Through the History of the Catalina Foothills and Tanque Verde Valle.* Obtained at www.ringbrothershistory.com accessed on 10/15/2016 at p.9; *see* LaSota, Kim. *Entertainment Magazine Online*. "Sabino Canyon – oasis in the Tucson Desert "explains how area was "first visited as a picnic area in about 1885." Obtained at http://www.emol.org/tucson/sabinocanyon/index.html accessed on 10/15/2016. An online map of Sabino Canyon at the Catalina Mountains is located at http://www.emol.org/tucson/sabinocanyon/map.html.

[2] At the time of this book's publication, no U.S. Department of Agriculture Forest Service records have been located to confirm the origin for the naming of Catalina Mountain's Sabino Canyon.

[3] Arizona Weekly Citizen. *A Day at the Dam: The Santa Catarina [sic] Water Right in Sabino Canyon.* Tucson, AZ. 12/15/1883 provided by the Arizona State Library, Archives and Public Records; Phoenix, AZ. http://chroniclingamerica.loc.gov/lccn/sn82015133/1883-12-15/ed-1/seq-4/

[4] Browne, John Ross. *Adventures in the Apache Country.* Harper & Brothers, Publishers. New York: 1869.

[5] Aguirre, Yjinio F. *The Journal of Arizona History.* "Echoes of the Conquistadores: Stock Raising in Spanish-Mexican Times." Arizona Historical Society. Vol. 16, No. 3 (Autumn 1975), p.275, 277. Obtained at http://www.jstor.org/stable/41695272 accessed 9/25/2016. ("…San Vicente…had been owned by the Otero family where there was a pond surrounded by a barbed-wire fence with a wire gate").

[6] DeLugan, Diana. *Otero Research Collection.* Email from Philip Halpenny dated 9/25/2016. According to Philip Halpenny, land/water expert, the actual location of the San Vicente and Santa Rosa Otero ranches cannot be located using the U.S. Bureau of Land Management records because the land is now part of the Tohono O'odham reservation, property likely taken by eminent domain at the turn of the 20th century. Records reflect that the ranches, likely numbered 2 and 3 of Section 18 of Township 18 South, Range 8, were near each other. The ranches could also be descending from the northwest corner of Section 18.

[7] United States. National Archives and Records Administration. US Bureau of Land Management. Affidavit of *The Arizona Citizen.*

[8] *Ibid.* Notice for Publication Homestead No. 1302. 8/9/1892.

[9] United States. National Archives and Records Administration. US Bureau of Land Management. Homestead Proof-Testimony of Witnesses George Martin, Sabino Otero, and Raimundo Vasquez. 9/10/1892.

[10] *Ibid.* Homestead Proof-Testimony of Witnesses George Martin, Sabino Otero, and Raimundo Vasquez. 9/10/1892.

[11] US Bureau of Land Management. Receiver's Receipt, No. 132 – Application No. 1302. 12/17/1889; and Final Affidavit Required of Homestead Claimants.

[12] United States Congressional Serial Set, Issue 9; Issue 3265, Section 2290 Revised. 1895.

[13] United States. Bureau of Land Management. *Sabino Otero Homestead Certificate No. 537.* 12/20/1892.
[14] Elkhorn Ranch. *History*. Obtained at http://elkhornranch.com/history/ accessed on 9/12/2106.
[15] True, Russell and Diana Madaras. *Dude Ranching in Arizona*. Arcadia Publishing. Charleston: 2016. p.123.
[16] Elkhorn Ranch. *History*. Obtained at http://elkhornranch.com/history/ accessed on 9/12/2016; *see also* Arizona Daily Star. *Marion Tyack Whitfield Obituary*. 4/5/2015.
[17] Elkhorn Ranch History. Obtained at http://www.elkhornranchmontana.com/about-us/history/ accessed on 11/27/2016.
[18] US Library of Congress. Chronicling America. Arizona Weekly Citizen. *Untitled.* 7/4/1891, image 4.
[19] DeLugan, Diana. *Otero Research Collection*. David Ballesteros initial contact summary taken 9/2016.
[20] *Ibid*. David Jesus Ballesteros Phone Interview Summary of interview taken 9/17/2016, Tucson.
[21] *Ibid*. Audio interview of David Jesus Ballesteros with author Diana DeLugan and Philip Halpenny on September 17, 2016 at Tucson, AZ. Ballesteros shared his recollection of living at the Sabino Otero House on Elkhorn Ranch.
[22] Interview of Pauline Clark, alleged witness who testified Dionicio Ballesteros stored arms and ammunition for Pancho Villa. *From U.S. Bureau of Investigation report by Robert L. Barnes, 5/16/1912. Case of U.S. versus Indalecio [sp] Ballesteros.*
[23] DeLugan, Diana. *Otero Research Collection.* Recorded lecture by historian and retired hydrologist Philip Halpenny at Tubac Presidio State Park and Museum on 10/22/2016. Halpenny gives guided tours of the Barrio de Tubac Archaeological site sponsored by the Tubac Presidio State Park and the Tumacácori National Historic Park.
[24] Baker, Robert D. *et al. Timeless Heritage: A History of the Forest Service in the Southwest. Land Grant Ranches.* U.S. Department of Agriculture Forest Service Publication No. FS-409. College Stations, TX: August 1988, p.21.
[25] United States. Senate. *Senate Documents, Vol. 187.* U.S. Government Printing Office. Washington: 1863, p. 14.
[26] Arizona Republic. *Sabino Otero Farm Bought by Rancher.* Phoenix, AZ. 7/12/1949.

[27] The Weekly Arizonian. *Extensive Improvement.* Tubac, AZ Territory. 3/03/1859.
[28] Browne, John Ross. *Adventures in the Apache County; A Tour Through Arizona and Sonora, with Notes on the Silver Regions of Nevada.* Harper & Brothers, Publishers. New York: 1869, p. 259.
[29] The Weekly Arizonian. *Extensive Improvement.* Tubac, AZ Territory. 3/03/1859.
[30] A "sutler" is someone who follows an army for the purpose of providing it provisions for its soldiers.
[31] *See* Brevoort. Elias. *New Mexico. Her Natural Resources and Attractions, Being a Collection of Facts, Mainly Concerning her Geography, Climate, Population, Schools, Mines and Minerals, Agricultural and Pastoral Capacities, and Spanish and Mexican Land Grants.* Elias Brevoort Publisher. Santa Fe: 1874. Available for free at Google Books online.
[32] Browne, John Ross. *Adventures in the Apache County; A Tour Through Arizona and Sonora, with Notes on the Silver Regions of Nevada.* Harper & Brothers, Publishers. New York: 1869, p. 259. Browne also reports that Brevoort was alleged to have some "connection with the Quarter-master's Department of the Army." *See* New Mexico Secretary of State. *New Mexico Blue Book.* 1915, p.16 reports Elias Brevoort was a "Receiver of Public Money" at the Santa Fe Land Office from 178-81; *See also* Evening Star. *Confirmations by the Senate.* 6/17/1878 reports Elias Brevoort was confirmed by the U.S. Senate as the "receiver of public moneys at Santa Fe," New Mexico, years after he left his El Reventon Ranch in Amado.
[33] NorthAmericanForts.com. *Camp El Reventon.* http://www.northamericanforts.com/West/az2.html#reventon
[34] Arizona Citizen. *Confiscation Cases.* Tucson, AZ. 12/3/1870.
[35] *Ibid.*
[36] Browne, John Ross. *Adventures in the Apache County; A Tour Through Arizona and Sonora, with Notes on the Silver Regions of Nevada.* Harper & Brothers, Publishers. New York: 1869, p. 259.

[37] Superior Court of Pima County. Probate Court. *Leonor Capan Otero and Ysidro Otero vs Leonardo Moreno et al. Deposition of Ana Maria Coenen. Docket No. 21094.* Held 10/17/1941, p.3
[38] U.S. Bureau of Land Management. *Clara M. Otero Land Patent No. 122.*2/6/1896.
[39] U.S. Bureau of Land Management Plat. *Township No. 20 South Range No. 13 East G&SRM.* Clara M. Otero homestead at Amado. The AZ General Land office surveyed Amado's township lines on 5/18 & 19/1885.Originally filed at the Tucson, AZ Surveyor General's Office on 11/4/1885 by Surveyor General Royal A. Johnson. Township lines were resurveyed in 1901 by Philip Cotzen.
[40] Superior Court of Pima County. Probate Court. *Last Will and Testament of Sabino Otero. Docket No. 2107.* Filed 2/4/1917.
[41] Superior Court of Pima County. Probate Court. *Inventory and Appraisement. Docket No. 2017.* Filed 3/9//1914.
[42] Superior Court of Pima County. Probate Court. *Inventory and Appraisement. Estate of Teofilo Otero.* Filed 8/13/1941.
[43] Blust, Kendal. *Rustic Gardens meet gilded-age glamour at Agua Linda Farm.* Nogales International. 4/4/2017. Accessed http://www.nogalesinternational.com/news/rustic-gardens-meet-gilded-age-glamour-at-agua-linda-farm/article_7aa0291e-18d3-11e7-9668-bba66f2e200b.html.
[44] The Otero family moved to Reventon in 1875. Clara Martinez Otero's land patent for El Reventon was finalized in 1896. The ranch was sold from the Teofilo Otero estate in 1949.
[45] Arizona Weekly Citizen. *Desert Land Locations in Arizona.* Tucson, Territory of AZ. 8/11/1877, p.2.
[46] Arizona Daily Star. *Official Records Locations.* Tucson, Territory of AZ. 4/5/1884.
[47] Wikipedia. *Pajarito Mountains.* Accessed https://en.wikipedia.org/wiki/Pajarito_Mountains on 2/29/2017.
[48] Arizona Daily Star. *Official Records Locations/Deeds.* Tucson, Territory of AZ. 8/10/1884.
[49] Arizona Weekly Citizen. *Untitled.* Tucson, Territory of AZ. 1/17/1891, p.3.
[50] Santa Cruz County Recorder Miscellaneous Bk 3, 447.
[51] Santa Cruz County Recorder Book of Deeds. Bk 15, 509.
[52] *Ibid.* Bk 5, 383.

[53] *Ibid.* Bk 5, 519.
[54] *Ibid.* Bk 8, 615.
[55] *Ibid.* Bk 9, 608.
[56] *Ibid.* Bk 10, 395.
[57] *Ibid.* Bk 10, 413.
[58] *Ibid.* Bk 10, 514.
[59] *Ibid.* Bk 11, 361.
[60] *Ibid.* Bk 14, 5.
[61] *Ibid.* Bk 16, 170.
[62] *Ibid.* Bk 14, 56.
[63] *Ibid.* Bk 14, 57.
[64] *Ibid.* Bk 15, 223.
[65] *Ibid.* Bk 15, 340.
[66] *Ibid.* Bk 14, 433.
[67] *Ibid.* Bk 14, 461.
[68] *Ibid.* Bk 14, 462.
[69] *Ibid.* Bk 14, 495.
[70] *Ibid.* Bk 14, 548.
[71] *Ibid.* Bk 16, 171.
[72] *Ibid.* Bk 16, 597.
[73] *Ibid.* Bk 18, 134.
[74] *Ibid.* Bk 19, 276.
[75] Arizona Daily Star. *Deed.* Tucson, AZ. 12/1/1917, p.5.
[76] *Ibid. Mortgage.* Tucson, AZ. 12/6/1917, p. 6.
[77] *Ibid. Mortgage.* Tucson, AZ. 2/28/1918, p.6.
[78] *Ibid. Public Documents.* Tucson, AZ. 5/14/1918, p.7.
[79] Arizona Daily Star. *Public Records.* Tucson, AZ. 12/18/1919, p.9.
[80] *Ibid. Untitled.* Tucson, AZ. 3/19/1921, p.4.
[81] *Ibid. Mortgages.* 9/9/1921, p.8.
[82] *Ibid. Deeds, Mortgages, Leases, Locations, Assignments, Filings and Discharges* Tucson, AZ. 5/24/1922, p.3.
[83] *Ibid. Suit on $7500 Note.* Tucson, AZ. 7/11/1919.
[84] *Ibid. Public Documents.* 9/26/1919, p.8.
[85] Tucson Daily Citizen. *Driscoll Street House Bought.* Tucson, AZ. 8/11/1942.
[86] *Ibis. Julianis Buy Property Here for $27,500.* Tucson, AZ. 8/25/1945, p.3.
[87] Eatherly, Charles. *Arizona State Parks......The Beginning.* Governor and Arizona Parks Board. 2006.

[88] United States. National Register of Historic Places Supplementary Listing Record. *NRIS Reference Number: 94001195.* 10/17/1994.
[89] Tubac Arizonian. *Presidio of Tubac, Resolution Accepting Gift.* Vol. II, No. II. Summer 1959. Courtesy of Arizona State Library, Archives & Public Records. Tubac Town News Clippings File.
[90] *Ibid.*
[91] Eatherly, Charles. *Arizona State Parks......The Beginning.* Governor and Arizona Parks Board. 2006: p.9.
[92] United States Department of the Interior National Park Service. *National Register of Historic Places Continuation Sheet, Tubac Townsite District.* 3/15/1993, p.7.
[93] Santa Cruz County Superior Court. *State of AZ vs Tubac Elementary School District No. 5. Case No. 6725. Final Order of Condemnation.* Tucson, AZ. 8/27/1973.
[94] United States Department of the Interior National Park Service. *National Register of Historic Places Continuation Sheet, Tubac Townsite District.* 3/15/1993, Section 7, p.5.
[95] Vandervoet, Kathleen. "Historic Tubac home gains new life." *Nogales International.* Online. 10/19/2006. Accessed at http://www.nogalesinternational.com/community/historic-tubac-home-gains-new-life/article_3bfbe8e3-b4ee-50d6-9904-e201f734f2b5.html.
[96] United States, Selective Service System. World War I Selective Service System Draft Registration Cards, 1917-1918. Washington, D.C.: National Archives and Records Administration. M1509, 4,582 rolls. Imaged from Family History Library microfilm. Arizona; Registration County: Santa Cruz; Roll: 1522650. "Francisco Rojas WWI Draft Registration Card." *Accessed from* Ancestry.com. U.S., World War I Draft Registration Cards, 1917-1918 [database on-line]. Provo, UT, USA: Ancestry.com Operations Inc., 2005.
[97] Arizona State Library, Archives & Public Records. *Plat of Tubac Townsite.* 1882.
[98] U.S. Federal Census. Year: 1910; Census Place: Precinct 3, Santa Cruz, Arizona; Roll: T624_42; Page: 9B; Enumeration District: 0115; FHL microfilm: 1374055. Obtained from Ancestry.com. 1910 United States Federal Census [database on-line]. Lehi, UT, USA: Ancestry.com Operations Inc., 2006.

[99] U.S. Federal Census. Year: 1920; Census Place: Tubac, Santa Cruz, Arizona; Roll: T625_51; Page: 2B; Enumeration District: 123. Fourteenth Census of the United States, 1920. (NARA microfilm publication T625, 2076 rolls). Records of the Bureau of the Census, Record Group 29. National Archives, Washington, D.C. Obtained from Ancestry.com. 1920 United States Federal Census [database on-line]. Provo, UT, USA: Ancestry.com.
[100] U.S. Federal Census. Year: 1910; Census Place: Precinct 3, Santa Cruz, Arizona; Roll: T624_42; Page: 9B; Enumeration District: 0115; FHL microfilm: 1374055. *Accessed from* Ancestry.com. 1910 United States Federal Census [database on-line]. Lehi, UT, USA: Ancestry.com Operations Inc., 2006.
[101] Vandervoet, Kathleen. "Historic Tubac home gains new life." *Nogales International.* Online. 10/19/2006. Accessed at http://www.nogalesinternational.com/community/historic-tubac-home-gains-new-life/article_3bfbe8e3-b4ee-50d6-9904-e201f734f2b5.html.
[102] City of Tucson. *Historic American Landscape Survey of El Tiradito – City of Tucson.* Accessed at https://www.tucsonaz.gov/files/preservation/ElTiradito_HALS_AZ-8.pdf, p.1.
[103] *Ibid*, pp. 1, 4; *see* DeLugan, Diana. *Interview of Ray Martinez La Pilita Docent.* Video. 10/18/2014.
[104] Ruiz, Vicki and John R. Chavez. "Memories and Migrations: Mapping Boricua and Chicana Histories." *La Placita Committee.* University of Illinois Press. Urbana and Chicago: 2008, pp. 60-61.
[105] City of Tucson. *Historic American Landscape Survey of El Tiradito – City of Tucson.* Accessed at https://www.tucsonaz.gov/files/preservation/ElTiradito_HALS_AZ-8.pdf, p.5-6.
[106] Arizona Historical Society. *MS 1454. Ana Otero Provencio Family Papers, 1901-1942. Letter from Sister Clara Otero to Teofilo Otero.* Tucson. 12/26/1901.
[107] Tucson Daily Citizen. *Travel to 'Town House' Was Perilous.* Tucson, AZ. 4/30/1965, p.2.
[108] Numerous reports that the Otero house on Main Street was built by Sabino Otero or Teofilo Otero and first occupied by his family in 1861 are incorrect. U.S. Census records report that Sabino and Teofilo's father Manuel moved his family from

Tubac to Tucson in 1863. The Otero family returned to Tubac frequently where it continued to maintain the Hacienda de Otero. Manuel died in 1870 when Sabino was # years old. *See* Tucson Daily Citizen. *Travel to 'Town House' Was Perilous.* Tucson, AZ. 4/30/1965, p.2 accurately reporting "The Tucson house was built by Tori[v]io's grandson, Manuel, some years after Sabino was born in Tubac in 1846." *See also* Tucson Daily Citizen. *Living Yesterdays.* Tucson, AZ. 2/18/1963, p.2 reporting that the home was built for Teofilo in 1861; Otero, Lydia. *La Calle.* University of Arizona Press. Tucson: 2010, p.159, reporting the home was built by Sabino in 1861.

[109] Arizona Weekly Citizen. *Untitled.* Tucson, AZ. 11/7/1874, p.3. ("Mr. Otero is going to soon rebuild his house on Main near McCormick [S]treet").

[110] See Tucson Daily Citizen. *Travel to 'Town House' Was Perilous.* Tucson, AZ. 4/30/1965, p.2.

[111] *Ibid.*

[112] *Ibid.*

[113] Lane, Betty. Tubac Historical Society Oral History Project Voices of the Valley. *Anna Maldonado Fimbres Interview.* Tubac: 2/27 & 3/16/1990, p.26.

[114] Tucson Daily Citizen. *Travel to 'Town House' Was Perilous.* Tucson, AZ. 4/30/1965, p.2.

[115] *Ibid. Letters to the Editor. Save Otero Home as Island of History.* Tucson, AZ. 10/27/1966, p.30.

[116] Tucson Daily Citizen. *Letters to the Editor. Save Otero Home as Island of History.* Tucson, AZ. 10/27/1966, p.30.

Conclusion

[1] NARA. *La Tierra de los Pioneros (Land of the Pioneers)* The National Archives in the Region. September 2011.

Otero Family of Tubac Biofile

[1] Arizona State Library, Archives & Public Records. *Defendant Teofilo Otero's Exhibits.* File 61. Pima Count. Superior Court. Civil. Civil Case, Territorial: 4740-4834. Case 4820 Anna B. Otero vs. Teofilo Otero, 1911, [RG 110]. Defendant's exhibits to the case included numerous letters exchanged between plaintiff Anna B. Otero and Teofilo Otero which support the inference that the couple did not cohabitate exclusively during the time alleged by plaintiff. Anna's letters to Teofilo profess her love,

petitions for them to reunite, and reference to other names she used.

[2] State of Arizona. *Arizona State Board of Health Bureau of Vital Statistics Certificate of Death of Anita B. Otero.* State File #1647, Registrar #251. Certified on 3/5/49.

[3] *Ibid.* File 61. Pima Count. Superior Court. Civil. Civil Case, Territorial: 4740-4834. Case 4820 Anna B. Otero vs. Teofilo Otero, 1911, [RG 110].

[4] *Ibid. Complaint.* File 61. Pima Count. Superior Court. Civil. Civil Case, Territorial: 4740-4834. Case 4820 Anna B. Otero vs. Teofilo Otero, 1911, [RG 110], p.1 §III.

[5] *Ibid. Complaint.* File 61. Pima Count. Superior Court. Civil. Civil Case, Territorial: 4740-4834. Case 4820 Anna B. Otero vs. Teofilo Otero, 1911, [RG 110], p.3 §VII.

[6] Arizona Historical Society. *Letter to Ana Provencio from E. Cusick on 4/6/1942. MS 1454. Ana Otero Provencio. Family papers, 1901-1942 (bulk 1928-1942).*

[7] State of Arizona. *Arizona State Board of Health Bureau of Vital Statistics Certificate of Death of Anita B. Otero.* State File #1647, Registrar #251. Certified on 3/5/49.

[8] J. Homer Thiel author of Presidio Families reports that Maria Elena de Jesus Otero and José Mauricio Maximiano Castro had two children, Eleanor Castro and Brigida Eloisa Castro. Although Thiel reports Eleanor was allegedly born between 1864 and 1866 and likely died young. Thiel suggests that Brijida and Eleanor may be the same person.

[9] Thiel, J. Homer. Presidio Families. Available online at archaeologysouthwest.org.

[10] 1930 US Federal Census. *Tucson, Pima, Arizona*; Page: *3A*; Enumeration District: *0065.*

[11] *Ibid. Certificate of Death of Brigida Castro Coenen.* State File #516, Registrar's # 73. Tucson, AZ. 6/17/22.

[12] *Ibid. Certificate of Death of Henry J. Coenen.* State Index #394, Registrar's # 456. Tucson, AZ. 5/31/1926. Henry was born on 3/29/1902 and died of Tubercular Meningitis on 5/30/1926. His usual occupation was accountant. He is buried at Holy Hope Cemetery and was married to Amparo Coenen. His last residence was 823 S. Third Avenue, Tucson, AZ.

[13] *Ibid. Certificate of Death of Luis J. Coenen.* State Index #394, Registrar's # 456. Tucson, AZ. 10/27/1924. Luis was born in

1897 and died of an abscess of the liver on 10/25/1924. He is buried at Holy Hope Cemetery and was married to Carmen A. Coenen.
[14] *Ibid. Certificate of Death of Mary Coenen Moreau.* State Index #375, Registrar's # 665. Tucson, AZ. 10/27/1924. Mary was born on 8/16/1905 and died of natural causes on 9/20/1935. She is buried at Holy Hope Cemetery and was married to Donato Moreau.
[15] AZ Division of Vital Statistics, State File No. 516.
[16] Thiel, J. Homer. Presidio Families. Available online at archaeologysouthwest.org.
[17] *Ibid.*
[18] O'Mack, Scott. Tucson National Cemetery: Additional Archival Research for the Joint Courts Complex Project. Prepared for Pima County Administrator's Office Archaeology and Historic Preservation. Contract No. 25-73-S-137689-0206. Work Order HYX153. Tucson: 2006, p. 122 citing page 18r, entry 1 of the Tucson Diocese Burial Registry 1863.1887. Accessed at http://www.tucsonfirefoundation.com/wp-content/uploads/2012/07/Tucson-National-Cemetery.pdf on 5/28/2018.
[19] State of Arizona. *Arizona State Board of Health Bureau of Vital Statistics Certificate of Death of Mauricio Castro.* State #310. Tucson, AZ. 6/17/22.
[20] Arizona State Library, Archives and Public Records. *Arizona Livestock Brand Book Mauricio Castro.* 12/14/1895.
[21] State of Arizona. *Arizona State Board of Health Bureau of Vital Statistics Certificate of Death of Mauricio Castro.* State #310. Tucson, AZ. 6/17/22.
[22] "United States World War I Draft Registration Cards, 1917-1918," database with images, *FamilySearch* (https://familysearch.org/ark:/61903/1:1:KZV4-C3V : 12 December 2014), Anthony Coenen, 1917-1918; citing Pima County, Arizona, United States, NARA microfilm publication M1509 (Washington D.C.: National Archives and Records Administration, n.d.); FHL microfilm 1,522,647. Anthony Coenen Jr. was born on 6/22/1895 at Tucson, AZ. Occupation: Music store clerk. Registration card signed on 6/8/17.
[23] Figures based on online conversion tool.

[24] Probate Court. County of Pima, Territory of Arizona. *In the Matter of the Estate of Luis [sic] Quesse, Order Appointing Administrator.* Tucson, Territory of AZ. 11/30/1892.
[25] Arizona Division of Vital Statistics. *Anthony Coenen Death Certificate.* State Index No. 384, Registrar No. 445.
[26] "United States World War I Draft Registration Cards, 1917-1918," database with images, *FamilySearch* (https://familysearch.org/ark:/61903/1:1:KZV4-C3K : 12 December 2014), Eugene Edward Coenen, 1917-1918; citing Pima County, Arizona, United States, NARA microfilm publication M1509 (Washington D.C.: National Archives and Records Administration, n.d.); FHL microfilm 1,522,647. Eugene Edward Coenen signed WWI Registration Card on 6/5/1917.
[27] Brownell, Elizabeth. *They Lived In Tubac.* Tucson: Westernlore Press, 1986, p. 119. *See* Tubac Historical Society. *Anna Maldonado Fimbres. "Voices of the Valley" Tubac Historical Society Oral History Project.* Tubac, 3/16/1990, p.2.
[28] *Ibid*, pp.2-4.
[29] State of Arizona. *Arizona State Board of Health Bureau of Vital Statistics Certificate of Death of Anna Maria Coenen.* State File #480, Registrar's # 83. Tucson, AZ. 6/17/22.
[30] Otero and Otero vs Leonardo Moreno, *et al. Deposition of Ana Maria Coenen.* No. 21094. Pima County Superior Court. Tucson, AZ. 10/17/1941.
[31] "United States Census, 1870," database with images, *FamilySearch* (https://familysearch.org/ark:/61903/1:1:MC2K-SP2 : 17 October 2014), Anna M Otero in household of Sabino Otero, Arizona, United States; citing p. 2, family 17, NARA microfilm publication M593 (Washington D.C.: National Archives and Records Administration, n.d.); FHL microfilm 545,545.
[32] U. S. Department of the Interior. National Park Service. Mission 2000 Searchable Database. "On January 28, 1871, I provided ecclesiastic burial for the body of an adult, Francisca Otero, widow of Ramón Comadurán, legitimate daughter of Manuel Otero, deceased, and Clara Martínez. She died on the 27th of the same month at the age of 30 years. = Augustín Moris (rubric), priest for Tubac." Event ID No. 7262, Book Tubac 2-D, p. 131.

[33] State of Arizona. *Arizona State Board of Health Bureau of Vital Statistics Certificate of Death of Alfonso H. Coenen.* State File #5881, Registrar's # 1114. Tucson, AZ. 610/30/1948. Alfonso was born on 1/14/1883 at Tucson, Territory of Arizona to parents Eugene Coenen and Ana Maria Comadurán and died on 10/30/1948 of Uremic poisoning. He is buried at Holy Hope Cemetery. His usual occupation is retired. He was divorced and his last residence was at 195 South Main Street, Tucson, AZ.
[34] Coenen, Sr., Jon D. Coenen Family History. *Manuscript.* 1988. Ramond born at Tubac died an infant. Antonio was born at Tubac in 1881 as was Alfonso in 1882. The latter married Anita Cajal and died in 1948. Only daughter Anita was born at Tucson in 1884. She married Juan Maldonado and died on 4/9/1964.
[35] "United States Census, 1930," database with images, *FamilySearch* (https://familysearch.org/ark:/61903/1:1:XH14-VM6 : accessed 28 May 2017), A M Coenen, Tubac, Santa Cruz, Arizona, United States; citing enumeration district (ED) ED 7, sheet 6A, line 7, family 113, NARA microfilm publication T626 (Washington D.C.: National Archives and Records Administration, 2002), roll 62; FHL microfilm 2,339,797. Sophia and Mercedes were children of close family friends and raised as Ana Maria Comadurán Coenen's own children.
[36] Thiel, J. Homer. Presidio Families. Available online at archaeologysouthwest.org.
[37] Officer, James. *Hispanic Arizona, 1536-1856. "The End of Mexican Rule."* The University of Arizona Press. Tucson: 1987, pp. 266, 331, 326.
[38] Officer, James. *Hispanic Arizona, 1536-1856.* The University of Arizona Press. Tucson: 1987, pp.266, 307, 389.
[39] State of Arizona. Digital Arizona Library, Arizona State Library, Archives and Public Records. *List of Taxed Brands. Territory of Arizona For Year 1903 to June 30, 1904.* Press Arizona Cattleman. 1904, p.38.
[40] "California Death Index, 1940-1997," database, *FamilySearch* (https://familysearch.org/ark:/61903/1:1:VGTF-Y5R : 26 November 2014), Leonor Kaphan Leon, 14 Feb 1943; Department of Public Health Services, Sacramento.
[41] Leonor Kaphan aka Leonor Kaphan Leon also gave birth to Ramon Kaphan Leon on 11/7/1896 at Tubac, Territory of AZ.

Ramon died on 11/14/1985 at San Bernardino, CA. ("California Death Index, 1940-1997," database, *FamilySearch* (https://familysearch.org/ark:/61903/1:1:VGPS-XV9 : 26 November 2014), Kaphan in entry for Ramon Kaphan Leon, 14 Nov 1985; Department of Public Health Services, Sacramento.) On 12/9/1903, she gave birth to a second child with Ramon Leon of Cucurpe, Sonora, Mexico named Juanita Leon. Juanita died of fever at 10 years of age on 12/29/1913 and is buried at the Tubac Cemetery (State of Arizona. *Arizona State Board of Health Bureau of Vital Statistics Certificate of Death of Juanita Leon.* State #716, Register #121. Tucson, AZ. 12/29/13. The informant at Juanita's death was her half-brother Ysidro Otero), and daughter Leonor Flores Kaphan Leon born 12/30/1906 who died on 12/31/1993 in Colton, San Bernardino, CA ("Find A Grave Index," database, *FamilySearch* (https://familysearch.org/ark:/61903/1:1:QVKS-87ZZ : 11 July 2016), Leonor Flores Kaphan Leon, 1993; Burial, Colton, San Bernardino, California, United States of America, Montecito Memorial Park; citing record ID 36005399, *Find a Grave*, http://www.findagrave.com).

[42] United States Census, 1910," database with images, *FamilySearch* (https://familysearch.org/ark:/61903/1:1:MVVZ-149 : accessed 3 June 2017), Jose Kaphan, Precinct 3, Santa Cruz, Arizona, United States; citing enumeration district (ED) ED 115, sheet 11B, family 213, NARA microfilm publication T624 (Washington D.C.: National Archives and Records Administration, 1982), roll 42; FHL microfilm 1,374,055. Jose Kaphan was born at Germany in 1828. He immigrated to the United States in 1871, and lived in Tubac, Territory of Arizona, Precinct 3, Santa Cruz County. His wife Juana Mendez was born in est. 1836.

[43] U.S. Bureau of Land Management. *Joseph Kaphan. Desert Lands Certificate No. 15, Land Patent 7783.* The Kaphan homestead was located at the current site of the Chavez Siding, Tubac, AZ. The patent contained Township 20 South, Range 13 E, NW ¼ NE ¼ of Section 31 for a total of 40 acres.

[44] "California Death Index, 1940-1997," database, *FamilySearch* (https://familysearch.org/ark:/61903/1:1:VPJJ-XFS : 26 November 2014), Kaphan in entry for Rita Avila, 25 Apr 1964; Department of Public Health Services, Sacramento. Entry reflects mother of Rita Avila.

[45] United Stated Federal Census, *Tubac.* 1860.
[46] Officer, James. *Hispanic Arizona, 1536-1856.* The University of Arizona Press. Tucson: 1987, p. 371, fn8.
[47] Thesis available online at http://biblioteca.colson.edu.mx:8081/e-docs/RED/RED000953/index.html
[48] State of Arizona. *Arizona State Board of Health Bureau of Vital Statistics Certificate of Death of Ana Brown Otero.* State File #[blank], Registrar #1013. Signed in Calexico, CA on 10/23/1933.
[49] *Ibid. Certificate of Birth of Ramon Armando Provencio.* State File #676, Register #537 signed 5/31/1938.
[50] Pima County Superior Court Electronic Documents Online. *Estate of Anna Otero Provencio. Case Number P29773.* www.agave.cosc.pima.gov
[51] Ancestry.com. *Mexico, Select Baptisms, 1560-1950* [database on-line]. Provo, UT, USA: Ancestry.com Operations, Inc., 2014. Original data: *Mexico, Baptisms, 1560-1950.* Salt Lake City, Utah: FamilySearch, 2013.
[52] Mission 2000. Accessed on 1/3/2014 at http://home.nps.gov/applications/tuma/search.cfm.
[53] Officer, James. *Hispanic Arizona, 1536-1856.* The University of Arizona Press. Tucson: 1987, p. 121.
[54] State of Arizona. *Arizona State Board of Health Bureau of Vital Statistics Certificate of Birth of Eduardo Brown Otero.* State # (none), Register #641. AZ. 7/17/1934. His sister was Ana Brown Otero Provencio. Eduardo's birth certificate differs from the number of siblings reported in his sister's birth record.
[55] "Find A Grave Index," database, *FamilySearch* (https://familysearch.org/ark:/61903/1:1:QV2D-SB9P : 13 December 2015), Edwardo Brown Otero, 1975; Burial, Tucson, Pima, Arizona, United States of America, Holy Hope Cemetery & Mausoleum; citing record ID 66666119, *Find a Grave,* http://www.findagrave.com.
[56] U.S. Federal Census. *Territory of New Mexico.* 9/10/1860., p.49 Fernando was 4 months old when the Territory of New Mexico Federal Census was taken at Tubac making his birth month May or June of 1860.
[57] Arizona State Library, Archives and Public Records. *Arizona Livestock Brand Book Fernando Otero.* 9/6/1883.

---

[58] Arizona Weekly Citizen. *Official Records.* 9/15/1883, p.4. A miscellaneous official record was filed by F.H. Garcia, Sabino Otero, Fernando Otero, and Manuela de Quesse.
[59] Arizona Weekly Citizen. *Mining Locations.* Tucson, AZ Territory. 3/20/1881.
[60] Rita Otero and Alberto Avila gave birth to Pauline Eva Avila on 10/12/1916. AZ Bureau of Vital Statistics State Index No. 414 with amendment; Albert Otero Avila on 10/14/1920. AZ Bureau of Vital Statistics State File No. 20-000643 with amendment; Ruben Arthur Avila on 10/22/1924. AZ Bureau of Vital Statistics State Index No. 661 with amendment.
[61] United States Department of Defense. *Fernando Kilbray Otero WWII Registration Card Serial #2884, Order #2406.* Tucson, AZ. Signed on 10/16/1940.
[62] United States Department of the Interior. National Park Service/Tumacácori National Historical Park. *Mission Burial Record, Event ID: 7262.* 1/28/1871.
[63] U. S. Department of the Interior. National Park Service. Mission 2000 Searchable Database. "On January 28, 1871, I provided ecclesiastic burial for the body of an adult, Francisca Otero, widow of Ramón Comadurán, legitimate daughter of Manuel Otero, deceased, and Clara Martínez. She died on the 27th of the same month at the age of 30 years. = Augustín Moris (rubric), priest for Tubac." Event ID No. 7262, Book Tubac 2-D, p. 131.
[64] *Ibid. Mission Marriage Record, Event ID: 4295.* 2/16/1779.
[65] Officer, James. *Hispanic Arizona, 1536-1856.* The University of Arizona Press. Tucson: 1987, p. 346, fn 38 stating Joseph was "possibly a son of Dos Santos."
[66] Arizona State Library, Archives and Public Records. *Arizona Livestock Brand Book Teofilo Otero.* 9/6/1883.
[67] "United States Census, 1910," database with images, *FamilySearch* (https://familysearch.org/ark:/61903/1:1:MVVZ-GZ4 : accessed 28 May 2017), Teofilo Otero in household of Ana Maria Coenen, Tucson Ward 2, Pima, Arizona, United States; citing enumeration district (ED) ED 106, sheet 16B, family 320, NARA microfilm publication T624 (Washington D.C.: National Archives and Records Administration, 1982), roll 41; FHL microfilm 1,374,054.

[68] Texas State Historical Society. *Alianza Hispano-Americana.* Obtained online at https://tshaonline.org/handbook/online/articles/vna02.
[69] Arizona Daily Star. *Neto's Tucson: La Alianza, a name to remember.* By. Ernesto Portillo Jr. Tucson, AZ. 1/23/2016.
[70] Arizona Daily Star. *New Officers.* Tucson, Territory of AZ. 1/9/1900, p. 4.
[71] *Ibid. Otero Will Lend Alliance $20,000; Plans for New Building on West Congress Will be Pushed.* Tucson, AZ. 5/2/1914., p.3.
[72] *Ibid. "Make it a Million" Is Slogan of Salesmen: Parade Inaugurates Day.* Tucson, AZ. 10/24/1917, p.7.
[73] Historic American Landscape Survey of El Tiradito – City of Tucson. *History of El Tiradito Wishing Shrine.* Accessed at https://www.tucsonaz.gov/files/preservation/ElTiradito_HALS_AZ-8.pdf
[74] "Arizona Deaths, 1870-1951," database with images, *FamilySearch* (https://familysearch.org/ark:/61903/1:1:FLN2-NY4 : 12 December 2014), Manuel Otero in entry for Teofilo Otero, 1941; citing Tucson, Pima, Arizona, reference , Department of Library and Archives, Phoenix, Arizona; FHL microfilm 2,114,696.
[75] Arizona Republican. *State Pioneer Taken By Death.* Phoenix, AZ. 5/16/1941, p.28.
[76] United States Department of the Interior. National Park Service/Tumacácori National Historical Park. *Mission Burial Record, Event ID: 2575.* 2/22/1821.
[77] There is an apparent discrepancy in Manuel Ochoa Otero's birthdate. The U.S. Federal Census reported he was 68 years old born in 1872. "United States Census, 1940," database with images, *FamilySearch* (https://familysearch.org/ark:/61903/1:1:VY43-2FD : accessed 28 May 2017), Manuel Otero in household of Angelita Otero, Ward 5, Tucson, Supervisorial District 2, Pima, Arizona, United States; citing enumeration district (ED) 10-30, sheet 20A, line 40, family 357, Sixteenth Census of the United States, 1940, NARA digital publication T627. Records of the Bureau of the Census, 1790 - 2007, RG 29. Washington, D.C.: National Archives and Records Administration, 2012, roll 111. Manuel's United States Department of Defense. *Manuel Ochoa Otero WWII Registration Card Serial # U2501.* Tucson, AZ. Signed on

4/27/1942 reports Manuel's birthdate as 6/24/1880. "United States World War II Draft Registration Cards, 1942," database with images, *FamilySearch* (https://familysearch.org/ark:/61903/1:1:QKC4-M2K9 : 9 April 2016), Manuel Ochoa Otero, 27 Apr 1942; citing NARA microfilm publication M1936, M1937, M1939, M1951, M1962, M1964, M1986, M2090, and M2097 (Washington D.C.: National Archives and Records Administration, n.d.).

[78] State of Arizona. *Arizona State Board of Health Bureau of Vital Statistics Certificate of Death of Manuel Otero*. State File #6850, Registrar's # 1309. Tucson, AZ. 9/3/1958. Information for Manuel Otero's Certificate of Death was obtained from his son Fernando Otero. He reported that Manuel's mother's name was Manuela.

[79] Tubac Historical Society. *Otero Family Papers. Civil Birth Registry of Fernando Otero*. Tubutama, Sonora, Mexico. 7/8/1910. Fernando Otero's paternal grandparents are listed as Sabino Otero and Concepcion Ochoa.

[80] Pimería Alta Historical Society. *Mexican Heritage Project Interview with Fernando Otero Courtesy of Teresa Leal, PAHS Curator*. 11/4/1982. Regarding the bequeath from Sabino Otero to his son Manuel: "Manuel was given a little money and the small freight business between Tubac and the mines and ranches" at p.2. Sabino Otero's Last Will and Testament makes no gift of a freight business to Manuel. The bequeath was for $2,500.00.

[81] Pimería Alta Historical Society. *Mexican Heritage Project Interview with Fernando Otero Courtesy of Teresa Leal, PAHS Curator*. 11/4/1982. "Sister Clara Otero, sister of Sabino Otero raised Manuel. He was sent to a college in California, but he didn't like it there because he missed the ranch life. Sabino paid Santiago Gastelum to take care of Manuel and it was he who taught Manuel to ride a horse" at p.2.

[82] State of Arizona. *Arizona State Board of Health Bureau of Vital Statistics Certificate of Death of Manuel Otero*. State File #6850, Registrar's # 1309. Tucson, AZ. 9/3/1958.

[83] Tucson Daily Citizen. *Deaths*. Tucson, AZ. 9/5/1958, p.4.

[84] Manuel Otero's birthplace was reported on contemporaneous U.S. Census records as Tubac. Upon his death, informant Arthur Carrillo reported that Manuel was born in Alamos, Sonora, Mexico. *See* State of Arizona. *Arizona State Board of*

Health Bureau of Vital Statistics Certificate of Death of Sabino Otero. State #250, Register #31. Filed 1/31/1914.
[85] 1831 Census of Tubac. *See* Brownell, Elizabeth. *They Lived in Tubac.* Tucson: Westernlore Press, 1986. Brownell misidentified Manuel Otero as the son of Don Torivio. Don Torivio's son and father of Manuel was Atanacio Otero. Brownell at 23.
[86] Officer, James. *Hispanic Arizona, 1536-1856.* The University of Arizona Press. Tucson: 1987, p. 183.
[87] Thiel, J. Homer. *Pioneer Families of the Tucson Presidio.* Accessed at https://www.archaeologysouthwest.org/pdf/presidio_families.pdf on 7/4/2014.
[88] Santa Maria Magdalena Church, Magdalena, Sonora, Mexico. *Baptismal Record* 9/8/1846.
[89] *Ibid.*
[90] O'Mack, Scott. Tucson National Cemetery: Additional Archival Research for the Joint Courts Complex Project. Prepared for Pima County Administrator's Office Archaeology and Historic Preservation. Contract No. 25-73-S-137689-0206. Work Order HYX153. Tucson: 2006, p. 122 citing page 18r, entry 1 of the Tucson Diocese Burial Registry 1863-1887. Accessed at http://www.tucsonfirefoundation.com/wp-content/uploads/2012/07/Tucson-National-Cemetery.pdf on 5/28/2018.
[91] *Ibid,* p.123 cites Elena Otero's death on page 22r, entry 1.
[92] Manuela O. de Quesse Probate Case #1346. Pima County Probate Court. Tucson, Territory of AZ. 1901.
[93] United States. *Town of Tubac, Pima County, Arizona Territory Census.* 1870, p.4.
[94] United States. *Town of Tubac, Pima County, Arizona Territory Census.* 1870, p.4. Louisa was 5 months old at the time of the 7/7/1870 census.
[95] United States. *Town of Tubac, Pima County, Arizona Territory Census.* 1870, p.4, line 12.
[96] Manuela O. de Quesse Probate Case #1346. Pima County Probate Court. Tucson, Territory of AZ. 1901.
[97] Arizona State Library, Archives and Public Records. *Arizona Livestock Brand Book Manuela (Otero) Quesse.* 9/6/1883.

[98] Manuela O. de Quesse Probate Case #1346. *Order of Appointing Administrator.* Pima County Probate Court. Tucson, Territory of AZ. 12/31/1901; Manuela O. de Quesse Probate Case #1346. *Inventory and Appraisement.* Pima County Probate Court. Tucson, Territory of AZ. 2/5/1902.

[99] *Ibid.* 2/5/1902.

[100] Officer, James. *Hispanic Arizona, 1536-1856.* "Cattle brands of old Spanish-Mexican families of Southern Arizona." The University of Arizona Press. Tucson: 1987, p.16.

[101] Manuela O. de Quesse Probate Case #1346. *Order of Appointing Administrator.* Pima County Probate Court. Tucson, Territory of AZ. 12/31/1901.

[102] *Ibid. Deed.* Pima County Probate Court. Tucson, Territory of AZ.11/20/1902.

[103] United States Department of the Interior. National Park Service/Tumacácori National Historical Park. *Mission Baptismal Record of Juan José Villaescusa, Event ID: 3177.* 7/21/1783. The baptismal was officiated by Fray Pedro Antonio de Arriquibar. Josefa Salazar was his godmother.

[104] Andrés Durán's parents were Juan Antonio Durán and Maria Guadalupe Ramirez.

[105] State of Arizona. *Arizona State Board of Health Bureau of Vital Statistics Certificate of Birth of Olga M. Otero.* State #489, Register # 518. Tucson, AZ. 6/6/1935.

[106] United States Department of Defense. Ricardo Otero WWI Registration Card Form I-572. Registration #132. Tubac, AZ. Signed at Silverbell, AZ by Ricardo. Ricardo's WWII Draft Registration Card lists 6/19/1891 as his date of birth. This information was taken by a witness signed by Ricardo's mark.

[107] State of Arizona. *Arizona State Board of Health Bureau of Vital Statistics Certificate of Death of Ricardo Otero.* State #555, Register # 24. Nogales, AZ. 3/20/1946.

[108] Rosa Otero was the eldest child of Ricardo Otero and Francisca Quijada. She was born on 9/16/1918. She married Leopoldo Sinohui and they had three children, Celia, Velia, and a son who died an infant. Leopoldo died on 5/22/1940. She remarried after Leopoldo's death and died on 1/8/1979 in San Diego, CA.

[109] *Ibid. Certificate of Birth of Ramon Otero.* State #560, Register # 534. Tucson, AZ. 6/10/1924. Susana Kaphan was the attending midwife. He died on 4/11/1937 due to a drowning

accident at Ruby, AZ. (*See* Arizona State Board of Health Bureau of Vital Statistics State File #543a, Register # 3). He was 12 years old. His death was considered a major event at Ruby. He died along with two other young boys. The mining town of Ruby held a wake for the young boys at the Ruby school house. (DeLugan Research Collection. *Interview of Thalia Calhoun*. Tucson, AZ. 8/13/2016. All three are buried side-by-side at the Arivaca Cemetery with matching silver crosses atop their graves adjacent to the grave of Ramon's mother, Francisca Quijada Otero.

[110] Manuel Quijada Otero was born in 1930 to Ricardo Otero and Francisca Quijada. He died in 1969. He is buried at the Fairview Cemetery at Superior, Pinal County, AZ. "BillionGraves Index," database, *FamilySearch* (https://familysearch.org/ark:/61903/1:1:QJDL-1RYV : 24 June 2015), Manuel Q. Otero, died 1969; citing *BillionGraves* (http://www.billiongraves.com : 2012), Burial at Fairview Cemetery, Superior, Pinal, Arizona, United States.

[111] State of Arizona, *Arizona State Board of Health Bureau of Vital Statistics Certificate of Birth of Ruben Otero*. State #565, Register #[None]. Ruben was born at the mining town of Harshaw. Mrs. Tereza Acevdo was the attending midwife. His birth certificate has two birth dates, November 13, 1928 and December 13, 1927. His WWII Registration Card confirms his actual birthdate as 11/13/1927. He was employed by the Baca Float Ranch, Nogales, AZ when he registered for the draft at 18 years of age. *See WWII Registration Card Form # 33-R012-42, Serial # W-219.*

[112] State of Arizona. *Arizona State Board of Health Bureau of Vital Statistics Certificate of Death of Ricardo Otero*. State #555, Register # 24. Nogales, AZ. 3/20/1946.

[113] "United States Census, 1930," database with images, *FamilySearch* (https://familysearch.org/ark:/61903/1:1:XH1Z-9Z5 : accessed 28 May 2017), Rita Avila in household of Albert Avila, Yuma, Yuma, Arizona, United States; citing enumeration district (ED) ED 24, sheet 12A, line 35, family 321, NARA microfilm publication T626 (Washington D.C.: National Archives and Records Administration, 2002), roll 63; FHL microfilm 2,339,798.

[114] State of Arizona. *Arizona State Board of Health Bureau of Vital Statistics Certificate of Death of Sabino Otero.* State #250, Register #31. Filed 1/31/1914.
[115] Arizona State Library, Archives and Public Records. *Arizona Livestock Brand Book No.1. Sabino Otero.* 9/6/1883 and Menager & Otero brand recorded 3/26/1896.
[116] Arizona Weekly Citizen. *Untitled.* 2/18/1871, p.3; Arizona Weekly Citizen. *Juries for the October Term.* Tucson, AZ. 9/23/1871, p.3; Arizona Weekly Citizen. *Local Matters; Jurors.* Tucson, AZ. 2/5/1876, p.3.; Arizona Weekly Citizen. *Untitled.* Tucson, AZ. 3/1/1873, p.3.; Arizona Weekly Citizen. *Grand Jurors.* Tucson, AZ. 2/5/1887, p.3.; Arizona Weekly Citizen. *Grand Jurors for October Court.* Tucson, AZ. 9/22/1877, p.3; Arizona Weekly Citizen. *Untitled.* Tucson, AZ. 2/1/1879, p.3; Arizona Weekly Citizen. *Jurors for 1881.* Tucson, AZ. 1/22/1881, p.3; Arizona Weekly Citizen. *Jurors Drawn.* Tucson, AZ. 9/4/1881, p.3; Arizona Daily Star. *Grand Jury.* Tucson, AZ. 3/3/1882, p.3; Arizona Daily Star. *Grand Jurors.* Tucson, AZ. 2/2/1887, p.4; Arizona Weekly Citizen. *Grant Jury Meets.* Tucson, AZ. 3/19/1892, p. 4.
[117] Arizona Daily Star. *Democratic County Ticket (Sabino Otero for Legislative Council).* Tucson, AZ. 9/28/1882, p.2; Arizona Daily Star. *Pima County Democracy (Sabino Otero for Assemblyman).* Tucson, AZ. 10/3/1884, p.4.
[118] Arizona Weekly Citizen. *The Election (Sabino Otero as Representative for AZ Territorial Congress).* Tucson, AZ. 11/2/1878, p.2; Weekly Republican. *Untitled.* Phoenix, AZ. 9/29/1882, p.3; Arizona Daily Star. *The Candidates.* Tucson, AZ. 8/22/1886, p.4.
[119] Arizona Daily Star. *Militia Captains.* Tucson, AZ. 10/17/1879, p.3
[120] Arizona Weekly Citizen. *Election Precincts.* Tucson, AZ. 10/15/1870, p.3; Arizona Weekly Citizen. *Untitled.* Tucson, AZ. 10/12/1872, p.2; Arizona Weekly citizen. *Supervisor's Proceedings.* Tucson, AZ. 10/10/1874, p.3; Arizona Weekly Citizen. *Board of Supervisors.* Tucson, AZ. 10/7/1876, p.3; Arizona Daily Star. *Election Precincts.* Tucson, AZ. 10/14/1880, p.3; Arizona Weekly Citizen. *Board of Supervisors.* Tucson, AZ. 9/17/1882, p.4; Arizona Daily Star. *Election Precincts.* Tucson, AZ. 9/12/1884, p.4; Arizona Weekly Citizen. *Untitled.*

4/25/1885, p.3.; Arizona Daily Star. *Voting Precincts.* Tucson, AZ. 10/17/1886, p.4.

[121] The Arizona Sentinel. *Double Murder.* Yuma, AZ. 8/9/1879.

[122] Arizona Weekly Citizen. Live *Stock.* Tucson, Territory of AZ. 9/6/1884, p.3.

[123] Arizona Daily Star. *Cattlemen's Attention.* Tucson, Territory of AZ. 9/2/1890, p.4.

[124] Arizona Weekly Citizen. *Untitled.* Tucson, Territory of AZ. 12/18/1886, p.4.

[125] *Ibid.* 9/28/1878, p.3.

[126] Manuela O. de Quesse Probate Case #1346. *Order of Appointing Administrator.* Pima County Probate Court. Tucson, Territory of AZ. 12/31/1901. Antonio Orfila acted as Attorney for Sabino Otero. Manuela O. de Quesse Probate Case #1346. *Receipts of Payments as Attorney.* Pima County Probate Court. Tucson, Territory of AZ. 12/13/1902.

[127] Arizona Weekly Citizen. *Notice re: Estate of Louis Quesse.* Tucson, Territory of AZ. 4/1/1871, p.2; In the Probate Court of the County of Pima, Territory of AZ, *In the Matter of the Estate of Louis Quesse for US government claim against the estate for $3,655.00.* Tucson, Territory of AZ. 11/18/1892.

[128] Arizona Daily Star. *Certificate and Articles of Incorporation of the Santa Cruz Land and Water Co.* Tucson, Territory of AZ. 12/15/1887, p.3.

[129] Arizona Weekly Citizen. *Untitled.* Tucson, AZ. 2/26/1887, p.2; The Arizona Sentinel. *Untitled.* Yuma, AZ. 5/11/1878, p.1; The Arizona Sentinel. *Untitled.* Yuma, AZ. 9/14/1878, p.3.

[130] State of Arizona. *Arizona State Board of Health Bureau of Vital Statistics Certificate of Death of Sabino Otero.* State #250, Register #31. Filed 1/31/1914.

[131] Arizona Daily Star. *Certificate and Articles of Incorporation of the Santa Cruz Land and Water Co.* Tucson, Territory of AZ. 12/14/1887, p.3; Arizona Weekly Citizen. *Untitled.* Tucson, Territory of AZ. 8/21/1886, p.3.

[132] United States Federal Census. 1860, 1866, and 1870. Tubac, Arizona.

[133] Arizona Weekly Citizen. *List of Premiums Awarded at St. Joseph's Academy on July 1, 1873.* Tucson, AZ. 7/5/1873, p.3. Gabriela (Sister Clara) Otero received awards for Deportment, Painting, English Studies, and Arithmetic.

[134] *Ibid. St. Joseph's Academy*. Tucson, AZ. 7/4/1874, p.3. As a student of St. Joseph's Academy, Gabriela (Sister Clara) Otero sang at the fourth annual exhibition of the Academy's students singing "The Midnight Moon," "The Lonely Bird," "The Murmuring Sea," and the "Hmno Nacional," as well as a dramatic role as "Sean-meis, A Chinese Widow" in the two-scene play *Pancratius*.
[135] County of Pima, Territory of Arizona. *Return of a Death, City of Tucson for Sister Clara Otero*. Burial Permit #2659. 9/4/1905.
[136] McMahon, Sister Thomas Marie. *A Heritage of Loving Service: The Sisters of St. Joseph of Carondelet in Tucson.* Accessed at http://parentseyes.arizona.edu/carondelet/mcmahon_chapter5.html Ch.5.
[137] Sisters of St. Joseph of Carondelet/Los Angeles. Facebook post. 5/12/2016.
[138] See Arizona Women's' Hall of Fame at https://www.azwhf.org/inductions/inducted-women/sister-clara-otero-1850-1905/
[139] United States Department of the Interior. National Park Service/Tumacácori National Historical Park. *Mission Marriage Record, Event ID: 4295*. 2/16/1779.
[140] United States. *Congressional Serial Set. (Tumacácori land grant)*. U.S. Government Printing Office. Washington: 1880, pp.19-24.
[141] United States National Archives and Records Administration. Record Group 49, Records of the Bureau of Land Management. *Arizona Court of Private Land Claims*. Miscellaneous Files 1789-1907. Folder Title: Spanish Documents from Miscellaneous Files, Box # 27.
[142] Officer, James. *Hispanic Arizona, 1536-1856*. The University of Arizona Press. Tucson: 1987, p.346 fn 38 stating "The original Otero (Dos Santos de Otero) may have been a relative of Pedro Luciano de Otero."
[143] United States Department of Defense. WWI Registration Card Form I-637, #28. Tubac, AZ. Signed on 6/5/1917 before William Lowe at Tubac, AZ reports Ysidro's birthdate as 12/18/1890. Ysidro's WWII registration card reports his birthdate as 4/26/1888.
[144] The Church of Jesus Christ of Latter-day Saints, "International Genealogical Index (IGI)," database,

FamilySearch (https://familysearch.org/ark:/61903/2:1:9X15-TTY: accessed 2017-05-28), entry for Ysidro Otero. Marriage reported in the Family Search International Genealogical Index submitted on 11/28/12 by asanford90948.

[145] State of Arizona. *Arizona State Board of Health Bureau of Vital Statistics Certificate of Birth of Francisco Otero.* State File #349, Registrar's # [illegible]. Tubac, AZ. 11/10/1913. He was born on 10/4/1913 at Tubac. Occupation: Miner. He married Maria Bejarano. (*See* United States Department of Defense. *Frank Olivas Otero WWII Registration Card Serial # 925, Order #1255.* Tucson, AZ. Signed on 10/16/1940 at Nogales, AZ.

[146] Ysidro was born on 2/19/1915 at Tubac, AZ to Ysidro Otero and Porfiria Olivas. He died on 1/15/1916 at Tubac where he was buried on 2/10/1916. The Church of Jesus Christ of Latter-day Saints, "International Genealogical Index (IGI)," database, *FamilySearch* (https://familysearch.org/ark:/61903/2:1:9NS2-H1R : accessed 2017-05-28), entry for Ysidro Otero. Vital record information was submitted on 11/28/2012 by ksanford32439.

[147] State of Arizona. *Arizona State Board of Health Bureau of Vital Statistics Certificate of Birth of Jose Otero.* State File #1366, Registrar's # 264. Tubac, AZ. 2/10/1917.

[148] United States Department of Defense. Joe Olivas Otero WWII Registration Card Serial #27, Order #457. Goldroad, Mohave County, signed on 10/16/1940. Joe was born on 12/16/1917 at Tubac. Occupation: Miner.

[149] State of Arizona. *Arizona State Board of Health Bureau of Vital Statistics Certificate of Birth of Elvira Otero.* State File #463, Registrar's # 678. Tubac, AZ. 1/10/1920.

[150] *Ibid. Birth of Rosa Otero.* State File #578, Registrar #678. Tubac, AZ. 4/10/1921.

[151] *Ibid. Birth of Elena Otero.* State File #617, Registrar's # 15. Tubac, AZ. 7/13/1926.

[152] The Church of Jesus Christ of Latter-day Saints, "International Genealogical Index (IGI)," database, *FamilySearch* (https://familysearch.org/ark:/61903/2:1:9NS2-H1T: accessed 2017-05-28), entry for Ysidro Otero. Record submitted on 11/28/2012 by ksanford32439.

[153] State of Arizona. *Arizona State Board of Health Bureau of Vital Statistics Certificate of Birth of Juan Ysidro Otero.* State File #551, Registrar's # 20. Tubac, AZ. 5/20/1934.

154 United States Department of Defense. WWII Registration Card Serial #135, Order #10,680. Tubac, AZ. Signed on 6/30/1942 at Nogales, AZ. Leonardo was born on 10/20/1923 and registered at age 18.
155 State of Arizona. *Arizona State Board of Health Bureau of Vital Statistics Certificate of Birth of Elena Otero.* State File #617, Registrar's # 15. Tubac, AZ. 7/13/1926.
156 The Church of Jesus Christ of Latter-day Saints, "International Genealogical Index (IGI)," database, *FamilySearch* (https://familysearch.org/ark:/61903/2:1:9X15-TTY: accessed 2017-05-28), entry for Ysidro Otero. Death date and location included in the FamilySearch International Genealogical Index on 11/28/2012 by asanford90948.
157 NARA. Regular Enlistments U.S. Army, *Descriptive and Historical Register of Enlisted Soldiers of the Army.*
158 United States. *Town of Tubac, Pima County, Arizona Territory Census.* 1870, p.4.
159 *Ibid.*
160 United States Department of the Interior. National Park Service/Tumacácori National Historical Park. *Mission Marriage Record, Event ID: 4295.* 2/16/1779.
161 United States National Park Service. Tumacácori National Historical Park Arizona. *Arizona / Planchas de Plata.* Accessed at https://www.nps.gov/tuma/learn/historyculture/arizona-planchas-de-plata.htm on 3/1/17. The Arizona ranch in Sonora was established between 1734 and 1736 by Bernardo de Urrea.

WORKS CITED

ARCHIVES AND COLLECTIONS

Arizona Corporation Commission *File Number 10585487.*

File Number L10412693

File No. L10412751

Arizona Historical SocieTy

MS 638, *Otero Family Papers, 1807-1957*

MV 1155. *James Officer Collection*

MS 1454 *Ana Otero Provencio Family Papers, 1901-1942*

Arizona State Library, Archives & Public Records

Bents, Doris. W. *The History of Tubac, 1752-1948. Call No. 979.1 H21B*

Field Notes of the Preliminary Survey of House lot in Tubac, Pima Co. Arizona Territory. Sabino Otero et al claim. Microfiche.

Sabino Otero Grant et al and Misc. Reels 10.1.21/22

Plan of Tubac Town site Pima County 1882

Tubac Town News Clippings File

U.S. Bureau of Land Management Assorted Grants & Miscellaneous papers. Filmfile #10.1.22.

Arizona State Supreme Court

Case No. 1630

Otero & Rojas v. Soto & Gonzalez. No. 2702

Arizona. *Territorial Census Records, 1860*

DeLugan, Diana. *Otero Research Collection*

Carol Cullen Email. 8/3/2016

David Jesus Valles Ballesteros Phone Interview Summary. 9/17/2016

David Jesus Valles Ballesteros. Audio Interview. 9/17/16

Maria Reina Otero Interview. 4/7/2010

Philip Halpenny Email. 7/24/2016

Philip Halpenny Email 9/25/2016

Philip Halpenny Audio Lecture. 10/22/2016

Dioceses of Tucson, AZ. Church Records.

Baptismal Registers

Burial Registers

District Court, First Judicial District. Territory of AZ

Sabino Otero et al v. Sacramento Granillo: Case No. 2087. 4/30/1892.

Fold3. *Mexican FBI Files*

M1085. "In Re: Mexican Activities." Wm. Neunhoffer. AZ. 6/28/1916

M1085. "Juan Ortiz-In Re: Mexican Activities." Wm. Neunhoffer. Tucson, AZ. 7/6/1916

M1085. "In Re-H. Yzurieta et al." Tucson, AZ. 7/17/1916

M1085. "In Re: Mexican Activities." Interview of General Santiago Riviero by Wm. Neunhoffer. AZ. 7/28/1916

M1085. "In Re: Mexican Activities." Interview of Colonel Francisco Cardenas by Wm. Neunhoffer. AZ. 8/10/1916

Gerald R. Ford Presidential Library

James H. McClintock Collection. Burton Barr Library, Phoenix AZ.

Pima County Superior Court, AZ

Anna Brown Otero, Ana O. Provencio and Edward Otero vs Leonardo Moreno et al. Docket No. 21553

In the Matter of the Estate of Teofilo Otero. Docket No. 8334

Last Will and Testament of Sabino Otero. Docket No. 2107

Leonor Capan Otero and Ysidro Otero vs. Leonardo Moreno et al. Docket No. 21094

Manuel Otero vs. Teofilo Otero. Complaint. Case No. 5835.

Manuela O. de Quesse Estate. Probate Court Journal 7

Otero vs Otero. Case 4820

T. Otero vs J. Otero. Case No. 5904.

Santa Cruz County Recorder, AZ

Book of Deeds. Book 3

Book of Deeds. Book 5

Book of Deeds. Book 8

Book of Deeds. Book 9

Book of Deeds. Book 10

Book of Deeds. Book 11

Book of Deeds. Book 14

Book of Deeds. Book 15

Book of Deeds. Book 16

Book of Deeds. Book 18

Book of Deeds. Book 19

Book of Deeds. Book 20

Plat of the Tubac Townsite. 3/3/1914

Santa Cruz County Superior Court, AZ

State of AZ vs Tubac Elementary School District No. 5, Case No. 6725

Tubac Historical Society, AZ

"Voices of the Valley" Anna Maldonado Fimbres Interview

Tucson City Directories, AZ

United States. Bureau of Land Management Records.

Accession No. AZAZAA 010528

Serial No. AZPHX-0011924

Serial No. AZPHX-0013005

Serial No. AZPHX-0013004

Homestead Certificate No. 537

United States. Federal and Territorial Census Records.

1831, 1860, 1880, 1910. 1920

United States Congressional Serial Set. 1895.

United States. National Archives and Records Administration. The National Archives at Riverside.

Record Group 49. *Records of the Bureau of Land Management.*

United States. National Register of Historic Places.

United States. Selective Service System

NEWSPAPERS CONSULTED

Arizona Citizen (Tucson, AZ)

Arizona Daily Star (Tucson, AZ)

Arizona Republic (Phoenix, AZ)

Arizona Republic Sun (Phoenix, AZ)

(The) Arizona Sentinel (Yuma, AZ)

Arizona Weekly Citizen (Tucson, AZ)

Arizona Weekly Enterprise (Florence, AZ)

(The) Border Vidette (Nogales, AZ)

Coconino Weekly Sun (Flagstaff, AZ)

Daily Alta California (San Francisco, CA)

El Fronterizo (Tucson, AZ)

El Paso Herald (El Paso, TX)

Nogales International (Nogales, AZ)

(The) St. Johns Herald (St. Johns, Apache County, AZ)

Santa Fe Daily New Mexican (Santa Fe, NM)

Tubac Arizonian (Tubac, AZ)

Tucson Daily Citizen (Tucson, AZ)

Yuma Weekly Examiner (Yuma, AZ)

(The) Weekly Arizonan (Tubac, AZ)

(The) Weekly Portage Sentinel (Ravenna, Ohio)

BOOKS, JOURNALS, AND MISCELLANEOUS WORKS

Baker, Robert D. *et al.* *Timeless Heritage: A History of the Forest Service in the Southwest. Land Grant Ranches.* U.S. Department of Agriculture Forest Service Publication No. FS-409. College Stations, TX: August 1988.

Bancroft, Hubert. *History of the Pacific States of North America: Arizona and New Mexico.* A.L. Bancroft & Company. British Columbia: 1888.

Bashford, Coles, Compiler. *The Compiled Laws of the Territory of Arizona including the Howell Code and the Session Laws from 1864 to 1871, inclusive, to which is prefixed the constitution of the United States, the Mining Law of the United States, and the Organic Acts of the Territory of Arizona and New Mexico.* Weed, Parsons and Company, Printers. Albany: 1871.

Bents, Doris W. *The History of Tubac, 1752-1948.* University of Arizona. Tucson: 1949, p.21 Courtesy of Arizona State Library, Archives & Public Records. Call No. 979.1 H21B.

Bingmann, Melissa. *The Journal of Arizona History.* "Prep School Cowboys: Arizona Ranch Schools and Images of the Mythic West. Vol. 43, No.3 (Autumn 2002).

Botsford, Gardner. *A Life of Privilege, Mostly: A Memoir.* St. Martins Press. New York: 2003.

Browne, John Ross. *Adventures in the Apache County; A Tour Through Arizona and Sonora, with Notes on the*

Silver Regions of Nevada. Harper & Brothers, Publishers. New York: 1869.

Brownell, Elizabeth. *They Lived in Tubac.* Tucson: Westernlore Press, 1986.

Confederate States of America. *Confederate War Journal,* Vol. 1. War Journal Publishing Company, 1893.

Dobyns, Henry F. *Tubac Through Four Centuries: An Historical Resume and Analysis.* Arizona State Parks Board. 1959.

Donaldson, Thomas. *The Public Domain Its History, With Statistics.* Waishington:1884.

Eatherly, Charles. *Arizona State Parks......The Beginning.* Governor and Arizona Parks Board. 2006.

Garcés, Francisco. *On the Trail of a Spanish Pioneer: The Diary and Itinerary of Francisco Garcés* (missionary Priest) in His Travels Through[ou]t Sonora, Arizona, and California, 1775-1776, Vol.1. F. P. Harper. New York: 1900.

Garcia y Alva, Federico. *"Mexico y sus progresos": "Albumdirectorio del estado de Sonora."Obra hecha con apoyo del gobierno del estado.* Impresa oficial dirigida por A.B. Monteverde. Sonora. 1905.

Gastelum, Luis A. "Memories of My Youth at Tubac: From the Old Homestead to Adulthood." *The Journal of Arizona History.* Vol. 36, No.1 (Spring, 1995). Arizona Historical Society. Tucson: 3.

Heintzelman, Samuel. *Sonora and the Value of Its Silver Mines. Report of the Sonora Exploring and Mining Co., Made to the Stockholders.* Railroad Print. Cincinnati: 1856.

Heintzelman, Samuel. *Report of the Sonora Exploring Co., Made To The Stockholders*. Railroad Record Print. Cincinnati: 1857.

Lane, Betty. Tubac Historical Society Oral History Project Voices of the Valley. *Anna Maldonado Fimbres Interview*. Tubac: 2/27/1990 and 3/16/1990.

Legislature of the Territory of Arizona. *Memorial and Affidavits Showing Outrages Perpetrated by the Apache Indians in the Territory of Arizona During the years 1869 and 1870.* Francis & Valentine Printers. San Francisco. 1871.

Longan, M.M. *Arizona in the Confederacy*. P.145. The Confederate Veteran Magazine. Broadfoot's Bookmark publisher. Wendell, N.C.: 1922.

Nathan F. *Ranching, Endangered Species, and Urbanization in the Southwest: Species of Capital*. The University of Arizona Press. Tucson: 2002.

Officer, James. *Hispanic Arizona, 1536-1856.* The University of Arizona Press. Tucson: 1987.

Poston, Charles. *Building a State in Apache Land*. The Overland Monthly Publishing Co. San Francisco: 1894.

Ruiz, Vicki and John R. Chavez. "Memories and Migrations: Mapping Boricua and Chicana Histories." *La Placita Committee*. University of Illinois Press. Urbana and Chicago: 2008.

Territory of Arizona. *Journals of the First Legislative Assembly of the Territory of Arizona.* Vol. 1. Prescott: 1865.

True, Russell and Diana Madaras. *Dude Ranching in Arizona.* Arcadia Publishing. Charleston: 2016.

Vegors, Wallace. *The Otero Solar at Tubac: "Home" for 150 Years.* History 399g class with Dr. Harwood Hinton.

Virrey of Spain. *Reglamento e instrucciones para los presidios que han de forman la linea de la frontera de la Nueva España.* La Aguila Printers. Mexico: 1834.

United States. *Annual Report of the Commissioner of the General Land Office.* Government Printing Office. Washington: 1882.

United States. *United States Congressional Serial Set, Volume 3115.* U.S. Government Printing Office. Washington: 1893.

United States. Department of the Interior National Park Service. *National Register of Historic Places Continuation Sheet.* Interagency Resources Division. 1994.

United States. *Report of the Commissioner of General Land Office to the Secretary of the Interior for the Year 1869.* Government Printing Office. Washington: 1870.

United States. *Report of the Governor of Arizona made to the Secretary of the Interior for the Year 1879.* Government Printing Office. Washington: 1879.

United States. *Report of the Acting Governor of Arizona Made to the Secretary of the Interior for the year*

1881. Government Printing Office. Washington: 1881.

United States. Report of the Governor of Arizona Made to the Secretary of the Interior for the Year 1883. *Government Printing Office. Washington: 1883* United States. *Report of the Governor of Arizona to the Secretary of the Interior*. Government Printing Office. Washington: 1885.

United States. *Report of the Secretary of the Interior for the Fiscal Year Ending June 30, 188*1. Government Printing Office. Washington: 1881.

United States. Senate. *Senate Documents, Volume 187.* U.S. Government Printing Office. Washington: 1863.

Wagoner, J.J. *History of the Cattle Industry in Southern Arizona, 1540-1940*. Social Science Bulletin No. 20. University of Arizona. Tucson: 1952.

Wasson, John. *Letter from the Secretary of the Interior transmitting the report and opinion of the surveyorgeneral of Arizona Territory, together with a duly authenticated copy of the title papers and testimony in the matter of the private land claim, No. 7, &c* (Tumacácori and Calabasas Land Grant). 46th Congress, 2d Session. Ex. Doc. No. 207.

Williams, Jack. The Center for Spanish Colonial Archaeology. *A Proposed Plan for El Presidio De Tubac Archaeological Park*. March 1989.

STATUTES

12 Stat. 392. *Homestead Act*. May 20, 1862.

26 Stat. 854 *An Act to Establish a Court of Private Land Claims*. (3 Mar 1891) [U.S. Comp. St. 1901, p.705].

3 Stat. 566, Ch. 51. *The Cash Act*. Enacted April 24, 1920.

Arizona Howell Code. *Of Probate Courts*. 10/3/1867.

Arizona Revised Statutes of the Territory of Arizona. Title 45, Chapter 1, Paragraph 3092, Section 6. 1901.

ONLINE REFERENCES

Aguirre, Yjinio F. *The Journal of Arizona History*. "Echoes of the Conquistadores: Stock Raising in SpanishMexican Times." Arizona Historical Society. Vol. 16, No. 3 (Autumn 1975). http://www.jstor.org/stable/41695272 accessed 9/25/2016.

Ancestry.com

Archaeology Southwest. www.archaeologysouthwest.org Arizona Department of Corrections. https://corrections.az.gov/

Arizona Department of Health Services. *Arizona Genealogy Birth and Death Certificates*. http://genealogy.az.gov/

Arizona State Parks. http://azstateparks.com

Arizona State Parks Board. http://parentseyes.arizona.edu

Author Unknown. *The Ghost of Matagorda Plantation*. https://wonderland1981.wordpresscom/2016/05/05/the-ghost-of-matagorda-plantation/

Biblioteca Digital Nacional de España. http://bdh.bne.es/

Bingmann, Melissa. *The Journal of Arizona History*. "Prep School Cowboys: Arizona Ranch Schools and Images of the Mythic West." Vol. 43, No.3 (Autumn 2002). https://www.jstor.org

Black's Law Dictionary Free 2nd Ed and The Law Dictionary. https://thelawdictionary.org/

Blust, Kendal. *Rustic Gardens meet gilded-age glamour at Agua Linda Farm.* Nogales International. 4/4/2017. http://www.nogalesinternational.com/

Bowden, J.J. Office of the State Historian, Division of the Commission of Public Records, State Records Center and Archives. http://newmexicohistory.org/

City of Tucson. *Historic American Landscape Survey of El Tiradito – City of Tucson.* https://www.tucsonaz.gov/

Cornell Law School. *WEX, Legal Information Institute.* https://www.law.cornell.edu/wex/

Davis, Ray Jay. *Antipolygamy Legislation.* Brigham Young University at http://eom.byu.edu/index.php/Antipolygamy_Legislation.

Davis-Monthan Aviation Field. *Register / Joan Fay Shankle.* http://dmairfield.com/

Elkhorn Ranch. http://elkhornranch.com/

Entertainment Magazine Online. http://www.emol.org

FamilySearch.org

Fold3. https://www.fold3.com

Historic Hotels of America. http://m.historichotels.org/

HRVH Historical Newspapers. Scarsdale Inquirer. *Goes to Arizona School.* Number 35, New York: 10/4/1935. http://news.hrvh.org/

Juarez Jr., Macario. The Arizona Daily Star. *Ronald D. Allred Acquired the Tubac Golf Resort for $7.28* *million; Visions the 400-acres as Potential World-class Resort.* http://www.hotel-online.com

NorthAmericanForts.com. *Camp El Reventon.* http://www.northamericanforts.com/

Oro Vally Historical Society. http://ovhistory.org/

(The) Pennocks of Primitive Hall website. *Surnames Index.* http://www.pennock.ws/surnames/nti/nti54797.html and Philly.com

Panchos. http://panchosdesign.com/

PRWeb. http://prweb.com

Ring, Bob. *Time Travel Through the History of the Catalina Foothills and Tanque Verde Valle.* www.ringbrothershistory.com

Rock, George. History of the American Field Services 1920-1955. *Roster of American Field Service Volunteers 1939-1955.* http://www.ourstory.info/library/Rock/roster.html,

Saint Ann's Church. http://www.gvrhc.org

San Xavier Mission. http://sanxaviermission.org

Santa Cruz County. http://www.co.santa-cruz.az.us/

Southern Pacific Lines. Brochure. *Guest Ranches on Lines of Southern Pacific.* 1934. http://uair.arizona.edu

State of Arizona. Department of Revenue. *Parceling Standards.* Revised 2/25/2011. https://azdor.gov/

Taylor Jr., Dr. Quintard. *United States History: Timeline:1800-1900.* University of Washington. http://faculty.washington.edu/qtaylor/a_us_history/1800_1900_timeline.htm.

Thiel, Homer. Archaeology Southwest. *Pioneer Families of the Presidio del Tucson.* www.archaeologysouthwest.org

Tubac Golf Resort and Spa. http://www.tubacgolfresort.com/

U.S. Bureau of Land Management. http://www.blm.gov

U.S. Department of the Interior, BLM General Land Office Records Online. https://glorecords.blm.gov/

U.S. Department of Interior, National Park Service. https://home.nps.gov/

U.S. Library of Congress. http://international.loc.gov

U.S. Library of Congress. Chronicling America. https://chroniclingamerica.loc.gov

Vandervoet, Kathleen. "Historic Tubac home gains new life." *Nogales International.* Online. 10/19/2006. http://www.nogalesinternational.com/

Wikipedia. *Pajarito Mountains.* https://en.wikipedia.org/wiki/Pajarito_Mountains

ERRATUM TO DEDICATION DATE

In the initial printing in 2018 there was a typographic error of the year of birth year listed as 1932 on p. iii. The 2 was replaced with 6 in this print version to reflect the correct year of 1936.

ABOUT THE AUTHOR

Author and historian Diana Hinojosa DeLugan earned a Bachelor of Arts degree in English, *magna cum laude,* from San Diego State University and a law degree from California Western School of Law at San Diego, California.

She lectures regularly on Hispanic genealogy and on topics related to pre-statehood Arizona.

Diana is happily married with three children, eight grandchildren, three great-grandchildren, and is a proud eighth generation Arizonan.

www.ingramcontent.com/pod-product-compliance
Lightning Source LLC
Chambersburg PA
CBHW051828230426
43671CB00008B/874
* 9 7 8 0 9 9 0 9 9 8 7 4 7 *